THE STRUGGLE FOR LIFE

A COMPANION TO WILLIAM JAMES'S
THE VARIETIES OF RELIGIOUS EXPERIENCE

Edited by
Donald Capps and Janet L. Jacobs

Printed in the United States of America

Library of Congress Number 95-71180

International Standard Book Number 1-882380-02-9

Printed by Mennonite Press, Newton, Kansas.

ACKNOWLEDGMENTS

Grateful acknowledgment for permission to reprint copyright material is made to the following:

Charles Y. Glock and Phillip E. Hammond for James E. Dittes, "Catching the Spirit of William James."

The Journal of the Psychology of Religion for Carol Zaleski, "Speaking of William James to the Cultured Among His Despisers."

Human Sciences Press, publishers of *Pastoral Psychology*, for Mary Jo Meadow, "The Dark Side of Mysticism: Depression and 'The Dark Night'."

W. W. Norton & Company for Erik H. Erikson, "William James's Terminal Dream."

The editors also wish to thank Princeton Theological Seminary for its generous contribution toward the costs of printing this volume. Also, special thanks to Katherine Meyer, SSSR Monograph Series Editor, to Edward Lehman, Executive Secretary of the SSSR, and to Steven Rudiger and Sharon Regier of the Mennonite Press, each of whom played an essential role in the publication of *The Struggle for Life*.

THE STRUGGLE FOR LIFE

A COMPANION TO WILLIAM JAMES'S
THE VARIETIES OF RELIGIOUS EXPERIENCE

INTRODUCTION

In 1897 William James was invited to deliver the Gifford Lectures at the University of Edinburgh. After some negotiations and postponements, they were delivered in 1901-1902. The first ten lectures were delivered to an audience of 250 persons in May and June of 1901, and the remaining lectures were delivered in the same months in 1902 to an equally large and appreciative audience. After delivering the first set of lectures, James (according to a recent biographer) "left Edinburgh with new heart in him because of the success of his lectures and looking toward the future ... with 'aggressive and hopeful eyes' "(Lewis, 1991:513).

In 1973 Charles Y. Glock and Phillip E. Hammond published *Beyond the Classics? Essays in the Scientific Study of Religion*, a collection of eight essays focussing on the "golden era" in the social scientific study of religion, the period from the middle of the nineteenth century through the first decades of the twentieth in which "a large number of highly gifted social scientists made contributions, now considered classic, to our understanding of the phenomena of religion" (Glock and Hammond 1973: ix). The purpose of their volume was to "take stock" of where the field of the social scientific study of religion has been and where it appears to be going, and to do this stock-taking by attempting to discover and assess what has happened over the course of fifty to a hundred years to the ideas, theories, and insights contributed by the classical writers in the field: "What has been their fate? How much do they continue to be the last word and in what ways have they been altered, extended, and elaborated upon by subsequent work? In effect, are we beyond the classics in the scientific study of religion or still mostly in the middle of them?" (Glock and Hammond 1973: x).

The Glock and Hammond book includes essays on Marx, Weber, Durkheim, Malinowski, Freud, James and H. Richard Niebuhr. In his essay on James (included in revised form in this volume), James E. Dittes pointed out that *The Varieties of Religious Experience* are the report of how one man, William James, "finds things to be." As James was "a man who happened to delight in the expectation that others would find things to be different," we have "the anomalous situation that the man most often and justifiably cited as the father of American psychology of religion has left no school or following or system or impact of the kind ordinarily regarded as a founder's heritage" (Dittes 1973:293-294). While other authors in the Glock and Hammond volume struggled with the question, "Have we gone beyond the classic in question, and if not, why not, and if so, in what sense?" Dittes, in light of his view that such a question implies a founder with a legacy, chose not to address it. Instead, he discusses what the word "beyond" in the title *Beyond the Classics?* might mean to James, and, in the course of discussing "beyond" as "outcome," he recounts the story of James's "scandalous" behavior while staying with his brother Henry, the famous novelist, in the latter's proper English home in Rye:

He heard that G.K. Chesterton was staying at the inn next door. He wanted to see Chesterton. So what else but to take the gardener's ladder, climb up, and peep over the wall .... (Dittes 1973:326).

As Dittes notes, James saw no reason to work through "proper mediators and according to proper forms" to discover what was "beyond" his present ken. If one wishes to "see" Chesterton, one contrives on one's own to see him. This episode, then, captures the "spirit" of James, and also makes the question of whether psychology of religion has gone "beyond" James seem irrelevant, for to claim to be engaged in going "beyond" a man who believed that the whole point of his work and life was to go "beyond" is to get caught in a rather hopeless self-contradiction. It is equally nonsensical, however, to claim to be a "follower" of James because this would be to contradict James's understanding of what he, you and I are about when we look into things.

The subtitle of this collection of essays, "A Companion to William James's *The Varieties of Religious Experience*," therefore avoids the grandiosity implied in phrases like "a new perspective" or "a supplement to" or even the very modest "commentaries upon." "Companion" suggests that the volume is "congenial" to *The Varieties*, but that it asks to be read alongside of, certainly not in the place of, the reading of *The Varieties* itself. The word "companion" should not, of course, be taken to mean that these essays are mere summaries of what James says, and says better, in *The Varieties*. True to the spirit of James himself, they are "critical" essays, reflecting James's own passion for incisive, toughminded inquiry. Like a true companion in human relationships, this volume—as Dittes says of James himself— gets close enough to wound (see his essay in this volume). There is no servile docility here, for this would surely, as nothing else could, enervate the spirit of James.

In September of 1993 we wrote to a fair number of colleagues in the psychology of religion and related disciplines, inviting them to write essays for this volume. In our letter of invitation, we said the following:

> Those of us who teach courses or seminars in the psychology of religion usually devote a significant part of the course to *The Varieties*, so we find ourselves returning to this text time and again throughout our teaching careers. Each time we return to *The Varieties*, we find ourselves responding to a feature of the text that we had not paid particular attention to in previous readings, or that had not struck us as forcibly before. We think it would be terrific if we, together, could produce a collection of essays on *The Varieties* in which each of us seeks to go beyond "textbook" readings of James's text and offer, instead, interpretations that grow out of our own readings and rereadings of the text. While the resulting volume would be a contribution to the psychology of religion, our hope would be that our essays would not be concerned so much with remarking on the importance of *The Varieties* for our field, but would instead be a reflection of the richly provocative nature of James's text and its capacity to evoke responses from the reader.

This invitation was based, in other words, on the assumption that a classic is never really gotten "beyond," but is instead returned to, again and again, for fresh insights that are possible, in large part, because we, the readers of the text, are not the same persons we were when we encountered the text before. If it made an appeal for going "beyond," this was an appeal to the authors to "go beyond 'textbook' readings" of James's text. While a "textbook reading" was not clearly defined in our letter, it *was* contrasted with the "interpretations that grow out of our own readings and rereadings of the text," implying, in other words, that "textbook readings" are usually those that are put forward when one has not engaged the text and allowed oneself to be engaged by it.

2

In our invitation to the authors of these essays, we did not assign topics, nor did we ask specific authors to address specific lectures (or chapters) in *The Varieties*. We felt that such assignments would fly in the face of the invitation to engage *The Varieties* on the basis of a fresh reading or rereading of the text. It is therefore a minor miracle that the essays in this volume are so evenly distributed across the lectures that comprise *The Varieties*. No major section of *The Varieties* has been neglected, and no single section of *The Varieties* is given significantly greater attention than other sections. Thus, the basic structure of the volume—its table of contents—follows the structure of *The Varieties* itself. (The perceptive reader will, however, note that there is no article that focuses specifically on conversion. See Capps 1990 for a possible explanation.)

As the volume began to take shape; that is, as the essays began arriving in the mail through the summer of 1994, we came to realize that our original, tentative theme for the volume—"the divided self"—was being superseded by the theme which is now the title, "the struggle for life." The word "struggle" kept reappearing in the essays, both in depicting James's own perception of the task he had set himself in the lectures, and in portraying how James thought about the role of religion in human life. On one hand, *The Varieties* marks a culminating point, though certainly not the end, of James's own lifelong struggle with religion. (The end of this struggle was coincident with his death, a fact that he not only knew would be the case but also was reflected in his effort to figure out what would be his "last words" to those he left behind.) His writings, whether represented as psychological or as philosophical, are always, in one way or another, about religion, and reflective of his own lifelong struggle with religion. Had he been able to come to some peace or equanimity about religion, or, conversely, had he been able to find a way to become indifferent to religion, the struggle would have ended, and he, one assumes, would have gone on to other topics. That he could *not* put the struggle to rest, that he could *not* come to some final peace with religion, goes a long way toward accounting for the fact that his writings up to the very time of his death, were either about religion or included significant discussions of it. A book that he was planning to write when death (at age 68) intervened, a book about the varieties of *military* experience, would surely have manifested his continuing struggle with religion (see on this point the article by Joseph Byrnes in this volume).

On the other hand, over and again, the essayists in this volume were picking up on James's perception of life itself as a struggle, and of the role that religion may play in reconciling the individual to the struggles of life. Several such struggles are addressed in these essays. There is the struggle to be whole, to experience oneself as less a "divided self" and more a "unified" or "harmonious" self. There is also the struggle to be strong, to experience oneself as capable of standing up to, or withstanding, the threats and blows that the world inflicts upon us. Then there is the struggle, perhaps—paradoxically—the most difficult of all, to "yield" to the powers that are "beyond" oneself, allowing these powers to take ultimate control over one's daily existence and over one's final destiny. Each of these struggles is, in its way, religious, and for each, religious language has been developed to describe and understand the struggle involved. "Conversion" and "regeneration" are words commonly used to express the struggle to be whole; "saintliness" is a word commonly used to express the struggle to be strong; and "mysticism" is a word commonly used to express the yielding of oneself to powers beyond oneself. These are words that the religious attach to these struggles, words that James is not hesitant to use in *The Varieties*, in large part because they are words with which he can personally identify, at least to a point. In commenting on his tendency to take an appreciative view of the religious testimony of others, he says, "No doubt there is a germ in me of something similar" (James 1973:124).

If these three comprise much of what James understands the religious struggle itself to be about, there is a fourth struggle with which *The Varieties* is also concerned, and this is the struggle for a living religion. This is a struggle in which humanity itself is continuously engaged, but is one that some individuals within society experience more acutely than others. Exemplary of this struggle were, for example, the Hebrew prophets, who were perceived by their contemporaries to be *enemies* of religion precisely because they were so intent on keeping religion itself alive and vital. The last several lectures in *The Varieties* may be viewed as James's own effort both to make the case for this struggle—we *should* work to keep religion truly alive—and to set forth his own sense of what constitutes living religion. Against the scientific community of his day that viewed religion as a mere survival of a more primitive era in human history, James believed that there was a profound wisdom in these primitives' view of the world as *animated*, and he throws his support behind the decision of these primitives to seek knowledge of the natural world through its most vivid and remarkable features and to give only secondary importance to charting its regularities and laws. We would expect this support of "animism" from a man of whom his father wrote: "He came down from his bedroom *dancing* to greet me.... He was an overflowing and inexhaustible fountain—a fountain, be it remarked, and not a channeled stream" (quoted in Dittes' essay in this volume).

On the other hand, James also throws his weight behind the new efforts to develop a "science of religion," one whose intention is to study religion as one would study any other human activity. For such a science to succeed, philosophy will necessarily play a most important role, for it is philosophy's task to engage in critical assessment of scientific theory and method. So James is *against* science when it proclaims itself to be the successor to religion, but *for* science when it sets itself the task of looking into religion and takes note of what it finds there. To do the latter right, however, we had better not take our cues from the systematic theologians who are curators of dead religion. James recalls reading as a boy Captain Mayne Reid's invectives against arm-chair naturalists:

> In the middle of the century just past, Mayne Reid was the great writer of books of out-of-door adventure. He was extolling the hunters and field-observers of living animals' habits, and keeping up a fire of invective against the "closet-naturalists," as he called them, the collectors and classifiers, and handlers of skeletons and skins. When I was a boy, I used to think that a closet-naturalist must be the vilest type of wretch under the sun. But surely the systematic theologians are the closet-naturalists of the deity, even in Captain Mayne Reid's sense. What is their deduction of metaphysical attributes but a shuffling and matching of pedantic dictionary-adjectives, aloof from morals, aloof from human needs, something that might be worked out from the mere word "God" by one of those logical machines of wood and brass which recent ingenuity has contrived as well as by a man of flesh and blood. They have the trail of the serpent over them... Did such a conglomeration of abstract terms give really the gist of our knowledge of the deity, schools of theology might indeed continue to flourish, but religion, vital religion, would have taken its flight from this world (VRE: 446-447).

If science, with its affinity for "mathematical and mechanical modes of conception," were to set itself the task of looking into religion, how will it manage to avoid leaving the same trail of the serpent over religion, killing it, as it were, with its "thin, pallid, uninteresting ideas" (VRE: 496-497).

This volume, then, is concerned with James's own investment in the struggle for a living religion, and his own effort in *The Varieties of Religious Experience* to articulate what living religion is. In this light, it is important for us to keep in mind that *The Varieties* was written when James was in his early sixties, when he was at the height of his career, but also at a time when he felt that he was running out of time, that he had only a few productive years remaining, and still so much to do, especially by way of completing several contemplated writing projects. The very fact that *The Varieties of Religious Experience* reflects his mature thinking on religion, as well as the fact that this thinking was still very strongly influenced by his psychological temperament in spite of the fact that, for all intents and purposes, he had long since abandoned the field of psychology, presents those of us who identify ourselves as psychologists of religion with a unique challenge. Knowing that we cannot address the book as though we can improve upon it—the rather unimpressive history of the psychology of religion field since *The Varieties* was written should be enough to disabuse us of that notion—the question is what we can do for *The Varieties* that it does not already do for itself. There is the danger that we will unintentionally engage in a kind of reductionism, that of reducing *The Varieties* to our own categories or systems of thought, and thereby kill the spirit that pervades the text. How to avoid, on one hand, being so awed by the text that one cannot engage in critical discussion of it, and, on the other hand, leaving the trail of the serpent over it, killing it, as it were, with our own thin, pallid, uninteresting ideas?

James's own commitment to pluralism in religion and all other important human activities is instructive in this regard, for this volume is not the work of a single author (as so many books on James tend to be) but of a very diverse group of individuals. This volume is inherently pluralistic, which is, it seems to me, precisely the right way to approach any work by William James, but especially *The Varieties of Religious Experience*, as it insures that no single theory about *The Varieties* will dominate, and no single perspective on *The Varieties* will have a controlling influence. In this sense, the volume is congruent with James's own method of inquiry and discovery. Each of us who have written essays for this volume believe in what we have written (as James might say, we believe in it precisely because this is what we found ourselves attending to), and we are all prepared to defend our point of view. But each of us is also committed to the premise that a classic like *The Varieties* can be viewed from various angles. If we did not believe this we would not have accepted the invitation to write for a volume of collected essays. If this implies that truth for us is relative to the perspectives of those who seek it, we believe that all of the contributors to this volume would disagree, arguing, in Jamesian fashion, that *The Varieties* is an existent *fact*, which means that while we may say various things concerning *The Varieties* about which there may be considerable disagreement among us, there are other things that, if said, would do such violence to the text—as an existent fact—that anyone who has read the text would be constrained to respond, "The text cannot bear the meaning you have ascribed to it." (For a fuller discussion of this issue of relativism, see the essay by John Capps in this volume).

In most essay collections, the editors' introductions include brief comments on each essay. Because of their selectivity, such comments inevitably fail to do the essay justice. Yet, this seems the only viable way to provide readers a general overview of what the volume offers. Our first set of readings centers on "The Spirit and Strategies of *The Varieties*." Since public lecturers are always introduced before they proceed with their lectures, and since *The Varieties* were public lectures, we begin with a brief, previously published essay by John Dewey entitled "William James." This essay was written shortly after James's death in 1910. When James retired from Harvard in 1907, he asked the philosophy department to recommend Dewey as his successor. Despite their recommendation, Harvard President Charles Eliot notified James that such an appointment would be "preposterous" (Myers 1986: 42). In his tribute to James, Dewey emphasizes James's concern as a psychologist not to become so enamored of technical details as to lose sight of the larger issue that attracted him to psychology in the first place, the study of human nature in all of its rich complexity. Dewey also notes that James did not so much lose interest in psychology in his later years but rather sought to apply psychology to issues of life (and death).

If Dewey introduces us to William James, the three remaining essays in this set of readings introduce us to *The Varieties of Religious Experience*. These essays, by James E. Dittes, Carol Zaleski and Troels Nørager, are distinguished by the fact that they view *The Varieties* wholistically, as opposed to centering mainly on one or another of its central themes. An adaptation of his 1973 essay entitled, "Beyond William James," James E. Dittes's essay centers on the spirit that pervades *The Varieties* and which gives rise to its principal strategy: "Generations before 'vulnerability' became fashionable, James relies on it; it can be regarded as the principal strategy of his lecture, disarmingly inviting his Calvinistic audience to drop their critical arms-length guard and to approach, to approach the experience afresh, and to approach his approach... " Dittes warns that the invitation to approach James, to catch his spirit, is an invitation to come close enough to be wounded, especially if one brings to the encounter with James a proclivity for thinking in systematic and propositional terms.

Carol Zaleski's essay is a defense of *The Varieties* against its detractors: "My sole purpose in this essay is to see whether James can be defended against some common charges. On the points where this defense fails, my strategy will be to consider whether James's thought is in principle corrigible, and hence of more than historical interest for interpreters of religion." Some of the charges that she takes up are that his account of religious experience is marred by his excessive individualism, privatism, and elitism; that he gives undue preference to feeling at the expense of intellect; and that his analysis of religious experience is founded on the false premise that there is such a thing as raw, immediate experience, and thus fails to recognize that all experience is interpreted experience.

Troels Nørager's essay draws attention to *The Varieties* at the level of discourse, where the "real drama" is enacted. For Nørager, *The Varieties* "is a text where you need to 'listen' very carefully to the way things are said. You need to be attentive to different types of discourse, rhetorical strategies, and generative metaphors." While James wants to interpret and explain religious experience psychologically, he "has intuitively felt the impossibility of introducing the psychological perspective directly. Instead, he employs a number of ... mediating strategies." Nørager focuses on James's use of interior metaphors that mediate between religion and psychology. All three authors agree that the "spirit" of the book is closely related to its discursive or rhetorical strategies. It is not only in what he says but how he says it.

The four essays by Donald Capps, Roger A. Johnson, Richard Chiles and Mark Ralls focus on the first major section of *The Varieties* (lectures 1-10). Donald Capps's essay argues that *The Varieties* challenges us to consider the possibility that religious experience may be "purely personal," and focuses on James's accounts of his own experiences of melancholy to explore this challenge. Capps gives particular attention to James's lectures on "The Reality of the Unseen" and "The Sick Soul," the two lectures in which James's experiences are anonymously presented. Noting that, for James, "the religious attitude involves belief in an *unseen order* whereas melancholy is an inability to take interest in, or give attention to, the world that *is* seen," he takes James to be saying that we can see from this "how the religious attitude and the melancholic temperament, rather than being mere polar opposites, might become conjoined, and why melancholic personalities might find themselves peculiarly attracted to the life of religion," as the two are "the mirror image of one another."

Roger A. Johnson's essay centers on James's judgment that "experiences of helplessness are an essential ingredient of religious experience," and then proceeds to make the case that, uncharacteristically, James "did not offer his readers a variety of experiences of helplessness, but consistently relied on one very specific type of helplessness," one whose resolution involves "a radical surrender of self for the sake of union with some greater power." Johnson considers other experiences of helplessness, especially ones resulting in the yielding of aspects of oneself in order to be united with the human family.

Mark Ralls's essay focuses on James's strategy of comparing and contrasting two religious figures (e.g. Tolstoy and Bunyan) as a means to demonstrate similarities in their religious temperaments while at the same time highlighting the differences in their religious struggles and resolutions. Ralls uses this same strategy to explore the dramatic personal changes that James and the German social theorist Max Scheler experienced as young men. On the basis of this biographical exploration, he suggests that James and Scheler both viewed religious experience as "resolution" involving surrender of the will to a greater power. Where they differed was that James emphasized the self's relation to itself whereas Scheler gave greater prominence to the self's relation to the other. Thus, for James, the "redeemed life is a birth to a new depth, to a universe that is 'two stories deep,'" while, for Scheler, "it is an opening to a new breadth, to the expanded horizons of universal solidarity."

Richard Chiles's essay focuses on "the divided self and its reparation," and is concerned "with the need to say more than James himself has said about the socio-cultural location of the self." Chiles addresses these concerns by relating James's distinction between the healthy-minded temperament and the sick-soul to psychoanalyst Melanie Klein's distinction between the "paranoid-schizoid" and "depressive" positions toward the world. By linking these two constructs, he shows that "James's healthy-minded and sick-soul orientations are ways of interacting with the social world," and are therefore not only psychological but also cultural types, "reflecting two socially constructed ways of being religious, with each having significant political implications, as each has its own understanding of how one is expected to behave with regard to issues of power and control."

A thread that runs through the essays by Johnson, Chiles and Ralls is what Zaleski refers to as a charge that "James's account of religious experience is marred by his excessive individualism, privatism, and elitism."

The three essays by Richard A. Hutch, Joseph F. Byrnes and Patricia H. Davis relate most directly to the large middle section of *The Varieties*, which is devoted to the topic of saintliness (lectures 11-15). These lectures are concerned with the ways in which religion not merely supports but truly empowers human life, enabling it to realize a higher level of significant achievement than might otherwise be possible. Noting that James wanted to use "human standards" to decide how far the "religious life commends itself as an ideal kind of human activity," Richard A. Hutch argues that James put forth two "working principles" to evaluate the religious life. These two principles, having their basis not in a "forensic metaphor" (sin/guilt) but grounded in human mortality, are the turnover of generations (i.e. that we live out of past generations and into new ones) and biological (and gender) complementarity (i.e. that males and females together create generational turnover). He concludes that "The question of whether these two general principles are affirmed together in a life ... provide us with a 'common sense' test of saintliness."

Patricia H. Davis is concerned with James's representation of women's religious experience in *The Varieties*. She notes that there are considerably more examples of men's than women's experiences in *The Varieties*, and that women are most likely to appear in the lectures on healthy-mindedness and saintliness and not in the lecture on the sick-soul. She gives particular attention to James's portrayal of Saint Teresa of Avila, noting that his "ambivalence toward her is revealed in striking fashion in the lectures on saintliness," where he professes profound admiration for her intellectual gifts, her great talent for politics and business, her buoyant disposition, and her first-rate literary style, and then ulti-mately dismisses her because she devoted these remarkable gifts to such "paltry ends." Davis concludes that "feminist literary critics have shown that we can no longer afford to read any text naively, no matter how interesting, important, or even classic." Her own essay is an important contribution in this regard. It is also, however, a plea for greater apprecia-tion of healthy-minded religion, whether encountered in women or in men, for even when healthy-minded religion is "grounded in denial," it is still profoundly "rooted (at least as much as sick-souledness) in personal struggle to survive and make sense of life."

Joseph F. Byrnes, a psychologist of religion and a historian who has written extensively on religion in France, centers on the experiences of French soldiers in World War I. Like Hutch, who views saintliness as being rooted in self-sacrifice, Byrnes centers on James's view that "the interior basis for this saintliness is a feeling of elated self-surrender to a wider world." What better examples have we of such self-surrender than the experiences of soldiers in battle. Also, for Byrnes, the confrontation with death may be a mystical experience, one having its place "within the broader awareness of reality-grounded exis-tential fear." Thus, Byrnes is interested both in the ways that war experience contributes to the increase of saintliness, as reflected, for example, in soldiers' profound respect for the remains of their fighting comrades, and in the fact that mystical experience is found in the seemingly unlikely setting of the battlefield.[1]

The essays by Wade Clark Roof and Sarah McFarland Taylor, Ralph W. Hood Jr., and Mary Jo Meadow are most directly related to James's lectures on mysticism (lectures 16-17). In the one coauthored essay in this volume, Wade Clark Roof and Sarah McFarland Taylor focus on James's concern to rehabilitate the element of feeling in religion and subordinate its intellectual part. They see James as concerned to "get back to the religious experience itself," and specifically with its felt sense, and are appreciative of his wariness of what today passes as "constructivist" interpretations of religion. In effect, they take up two of the charges commonly made against James (see Zaleski's article in this volume), that James gives undue preference to feeling at the expense of intellect and that his analysis of religious experience (mysticism in particular) is founded on the false premise that there is such a thing as raw, immediate experience, and they come out strongly in James's corner, noting that these charges reflect a particular social and cultural bias. They argue: "Today, the 'feel-ing self' is a self that is transformed through its own emotional expansion, and, for James, there is no more likely way for this to happen than by means of religious experience."

Key to Ralph W. Hood Jr.'s argument that James makes a case in *The Varieties* and espe-cially in his lectures on mysticism for "methodological theism" is his observation that James excluded the soul from *The Principles of Psychology* for scientific reasons but includ-

---

1. Relevant to Byrnes's study of war experiences is the following footnote in Gerald E. Myers's *William James: His Life and Thought* (1986: 600-601):

   In a letter of 21 April 1923, Henry James III, writing on behalf of the James family to the President and Fellows of Harvard to present much of his father's library, noted that the books fell into four groups: about four hundred on philosophy and psychology; about six hundred on abnormal psychology and psychical research, many not easily obtainable; approximately fifty on philosophy and religion; and about "a score of books, somewhat annotated, which my father placed together shortly before his death with the intention of working up the subject of military psychology." James thought he might one day write a book called *A Psychology of Jingoism* or *Varieties of Military Experience*.

   Myers adds that the closest he came to writing a book on military psychology was "The Moral Equivalent of War," an essay that appeared in the year of his death, in which he called for "a con-scription of the whole youthful population to form for a certain number of years a part of the army enlisted against *Nature*."

ed it in *The Varieties* for religious reasons. Hood is especially concerned with the "evidential force of mystical experience," and notes that "in *The Varieties* the language of soul and the reality of the unseen order loom large as appropriate language for the facts of religious experience." He notes that, for James, the soulful self may be construed as "merely a subjective expansion in which the subconscious is confronted," but that a "richer option" is provided when one experiences an "objective expansion in which God or the Absolute is encountered." Religious mystical experience involves belief that God or the Absolute is encountered; that, as James puts it, "the conscious person is continuous with a wider self through which saving experiences come." Hood thus sees the mystical experience as both a *belief* in the reality of God or the Absolute and an experience of *yielding* to "the higher powers." Its effect is personal salvation, or "the soulful self at rest."

Mary Jo Meadow's essay focuses on the "dark side" of mysticism and explores the relationship between mysticism and clinical depression, setting the discussion of clinical depression within the framework provided by James's lecture on the sick or melancholic soul. Following a strategy employed by James himself of discussing two religious individuals together so as to identify similarities and differences, Meadow explores the mystical experiences of Dag Hammarskjöld and Simone Weil, who were roughly contemporaries of one another, and from these illustrations draws the conclusion that mystics have an "intense awareness of ultimate human aloneness and emptiness" which reveals "their sensitivity to loss." They are also highly sensitive to their own failings and, while they are often "prestigious accomplishers in their endeavors," they display inwardly tendencies toward passivity and feelings of impotence. She concludes that "darkness" has many negative connotations, but also has positive ones as well: "terrible aloneness" but also "perfect peace."

This group of essays on mysticism and yielding to the "more" of life concludes with Erik H. Erikson's brief discussion of a dream report by James himself. This dream, which occurred in San Francisco two months prior to the San Francisco earthquake, is represented by James as the "exact opposite of mystical illumination," and yet, because it also afforded "the sense that reality was being uncovered," it was "mystical in the highest degree." Erikson views the dream as reflective of acute identity confusion, especially owing to James's impression that he was being dreamed by the dream rather than actively "having" the dream, and he also interprets it as "a product of the conflict between man's lasting hopes for a higher integrity and his terminal despair."

The essay by John Capps and the second essay in this volume by Donald Capps focus on the last three lectures in *The Varieties*. John Capps addresses James's concern in the closing lectures of *The Varieties* with the question of the objective truth of religious experiences. Focusing on James's distrust of both philosophy and science on the grounds that they are unable "to provide an adequate rational foundation for religious experience," Capps takes up the "familiar but serious criticism" that *The Varieties* "lacks a normative, regulative foundation." In place of a "moral order" and "objective truth," we "seem to be left at the mercy of passion and desire." (This is the fifth charge against James identified by Zaleski in her essay in this volume.) The question then, for Capps, is "whether [James's] strategy in *The Varieties* contains a coherent regulative component." Capps cautiously argues that it does, and that its roots are to be found in James's assumption, in his discussion of religion, of an "evolutionary standpoint" and, more specifically, in his view that experience itself obeys a principle of evolution. Furthermore, James grounds both philosophy and science "in a pure experience that is prior … to the formulation of subjective and objective spheres." Thus, precisely because *religious* experience raises with special urgency the question of what is "subjective" and what is "objective" about an experience means that it proves to be a particularly rich resource for a re-appraisal of both philosophy and science, and of the regulative role they claim for themselves in the matter of truth.

The article by Donald Capps centers on James's interest in prayer and his rather startling claim that prayer "is the very soul and essence of religion." Capps is especially concerned with the connections that James makes between prayer, melancholy and the transfiguration of the seen world. If the seen world is dead and lifeless for the melancholic, prayer is the religious means whereby the world is transfigured and the face of nature is revivified. If, therefore, James wants to protect religious experience from science, and declares that it is in a sense impervious to scientific criticism, this is because the religious person, largely through personal prayer, is enabled to perceive the world as alive and inviting, whereas science tends to perceive the world much as the melancholic type perceives it, as lifeless and dead. Capps contends that the "metaphor of the portrait is perhaps, then, a particularly apt way of describing what James has accomplished in *The Varieties*" because "portraiture illustrates his point about the world 'out there' not being an undifferentiated mass, but as having features that stand out from the rest, that are more animated than the other features. For the portrait artist, it is the face that portrays the 'life' of the subject."

This section on James's concern for living religion concludes with his own essay entitled, "Is Life Worth Living?" We have included it here because it seemed appropriate that James should be allowed the last word, and because this essay especially catches the spirit of James. The essay is invitational in spirit—"I ask you to join me in turning an attention, commonly too unwilling, to the profounder bass-note of life"—but this invitation is put forth in response to what James took to be the invitation that had been extended to him: "I know not what such an association of yours intends, nor what you ask of those whom you invite to address you, unless it be to lead you from the surface-glamour of existence" into "the deepest heart of all of us" wherein "there is a corner in which the ultimate mystery of things works sadly." Is life worth living? The jocular response to this question is that "it depends on the *liver*" (a double-entendre that James will use again the *The Varieties* when, in his lecture on religion and neurology, he refers to "William's melancholy about the universe" being said to be "due to bad digestion—probably his liver is torpid"). The more serious response is that it does indeed "depend on you *the liver*":

> If you surrender to the nightmare view and crown the evil edifice by your own suicide, you have indeed made a picture totally black ... Your mistrust of life has removed whatever worth your own enduring existence might have given to it; and now, throughout the whole sphere of possible influence of that existence, the mistrust has proved itself to have had divining power. But suppose, on the other hand, that instead of giving way to the nightmare view you cling to it that this world is not the *ultimatum* .... Suppose, however thickly evils crowd upon you, that your unconquerable subjectivity proves to be their match, and that you find a more wonderful joy than any passive pleasure can bring in trusting ever in the larger whole? Have you not now made life worth living on these terms?

From whence comes this conviction that *this world* is not the *ultimatum*? James returns, as he began, to "the deepest heart of all of us," and to our need "first of all to redeem our own hearts from atheisms and fears":

> The deepest thing in our nature is this ... dumb region of the heart in which we dwell alone with our willingnesses and unwillingnesses, our faiths and fears .... Here is our deepest organ of communication with the nature of things; and com-

pared with these concrete movements of our soul all abstract statements and scientific arguments—the veto, for example, which the strict positivist pronounces upon our faith—sound to us like mere chatterings of the teeth....

Speaking for—and from—this dumb region of the heart in which we dwell alone with our willingnesses and unwillingnesses, our faiths and fears," James offers this final benediction, the "last words" that an older man has the right and even the responsibility to speak to the younger generation:

These, then, are my last words to you: Be not afraid of life. Believe that life *is* worth living, and your belief will help create the fact. The "scientific proof" that you are right may not be clear before the day of judgment ... is reached. But the faithful fighters of this hour, or the beings that then and there will represent them, may then turn to the faint-hearted, who here decline to go on, with words like those with which Henry IV greeted the tardy Crillon after a great victory had been gained: "Hang yourself, brave Crillon! We fought at Arques, and you were not there."

"Be not afraid of life"—one catches in this simple heartfelt admonition the spirit of William James.

The volume concludes with an annotated bibliography by David M. Wulff. Especially noteworthy are the reviews published shortly after *The Varieties* appeared in print. As Wulff's annotations indicate, *The Varieties* was controversial then as it is now. We might say that where religionists sought to convert, James sought to controvert. He knew that controversy wounds, but he also knew that certain ideas are worth fighting for, especially those that have the capacity to energize our struggle for life.

REFERENCES

Capps, D. (1990). Sin, narcissism, and the changing face of conversion. *Journal of Religion and Health*, 29: 233-251.

Dittes, J. (1973). Beyond William James. In C.Y. Glock & P.E. Hammond (Eds.) *Beyond the Classics: Essays in the Scientific Study of Religion*. New York: Harper and Row (pp. 291-354).

Glock, C.Y. & P.E. Hammond (Eds.) (1973). *Beyond the Classics: Essays in the Scientific Study of Religion*. New York: Harper and Row.

James, W. (1973). Answers to Pratt's Questionnaire. In L.B. Brown (Ed.). *Psychology and Religion: Selected Readings*. Baltimore: Penguin Books (pp. 212-215). Originally published in Henry James III (Ed.) *The Letters of William James*. London: Longmans, 1926.

_____ (1982). *The Varieties of Religious Experience*. New York: Penguin Books.

Lewis, R.W.B. (1991). *The Jameses: A Family Narrative*. New York: Farrar, Straus and Giroux.

Myers, G.E. (1986). *William James: His Life and Thought*. New York: Yale University Press.

I. THE SPIRIT AND STRATEGIES OF *THE VARIETIES*

WILLIAM JAMES

JOHN DEWEY

By the death of Prof. William James, at the age of sixty-eight, America loses its most distinguished figure in the field of philosophy and psychology. A teacher of philosophy and psychology at Harvard from 1880 to 1907 (after having taught physiology eight years in the Harvard Medical School), he was much more than the professor. Lecturer upon the Gifford Foundation at Edinburgh in 1899-1901; Hibbert lecturer at Oxford in 1908; recipient of every type of honorary degree from American and European universities; member of almost every learned academy in Europe, he was much more than the erudite scholar. He was essentially the man of letters, but the man of letters who makes literature the medium of communicating ideas for the sake of public instruction. Never didactic, he was always the teacher. Always brilliant in literary style, he never indulged in literature for its own sake. If the common people read him gladly, it was not alone for a clearness and picturesqueness that will long be the despair of other philosophers, but because of their instinctive recognition that here at least was a philosopher who believed in life and who believed in philosophy because of his belief in life.

It is a significant fact that many of his most noteworthy books originally appeared as lectures before semi-popular audiences. His *Varieties of Religious Experience* are Gifford lectures; his *Pragmatism*, Lowell lectures; his *Pluralistic Universe*, Hibbert lectures; his *Human Immortality*, an Ingersoll lecture; his application of psychology to education is a series of *Talks to Teachers*. Of the various essays that compose his *Will to Believe*, the greater number are addresses delivered before various philosophical societies. This fact is significant, I say, for it indicates how essentially Professor James's thought is a human affair. He could not help making the expression of his philosophy intelligible, because to him a philosophy that was merely technical and professional missed the point of philosophy: the illumination and enlargement of the human mind on the things that are its most vital concern. William James did not need to write a separate treatise on ethics, because in its larger sense he was everywhere and always the moralist. He believed in his ideas and in his public, and the public's eager response to his ideas justified his confidence. He is almost the only philosopher of the day whose death marks an event in the world of letters and of public affairs, as well as in the realm of university teaching and scholarship.

Mr. James first won his standing as a psychologist. In 1890 appeared his large two-volumed *Principles of Psychology*. In some of its scientific detail the book has, of course, been

Originally published in *Independent*, 69 (1910): 533-536

superseded by later experimental work; the book itself initiated a movement which is already carrying psychology away from some of the positions of the original text. Nevertheless, the book is likely to become a classic—a classic of the order of Locke's *Essay* or Hume's *Treatise*. In a review of Wundt's monumental work on physiological psychology, Mr. James expressed the opinion that it ranked after Darwin's *Origin of Species* in the variety of its original contributions to important scientific matters. I am not sure that this saying could not better be applied to Mr. James's own work. One advantage, at least, he had; he never lost sight of the forest on account of the trees. Even when dealing with details of physiological and laboratory technique, he never forgets nor allows the reader to forget that the real subject-matter is human nature, not technical details. Comparison with his brother Henry seems to be made inevitable by the popular epigram, which I think is even more inept than such supposed epigrams are wont to be. The difference between the two is not that William James was a literary man and Henry a psychologist, but that the former was concerned with human nature in its broad and common features (like Walt Whitman, he gives the average of the massed effect), while the latter is concerned with the special and peculiar coloring that the mental life takes on in different individualities.

Professionally speaking, the distinctive trait of James's psychology is its remarkable union of the physiological and laboratory attitude with the introspective method. In spite of some efforts by Bain and Spencer, James was practically the first author using the English language to base his psychology on the biological method, with which he had become familiar as medical student and teacher. The reader feels that he is following a man whose training has been in the *natural* sciences, not in the metaphysical. This alone would, however, have secured only the honor of being a pioneer on a road in which he must inevitably have soon been overtaken and surpassed. His lasting achievement is to have laid upon this firm basis of scientific method a superstructure of unrivaled introspective refinement, accuracy and breadth. After reading James one sees that most of what had been called introspection, and that had brought the method into disrepute, was not introspection at all, but simply the spinning out of certain ready-made ideas. With William James introspection meant genuine observation of genuine events, events that most persons are too conventional or too literal to note at all, even though the facts lie close to them. He was almost a Columbus as an explorer of the inner world; even the better of those who preceded him seem by comparison clumsy and coarse, or bent on supporting some preconceived theory, while the joy of James was the delight of the explorer in pure discovery. It is impossible to overstate the originality of many portions of his treatise in directions where originality means sincere, unbiased, subtle and sympathetic observation.

The decade from 1890 to 1900 marked a decline of Mr. James's direct interest in psychology, or, rather, a transfer to some applications of psychology to life. The Gifford lectures on *Varieties of Religious Experience* signalized the fruition of his psychological method in a definite philosophic attitude; the ten remaining years of his life were courageously devoted, in spite of continual attacks of the heart trouble to which he finally succumbed, to the elaboration of this philosophy. From the standpoint of method he called it "pragmatism"; from that of substance of doctrine "radical empiricism." The germs of his pragmatism flourish in his psychology; the main ideas of his radical empiricism were outlined in his *Will to Believe,* the essays of which date from the late eighties and the nineties. To understand the roots of his philosophy one must turn to the ideas dominant after 1870.

Broadly speaking, there were just two types of philosophy to choose between at that time. Darwinism had finally won a definitive victory. Herbert Spencer was the guide and philosopher, if not the friend, of an aggressive group of thinkers. On this side, there was a dogmatic, militant philosophy which claimed to speak in the name of science; and in the name of science to banish to the unknowable all that was vague and mystical, or in any way beyond the realm of facts verifiable by the senses. This philosophy, when not materialistic, was positivistic or agnostic. Probably what turned Mr. James from it was its crudity and insensitiveness upon the esthetic side, and its somewhat blatant know-it-all air, as well as the doom it seemed to pronounce, in the name of science, upon man's ideal aims—upon all that goes, vaguely, under the name of the life of the spirit. Mr. James always had a keen eye for the under dog, and I imagine that "scientific philosophy" was so openly the upper dog of the day as to repel him.

Most of those who turned away from materialism and positivism sought refuge in German idealism. Thomas Hill Green, the Cairds, Bradley and their active disciples naturalized the thought of Kant and Hegel in England; William T. Harris, George S. Morris and others made it at home in this country. Now, Mr. James could not find satisfaction in this school any more than in positivism. His training in the methods of natural science made him find neo-Kantianism and Hegelianism rather formal and empty. They proceeded with too much respect for concepts in general and with too little for brute facts in the concrete.

But more than that, they were tarred, to his mind, with that which made the "scientific" philosophy so objectionable to him. Idealism as well as materialism were "absolutistic" in tendency; they made the universe what Mr. James called a "block universe"—a world all in one piece. Such a world left no place for genuine novelty, for real change, for adventure, for the uncertain and the vague, for choice and freedom—in short, for distinctive individuality. It made little difference to Mr. James whether the hard and fast unity to which these things were sacrificed was called Matter or Thought; the intolerable thing was that they were—or seemed to him to be —sacrificed.

One may say, with as much truth as is possible in such a summary statement, that Mr. James's philosophy took shape as a deliberate protest against the monisms that reduced everything to parts of one embracing whole, and against the absolutisms which regarded reality as having a fixed, final, unalterable character. His was the task of preserving loyalty to fact, respect for the humble particular, so long as it was concretely verifiable, against the pretentious rational formula. This loyalty constituted the empiricism he learned from science. But when "science" presumed to set fixed meters and bounds, when in the name of some general law it denied freedom and reduced individual life to a meaningless bubble, he protested that science itself was a human product whose justification was in the service it rendered in making human life freer and happier. Idealism means one thing to the technical philosopher—a theory of knowledge. To the common man it means something quite different—faith in the supremacy of moral values. This latter faith Mr. James had, but he held that idealism in this sense was a matter of will—of the will to believe—not something to be demonstrated by rationalistic formula.

It may perhaps seem strange to the layman to learn that a new and vital movement could be launched in philosophy by insisting upon novelty, plasticity or indeterminateness, variety and change as genuine traits of the world in which we live. But so fixed in the contrary sense, so intellectualistic, were the traditions of philosophy, both from the materialistic and the idealistic sides, that for a long time, for almost twenty years, in fact, Mr. James stood practically alone—a voice crying in the wilderness. He was listened to with respect and with admiration, because he said inspiring and suggestive things in a brilliant way. But few or none took him seriously as a philosopher, even when proclaiming his preeminence as a philosopher. By the beginning of this century, however, the tide had turned. The *Zeitgeist* has been visibly with Mr. James instead of against him. Somehow the temper of imagination changed; positivism and idealism had, for the time at least, exhausted themselves. The pragmatism which Mr. James urged with apostolic fervor as a *via media* between natural science and the ideal interests of morals and religion, seemed to be in the air, only waiting the word of a master to precipitate itself. Instead of being at cross-purposes with his generation, as he had been during the period when most philosophers are finding their audience and elaborating their systems, he found an eager audience waiting. The result was an immediate efflorescence. The ideas that he long entertained grew and expanded in the new genial warmth. Three books and many articles appeared in the last five years. I do not know whether there is any precedent for a man finding himself as a philosopher and presenting himself as a master after the age of sixty. Yet this is what happened in the case of Mr. James. It is characteristic of the man that one does not associate years with Mr. James, to say nothing of thinking of him as old. Even to say that he was sixty-eight is like mentioning some insignificant external fact, like his weight. His intellectual vitality, his openness of mind, his freedom from cant, his sympathetic insight into what other people were thinking of, his frank honesty, his spirit of adventure into the unknown, did more than keep him young; they made age an irrelevant matter.

Whatever fate may have in store for Mr. James's pragmatism as a system, it is a great thing for university life and for higher culture in America that Mr. James united the wise maturity of rich experience with the ardor and enthusiasm of youth, and both with the gallantry of a free soul that was all his own.

America will justify herself as long as she breeds those like William James; men who are thinkers and thinkers who are men. I love, indeed, to think that there is something profoundly American in his union of philosophy with life; in his honest acceptance of the facts of science joined to a hopeful outlook upon the future; in his courageous faith in our ability to shape the unknown future. When our country comes to itself in consciousness, when it transmutes into articulate ideas what are still obscure and blind strivings, two men, Emerson and William James, will, I think, stand out as the prophetic forerunners of the attained creed of values.

CATCHING THE SPIRIT OF WILLIAM JAMES

JAMES E. DITTES

For those of us who venture to appraise and appropriate *The Varieties* in this volume, William James has a word of warning. It's the same good-natured rebuke he offered, near the end of his life, to a bright and aspiring Ph.D. candidate, Miss S. Her dissertation had painstakingly catalogued and appraised the propositions she had found in his writings, but had disregarded the spirit that animated them. So he chided her:

> "... from the technical point of view you may be proud of your production ... the number of subdivisions and articulations which you make gives me vertiginous admiration. Nevertheless, the tragic fact remains that I don't feel wounded at all by all that output of ability ... as a Ph.D. thesis your essay is supreme, but why don't you go farther? ... This is splendid philology, but is it live criticism of anyone's *Weltanschauung*? ... the whole Ph.D. industry of building up an author's meaning out of separate texts leads nowhere, unless you have *first grasped his centre of vision, by an act of imagination*" (H. James 1920, II: 355 my italics).

The legacy of *The Varieties*, nearly a century after they were spoken at Edinburgh, is not as a system of ideas, a set of propositions—though some (e.g., Uren 1928; Browning 1980) have joined Miss S in efforts to codify James's thinking as though it were. The legacy is not in the "content" but in the "method," except that "method" is much too pallid and formal a term. The legacy is in the "centre of vision," the *"Weltanschauung,"* in the personal outlook, the personal spirit. James wants us to see *how he* (each word separately emphasized) sees things, so that *we can* better see things our way, not so that we can see things his way. In the parlance of our day (on which he would improve) he wants to empower us. In the parlance of his day, we are invited to a personal conversion. We are challenged to catch his spirit.

> "... since you have shown what a superb mistress you are in that difficult art of discriminating abstractions and opposing them to each other one by one ... may I urge, I say, that you should now turn your back upon that academic sort of artificiality altogether, and devote your great talents to the study of reality in its concreteness" (ibid).

Adapted from "Beyond William James" in Charles Y. Glock and Phillip Hammond (Eds.) *Beyond the Classics?: Essays in the Scientific Study of Religion*; (New York: Harper and Row, 1973), pp. 291-354. The challenge of following "In the Spirit of William James" has long since been authoritatively claimed as a title (Perry 1938), but it is too apt, too "in the spirit," not to be reclaimed here.

Propositions and structures of ideas must have been among the "the big successes and results" he had in mind when he wrote, as the Gifford lectures approached, what we may legitimately take not only as a political manifesto, but also as a principle of intellectual inquiry:

"I am against bigness and greatness in all its forms, and with the invisible molecular forces that work from individual to individual, stealing in through the crannies of the world like so many soft rootlets, or like the capillary oozing of water, and yet rending the hardest monuments of man's pride, if you give them time...against all big successes and big results; and in favor of the eternal forces of truth which always work in the individual and immediately unsuccessful way, underdogs always, till history comes after they are long dead, and puts them on the top" (H. James 1920, II: 90).

Generations before "vulnerability" became fashionable, James relies on it; it can be regarded as the principal strategy of his lectures, disarmingly inviting his Calvinistic audience to drop their critical arms-length guard and to approach, to approach the experiences afresh, and to approach his approach to them. As his choice of words recognized when he wrote Miss S, the invitation to approach him, to catch his spirit, is a risky invitation to come close enough to *wound*.

I think we approach William James most authentically and most usefully, when we approach *him* as intimately and as naively as he approached the persons who people *The Varieties*, intimately enough to catch his spirit. We snub William James when we catalog his propositions.

"Propositions" is the language of structure. But, for James, structure entombs the mind. Experience is so much richer than any success of the mind in comprehending it that efforts to locate and organize thought are as likely to hinder as to aid the mind in its proper quest, which is always to seek that which is "beyond" its present confinements.

To focus on "propositions" may suggest that disciplined thinking is an end in itself or that it yields products to be arrayed and admired in a museum (including those museums called scholarly journals or books or classrooms or even, perhaps, Gifford Lectures). But, for James, critical, disciplined thinking has a *purpose*—to enable us to live more effectively in our world—and in such *use* is its importance and its validity.

"Propositions" implies dicta that claim attention as insights of permanence and wide generalizability, a kind of building block added to humanity's gradually accumulating tower of knowledge. But, for James, the discoveries and formulations of the mind have a type of validity that is "here and now," "for me," as well as "maybe." To build with them is to build a futile tower of Babel; solid towers can be built only of inert, inorganic, squared and smoothed blocks; and thought, for James, is living, organic, magnificently uneven in contours, and wonderfully rough in texture.

James's ideas were not offered, the lectures were not intended, the book was not written for the purpose of contributing to a common enterprise of accumulating scientific generalization. They were offered to express a personal outlook, an attitude, a philosophy, a spirit. In James's own view nothing is more crucial than the context and the function of an idea. Ideas for him do not have, as they do for the contemporary scientific outlook, reference to a constant, objective reality, equally perceptible to all observers in the same way, observers whose perception is gradually clarified, gradually made more like the reality itself, as they share their individual perceptions and ideas about this reality. For James, an idea about reality and, for that matter, reality itself, exists for particular persons in particular circumstances. The ideas are *for* the thinker, here and now. Since their purpose is not to make a rendering as isomorphic as possible with some objective reality "out there," there is no point in talking about James's ideas as though they were to be validated or corrected by rigorous test to see how accurately they do render the objective reality.

James's ideas are the report of how one man, a man who happened to delight in the expectation that others would find things to be different, finds things to be.

Thus we have the anomalous situation that the man most often and justifiably cited as the father of American psychology of religion has left no school or following or system or impact of the kind ordinarily regarded as a founder's heritage. There is no distinctive Jamesian psychology of religion any more than there is a distinctive Jamesian psychology.[1] James can be appropriately regarded as the founder of American psychology of religion not for the psychological theories or psychological data or psychological method he offered, but for his philosophical position or perhaps more accurately, philosophical temper or outlook. He championed an attitude toward religion and toward the universe and toward investigation which justified, even encouraged, psychological study.

James was a philosopher. Or, perhaps more accurately, he was philosophical, not the possessor or announcer of a philosophy. What he had to offer and has to offer is a distinctive philosophical temper, an outlook, a *spirit*, to use the highly appropriate word chosen by his literary executor and biographer Ralph Barto Perry for his own exposition of William James's mind, *In the Spirit of William James* (1938).

As John Smith (1967) writes:

James was philosophical in a way that is, unfortunately, not as widespread today as it was at some time in the past. For him, to be philosophical meant viewing every subject against the background of man and his place in the universe; it meant being aware that there is always more to your subject than you are able to capture at one time and from one perspective. Being philosophical on his terms was as much an attitude and a temper of mind as a standpoint or a position to be articulated in a particular system ... the philosophical influence was evident less as a matter of doctrine and more as the persistent attempt to think critically and comprehensively.

James not only thought *with* the concepts and principles he found necessary for expressing the results of his investigations, but thought *about* them as well.

Perhaps we could even venture to say that he thought *through* them. He made his concepts transparent—and his English style cannot be separated from his thought—enough that his mind/spirit shows through as much in spite of them as with them.

If, with any integrity, we are to consider William James with reference to contemporary social scientific study of religion, it must be this philosophy, this spirit that we consider, this attitude toward religion, toward the realities religion points to, and toward the

---

1. The most frequently cited contribution by James to psychological theory, as such, is the exception that proves the rule. The theory of emotions to which James's name is often attached, along with that of the Dane, C. Lange, may be and has been taken as a straightforward psychological theory of the kind I have argued here James did not produce, at least in the psychology of religion theory to be tested against data to see how accurately it can account for them. It patently does not fit the data. The "theory" can be read much more plausibly and much more straightforwardly as an expression of James's radically empirical or pragmatic or functional epistemology. The theory, in James's own epigrammatic formulation, "we feel sorry because we cry, angry because we strike, afraid because we tremble" (1890: 450), clearly does not arise from analysis of data nearly so much as from James's philosophical and dispositional preference to give priority to the more behavioral elements and to make the more cognitive elements derivative, having validity only as they are rooted in overt function, in the empirical.

processes of knowing and of investigating. If we consider particular psychological statements, it must be as these express this spirit, not to see how closely these psychological statements correspond with any particular facts or other theories at our disposal. The next section will demonstrate in some detail how even James's most striking psychological statements are better understood as expressions of this outlook or philosophy or spirit than they are as scientific propositions.

This exercise may or may not seem fruitful to contemporary scientists. On one hand, James's spirit seems remarkably contemporary. Secularism, pluralism, existentialism, confrontation, involvement, search for authenticity, the struggle of the individual against the establishment—these are the characteristics of James's spirit. However, though these may be the characteristics of some parts of our culture, they are not the characteristics of the scientific parts of our culture. Some of the battles James was fighting would be viewed by contemporary scientists as on their behalf; he can be quoted and proof-texted for his opposition to a monolithic, supernatural, reductionistic understanding of religious phenomena, a view that precludes psychological investigation. Because his philosophy insisted on taking religious phenomena seriously as *phenomena*, he fought battles that paved the way for scientific study. But, on the other hand, because James was opposed to established, exclusivistic, monolithic reductionism of any kind, not just *religiously* established monopolies, his philosophy can be turned against much of contemporary science just as well. Because he insists on taking religious phenomena seriously, as *phenomena* with an authority and importance in themselves, he raises constant objection against attempts to capture these phenomena in the name of science.

Psychology, and indeed all science, is beset with a persistent and ongoing battle between those who place the highest values on regularity, generalizability, reproducibility, and those who would place still higher values on individuality, depth, richness, and "meaning." James stands with the latter, endorsing, even insisting upon individual distinctiveness and depth. Since the debate is still so lively and James has so many allies, it might seem of no more than historic interest to retrace his early arguments. Yet his own formulation—a blend of pluralism in ontology and radical empiricism and pragmatism in epistemology—may still represent a distinctive, important, and instructive position, a somewhat different and more sophisticated formulation of the issues than, for example, many of his disciples and spokesmen may achieve today.

This essay will now proceed in two sections. First, it will try to make good on the assertion that the pronouncements in *The Varieties of Religious Experience* are better seen as expressions of a philosophy or spirit than they are as entries into an accumulating scientific corpus. Those of James's observations that seem the most likely candidates for "central propositions" will be reviewed, and it will be seen how these, rather than formulating propositions, express a spirit. This kind of inductive, empirical, case study approach to discerning James's spirit is the most characteristically Jamesian method we could use. So, after having examined several materials in the book, we should have an understanding of the spirit which animates it. Second, however un-Jamesian as may be such a concession to would be synthesizers, the last section will attempt a more systematic statement of the philosophy or spirit.

I. BEYOND THE PSYCHOLOGY TO THE SPIRIT

If the study of religion has yielded any insight in our time, it is an understanding of the paradox of institutionalization: the religious spirit demands a body, but this body preempts the spirit. The transcendent, or the response to the transcendent, finds cultural forms and expressions which are supposed to reflect and point to the transcendent but which turn out to veil the transcendent; and forms receive the response due the transcendent. Something like that has happened to the spirit of William James. He delivered the Gifford Lectures, *The Varieties of Religious Experience,* as a series of rich and varied expressions of his outlook, his spirit. *"The Varieties* can scarcely be called a systematic treatise on the psychology of the religious life. Professor James had a thesis to prove. The philosophy that appealed at once to his heart and mind was pluralistic idealism. James therefore sought support in the religious life for his hypothesis that the universe is a protean world of spiritual beings"[2] (Uren 1928: 61). James's skepticism for questionnaires and his use of case studies, his arguments on the validity of mysticism and the constructive potential of mental illness, his affirmation of a "beyond" and "over belief," his construction of types—rightly read, all these and other parts of the book point us not just to themselves but to the spirit that has called them into being. But, as idolatry and fundamentalism are easier than faith in a transcendent beyond form, so it is easier to select certain "fruits" of James's spirit and to hold these up as the "central propositions" which most of us prefer to find. We tend to absolutize, as *the* key to James, expressions and arguments that James was content, even insistent, to leave tentative and open and even to leave behind, as he moved "beyond." Even Uren (1928), whose insight into the unsystematic nature of this book was quoted with approval above, subsequently insisted on the systematic codification of these lectures. He endeavors "to isolate and classify the numerous types which are treated by James with irritating desultoryness" (Uren 1928: 80), and he offers an elaborate scheme of well-labeled and well-defined types and subtypes, and the insights that James wanted such excursions to yield for the reader are utterly obscured.

If it is tempting and easy to rend selected elements of James's thinking out of context and to nominate these to a centrality they do not deserve (a pseudocentrality that obscures the communication of his spirit), part of the problem is that James also writes "out of context." He threw himself into each chapter in his *Psychology* as though it *were* the key to all psychology, and then he abandoned it and moved beyond to the next chapter and threw himself into *that* in the same way. So he conducts himself in the Gifford Lectures. He ventures to write about each "variety" as though it provided the key, then he moves on. One can, like Uren (1928) or Browning (1980), be irritated at such carelessness, discount such lapses, and proceed to arrange all in a super organization. Or one can suppose that James means to do exactly what he is doing and that this style is only one more clue to the message he wants to get across. He does after all make the message obligingly explicit from time to time.

> The obvious outcome of our total experience is that the world can be handled according to many systems of ideas, and is so handled by different men, and will each time give some characteristic kind of profit, for which he cares, to the handler, while at the same time some other kind of profit has to be omitted or postponed (VRE: 120).

This section proposes to consider, one after another, several of the ideas that could be, and have been, offered as "central propositions." It will show that James did discuss each one as though it were the key. It will also show that James clearly invited his hearers and readers to move "beyond" each one. I propose to "demythologize" each of these central propositions to discover the spirit of William James.

---

2. Uren shares the understanding I am proposing as to James's strategy and as to what the book is and is not. But I think it clear that James had not only a thesis of a pluralistic universe to demonstrate but also his pragmatic theory of knowledge. By the same token the way James goes about presenting the lectures is as much a clue to these dimensions of his spirit as is the material he desribes in them.

Two Types

If William James is to be cited for actual, constructive theorizing in the psychology of religion, it is for his famous types: "The contrast between the two ways of looking at life which are characteristic respectively of what we called the healthy-minded, who need to be born only once, and of the sick souls, who must be twice-born in order to be happy. The result is two different conceptions of the universe of our experience" (VRE: 163). It is with these types that he is most often represented in textbooks whose writers and readers have typically tried to see how they could make still other instances fit into these types.

But rather than trying to make these types *the* distinctive Jamesian key to comprehending religious experience, they might be advised to linger over these types no longer than did James. "It is true that he introduced distinctions such as 'once-born' and 'twice-born,' for purposes of classification. But he attached little importance to them" (Perry 1948: 333). The distinction that James seems to offer so absolutely on page 163 looks different on pages 477f.

> From this point of view, the contrasts between the healthy and the morbid mind, and between the once-born and the twice-born types, of which I spoke in earlier lectures, cease to be the radical antagonisms which many think them ... But the final consciousness which each type reaches of union with the divine has the same practical significance for the individual; and individuals may well be allowed to get to it by the channels which lie most open to their several temperaments ... so that in many instances it is quite arbitrary whether we class the individual as a once-born or a twice-born subject (VRE: 477ff).

These types are important, but they are important for the representations they give in *their* chapters of the philosophy-spirit-method approach of James to the study of religion. And it contradicts that spirit with ironic severity to wrest these types out of context and try to discover how religious persons or experiences can be sorted into one type or the other. In presenting these types, James wanted us to understand something about religious experience and human nature (that *is* the subtitle of the volume, "A Study in Human Nature"), but what he wanted his hearers to understand was not simply that these two types can be distinguished.

James's distinction between the healthy-minded and the sick soul bears an obvious, though perhaps superficial, correlation with the still more famous types to be suggested by Max Weber within three years of the Gifford Lectures and to be elaborated and solidly established within a decade by Ernst Troeltsch: the distinction between the church and the sect.[3] Church-sect has been subjected ever since to seemingly endless (in both meanings of the word) debate: Which are the crucial defining characteristics? What instances fit which category?

There is, undoubtedly, a variety of reasons that James's types have escaped the degree of obsession and preoccupation that have harassed church-sect. There have been fewer psychologists of religion than sociologists of religion to argue with each other, for one thing. And these psychologists of religion have generally been attracted to the more dynamic formulations of the same distinction (between the suppression and acknowledgement of conflict and "evil") announced by Sigmund Freud in his manifesto *The Interpretation of Dreams* while James was preparing the Gifford Lectures (without, so far as

---

3. Weber first pairs the terms "church" and "sect" after a sentence that could be mistaken for James's account of his distinction. Weber describes the one "as a sort of trust foundation for supernatural ends," and the "other as a community ... of the reborn". (Weber 1958: 144ff).

is apparent, being informed by or about Freud's thinking at the time). But perhaps psychologists have avoided preoccupation with how well the types fit the facts because they implicitly recognize a different intention for James's types.

Perhaps the difference in intention between James's types and the sociologists' is as simple as hearing James want to say "there *are* two types" and hearing Troeltsch want to say "there are *two* types." Theoretical types, like their more recent statistical counterparts, factors, do two things. They collect like characteristics, and they separate unlike. But James, like the most sophisticated users of factor analysis, was totally unwilling to generalize beyond his own accumulation of data; the groupings that emerged made sense of the instances at hand, but different data, or even a different way of viewing the same data, could easily yield different groupings. James was particularly unwilling to suppose that his "factors" exhausted the "space." Nothing could have been more repellent to him than the aspiration "to account for all of the variance." It was enough for James to poke gentle fun at the established view of religion held by his hearers by calling it, ironically, "healthy-minded," and by demonstrating one alternative style, an underdog that turned out to have at least as strong claims for validity. (He could never assume Freud's more radical contention that the self-repressive style that the Establishment preferred could actually be dysfunctional, yielding pathology. In James's father's house there were many rooms, enough even for Victorian Henry as well as Yankee William.)

The description of the two types comes early in the book, the first thing after three essentially introductory lectures. This is not, in my judgment, to announce these as the banner psychological concepts to be announced in the lectures, but to establish, in their own way, that there *is* variety. It just takes two. Having established this decisively, the types have served their purpose, and there is not the slightest hesitation about going on to looking at similar and different data in different ways. The very next chapter introduces the "divided self," a category that has troubled no end of more "logical minded" (James's epithet) readers (e.q., Uren 1928), who have agitated themselves over whether this is a third type or a subtype or whether it fits in to the overall scheme begun by "healthy-minded" and "morbid-minded" in some different way. The difficulty makes James's point for him, even though it goes too often unheeded: there is no "overall scheme," experience is too rich for one.

He concludes the chapter on healthy-mindedness with as eloquent and explicit appeal for pluralism as is found in the book, including such resounding sentences as

> But why in the name of common sense need we assume that only one such system of ideas can be true...and why, after all, may not the world be so complex as to consist of many interpenetrating spheres of reality, which we can best approach in alternation by using different conceptions and assuming different attitudes, just as mathematicians handle the same numerical and spacial facts by geometry, by analytical geometry, by algebra, by the calculus, or by quarternions, and each time come out right? (VRE: 120).

He is characteristically tactful enough not to address this attack directly against the Establishment's view of religion, which I do think he means to be chiding. But its climactic position at the end of this chapter can hardly intend otherwise.

All this contrasts with the treatment commonly given church-sect. Sociologists have generally succeeded in discussing their types as though they were intended to give a mapping of the universe, rather than an account of the inner coherence of certain segments of it. However, this turns out to be a misunderstanding of Troeltsch's intentions, too. Paul Gustafson (1967) has argued impressively that Troeltsch intended to be developing the coherent implications of two theologically derived dimensions, rather than account for all possible empirical observations. And others (for example, Johnson 1957, 1971; Eister 1967) have suggested that Troeltsch, too, was chiefly concerned to peg his types "simply as two among other alternate or variant forms" (Eister 1967: 88).

The style with which James works is also important to notice in connection with these types as elsewhere. One looks in vain for the definition for these types, for the itemization of those characteristics which definitively put an instance in one or the other. He enumerates rather than defines. He adds instance to instance, loosely linked. Careful conceptual summary would subtract from, not add to, the description of actual events, which is where the "essentials" lie.

If the chapter on healthy-mindedness has, as its end, the appeal for pluralism quoted above, and the chapter on the sick soul continues this appeal by demonstrating the greater adequacy of this underdog of religious styles, these two chapters carry another message as well. The criterion of adequacy is made clear. "The world *can be handled* according to many systems of ideas, and is so handled by different men, and will each time *give* some characteristic kind of *profit,* for which he cares, to the handler, while at the same time some other kind of profit has to be omitted or postponed" (VRE: 120, my italics). "The method of averting one's attention from evil, and living simply in the light of good is splendid *as long as it will* work. It will work with many persons; it will work far more generally than most of us are ready to suppose ... But it breaks down *impotently* as soon as melancholy comes" (VRE: 160, italics added). In the middle, then, of his essentially descriptive, static account, James introduces functionalism—pragmatism, as he will later call it—not as a style of psychological analysis, but as a criterion of philosophical evaluation. "Here is the real core of the religious problem: help!" (VRE: 159). Validity is more likely to be found where responses to such need are found. Such judgment is closer to the judgment of the religious traditions themselves ("In as much as ye did it unto the least of these ...") than it is to those contemporary judgments which presuppose that functional analysis invalidates rather than validates. If a social scientist ventures to demonstrate the functions of religion, to show how religion answers the cry for help, perhaps even in ways not consciously recognized by the religionist, he or she may be ennobling religion, in James's view, but debasing it ("reducing" it, we say) in others' eyes. Not just religionists, but social scientists, too, are suspicious of the functional and seem to assume that *either* religion serves discernible functions *or* it is true. The serving of functions, which James exalts as a criterion of value, is still apologized for (e.q., Bellah 1970) or scolded (e.q., Berger 1967) as degrading.

But another criterion intrudes, partly between the lines, a familiar criterion by now. Healthy-mindedness, the spirit of the once-born, is dubious in part just because it suggests a oneness. James must have in mind here, in part, the buoyant absolutism of Emerson and, perhaps, even of his own father, which he found wanting. It too simply denies the conflicting components of experience.[4]

The two types, in summary then, point more to the philosophical principles of pluralism and pragmatism than to any empirical ordering of phenomena.

---

4. I say that healthy-mindedness implies a monism, despite James's apparent word to the contrary, "Now the gospel of healthy-mindedness, as we have described it, casts its vote distinctly for the pluralistic view" (VRE: 130). If James was not above a gentle irony in his designation of "healthy-mindedness," it may be recurring here. In any case, James is speaking here of what might be called—though he had more regard for the niceties of language than to do so—"vertical pluralism." Health-mindedness is pluralistic to the extent that it discards (James's younger Viennese contemporary would have said "represses") evil and conflicts into a distant and distinct world, beyond its own conscious experience. The remaining world of experience remains safely monistic.

Mysticism

If the healthy-minded-morbid-minded distinction occupies the prime place after the introductory lectures, mysticism occupies the climactic place. James contributes to this notion of the climactic status of mysticism by saying at the outset of the chapter that he has been building up to it throughout the lectures. And here he offers the oft-quoted statement, "One may say truly, I think, that personal religious experience has its root and center in mystical states of consciousness ... Such states of consciousness ought to form the vital chapter from which the other chapters get their light"[5] (VRE: 370).

Is mysticism, then, the key, the epitome, the model, the essence, the foundation of religious experience? Well, James is capable of treating any current topic as though it were the whole or the key to the whole, for the very simple reason that while he is discussing it, it is. But we need to read to the end of his chapter on mysticism and also, of course, consider the other topics which alternatively serve the same function. At the end of the chapter we discover that, far from an absolute, mysticism is characteristically relative. It may claim an authority over those who experience it, but none over the rest of us. James writes with an absolute firmness only when he is combating absolutism.

> Once more, then, I repeat that non-mystics are under no obligation to acknowledge in mystical states a superior authority ... They offer us *hypotheses* ... What comes [in mystical experience] must be sifted and tested, and run the gauntlet of confrontation with the total context of experience, just like what comes from the outer world of sense (VRE: 417-19, italics in original).

James does not dispute it as a fair reading of his purposes to suppose that "I have undermined the authority of mysticism" (VRE: 421).

James, indeed, wants us to have respect for mysticism, not because it represents the essence of religious experience so much as because it represents the essence of some values very important to his spirit. James used his lectures on mysticism to carry on two running battles, each occupying about half of the chapter. The first half of the chapter wages battle against the absolutistic pretensions of rationalism (and in favor of a pluralism of consciousness). The second half battles against the stultified pretensions of "established" mystical traditions (and in favor of more functional understanding and of attention to pragmatic effects). Actually, in a sense, it is a single running battle, the same that occupied most of his career. He challenges the pretensions of the established system wherever he finds it oppressive and idolatrous, which seems to be about wherever he finds it, in this case both among mystics and among antimystics.

Mysticism: Alternative to Rationalism

Mysticism is defined as an experience of knowledge that "defies expression" (VRE: 371). The principal mark of mysticism is, on purpose, a negative one. Mysticism provides a repudiation, if its validity can be acknowledged, of the primacy of rationalism. This was a repudiation devoutly to wished; "our normal waking consciousness, rational consciousness as we call it, is but one special type of consciousness, whilst all about it, parted from

---

5. Mysticism, interestingly enough, was a type that Troeltsch added to church and sect, apparently to move in two directions which correspond to the two dimensions we are finding fundamentally in James's thought. Troeltsch apparently wanted to demonstrate more of the diversity of religious types. He also apparently wanted to find more opportunity for discussing their function.

it by the filmiest of screens, there lie potential forms of consciousness entirely different"(VRE: 378). James set out in this chapter not so much to describe the essence of religion as finally and climactically to help his hearers rend that filmy screen and to discover that they, too, are capable of experiencing forms of consciousness quite different from the feeble rationalism on which they were wont to rely. He starts out with innocent guile assuring his hearers in the first paragraph that he is on *their* side of the filmy screen. He is separated from mystical experience "almost entirely." Then step by step, with gradual escalation, he reminds them—us—that after all we do have glimpses of such things, glimpses which we can find nonthreatening and even authentic. First, "aha" experiences of recognition and perception, then *déjà vu*, then dreams, then, briefly, trances. Then alcohol, which he wryly suggests has been "long since branded as pathological," apparently wanting to remind us how far behind the filmy screen we have already gone. Then nitrous oxide which James had experimented with.

At this point his presentation reaches a climax. He has led his hearers and readers gradually into an appreciation of mysticism, not just so they could appreciate and understand mysticism—one is hard pressed to find any "psychology of mysticism" anywhere in the chapter—but so that they would come to appreciate that understanding of reality that mysticism points to. "No account of the universe in its totality can be final which leaves these other forms of consciousness quite disregarded ... They forbid a premature closing of our accounts with reality." *This* is the message: do not cheat yourself by closing your account with reality. This is the message to which much of the book is directed; mysticism is in its climactic place in the book because it makes the point insistently. And James has been especially careful in constructing this lecture to make sure his hearers are led gently enough to this point so that they can accept the message as deriving from their own experience and not as alien and exotic. James can end his brief homiletic pressing of the point, as he does ("those who have ears to hear, let them hear") with some confidence that he has opened ears to the hearing of his message of an open, pluralistic universe. Having opened ears and having announced the message they are to hear, James bombards his hearers with ten pages of personal accounts of mystical experiences—some drug-induced and some "religious mysticism pure and simple"—with virtually no comment.

Mysticism: Not the Final Authority, Either

The end of this series of cases almost certainly must have been the end of Lecture 16. For at this point James makes the transition from the discussion of mysticism "as it comes sporadically" to a discussion of "its methodical cultivation" within the established religious traditions (VRE: 391), which have sometimes even generated "a codified system of mystical theology" (VRE: 397). This transition is the signal to make the transition in mood from the trust and openness accorded the disestablished to the guardedness and suspicion accorded the established. Testimony is still taken even from these "methodical" mystics when this is useful to attack the pretensions of rationalism. "Saint Ignatius confessed one day to Father Laynez that a single hour of meditation at Manresa had taught him more truth about heavenly things than all the teachings of the doctors put together could have taught him" (VRE: 401). But a new note of challenge creeps in, lest these established mystics lay claim to too much authority over the rest of us. The challenge gradually escalates from this mid-point to the end of the chapter where the claims of mysticism to be a decisive religious authority are soundly repudiated with such remarks as I have quoted above.

The challenge is, in part, on familiar ground, that of pluralism of consciousness and, hence, pluralism of reality and, hence, pluralism of authority. We are reminded that religious mysticism itself comprises richly varying moods and experiences, so that any one can hardly be norm or authority. We are reminded that "religious mysticism is only one half of mysticism" (VRE: 417); although the "other half" is presently largely relegated to "textbooks on insanity," it too still needs to be heard from. And we are finally reminded that mysticism is only one of the varieties of religious experience. If the call, "those that have ears to hear, let them hear," is an appeal to unblock ears too long tuned to only a narrow band of hearing, it must also, in the last analysis, remind us that there are those who do not have ears to hear.

But the challenge comes too from the other principal force within James's spirit, his pragmatism. Mystics may report many wonderful and amazing experiences and even develop means for codifying and cultivating these. But such an experience has value and deserves to be taken seriously—even for the mystics themselves, much less by the rest of us—only if it meets one clear test. "Its fruits must be good for life" (VRE: 392). "To pass a spiritual judgment upon these states, we must ... inquire into their fruits for life" (VRE: 404). James's seemingly unqualified enthusiasm for mysticism in the first half of the chapter now gives way to the guardedness with which he puts mystics to this test; notice the conjunction he chooses now that he is well into this part of his discussion: "Saint Ignatius was a mystic, *but* his mysticism made him assuredly one of the most powerfully practical human engines that ever lived" (VRE: 404, my italics added).

One could try to tease out of James's discussion some fragments of actual psychological study of mysticism. The most notable such fragment would be his summary description (VRE: 407-13) of the qualities of mystic consciousness. He summarizes this by saying that mystic consciousness is optimistic "or at least the opposite of pessimistic," and that it "harmonizes best with twice-bornness." But several things need to be noted to put this description into context. First and most amusingly almost, is the polite disregard he shows here for the distinctiveness of the types of healthy-mindedness and morbid-mindedness to which he earlier devoted so much attention, a disregard which was interpreted in our last section. It doesn't offend James, as it does the systematizers of his thought, to find mysticism both optimistic and twice-born. Second, this descriptive summary is exceedingly brief and tucked in near the end of the chapter. Third and crucial, this description has a context and an explicit purpose, a "function." He says at the outset that he is going into this description to see what evidence he can find for the authority of mysticism.

Summary. What Mysticiam Teaches Us

He follows this descriptive material and concludes the chapter with a systematic three-point statement. These summarize the three principal messages he has wanted to get across in the course of his discussion of mysticism. He summarizes them in the reverse order from that in which we have found them in the chapter. First, whatever authority mysticism possesses, it comes from its pragmatic outcome, the "truth that comes to a man [that] proves to be a force that he can live by" (VRE: 414), and this becomes a very strong authority indeed, rendering the mystic even *"invulnerable"* (VRE: 415) to whatever demands social propriety and rationalism may want to inflict upon him. Second, however, even the claims of mysticism are severely limited by the consideration of pluralism within and without mystical consciousness. And third, the appeal of the first half of the chapter is now recapitulated: mysticism holds out a hope to all of us to move beyond the confining rationalistic cells in which our own consciousness may be fettered. William James's discussion of mysticism is far less important for what he wants us to know about mysticism than it is for what he wants us to know through mysticism about the spirit with which he approached this subject and all matters.

Saintliness

With this new affirmation of the pragmatic (or, as James was then still calling it, the "empirical") test, perhaps we should look to what he says about the "fruits" of religion for a "central proposition." What counts is the pay-off of religious experience in helping a person move through actual life experiences. This must be a clear deduction from James's presuppositions, and he obliges us in making it and in providing a total of five lectures—a fourth of the total and by far the most pages given to any topic—to "saintliness." He opens this section by calling this discussion of "the practical fruits for life" the "really important part of our task" (VRE: 254). "The collective name for the ripe fruits of religion in a character is Saintliness. The saintly character is the character for which spiritual emotions are the habitual centre of the personal energy" (VRE: 266). And at the outset of such a crucial discussion, James even ventures to write as though he had hold of a universal: "and there is a certain composite photograph of universal saintliness, the same in all religions, of which the features can easily be traced" (VRE: 266). He proceeds with an elaborate and definitive-sounding catalogue. Having itemized these validating fruits for 100 pages, he is still ready to answer "yes" to the question "as to whether religion stands approved by its fruits... The whole group [of saintly attributes] forms a combination which, as such, is religious, for it seems to flow from the sense of the divine as from its psychological center" (VRE: 361). But then, two paragraphs before the end, the real William James stands up, after this long but temporary investment in the promotion of saintliness.

> Let us be saints, then, if we can... But in our Father's house are many mansions, and each of us must discover for himself the kind of religion and the amount of saintship which best comports with what he believes to be his powers and feels to be his truest mission and vocation. There are no successes to be guaranteed and no set orders to be given to individuals, so long as we follow the methods of empirical philosophy (VRE: 368).

His discussion of saintliness, as thorough and commanding as it is, is not to describe or endorse any of these particular fruits of religion so much as it is to insist that it is to the fruits, the pragmatic outcome, that we must look for validation, not to premises or to logic or to absolute givens. James would hardly be surprised or chagrined that the catalogue of virtues and other outcomes, to which he devoted one-fourth of his lectures, would appear today to be the most dated and the most neglected. What counts as a good outcome depends in large measure on the culture and the expectations and values within which the outcome occurs. Pragmatism is hardly a criterion of value, but only a direction, showing one where to look for criteria. "How is success to be absolutely measured when there are so many environments and so many ways of looking at the adaptation?" James asks at the end of his discussion of saintliness (p. 367). "It cannot be measured absolutely; the verdict will vary according to the point of view adopted." The pragmatism does not so much yield to the pluralism as blend with it. And new "environments" and new "ways of looking at the adaptation" will generate new catalogues of desirable outcomes.

Religion as "Sui Generis"

There is one other strong candidate for the position of "central proposition." Though it has no chapter by itself, proof-tests can be found distributed throughout the lectures. William James is frequently taken as a champion of those who would regard religion as *sui generis* and oppose the "reduction" of religion by analyzing it with categories rooted "outside" religion. He was indeed such a champion—in a sense and in a context. It is important, though, to understand just what he did say. For he patently did not mean and would not approve of some of the views he is sometimes taken as endorsing.

The *sui generis* argument, in varying form and on varying grounds, claims that religion or religious phenomena are inadequately understood if they are understood with categories or variables or theories that could be or have been used to analyze other, nonreligious phenomena.[6] There are grounds for invoking James as a supporter of this argument: the undoubted respect which he accorded religious experiences and those who reported them, the scorn he heaped upon "medical materialism" and other such simple-minded reduction of religious experience to organic and pathological causes, and the fact that he does not invoke in his discussion of religious experiences any of the psychological concepts he had labored through a decade earlier in his general psychology text.

But the principal purpose of *The Varieties of Religious Experience* was to wrest religion from a distinctive preserve under the sovereignty of a religious Establishment and to claim the same rights for psychology in this former preserve as in all other domains of human experience. As Paul Pruyser puts it clearly in listing the propositions advanced by James, the first is "that religious phenomena are continuous with other psychic phenomena" (Pruyser 1969: 3).

As part of his strategy to make this point, James's first chapter—in this connection, we should probably remember that it was his first *lecture*—is of considerable importance. Except as such a tactic, it seems otherwise unaccountable why he would begin the entire lecture series with a discussion of "Religion and Neurology." This lecture accomplished two things. (1) He identified the most extreme of the reductionists—those referring religious experience to the bodily functions—and thereby acknowledged the chief apprehension and resistance his audience would have to his lectures; by being able in good conscience to share the offense they felt by this extreme (physical) reductionism, he was able to win a hearing for his own more moderate reductionism. (2) He was also able, continuing the task which belonged to his times and to his own personal vocational development, to emphasize the distinction between physiology and psychology and to make his vigorous claim for the propriety of purely psychological investigation of religious experiences. To attack the sovereignty of the medical Establishment over his topic was good warm-up, perhaps even throwing his listeners off guard, for his attack on the religious Establishment's claim to sovereignty over religious experience.

Having thus claimed his right to treat religious experience as he would any other object of psychological investigation, James proceeded to do just that. It happens that his way of treating anything was to take it very seriously in its own right and to take it fresh. It is on principles far more fundamental than the *sui generis* character of religious experience that he treats his material with respect and does not try to employ psychological categories developed elsewhere. His affirmation is of the *sui generis* character of each experience, not just religious experience. He does not bring categories from his psychology textbook into his study of religion anymore than he carries categories from one chapter to another of his psychology text or anymore than he carries the same analytic categories from one chapter to another in *The Varieties of Religious Experience*. He treats religious

---

6. The *sui generis* argument is often accompanied by or confused with, but is logically quite distinguishable from the more extreme phenomenological argument: Religious phenomena are inadequately understood if they are understood with categories different from those used by the subjects experiencing the phenomena. The *sui generis* argument is often accompanied by or confused with, but is logically quite distinguishable from the more general, antiscientism argument: the validity of the religious experience may not be challenged by any psychological analysis, of whatever variety.

experience as no less *sui generis* than any experience, but also no more so. In analyzing any particular instance of religious experience, he does not hesitate to move freely through the total psychological experience, so far as he has it accessible. He sets up no boundaries marking religious off from other experience.

I can find no counterpart in James's thinking and certainly no warrant in his spirit for such notions as a distinctive religious sentiment or the idea that "peak experiences" are removed from other psychological functions and somehow of a different order, to mention characteristic suggestions of two later Bostonian psychologists (Allport and Maaslow) with whose names and ideas James is often linked in this matter. Indeed, James is quite explicit about the notion of a "'religious sentiment' which we see referred to in so many books, as if it were a sort of mental entity" (VRE: 28). "As there just seems to be no one elementary religious emotion, but only a common storehouse of emotions upon which religious objects may draw, so there might conceivably also prove to be no one specific and mutual kind of religious object, and no one specific and essential kind of religious act" (VRE: 29)[7]

There is another issue closely related to that of the *sui generis* question. The genetic fallacy is frequently attacked, scientism put in its proper place, and the validity of religious experience protected by insisting on the sharp distinction between psychological analysis and judgments of validity. To know, even with certainty, the psychological history and function of a belief or a practice says nothing for or against the truth of the belief, the appropriateness of the practice, or any objective reference for either; adjudicating such questions as these presumably is the business of philosophy or some other discipline, not psychology. That kind of division of questions may be appropriate; indeed, it is one I would advance (1969: 605), but it is far from James's position. This kind of separation of scientific questions from questions of value and validity—the "we build the bomb, you decide how to use it" mentality—is absolutely antithetical to James's own spirit, especially in its pragmatic emphasis. There is no world apart from the working, functioning world. So there is no world of value and no references or criteria for validity apart from the world of psychological functions. Value and validity are established precisely by and only by function.

How then must we understand the passages which can be and are proof-texted as indicating James's support of such a distinction? He indeed casts livid and unambiguous scorn on attempts to disparage and discredit religious experience by relating it to pathological or glandular or other mean origins and functions. But if William James scorned the evaluation of religious experience according to its origins and roots we need to be clear what he advocated instead. It was not the separation of the evaluative question from functional analysis. Rather, it was the distinction between what amounts to two different kinds of functional analyses. He did not oppose *evaluation* based on *origins* because he wanted to separate evaluation from fact, but because he insisted on evaluation based on *outcome*. It was not that William James as philosopher refused to evaluate religious experi-

---

7. It is another definitional question, not particularly relevant here, as to whether religion is psychologically single or multiple. Theorists' positions on *this* question, however, are closely correlated with their positions on the *sui generis* question. This is perhaps predictable both logically and psychologically. Those who draw a tight boundary between religious and other experience tend to make it a single boundary. Religion is more clearly distinct from other phenomena when it is a single phenomenon. To admit of differentiation within the domain of religion, as to speak of *The Varieties of Religious Experience*, seems to be associated with a willingness to permit the lowering of the (protective?) barrier between religion and other human realms; just as the society that most acknowledges pluralism and differentiation within is most likely to admit contacts outside of its borders.

ences on the basis of what William James as psychologist could discern. It was rather a question of what the psychologist would look at and, hence, what the philosopher would judge by. It was the fruits, not the roots, of religious experience—as of any experience—which were to provide the criteria. James disposed of the mean origins quickly in his first chapter but devoted five chapters, one-fourth of the book, to "Saintliness." The origins of the experience, that is past, and like all pages once turned, is of little interest to the here and now. What effects does the religious experience have on his behavior now? That is the crucial question. What if authoritarians and the prejudiced are attracted to established religions these days, as we now know from unequivocal research findings that they are. (Dittes 1969). That would hardly even be interesting information to James. The question is whether the religion does anything to affect them.

James had one more important comment to make on the problem of reductionism. This derives more from his pluralism than his pragmatism. It consists of taking the meanness out of mean origins. If his move just discussed above consists of bringing the "big questions" down to the level of experience, perhaps the move mentioned here consists of bringing the "lower origins" up to the level of experience. Even if one were to grant pathological roots, for example, what is so discrediting or disparaging or devaluating or invalidating about that, anyhow? As James would not put it, (though C. G. Jung. e.q., could), pathology is part of the creation with equal rights and equal likelihood of yielding truth and value. To suppose otherwise is a prejudice and stereotype not unlike any other social prejudice. To discredit any idea by pointing out that the speaker is insane is not so different from trying to discredit it by pointing out that the speaker is, for example, Asian or female. In fact, of course, there is more than a hint in James's celebration of the other and of the different, in his suspicion of the established, in his sympathy with the underdog, that, if anything, he expects a little more validity and insight and goodness to come from the outcast.

Summary of "Central Propositions"

This search through the beginning, the climax, and the heart of VRE for "central propositions" leaves us with one disconcerting impression. James was capable of writing as though he were offering firm absolutes—highly generalizable, tightly defined analytic categories; a descriptive catalogue of universal phenomena; definitions and criteria of authentic religion—then of renouncing these. The reader may well feel abandoned and exposed if he thought the structure James was inviting him to enter was a solid abode; for James it turns out to be only a transient tent, serving James fully and well and serving him temporarily. This nomadic style of mind, delighting in movement and thriving in the anticipation of what is yet to come, baffles and offends some, who can live only in clearly located stable structures; James's younger colleague at Harvard, Josiah Royce, found him verging on irresponsibility. This is why there is on purpose no Jamesian school of psychology. In writing his *Principles of Psychology*, as in writing *The Varieties of Religious Experience* he becomes totally immersed in the substance and tools of each chapter, as though *it* were the key to the whole; then moves on feeling no more desire to "integrate" the chapters one with another or to fashion a comprehensive system than he would want all his dinner guests or all the members of his family cast in the same mold.

Boring (1950) epitomized James's mind as "positive yet tolerant" and Allport (1961) celebrated his "magnificent tentativeness." But to call William James "tolerant" or "tentative" is like saying that his writing style was "not cumbersome." There is a fierce, positive affirmation in this nomadic style of mind which is the whole point of James's message and is his legacy. This message is on purpose in the way he worked, fully as much as in what he said.[8] The shiftiness which may frustrate the systematizing reader looking for the essence of James's thought should be heeded by that reader as the best clue he may get to that "essence." To understand William James best on his own terms we must not listen and appraise what he says (propositions, central or otherwise) so much as we discover what his statements are doing for him; what function do they serve in the largest context of his life that we can apprehend? What *process* do they reflect? So, to know William James best, we find ourselves assessing not the content of his mind but its quality, his style, his temper, his basic attitudes, his spirit.

"On the whole" is a frequent and telling phrase in VRE, one about which James became self-conscious toward the end of the lectures (see, for example, pp. 321, 368), perhaps challenged by the more systematically minded and therefore impatient Scotch listeners. The phrase of course, expresses his essential "tentativeness," to stick with Allport's word. "'On the whole'—I fear we shall never escape complicity with that qualification, so dear to your practical man, so repugnant to your systematizer" (VRE: 321). But the phrase also points to the grounds for that "tentativeness"; it expresses the affirmation that is expressed by the tentativeness.

The authority William James acknowledged was that of experience itself the "blooming, buzzing confusion" from which one fashions a *Weltanschauung* and to which one then submits cognitive abstractions for correction and renewal. This ore of experience, though crude, remains richer and grander than any attempts to refine it. There is always a "more" to experience, both a qualitative "more" and a quantitative "more," into which one may, nay must, dip again and again.

To identify this root conviction, from which so much else derived, one might speak of James's "reverence for life." But this phrase has now been preempted to cover a decidedly unJamesian pallid, constricted, imperious legalism. For Schweitzer, the phrase expresses and generates restriction; it emphasizes the distinction between self and others and yields mostly a narrowing of choices. It mostly adds to the "thou shalt nots" of life. To reclaim the phrase to suit James, we should have to refuel it with relish and gusto and openness, with a lust to relate to life, to be subject to its discoveries.

Here is the personal zest, the "chivalry of sou"—Royce's phrase—reaching out to embrace others, all others, in conversation and correspondence that made immediate intimates of all and antagonized none. As James Ward wrote to William James ten days before he died, "Yours, my dear friend, has been a successful life and surely it has been a happy one, for I know of no-one more universally beloved. I, at least, never heard an ill word of you from anyone" (Perry 1948: 355ff). Dwight Eisenhower (1967) described his method of handling someone who "has acted despicably, especially toward me. I try to forget him. I used to follow a custom—somewhat contrived, I admit—of writing the man's name on a piece of scrap paper, dropping it into the lowest drawer of my desk, and saying to myself, That finishes the incident, and so far as I am concerned, that fellow." Somehow people did not seem to act despicably toward William James, and such disposal would have meant to William James an avoidable loss, a loss not to the "fellow" but to himself. James welcomed, even celebrated the different *other*—other person, other idea, other culture—not in spite of the difference, but, with an insight only now being forced on American society's attitude toward social minorities, *because* of the difference. The different is beautiful.

To go "beyond" is always urged by James because in the "beyond" is still more of the rich rewarding life which James finds in the here and now.

---

8. And, in poor imitation, it is a message I have tried to communicate as much in the way I have presented the preceding paragraphs fully as much as in their content.

II. THE "BEYOND" IN JAMES:
ALWAYS A "MORE" AND AN "OUTCOME"

"Beyond" as "More": A Throbbing Pluralistic Universe

William James grew up in a family of strong, distinctive personalities, of diverse talents, of interests pulling in all directions, of vigorous convictions constantly contending across the dinner table and across the Atlantic, perpetually on the move, seldom living in the same house for as long as a year, its own diversity regularly augmented by a stream of stimulating household visitors; yet he grew up in a family remarkable also for its mutual support and affectionate cohesiveness. The final book James published was a celebration of *A Pluralistic Universe,* and some of his most memorable contributions to psychology are caught in such phrases as "a stream of consciousness" and "blooming, buzzing confusion." There is a straight line from the experience to the philosophical position and psychological insights. James had every reason to conclude that people not only did, but perhaps more importantly, *could* live in the context of a reality that was "redundant and superabundant," to quote Bergson's summary of James's metaphysical position.[9] Where some people can find support for a sense of rightness and direction, an identity, a satisfaction of fundamental personal religious and metaphysical yearnings only in closely structured social and ideological systems, James had every reason to suppose that a person most readily found self not in spite of, but verily in the middle of contention and multiplicity and change, the tug and pull of sensations and ideas and wills. And, given his pragmatic, radically empirical epistemology (to be discussed later), if this is how and where people found themselves, this is how the universe is. Educated throughout boyhood by a succession of tutors who came and went or, more accurately, were found here and there as the James family came and went; forbidden by his father's suspicion of organized education to accompany a friend to college; even when James was finally permitted to subject himself to the formal structures of scientific study at Harvard; these scientific studies remained only a fragment of his ever-fragmented education.

He was perpetually grazing and ruminating, wandering wherever the pasturage was good. Fortunately two notebooks of the year 1862-63 have been preserved, in which appear—along with items extracted from the lectures of Agassiz on "Geology and the Structure and Classification of the Animal Kingdom," and Joseph Lovering on "Electrostatics, Electrodynamics and Acoustics"—pencil drawings, historical and literary chronologies, sayings of Charles Pierce, an outline of the French Revolution, and abstracts of Buchner's *Kraft and Stoff,* Max Muller's *History of Ancient Sanskrit Literature,* Farrar's *Origins of Language,* and Jonathan Edward's *Original Sin.* The entries in these books, and in an Index Rerum begun in 1864, range over the whole field of literature, history, science, and philosophy. They indicate a mind as energetic and acquisitive as it was voracious and incorrigibly vagrant (Perry 1948: 71).

Fully satisfied by such knowledge that came in illuminating bursts, feeling no need to struggle for synthesis, James could readily suppose that the reality itself was similarly burstlike with an infinite plurality of bursts always to come. The "beyond" which constantly lured his restless mind from one idea to another, from one solution to another, was always the beyond of others, never the beyond of the One which lay behind or above or around the immediate.

---

9. In his introduction to the French translation of *Pragmatism* cited by Perry (1948: 351).

The power of his mind lay largely in its extreme mobility, its darting, exploratory impulsiveness. It was not a mind which remained stationary, drawing all things to itself as a centre; but a mind which traveled widely—now here and now there—seeing all things for itself, and making up in the variety of its adventures for what it lacked in poise (Perry 1948: 66).

And if the diversity of ideas one person found was to be welcomed, so also was the diversity of ideas brought by the confrontation of one person with another. His most faithful and staunchest philosophical adversary was his younger colleague and friend Josiah Royce. Near the end of James's life, Royce testified to the nature of the relationship and to the nature of James's attitude toward those who held contradictory ideas:

James found me at once—made out what my essential interests were at our first interview, accepted me, with all my imperfections, as one of those many souls who ought to be able to find themselves in their own way, gave a patient and willing ear to just my variety of philosophical experience, and used his influence from that time on, not to win me as a follower, but to give me my chance... Whatever I am is in that sense due to him ...
Sometimes critical people have expressed this by saying that James has always been too fond of cranks, and that the cranks have loved him. Well, I am one of James's cranks. He was good to me, and I love him. The result of my own early contact with James was to make me for years very much his disciple. I am still in large part under his spell. If I contend with him sometimes, I suppose that it is he also who through his own free spirit has in great measure taught me this liberty (Perry 1948: 162).

In his social judgments James was a liberal but most definitely not of the brand who proposed the management of other people's lives for their own welfare. He might today even be called a radical for his unequivocal endorsement for letting each one do his or her own thing or, as he put it with characteristic greater elegance, letting the "bird fly with no strings tied to its leg" (Perry 1948: 140).
James's celebration of this diversity in each person's experience and between persons, was suggested and was justified by his conviction that the nature of things is just so diverse. James does *not* see us in the position of the blind men feeling different parts of the elephant—exactly the opposite. For that image implies several things which are not true for James: (1) that there is a synthesis, a oneness which could be built from our multiple perceptions; (2) that our individual distinctive perceptions are somehow the product of an inadequacy or defect in our own perceiving; and (3) that the particularity we happen to comprehend is somehow an accidental product of where we happen to be standing, rather than, as James would have it, the particular validating and validated product of our own directed energy and searching. (If one observer perceives a leg and another a tusk, in James's view it is because one in some sense, is "looking for" a leg the other "looking for" a tusk.)
When one has perceived a truth or insight to the satisfaction of his criteria for the validity of evidence (in James's case the pragmatic radically empirical functional criteria), then that is truth. That is as absolute a truth as one can expect or needs to find and, by James's extension, as there is. Though aware and delighted that there are other truths, one does not disparage his own personal finding by thinking of it only as a shadow of a truth which is potentially clearer, or a part of a truth which is potentially more complete or to be integrated with other truths. This would be illusion and futility.

The affirmations of pluralism *can* be grudging, merely tolerant and not really affirmations at all. One can concede, as a kind of practical inconvenience or an embarrassment to be overlooked, that there are realities other than those one has perceived, discoveries other than those one has made, but without being affected by this acknowledgement. But James actively pursued the "beyond." He genuinely celebrated the "other." One solution was no sooner formulated than the question had to be reopened in search for new solutions. He eagerly moved from chapter to chapter in the *Psychology* and *The Varieties of Religious Experience*, moving from one conceptual framework to another, exploring and exploiting each fully and decisively but no more feeling the need to stick with the framework adopted in one chapter while he was in the next than he did the need to integrate all the frameworks into a single systematic whole.

The affirmations of pluralism *can* be inhibiting and stifling. If there is such an infinite variety of reality and of approaches to reality, why take any one seriously? "Sure, I'll be on the symposium; what do you want me to talk about?" "Find out which research grants are easiest to get this year; we'll submit a proposal for that." Against such stifling carelessness, James's epistemology is a vigorous corrective. One does not pick truth off a cafeteria serving table, passively accepting something that has been served up by someone else. Truth is harder earned than this and, therefore, well earned. Truth yields only to more active, directed search. One approaches the food table with a specific *appetite* and *this* must be satisfied, or there is no meal. Perhaps it can be satisfied from the cafeteria line but, more characteristically, the appetite must move on to the kitchen and there direct preparations afresh. The truth has to work for you, or there is no truth. To be a philosopher—and, presumably, a scientist—one must be an active participant, even a partisan, never a mere spectator. If one does not have a specific *will* to believe, there is nothing to believe. Reality must be wooed and courted before it will yield its secrets, and then only to the particular suitor. Nothing could be more different from pallid relativism—anything goes—than James's demand for energetic self-direction and self-investment in the approach to reality. James's empiricism could not be further removed from the shotgun empiricism of heedless, mindless searching to which questionnaire respondents, computer programmers, and journal readers are too much subject today. One approaches reality with a clear question, formulated out of the heat and heart of one's own searching—we might say scientific theories—or one does not get an answer.

The affirmation of pluralism, the affirmation of the beyond, of the discovery yet to come, is always an extension of the affirmation of the validity and vitality of the discovery already made; it is not a compensation for the defects of the present discovery. James is affirming a doctrine of creation and, perhaps, of redemption far more readily than he can countenance a doctrine of the fall or of sin. You *can* be humble about your own views, tolerant of others', and hopeful for new insights all on the basis of your awareness of the defects of your own views. You can believe, on the principle of human fallibility, that you must expect to move beyond any conclusion, however hard won and however valid it may seem. Yet not so with James. He moved joyfully from idea to idea, from solution to solution, even as he moved from friend to friend, from career to career, from place to place, expecting the most from the next because the last had had so much to offer him. James abandoned painting as a career only after he was good at it and was sure he enjoyed it through a period of total immersion in painting. He almost left Agassiz's botanical collection expedition in the Amazon out of despair—"If there is one thing I hate it is collecting" (Perry 1948: 21)—but he stuck it out and came to write nostalgically about the trip. And he came home to make a career and a philosophy of being a collector. James rejected the absolutism that he found in his father and in Emerson, for example, and later in Royce, not because he found this absolute so overwhelming and terrifying that its yoke had to be thrown off—a view that makes relativists of some as they experience the absolute's judgment—but, rather, James discarded the absolute as too puny. He found life too rich, the universe too fast-moving and full to be gauged by a single absolute. "James relished this...chaotic plenitude which experience exhibits when it is restored to its primitive unselectedness" (Perry 1938: 127). "He was scarcely out of his infancy before he began to be a nostalgic cosmopolitan, flying from perch to perch, now yearning for home, now equally eager to escape—liking it where he was *and* longing for the better far away" (Perry 1948: 48). It is that final "and" (which I have italicized), the affirmation of the beyond out of the affirmation of the here and now, that is James's spirit. Is this "healthy-mindedness?" Hardly. Is this "tough-mindedness?" Perhaps. But those are categories developed for other purposes, and why suppose that they have to be found appropriate for this occasion?

"Beyond" as "Outcome": Knowledge is in the "Happening"

Before finding himself in the academic career of philosopher and psychologist, William James experimented with two other careers, one which he enjoyed and one which he disliked. At the age of eighteen he became a painter, but having tested his talents and found them substantial, he left the career, satisfied, to move on. In his early twenties, he began studying science and medicine, found much of this not to his liking, and, accordingly, was able to wrench himself from it only after prolonged torment.

When James's philosophy is called "empiricism," we would do better to think of the empiricism of the painter rather than the empiricism of the scientist. To know something, for James, is to take a very active role in the discovery, to make perceptions that are shaped by the vigorous interaction and expectation and actual experience. To know "empirically" is no more to be the passive recorder or collector of events and objects, as James too often found science to be, than the painter is engaged in making a photographic reproduction. The knowledge one thus gains from expectation consummated by experience is a person's knowledge. Presumably, it does not contradict others' knowledge, just as the painter's product can be viewed by others intelligibly and with appreciation. But one hardly expects, as the scientist typically does, that the validity of his knowledge will be tested precisely by the degree that it is identical with the knowledge of others. The reason for this is not just the metaphysics of pluralism—reality does not just present itself differently to different persons—but is also in the necessity for personal investment in the act of knowing.

"To know" carries two rather distinct kinds of meaning in English. To know is to have information about, usually of impersonal facts. To know is also to be acquainted with, to be familiar with; in this sense, perhaps the word's basic usage is with reference to persons. "I know John Smith's telephone number" suggests a very different type of knowledge from "I know John Smith." Perhaps the archaic usage of "to know," referring to sexual familiarity, is an intense form of the second usage. Other languages have two different words for these two different meanings. But the single word in English permits the more ready extension of knowledge as personal acquaintance and familiarity to apply to impersonal objects and events and experiences. Perhaps this is why English-speaking philosophers have seen the richest possibilities in empiricism. In any case, this is what James does.

"Pragmatism" is the particular radical form of empiricism which is generally applied to James's theory of knowledge. (Actually, the pragmatism is offered by James as a kind of supplement or a substitute for the more immediate, intuitive familiarity which is the preferred, but seldom accessible, form of knowledge. But if one has to have mediated "knowledge about," then let it follow from the principles of pragmatism.) Knowledge is validated by its practical consequences. Something is true to the degree that it works, rather than something works to the degree that it is true, to follow the aphorismic formulation of which James's theory of emotion is a direct echo (we are sad because we cry and angry because we strike).

At first glance, such a theory of knowledge would seem to give primacy to external events and practical pay-off; and in the political sphere today, the notion of pragmatism does conjure up the image of a mindless politician without inner conviction or principle led to decisions by the calculation of maximum votes in the next election. But this is exactly the wrong way to understand James. Pragmatism actually calls our attention much more to inner direction and personal initiative in the process of knowing than it does to "objective" events. Though it is the pay-off that is decisive; something has to be paid off. Though the results are essential to establish knowledge, the results are defined by *expectations* which are even more fundamental and equally indispensable. An event *is* a result only as it is a response to directed probing. There is no answer without a question. Much as some conditioning theorists would like to overlook the fact, it still seems to be a fact that "reinforcement" or "reward" is effective only insofar as it meets an inner need or drive. Even Pavlov's dogs had to be hungry to salivate even to food, much less to bells, which is just as important to understand as the fact that they would stop salivating to bells if they never got food. James would enjoy, for his illustration of such self-direction and especially for its illustration of the dominance of the underdog's self-direction, the cartoon in which the rat brags that he has the psychologist trained: "Everytime I press this bar he gives me something to eat." He might also understand that advertisers are as hooked on the particular motive they are trying to appeal to as their audience is hooked by their manipulation of those motives.

It is no wonder that a commentator finds himself almost anthropomorphizing pragmatism.

> It stresses the act of initiative. Such knowledge is not a pure receptivity, but an attack—inspired by a desire for truth or a state of discontent, and guided by a plan of campaign. It is a project framed or expectation entertained in advance, and then executed, so far as experience permits ... It does not attack at random, but selects an objective which promises to remove its present quandary (Perry 1938: 72).

One takes aim at a target, then hurls self at the target to see if the sighting was true. In such an account of how truth is wrested from experience, we are undoubtedly justified in hearing more than a slight autobiographical overtone. This was James's style of life. Perhaps it is epitomized in an incident recounted by H. G. Wells in his *Autobiography* (Knight 1950: 61). James was visiting his brother Henry in the latter's proper English home in Rye. He heard that G. K. Chesterton was staying at the inn next door. He wanted to see Chesterton. So what else but to take the gardener's ladder, climb up, and peep over the wall—a move of "scandalous directness" that "terribly unnerved" the thoroughly Europeanized Henry who, of course, would have all experience as muted and indirect—and sometimes, it even seems, as pointless—as possible. The correct way to meet Chesterton was through proper mediators and according to proper forms.

> This vivacity, this eagerness and gusto, marked James from an early age—as a "son and brother." His sister Alice once said of him that he seemed "to be born afresh every morning." "He came down from his bedroom *dancing* to greet me," said his father ... He was an overflowing and inexhaustible fountain—a fountain, be it remarked, and not a channeled stream (Perry 1948: 373).

James apparently took more congenially to lectures and to letter writing than to more formal book writing, probably because the former has a clearer target to which the author can direct himself; and self-direction is the name of the game.

If William James's pluralism is, to some degree, a reaction against his father's search for and claim for absolutes, his insistence on personal investment—with pay-off of the investment—as the necessary condition for discovery, stands in counterpoint to his brother's placid, passive, interminable, and indirect descriptions. William once posed the contrast in a letter to his brother: "but why won't you, just to please Brother, sit down and write a new book, with no twilight or mustiness in the plot, with great vigor and decisiveness in the action, no fencing in the dialogue, no psychological commentaries, and absolute straightness in the style?" (Perry 1935, I: 424) (Notice that by 1905 "psychological commentaries"—at least Henry's, and perhaps others'—belonged among those verbal exercises that miss the point of experience.)

His brother's prose meanderings annoyed James for the same reason that he had no patience with what he regarded as the trivial preoccupations of the religious and scientific Establishment. Such indirectness, such infatuation with peripheral and unsorted details denied and prevented authenticity. To be genuine is to be carried to the heart of a matter and to a clear pay-off by the "acute fever" of one's own inner experience by the active anticipation of the encounter. An important part of the agenda for *The Varieties of Religious Experience* is the search for the criteria of authentic religion. This is important testimony to the impossibility in James's view of separating "fact" from "value," but it is even more important to notice the criteria he chooses. Early on (VRE: 8) he links the "acute fever" with "effective fruits" and before the first chapter is over has referred to "inner happiness" and "serviceability for our needs" and to "immediate luminousness" and to "moral helpfulness." These criteria, like the five lectures James gives to "Saintliness," refer, as those of a pragmatist should, to fruits, to good effects. But these fruits, these effects, all refer, as those of a Jamesian pragmatist should, to the personal search that forms the target for the outcome.

It is ironic that Gordon Allport, who in many ways should be regarded as a disciple of James, lost this tension of pragmatism when he came to establish criteria for authenticity. "Extrinsic" religion was to be disparaged, in contrast with the more committed and personal "intrinsic" religion, in large part for its "utilitarianism" (Hunt and King 1971). The extrinsically religious person "uses" his religion, and this makes it degraded religion in Allport's view. But to James usefulness belongs more clearly on the side of authentic religion than its opposite. James would, of course, want to share with Allport some concern for better and poorer uses. Perhaps, paradoxically, the pragmatist is more readily alerted by his very concern for function, to different quality of functions being served, as contrasted with the one who, offended by utilitarianism, dismisses all outcome as a criterion in favor of the more static and remote concept of sentiment.

James was hardly disposed to separate religion and the psychological investigation of it as somehow entirely different types of human enterprise. The criteria for value and authenticity in the one are criteria for value and authenticity in the other. Whether in religious inquiry or scientific inquiry or any other enterprise, pragmatism refers to the investment of the self in a particular set of circumstances and to the pay-off by those circumstances of that investment. With only casual or slight investment there can be only slight pay-off and, hence, slight "knowledge." This must be the fate of the atheoretical, purely "empirical" foray, even also of the study guided by relatively trivial hypotheses. Only the risky plunge of the big expectation, mobilizing one's most significant expectations, is likely to have a big pay-off and, hence, important knowledge. But what if the risk proves too risky and the circumstances do not pay off the expectation? Much as William James admires and trusts moral and psychological struggle, he is almost too "healthy-minded" to consider the possibilities of epistemological failure, that the circumstances will say "no" to one's expectations. And he is definitely too healthy-minded and non-Freudian to consider the possibility that expectations and investment will make one continue to perceive "yes" even after circumstances have said "no." But there is, after all, the completely open-ended, pluralistic universe, rich with possibilities and awaiting one's next investment.

REFERENCES

Bellah, R.N. (1970). Confessions of a former establishment fundamentalist. *Bulletin of the Council on the Study of Religion*, 1(3): 3-6.
Berger, P.L. (1967). A sociological view of the secularization of theology. *Journal for the Scientific Study of Religion*, 6: 3-16.
Boring, E.G. (1950). *A History of Experimental Psychology*, 2nd. ed. New York: Appleton-Century-Crofts.
Browning, D.S. (1980). *Pluralism and Personality: William James and Some Contemporary Cultures of Psychology*. Lewisburg, PA: Bucknell University Press.
Dittes, J.E. (1967). *The Church in the Way*. New York: Scribner's Sons.
———— (1969). Psychology of religion. In Gardner Lindzey and Eliot Aronson (Eds.) *Handbook of Social Psychology*, vol. 5. Reading, PA: Addison-Wesley (pp. 602-659).
Eisenhower, D.D. (1967). *At Ease: Stories I Tell My Friends*. Garden City, NY: Doubleday.
Eister, A.W. (1967). Toward a radical critique of church-sect typologizing. *Journal for the Scientific Study of Religion*, 6: 85-90.
Gustafson, P.M. (1967). UO-US-PS-PO: A restatement of Troeltsch's church-sect typology. *Journal for the Scientific Study of Religion*, 6: 64-68.
Hunt, R.A. (1968). The interpretation of the religious scale of the Allport-Vernon-Lindzey study of values. *Journal for the Scientific Study of Religion*, 7: 65-77.
———— (1971). The intrinsic-extrinsic concept: A review and evaluation. *Journal for the Scientific Study of Religion*, 10: 339-356.
James, H. (ed.) (1920). *Letters of William James*, 2 vols. Boston: Atlantic Monthly Press.
James, W. (1890). *The Principles of Psychology*, 2 vols. New York: Henry Holt.
———— (1902). *The Varieties of Religious Experience*. New York: Longmans Green. New York: Random House Modern Library.
Johnson, B. (1957). A critical appraisal of the church-sect typology. *American Sociological Review*, 22: 88-92.
———— (1971). Church and sect revisited. *Journal for the Scientific Study of Religion*, 10: 124-137.
Maslow, A.M. (1964). *Religions, Values and Peak-Experiences*. Columbus: Ohio State University Press.
Perry, R.B. (1935). *The Thought and Character of William James*, 2 vols. Boston: Little, Brown.
———— (1938). *In the Spirit of William James*. New Haven, CT: Yale University Press.
———— (1948); 1964). *The Thought and Character of William James, Briefer Version*. Cambridge, MA: Harvard University Press. New York: Harper and Row.
Pruyser, P. W. (1969). *A Dynamic Psychology of Religion*. New York: Harper and Row.
Smith, J. (1967). William James as philosophical psychologist. 75th Anniversary Address for the Division of Philosophical Psychology. American Psychological Association, Washington, D.C., September 3.
Troeltsch, E. (1912). *The Social Teachings of the Christian Church*. Olive Wynn (Trans.) New York: Macmillan.

Uren, A.R. (1928). *Recent Religious Psychology: A Study in the Psychology of Religion.* New York: Scribner's Sons.

Weber, M. (1958). *The Protestant Ethic and the Spirit of Capitalism.* Talcott Parsons (Trans.) New York: Scribner's Sons.

SPEAKING OF WILLIAM JAMES
TO THE CULTURED AMONG HIS DESPISERS

CAROL ZALESKI

In his eighteenth Gifford Lecture ("Philosophy"), William James anticipates the main objections that will be voiced by critics of his account of religious experience:

Religion, you expect to hear me conclude, is nothing but an affair of faith, based either on vague sentiment, or on that vivid sense of the reality of the unseen of which in my second lecture and in the lecture on Mysticism I gave so many examples. It is essentially private and individualistic; it always exceeds our powers of formulation; and although attempts to pour its contents into a philosophic mould will probably always go on, men being what they are, yet these attempts are always secondary processes which in no way add to the authority, or warrant the veracity, of the sentiments from which they derive their own stimulus and borrow whatever glow of conviction they may themselves possess. In short, you suspect that I am planning to defend feeling at the expense of reason, to rehabilitate the primitive and unreflective, and to dissuade you from the hope of any Theology worthy of the name (VRE: 340-341).

James admits some truth to this characterization: "I do believe that feeling is the deeper source of religion, and that philosophical and theological formulas are secondary products, like translations of a text into another tongue." Nonetheless, he affirms his commitment to philosophical reason, in a passage that should at least give his critics pause. The passage deserves to be quoted in full:

To redeem religion from unwholesome privacy, and to give public status and universal right of way to its deliverances, has been reason's task.
    I believe that philosophy will always have opportunity to labor at this task. We are thinking beings, and we cannot exclude the intellect from participating in any of our functions. Even in soliloquizing with ourselves, we construe our feelings intellectually. Both our personal ideals and our religious and mystical experiences must be interpreted congruously with the kind of scenery which our thinking mind inhabits. The philosophic climate of our time inevitably forces its own clothing on us. Moreover, we must exchange our feelings with one another, and in doing so we have to speak, and to use general and abstract verbal formulas. Conceptions and constructions are thus a necessary part of our religion; and as moderator amid the clash of hypotheses, and moderator among the criticisms of one man's constructions by another, philosophy will always have much to do. It would be strange if I disputed this, when these very lectures which I am giving are...a laborious attempt to extract from the privacies of religious experience some general facts which can be defined in formulas upon which everybody may agree (VRE: 341-341).

Has James answered his critics with this passage? Apparently not, for the same old charges of romanticism, privatism, and subjectivism continue to be levelled against him today, even

---

Originally published in *Journal of Psychology of Religion* 2 (1993-94):127-170.

by some of his most sophisticated readers. While they have not managed to dislodge *The Varieties of Religious Experience* from its status as a classic (and as a work with enduring popular appeal), I believe that these criticisms have stood in the way of our ability to *use* James as effectively as we might, either for psychology of religion or for theological reflection.

Despite what Henry Samuel Levinson calls James's "cultural canonization" (or perhaps partly because of it), James's influence on psychology of religion and theology waned in precisely the same measure as the spirit of academic professionalism, against which he so vehemently protested, overtook these two fields (Levinson, 1981: 270).

For psychology of religion, James was a tutelary spirit, but not in a practical sense its founder. As a behavioral science relying on experimental and quantitative methods to the exclusion of anecdote and introspection, psychology of religion is characterized by a "promiscuous empiricism" (to use James Dittes's phrase) quite alien to the empiricism James hoped to bring to the study of religious consciousness (Dittes, 1973). Even among humanistic and trans-personal psychologists, James has been more admired than followed. David Wulff puts this succinctly in his lucid textbook, *Psychology of Religion: Classic and Contemporary Views:*

> In our day as well as its own, James has often served as little more than a prestigious source of striking examples and mellifluous prose. His commonly misunderstood methods, if not simply criticized, have been largely ignored. What *The Varieties* has most often been thought to offer, then, is the possibility of a viable psychology of religion rather than its prototype (1991: 499).

With a few brilliant exceptions, theologians have also tended to ignore *The Varieties*, under the impression that his approach to religion undermines the autonomy of the theological enterprise. As James himself predicted, *Varieties* was "too biological for the religious, too religious for the biologists (Perry, II: 199). Signs of the enduring influence of *The Varieties* are to be found spread abroad widely in our culture, rather than confined within the professional disciplines. James's influence on Bill Wilson, the co-founder of Alcoholics Anonymous, has become part of the AA legend. His general readers appreciate *The Varieties* above all for its humane defense of the individual's right to believe in his or her religious experiences, and for its vivid sense of human possibilities.

The present essay in an experiment in making *The Varieties of Religious Experience* more usable, even for us "closet-naturalists of the deity." As such, it will be necessarily one-sided. I will throw my lot in with James, reading him in such a way as to answer the chief objections. I will not attempt to portray the genesis or the historical context of James's way of thinking about religious experience; neither will I do justice to his "cultured despisers," who certainly deserve a full hearing on their own terms. My sole purpose in this essay is to see whether James can be defended against some common charges. On the points where this defense fails, my strategy will be to consider whether James's thought is in principle corrigible, and hence of more than historical interest for interpreters of religion.

Readers of Henry Samuel Levinson's masterful study of *The Religious Investigations of William James* will find in this essay signs of what he calls a "presentist" interpretation of James: examining James's thought with an eye to questions of our own time, rather than stressing those characteristics of his historical situation that distance him from us (Levinson 1981: 280-283, 293, 298). I own up to this from the start. I trust that it is possible, without becoming completely ahistorical, to stage a meeting of minds across the century.[1]

---

1. My understanding of James is indebted to R.R. Niebuhr (see especially Niebuhr, 1983).

The charges against James are, to wit:

1. James's account of religious experience is marred by his excessive individualism, privatism, and elitism.
2. James gives undue preference to feeling, at the expense of intellect.
3. James's interest in extreme instances of religious experience leads him to overlook more ordinary and wholesome forms of piety.
4. James's analysis of religious experience (in particular, of mysticism) is founded on the false premise that there is such a thing as raw, immediate experience. He is blamed for failing to possess the insight—which since his time has become ubiquitous and easily won—that all experience is interpreted experience.
5. James confounds truth with common expediency, with therapy, or—worst of all—with the satisfaction of arbitrary desires.
6. *The Varieties* is an exercise in natural theology, a rather unkempt version of the theistic argument from religious experience.
7. The God of *The Varieties* is unworthy of the conception of God found in the world's great theistic traditions.

John E. Smith, in his introduction to *The Varieties of Religious Experience*, identifies five topics of criticism: the prominence in *The Varieties* of abnormal and exaggerated cases; James's "American Protestant conversionism"; his neglect of the social dimension of religion; his subjectivism; and his tendency to equate the subliminal self with man's "better nature" (pp. xvii-xxii). David M. Wulff also cites many instances of James being charged by his own contemporaries with an irresponsible confusion of genuine religion with pathological states, an overemphasis on feeling, obscure appeals to the subconscious, and selective use of experiential testimony to bolster his own pragmatic program and pluralistic metaphysics (with its alarming spiritualist and pan-psychic undertones) (Wulff 1991: 494-498). James himself has from time to time provided his future readers with roughly similar lists of objections raised against his views on pragmatism, personal religion, pluralism, and radical empiricism.

I will consider the criticisms roughly in the order I have listed above.

JAMES'S INDIVIDUALISM

James is frequently rebuked for being individualistic, privatistic, and elitist. Recently this charge has been made most vigorously by the Cambridge philosopher/theologian Nicholas Lash (1988) as part of a general critique of the narcissism inherent in contemporary preoccupation with discrete religious experiences.

Much of what James says in *The Varieties of Religious Experience* supports Lash's critique. Certainly he is an individualist; in his own day, this was not a term of opprobrium. A more complex picture emerges, however, if we step back and consider what James was trying to accomplish in his role as an interpreter of religious life.

James has supplied several different accounts of the task he set for himself in the Gifford Lectures, and John E. Smith judiciously warns against taking any of these statements as definitive (VRE: xiv). What they have in common, however, is a sense of mission. James clearly saw himself as undertaking far more than a merely descriptive task, even in the first series of lectures. In a letter written to his friend Frances Morse in April 1900, he offers one version of his mission:

First, to defend (against all the prejudices of my class) "experience" against "philosophy" as being the real backbone of the world's religious life—I mean prayer, guidance, and all that sort of thing immediately and privately felt, as against high and noble general views of our destiny and the world's meaning; and *second,* to make the hearer or reader believe, what I invincibly do believe, that, although all the special manifestations of religion may have been absurd, (I mean its creeds and theories), yet the life of it as a whole is mankind's most important function. A task wellnigh impossible, I fear, and in which I shall fail, but to attempt it is *my* religious act (H. James 1920, I: 127).

James's conviction that his interpretation of religious experience had a public significance, and a civic duty attached to it, was consonant with his general view of the philosopher's role in society. Several recent studies have brought out this feature of James's thought. Henry Samuel Levinson speaks of a "statesmanship model of interpretation" that James shared with Royce and Santayana: "Harvard teachers simply assumed that exemplifying republican virtues, especially the virtue embodied in the nation's motto *e pluribus unum,* was one of their role-specific duties" (1984: 39, 41; see also Cotkin, 1990).

James's sense of his public responsibility as a philosopher, was part of his reason for cultivating a "popular," that is, non-technical, philosophical style. This did not mean pandering to mass tastes, but it did mean attempting to reach a wide audience. He believed that philosophy was of concern to every thinking person. He also believed philosophers owed it to humanity to be willing to let practical reality disrupt their cherished systematic schemes.

His public responsibility as a philosopher was not just a case of *noblesse oblige* attaching to his position as a Harvard professor, but a recognition of a much more pervasive fact: the social character of all human thought and experience.

James underplays the social character of human thought and experience in *The Varieties,* for reasons to be discussed below. He was to lay great stress on it, however, in *Pragmatism,* with statements like the following:

All human thinking gets discursified; we exchange ideas; we lend and borrow verifications, get them from one another by means of social intercourse. All truth thus gets verbally built out, stored up, and made available for everyone Hence, we must *talk* consistently just as we must *think* consistently .... (1975: 102-103).

Paradoxically, it is precisely because he assigns public significance to philosophy that he feels duty-bound to make a place for the private impulse; for the solitary contemplative, mystic, ecstatic; for the dissenter who heeds the private dictates of conscience; for the metaphysical crank, the odd-ball inventor, the unorthodox healer, who might otherwise never have a hearing in the public forum. His philosophy may have been more individualistic than is fashionable today, but his sense of philosophical and cultural community was more robust.

Today, insistence upon the social character of discourse and experience has become something of a shibboleth—either because of nostalgia for a vanished sense of community, or because of the paranoid suspicion that experiences are being engineered by power elites. James, on the other hand, was gifted at finding and also creating community within the academic world (where it is notoriously lacking), and within the wider cultural circles to which he belonged. He knew how to argue without damaging trust, as Josiah Royce testifies:

Nothing is more characteristic of Professor James's work as a teacher and as a thinker than is his chivalrous fondness for fair play in the warfare and in the cooperation of ideas and of ideals. We all of us profess to love truth. But one of James's especial offices in the service of truth has been the love and protection and encouragement of the truth-seekers ....

My real acquaintance with [James] began one summer day in 1877, when I first visited him in the house on Quincy Street and was permitted to pour out my soul to somebody who really seemed to believe that at young man might rightfully devote his life to philosophy if he chose .... James found me at once—made out what my essential interests were at our first interview, accepted me, with all my imperfections, as one of those many souls who ought to be able to find themselves in their own way, gave a patient and willing ear to just my variety of philosophical experience, and used his influence from that time on, not to win me as a follower, but to give me my chance ....

Sometimes critical people have expressed this by saying that James has always been too fond of cranks, and that cranks have loved him. Well, I am one of James's cranks. He was good to me, and I love him (Perry 1935, I: 779-780).

This testimonial comes from a friend who had been James's chief philosophical adversary in what Ralph Barton Perry called "the battle of the absolute" (p. 797). It was to Royce that James wrote, affectionately, "When I compose my Gifford lectures mentally, 'tis with the design exclusively of overthrowing your system, and ruining your peace. I lead a parasitic life upon you, for my highest flight of ambitious ideality is to become your conqueror and go down into history as such ...." (Perry 1935, I: 817).

James knew how to judge an argument on its own merits, without regard for the academic pedigree of its author. What is this if not a living belief in truth-seeking as a communal ideal, and a reasoned hope for an intellectual life animated by this ideal rather than capriciously ruled by the competition between power-interests?

To those who would reject *The Varieties* because it neglects the role of community in religious life, John E. Smith points out, "... it will not do to base an evaluation of what James did accomplish on what he failed to include, no matter how serious the omission (VRE: xix). The question still to be faced is whether or not there is something programmatic in James's account of religion that would forever preclude filling it in.

In the second Gifford Lecture, "Circumscription of the Topic," James gives the impression (perhaps disingenuously given his strong bias), that the decision to omit institutional religion is merely a tactical one. He is a psychologist; therefore he concentrates on emotions and impulses. He is an anatomist, therefore he trains his attention on isolated parts of the religious corpus—but again, only for the purpose of analysis. Above all, he is a modest man, not an expert on the history of religion; therefore he does not presume to cover the whole field. In short, James seems to say that he is not programmatically *excluding* institutional religion from any definition of the core or essence of religion; he is merely setting it aside temporarily from the program of investigation. Presumably nothing should bar other investigators from exploring the institutional dimension in a Jamesian fashion, as, for example, James Pratt set out to do.

We must admit, though, that as soon as the institutional dimension is brought back into the picture, it calls into question the pivotal distinction James draws between personal and ritual acts. Despite the provisional way in which James introduces it, this is no innocuous dichotomy; it inevitably causes some distortion even of the most personal religious testimony. Yet neither is it merely arbitrary. His claim that personal, inward religiousness is more primordial than its culturally mediated forms reflect a common distinction that religious people themselves often make, between ritual experienced as vitally charged, and ritual experienced as empty and repetitive. It reflects the real difference between adhering to a tradition out of dull habit, and appropriating a tradition in such a way that it may become, with all its ancient observances intact, a vehicle for "first-hand" religious experience.

James himself notes in passing that it is not chronological priority that gives to personal religious experience its primordial, first-hand quality. If only James had lingered over this thought, he might have realized that dogmas, traditions, rituals, and ecclesial communities are supreme custodians and shapers of the very kinds of religious experience that most readily pass all of his pragmatic tests.

But would James have been willing to acknowledge this, given his pronounced bias against "the ecclesiastical spirit?" Not without a struggle, I suspect. Yet it is tempting to speculate—even at the risk of "presentism"—about how his thinking might change if he were with us today, in our more historicist and pluralist philosophical climate.

James's great intellectual virtue is openness and educability; this is the hallmark of his pragmatism and it is also what has made him vulnerable to the charge of being inconsistent. How might James educate himself if he were with us today? Surely he would see the break-down of community, and realize that what is called for now is a religious philosophy more adequate to the task of repairing that break-down. His own vision of the social character of philosophy would contribute to that end. Perhaps he could even be taught to recognize his blind spots: his inherited prejudice against Roman Catholicism, and his less explicit but no less damaging lack of sympathy for Judaism.

There are some passages in *The Varieties*, however, which do give me pause. While I believe that James's philosophy could survive the uprooting of the exaggerated dichotomy between personal and institutional religion, it would not have been an easy matter to persuade James himself of this; nor would it be easy to overcome the bias against Catholicism, given his deep-rooted tendency to see Protestantism as the very spirit of the great American experiment, standing for modernity, toleration, individual freedom of conscience, and personal experience, over against the monarchical, baroque, hierarchial Catholic spirit with its impossible tangle of intermediaries, external devotions, and arbitrary restrictions standing in the way of personal experience. The irony is that James's own Protestantism—the Protestantism of such passages as "examples ... which make us rub our Protestant eyes;" "our Protestant and modern education"; and "We English-speaking Protestants ... seem to find it enough if we take God alone into our confidence"—is itself a figment (VRE: 265, 276, 365). The abstract conception of Protestantism that lies behind these passages presupposes a most unlikely marriage: some features of evangelical Protestantism (its emphasis on conversion and intense personal religious experience, but not its exclusivism) wedded to some features of liberal Protestantism (its modernism, but not its "pale negations").

Could James be cured of his blind spot by the new discipline of "science of religions," which he hopes will win the day? Yes, if by "science of religions" he means the empathetic study of world religions, *in situ,* rather than merely cobbled together from European-language books. But what James tells us of his plan for the science of religions is not entirely encouraging. As a method of testing religious claims against human standards and the evolving canons of common sense, "It is but the elimination of the humanly unfit, and the survival of the humanly fittest, applied to religious beliefs" (VRE: 266). Its job is not "thick description" in Clifford Geertz's sense. Rather, it is to "eliminate the local and the accidental," to sift out "unworthy formulations," and to confront the claims of religious experience with the findings of the natural sciences (VRE: 359). Eventually, James hoped, this method would lead to a consensus on what is common and essential in religious life.

While James defends religion, in general, against the charge of being a mere atavism, he believes that *some* forms of religion do represent an atavism; and that this is the sort of thing that we know by common sense: "the older gods have fallen below the secular level, and can no longer be believed in" (VRE: 264).

Unlike Chesterton, who said that the only problem with Christianity was that it had never been tried, James believes that the "old" version of Christianity *has* been tried—and found wanting—before the tribunal of common sense and empirically evolved values. If Catholicism and its ilk continue to flourish, that is no vindication of their merits, but only a sign that some people (and this puzzles James) actually *like* all that scholastic mumbo-jumbo and ecclesiastic pomp.

James is particularly puzzled by John Henry Newman, perhaps because he senses that Newman is a kindred spirit facing him from the other side of the looking-glass. It troubles James, for he cannot fathom how a great mind like Newman got there. Newman makes several appearances in *The Varieties,* almost in the fashion of an allegorical type Ecclesiastical Man, who intones absurd long lists of divine attributes as if they were Gregorian antiphons; whose "imagination ... innately craved an ecclesiastical system ..." who in guarding his dogmatic articles was "as jealous of their credit as heathen priests are of that of the jewelry and ornaments that blaze upon their idols (VRE: 361-362).

James makes an effort to understand the Catholic sensibility as an imaginative need for richness, hierarchy, and complexity; but he is unable to press his sympathies very far in this direction. As soon as the subject comes up, the old antipathies kick in. James is at his most un-original in these passages.

On the other hand, in James's defense, we should consider the possibility that the current temper of heightened sensitivity to "bias-crimes" in language keeps us from catching a certain deliberate irony and playfulness in James's "we Protestants" remarks. Perhaps he is not vaunting his inherited Protestant world-view so much as playing off it—much as he plays off "the clerico-academic-scientific" world-view—in order to highlight the strangeness, and thereby rediscover the familiarity, of the full range of human religiousness. We must remember that this is his real aim, even on those occasions when he misses the mark.

But what really saves James, in my estimation, is his fallibilism, which finds expression—almost in the same breath with his most egregiously anti-Catholic remarks—in the lecture on "The Value of Saintliness." James freely admits his own bias: "how can any possible judge or critic help being biased in favor of the religion by which his own needs are best met? He aspires to impartiality; but he is too close to the struggle not to be to some degree a participant ...." (VRE: 268). The solution, for James, is not to retreat into skepticism or fideism (it is instructive to note the contrast between his position and that of Kierkegaardian or Wittgensteinian fideists). Nor, I venture to say, would James approve of the deterministic historicisms of our day. Rather, he trusts that one can have a coherent philosophy and still be open to change: "... it would be absurd to affirm that one's own age of the world can be beyond correction by the next age" (VRE: 266).

James's diagnosis of institutional religion is unsustainable, granted. Yet it may be forgivable insofar as it is in principle open to revision. "The wisest of critics is an altering being," James declares (VRE: 267). If we take him at his word, then we are justified in imagining a Jamesian "science of religions" cured of its besetting vice, that narrow-mindedness which (under the guise of open-mindedness!) would block the way to understanding the ways in which dogma (as distinguished from misplaced dogmatism) and sacrament (as distinguished from empty ritualism) may produce their own abundant "fruits for life."

A related problem, which contemporary interpreters of religion are bound to notice, is the skewed nature of the sources on which James depends, his *documents humains.* As David Wulff tells us, James's sources amount to nearly two hundred excerpts, most coming from works Wulff describes as "spontaneous" ("confessions, biographies, or inspirational works") (Wulff 1991: 483). Roughly twenty percent come from other sources, according to Wulff; about half of these from Starbuck's questionnaire responses, and most of the remainder from personal acquaintances of James.

Since the majority of these accounts have a Christian or at least a post-Christian provenance, it is no wonder that the category of conversion figures so largely, while related categories—such as initiation—suffer neglect. If this is to be the beginnings of a science of religions, then it is a neglect that demands to be redressed.

James does make use of excerpts from Hindu, Buddhist, and Islamic sources. He is limited, he says, by the lack of personal testimony from non-Christian traditions (VRE: 319; discussed by Wulff 1991: 483). One explanation for this is that non-Christian religious testimony was only beginning to become available to European and American readers. Another is that the personal confession is a particularly well-developed Christian genre, beginning with—and still informed by—Augustine.

Interestingly, the genre of Christian confession is directly tied to the theme of conversion experience. The personal narrative is the precise literary counterpart to the conversion experience. James's discussion of conversion may be viewed as a contribution to this genre, for it is far from being a disinterested account; it even includes, attributed to an unnamed French correspondent, a personal confession of his own terrifying brush with religious melancholy (VRE: 134-135).

James evidently finds in the classic Christian conversion narratives (Augustine, Bunyan, Edwards, Tolstoy) the supreme expression of the experience of salvation; he has only to naturalize this experience in order to make universal its claim that despair and rebirth provide the most profound key to the secrets of the universe.

Of course, the original purpose of Christian confessional literature was not to provide data for psychological or sociological analysis; nor was it mere self-expression. Rather, the conversion narrative was an act of personal and communal remembering and self-offering, with pointed didactic intent. What happens, then, when such material is made the basis for a psychological study? That study is bound to be drawn into theological questions or, as James puts it, spiritual judgments. James tries to put these judgments into neutral religious language in order to naturalize what would seem otherwise to be a merely intra-Christian investigation.

James's vision of a "science of religions" may be understood as an expression of his wish for a richer neutral vocabulary with to accomplish this naturalization and thus make more efficient the transition from description to what James calls appreciation (that is, evaluation). As David Wulff points out, James does not linger very long over phenomenological description; he begins the Gifford Lectures in an apologetic vein, and moves rather quickly into questions that call for theological judgment (Wulff 1991: 488). All the more reason to re-think the theological assumptions involved.

THE CULT OF FEELING

James is widely criticized for elevating feeling at the expense of intellect. "At the end of the day," writes Nicholas Lash, "it was the feeling and its fruitfulness, the temperature and temper of the ego when happily accepting nothing in particular, but just the universe, which interested him" (Lash 1988: 41-42). It is this charge that James anticipates and attempts to answer in the passages I quoted at the beginning of this paper, in which he pledges his faith in philosophical reason.

It is easy to see why James's protestations on this point have not satisfied his critics. He commends philosophical reason simply on the grounds of its humanity, not on the grounds that it provides a superior vantage point. The intellect is part of our total organic and social life; therefore it must be counted into any analysis of religious experience that ventures to be, as the subtitle of *The Varieties* indicates, "A Study in Human Nature."

Philosophy, as James characterizes it here, is a human tool, whose purpose is to help human beings adapt to the world in which we live. Its main contribution is to mediate among conflicting interpretations. Its authority is modest, however; for the conceptions we frame as well as the questions we think to ask are shaped by the shared philosophical climate and limited by whatever happens to be in our stock of available experience. The primordial living source or "current" (to use one of his favorite metaphors) of this experience is what James calls "feeling."

James has provoked misunderstanding by speaking of feeling as something private and mute. His critics have taken this rhetorical practice rather too literally, assuming that feeling is for James irretrievably subjective: bottled up, as it were, in the private chamber of the heart. But for James feeling is like a wellspring or current that pours forth in action. He writes in "Reflex Action and Theism": "The current of life which runs in at our eyes or ears is meant to run out at our hands, feet, or lips" (James 1979: 92). An exclusively subjective feeling or sensation would be "either pathological or abortive" (p. 92).

James describes the processes of emotion, sensation, and thought in similar ways. An inflow of vital impressions leads (unless blocked by inhibitions) to an outflow of action and decision. Inhibitions have a vital role to play in these processes, but there are times when their over-production clogs the stream of life and thought. One of James's aims in *The Varieties* (as in "The Will to Believe") was to clear away the superfluous inhibitions that prevailing intellectual fashions had set in the path of the religious impulse; hence his desire to let feeling have its day.

THE CULT OF GENIUS AND THE PREOCCUPATION WITH EXTREMES

In *The Varieties* James chose to focus on exceptional, intense, transforming, sudden, apparently spontaneous, discrete religious experiences. This is congruent with the interest he displayed elsewhere in paranormal phenomena and exceptional mental states. He could have written a different book, one that would stress the religious character of everyday experience—this is the current trend, and it is a very wholesome one. But such a book would not have to displace *The Varieties*. Indeed, if it were made out to do so, much would be lost from our account of the religious character of everyday life. Many people are first alerted to a sacramental quality in existence by way of an extraordinary religious episode. James gives permission to take such extraordinary states seriously, and thus to integrate them into a religious interpretation of the whole of life.

James's remarks on the crucial role of the religious genius have provoked a reaction on the part of critics who find the very word "genius" suspect. It is claimed that he considers only the virtuosos of religious experience capable of an authentically grounded faith.

The chief drawback of the "genius" paradigm is that it causes James to neglect religious movements that are not centered on founder figures. James's fascination was not a matter of romantic individualism run amok, however, but a corrective reaction against the bulldog Darwinism that—illicitly imported into social psychology—decreed that individuals cannot make a difference. This misuse of Darwinism was one of James's lifelong concerns, expressed in such essays as "Great Men and their Environment" and "The Importance of Individuals" (see Rambo 1982).

James has been charged with stressing first-hand religious experience to an extent that would shut out mere bystanders from a full participation in religious life. He is said to be positively disdainful of the religion of ordinary folk. How, then, shall we account for the enduring popular appeal of *The Varieties*? There are two possibilities:

1. James's readers have responded favorably to *The Varieties* because they believe themselves to have had similar experiences and are gratified to find those experiences empathetically described and vindicated—a supposition to which support is given by recent surveys on the prevalence of reported mystical experience. We are, as Andrew Greeley put it years ago, "a nation of mystics" (See Greeley 1974).

2. James's readers, on the whole, apparently have not felt put off or put down by the distinction he draws between first-hand and second-hand experience. They have not felt thereby excluded from James's general account of the religious life of humanity.

Perhaps this is because James is notably less the esotericist that Schleiermacher is in his *Speeches on Religion* or Otto in his *Idea of the Holy*. James does not find it necessary, as Otto does, to issue warnings to the uninitiated. James never suggests that it will be difficult for his readers to enjoy accounts of extraordinary religious experience vicariously, and to take to heart the messages they bear. It would indeed be odd if James had suggested such a thing, for he remarks on several occasions that he is constitutionally incapable of having many of the kinds of religious experience he describes; and yet he feels qualified to interpret them on the strength of sheer sympathy (see Smith, intro. to VRE: xvi).

James's use of extreme examples must be seen alongside his use of familiar analogies. James frequently invites his audience to think of comparable, though less dramatic, instances from their own experience, like the thrill of looking into a mountain gorge, odd deja-vu sensations, or the discovery that letting go of conscious struggle is the best way to retrieve a forgotten name. Here are two typical instances: "The rest of us can, I think, imagine this by recalling our state of feeling in those temporary 'melting moods' into which either the trials of real life, or the theatre, or a novel sometimes throw us" (VRE: 216); and "apart from anything acutely religious, we all have moments when the universal life seems to wrap us round with friendliness. In youth and health, in summer, in the woods or on the mountains, there come days when the weather seems all whispering with peace .... (VRE: 221).

Taken together (and he never intended for them to be taken apart) the extreme cases and the homespun analogies provide the material for James's "method of serial study," which he explains, at the beginning of the Mysticism lectures, as follows: "phenomena are best understood when placed within their series, studied in their germ and in their over-ripe decay, and compared with their exaggerated and degenerated kindred" (VRE: 303; James often uses the analogy of the series scale, range, or ladder; see also VRE: 28, 41).

The exaggerated cases are needed in order to accumulate the all-important *differentia* that reveal what is distinctive about a phenomenon; for instance, what distinguishes religious from moral ways of accepting the universe (VRE: 42, 44). The cumulative effect of these *differentia* is to show that religious feeling is "an absolute addition to the Subject's range of life" (VRE: 46). An *absolute* addition, yet James has led us to its threshold by small increments.

Contrast this to the characteristic Romantic defense of religious experience (Schleiermacher, Otto), which insists on its categorical uniqueness. James lampoons the quest for uniqueness in a way that speaks tellingly to the Romantic defense: "any object that is infinitely important to us and awakens our devotion feels to us also as if it must be *sui generis* and unique. Probably a crab would be filled with a sense of personal outrage if it could hear us class it without ado or apology as a crustacean ...." (VRE: 17).

James's aim is to take the whole range of religious experience together—from the far end, where its characteristic features are set in sharp (though sometimes pathological) relief, to the near end, where they shade off into common and apparently non-religious phenomena (VRE: 26). In the long run, he suggests, this provides a more stable basis for the vindication of religious phenomena than can be achieved by "refusing to consider their place in any more general series, and treating them as if they were outside of nature's order altogether" (VRE: 28).

A fair appraisal of what James achieved in *The Varieties* must also take into account its frankly apologetic intent. James is addressing a generation of intellectuals whose religious instincts were being thwarted (or so they thought) by inhibitions set down by scientific and religious orthodoxies. If James is to reach such an audience, his starting-point cannot be that of adherence to a concrete religious tradition. Inevitably this puts him at a disadvantage, if he is compared to the more seasoned masters of spiritual life. When it comes to framing a rich and balanced theology of religious experience, he will be no match for a Jonathan Edwards or a John of the Cross (Jantzen 1989; Proudfoot 1989).

By way of contrast to James, Grace Jantzen cites the spiritual advice of Bernard of Clairvaux: "Experiences of God are not to be sought for their own sake, for their delightfulness, or out of intellectual curiosity. They are to be sought only and solely as the opening of the heart to God in communion with Christ through scripture and sacrament, which is the pathway of increasing union with God" (Jantzen 1989: 306).

Bernard "is not interested in odd psychic states," writes Jantzen. It should be noted, however, that for all James's fascination with odd psychic states, he does not make them the sole test of a religious sensibility. For one thing, a psychic experience that is so special, so set apart from the rest of life as to be merely interruptive, would fail James's "fruits for life" criterion. Excessive preoccupation with discrete religious experiences, pursued for their own sake, is one of the marks of what James calls a "theopathic" personality.

While there is no question that Bernard has the more developed religious world-view, James has the apologetic advantage. For James himself, and for his audience, scripture is already essentially a closed book, and a disciplined religious life at best a distant prospect. James makes entry into a more developed religious world-view—of some kind—possible again for many to whom the way seemed blocked. When he focuses on visions and other extraordinary psychic states, this is part of a larger strategy to defend religious experience and assure it a place of honor in modern understandings of human nature.

THE INEFFABLE AND THE IMMEDIATE

Another set of criticisms and misunderstandings (misunderstandings for which James bears at least partial responsibility) have to do with a class of religious experiences for which claims of "immediacy" and "ineffability" are frequently made.

Today, one has only to say something like "all experience is interpreted experience" in order for heads to nod sagely all around. In James's day, this insight was beginning to be voiced, but had not yet achieved the status of academic credendum. James was therefore unaware of the offense he would cause later readers when he defined "experience," for Baldwin's Dictionary, as

... the entire process of phenomena, of present data considered in their raw immediacy, before reflective thought has analysed them into subjective and objective aspects or ingredients" (James 1978: 95).

Nicholas Lash speaks for many of James's critics when he says:

... any general account of human experience is mistaken, bewitched by the form of our language, if it proceeds on the supposition that there is any such thing as experience. There is no such thing, and hence there is no such thing as pure or raw experience, any more than there is any such thing as pure or raw size or quantity or color (Lash 1988: 12).

Lash hears "infantilist overtones" in James's expression "raw immediacy" (p. 86). "What kind of people would we have to be, " asks Lash, "in order to enjoy 'experience' in what he took to be its 'pure' condition?" (p. 68) Babies!

Lash assumes that James identifies mysticism with pure experience, and pure experience with the dissolving of ego boundaries. There are two problems with this reading. First, it commits the Freudian error of equating the complex states of unification to which mystical literature attests with a simple regression to non-differentiation. James was too much a lover of diversity and complexity to make such an error. Second, Lash overlooks the fact that, for James, raw immediacy characterizes the entire process of phenomena *prior to* the division into subject and object.

James does not claim raw immediacy, in the technical sense, for the religious or mystical experiences described in *The Varieties*. All of these are experiences that belong to experiencing subjects. Although intense unitive states carry with them what Wayne Proudfoot has conveniently designated the *felt sense* of immediacy, this felt sense of immediacy is actually, if we follow James, a particular state of consciousness, a particular modification of the subject's inner life (Proudfoot 1985: 36). It is an experience of wondrous intimacy and communion; as such, it is already defined by a subject/object dichotomy. Only this dichotomy accounts for the rapture that accompanies the unitive experience, with its sense of boundaries dissolving. Pure experience, on the other hand, is not a rapture, not a merging of self and other; rather, it is a name for the whole field of phenomena; the "immediate flux of life," the "primal stuff" of existence.

When James calls philosophy back to the sense of the immediate flux of life, what he is asking for has nothing in common with either mysticism or infantile regression; rather, as Charlene Seigfried has shown, it entails a creative reconstruction of experience (Seigfried 1981).

James's observations, in *The Varieties* and elsewhere, about the ineffability of mystical experience and the private and inarticulate character of feeling, have led his critics to overlook James's confidence that a sympathetic interpreter who attends to such phenomena may be able to say something useful by way of description. In a letter to Münsterberg, James writes, "I still believe the immediate living moment of experience to be as 'describable' as any 'scientific' substitute therefore can be" (In Seigfried 1981: 499). The Gifford Lectures themselves are a substantial wager on the describability of religious experience. When, in the course of describing religious experience, James stresses its indescribability, he is simply trying to do justice to a pervasive fact of experience: that people find themselves sensing things without knowing how to find the words to express them. This much must be admitted, however one views the relationship between language and experience. James's other point is to highlight the difference between first- and second-hand experience, the difference between knowing the symptoms of drunkenness and being drunk.

If religious experience were completely indescribable, however, there would be no rationale for the science of religions at whose birth James hopes to assist. It is only because religious experience is describable that James can make it a matter of obligation for philosophy to count it in: "To describe the world with all the various feelings of the individual pinch of destiny, all the various spiritual attitudes, left out from the description—they being as describable as anything else—would be something like offering a printed bill of fare as the equivalent for a solid meal" (VRE: 394).

If we re-read James's account of the four marks of mystical experience with these observations in mind, then James's view comes closer than we might otherwise have suspected to the position recently advanced with exceptional clarity by Wayne Proudfoot—that the ineffability of mystical experience is itself part of the very description by which that experience is characterized (Proudfoot 1985: 124-136).

As important as *Essays in Radical Empiricism* was to the development of James's religious thought, we should avoid reading it back into *The Varieties*. James's pragmatism and pluralism play a more important role than his radical empiricism in the shaping of *The Varieties*. In his own Preface to *Pragmatism*, James remarks that "there is no logical connection between pragmatism, as I understand it, and a doctrine which I have recently set forth as 'radical empiricism.' The latter stands on its own feet. One may entirely reject it and still be a pragmatist" (James 1975: 6). Similarly, James would not want his defense of religious experience to stand or fall on the merits of his radical empiricism. In *The Varieties* he makes every effort to ensure that his account of religious experience, and his defense of it, are compatible with more than one philosophy of mind, more than one psychological model, and more than one metaphysical world-picture—even though he scatters the lectures with hints at the pluralistic pantheism which is his own inclination and towards which he sees the collective weight of religious testimony leaning.

ANYTHING GOES?

"The Will to Believe," *The Varieties* and *Pragmatism* each in turn provoked the criticism, from philosophical friend and foe alike, that James was playing fast and loose with the question of truth. Dickinson S. Miller, Josiah Royce, Bertrand Russell, and G.E. Moore may not have agreed on much else, but they did agree in finding James guilty of equating truth simplistically with emotional expediency (see Levinson 1981: 220; also Lash 1988: 81).

James finally gives an exasperated response to this criticism in *The Meaning of Truth*: "All this rubbish. The coincidence of the true with the emotionally satisfying becomes of importance for determining what may count for true, only when there is no evidence" (in Levinson, p. 236).

The question of whether James, in *The Varieties*, advocates a simple voluntarism in matters of belief is raised and settled in the very first lecture, in which he defends religious claims against "medical materialism." James begins by making the point that if one admits (as he does), that *all* mental states depend upon bodily states, then organic causation cannot be a basis for discrediting religious states. Another standpoint must be found for judging the validity of an insight to which experience (all of it organically explainable) has led.

That standpoint is fundamentally a rational one; one should not automatically assent to an insight just because it is keenly felt to be true. James is easily misunderstood on this point, by readers who mistake descriptive passages for his normative account of the process of judgment. Speaking descriptively, James says that when we judge experiences or states of mind to be valid, we do so "either because we take an immediate delight in them; or else it is because we believe them to bring us good consequential fruits for life" (VRE: 21). Similarly, "It is the character of inner happiness in the thoughts which stamps them as good, or else their consistency with our other opinions and their serviceability for our needs, which make them pass for true in our esteem" (VRE: 21-22). Observe the optional character of these criteria: *either* inner happiness, *or* consistency, *or* serviceability suffice, according to James, for us to count an insight delivered to us by experience as true.

Even more basic is the "primitive credulity" (an expression James takes from Alexander Bain) with which we ordinarily meet our mental states. In *The Principles of*

Psychology, James maintains that "Any relation to our mind at all, in the absence of a stronger contradicting relation, suffices to make an object real .... As a rule we believe as much as we can. We would believe everything if we only could" (James 1981, II: 928). Belief, for James, is a movement of the affection and the will towards an object to which the mind attends. In its earliest stage, this movement is only barely susceptible of analysis. Even at later stages of reflection, when we are inwardly debating the truth or falsehood of a thought, our primitive credulity remains largely in effect.

Cognitive habits are not the same as cognitive principles, however, and James points out that when we reflect upon our habitual ways of counting thoughts true, we soon discover that "inner happiness and serviceability do not always agree" (VRE: 22). Hence the need for critical testing. James's model for such testing is a Darwinian one; our ideas, once set out in the surrounding environment, will survive only if they are fit to do so.

At first blush, James acknowledges, many of the ideas delivered by religious experience seem ill-fitted to survive in our environment:

> There are moments of sentimental and mystical experience ... that carry an enormous sense of inner authority and illumination with them when they come. But they come seldom, and they do not come to every one; and the rest of life makes either no connection with them, or tends to contradict them more than it confirms them (VRE: 22).

What shall we make of such moments? James asks us neither to credit nor to discard them out of hand, but to subject them to pragmatic testing, which—if they pass the test—will in turn help us to cultivate them (even in a seemingly hostile environment) and thereby bring them into ever more productive and enduring connection with life.

It is with this aim in mind that James first introduces principles that may be considered normative rather than merely descriptive: "*Immediate luminousness*, in short, *philosophical reasonableness*, and *moral helpfulness* are the only available criteria" (VRE: 23). Here we are dealing no longer with an array of options, but with a set of principles that must be taken all together; none suffices by itself to make assent rationally warranted.

As William Wainwright argues, what James offers is a balance: our passional nature is counted in, and kept in sight; but it is also kept in check by reason (Wainwright 1991). John E. Smith concurs: "the appeal to the function, fruits, and value of religion does not tell the whole story about James and the problem of religious truth" (Introduction to VRE: xvii). The whole story, if it is ever told, will retain its unfinished look; for truth has for James an eschatological character.

James was interested in how ideas become true for us, and how we come to stand in a relationship of truth to the objects of our knowledge. Applied to the religious sphere, James's pragmatic method is not very different from the methods for discernment used throughout the ages by seasoned spiritual directors; as a theory of truth, it is sapiential (like the views of truth one finds in Patristic and monastic Christian literature) rather than epistemological. As Henry Samuel Levinson puts it, James renounced the quest for certainty, not for reality (Levinson 1981: 220-230).

AN ARGUMENT FROM RELIGIOUS EXPERIENCE?

Is James trying to construct an empirical argument for the existence of God? A few stray remarks suggest that he may have thought so. Consider his passing statement, in *Pragmatism*, that "I have written a book on men's religious experience, which on the whole has been regarded as making for the reality of God;" or his confession, "I myself believe that the evidence for God lies primarily in inner personal experiences" (James 1975: 143, 156).

On the other hand, in the Gifford lecture on "Philosophy," James summarily rejects the classic theistic proofs:

> The arguments for God's existence have stood for hundreds of years with the waves of unbelieving criticism breaking against them, never totally discrediting them in the ears of the faithful, but on the whole slowly and surely washing out the mortar from between their joints. If you have a God already whom you believe in, these arguments confirm you. If you are atheistic, they fail to set you right (VRE: 345).

If James thought he had a more compelling argument to offer, would this not be the opportune moment to unveil it?

I can only conclude that when James speaks of religious experience as "evidence for God," he is using the word "evidence" rather loosely. We know that for James religious testimony constitutes a mass of experiential facts that must be counted in. At times he suggests that he finds in religious experience positive hints of divine activity. Yet he never presses this point very far; clearly, James was not attempting to marshal evidence that would logically compel theistic belief. The phrase "on the whole" is the telling one.

What James was attempting to do was to provide permission to take religious experience seriously, thus removing some of the obstacles to theistic belief. *The Varieties* is "a study of human nature," not an exercise in natural theology. God's credentials are not the issue. Once we realize this, it becomes less problematic that developed conceptions of God enter in only through the back and side doors, in the form of diverse and tentative "over-beliefs."

CRASS SUPERNATURALISM

In his "Postscript" to *The Varieties* James tells us what he thinks about God. His point of departure, as always, is the cumulative evidence of human experience, and his intention is to sketch only the minimal conclusions to which such evidence points. While classical philosophical theism requires a God that fills the firmament, commands the elements, and legislates to all realms, James's minimal conception of God is merely that of a presence or "energy" that makes incursions into human consciousness through its fringes:

> ... the practical needs and experiences of religion seem to me sufficiently met by the belief that beyond each man and in a fashion continuous with him there exists a larger power which is friendly to him and to his ideals. All that the facts require is that the power should be both other and larger than our conscious selves. Anything larger will do, if only it be large enough to trust for the next step. It need not be infinite, it need not be solitary. It might conceivably be only a larger and more godlike self, of which the present self would then be but the mutilated expression, and the universe might conceivably be a collection of such selves, of different degrees of inclusiveness.... (VRE: 413).

With the delight he always takes in championing the popular and practical view of things against the "clerico-academic," James readily labels his proposal a "crasser" form of supernaturalism. His critics could not agree more.

French Catholic theologian Jean Mouroux, whose theology of religious experience has deeply influenced Catholic thinkers of the *ressourcement* generation, finds that James's God is merely secondary in religious experience. He is reduced to the stature of an unknown quantity who exists solely that we may live: we do not serve him, we make use of him, James says, repeating a phrase of Leuba's—and the really interesting and typical element in religious experience is to be found in the power which is attributed to God and which flows from him into us. This deliberately utilitarian conception—the utter negation of any genuine God of religion—ends in the most unmitigated anthropocentricism...." (Mouroux 1954: 4).

For a theologian like Mouroux, accustomed to the architectonics of a fully elaborated Christian faith, a faith which conjoins the philosophical vision of absolute reality with a concrete revealed and sacramental tradition, James's piecemeal, experimental, pluralistic theism is bound to seem scandalously insufficient. The shock effect of reading James after immersion in an orthodox theistic tradition renders even the most profound and sensitive of such theologians poor judges of James's message.

Once again, James's rhetoric is partly to blame for the misunderstanding. He speaks of God in terms of use and function, in much the same way that he speaks of truth as instrumental. Yet surely there is nothing controversial about saying that God's presence may be discerned through human needs. James's stronger statements, which suggest that God is somehow vindicated by concrete benefits, are simply facing the pervasive facts of ordinary piety.

James is neither a utilitarian nor a programmatic anthropocentrist; if he were, he would have come out sounding more like Feuerbach. It is hard to imagine James utterly negating anything, let alone "the genuine God of religion." Nor does he utterly affirm anything strictly theological; his attention is focused on the provisional nature of human efforts to conceive of the God whose reality they sense.

THE "BATTLE OF THE ABSOLUTE"

The story of James's battle against absolutism in theology is a complex one, beyond the scope of the present essay. Suffice it to say that the absolute James rejected was not really the absolute God of any concrete religious tradition. He knew the absolute primarily as the brain-child of philosophical idealism. In this philosophical tradition, James believed, the absolute is nothing more than a sterile abstraction, which explains everything—and changes nothing.

James was not acquainted to a comparable degree with the way the absolute functions in concrete religious traditions like Judaism, Christianity and Islam; therefore he was not in a position to avail himself of the resources that these traditions provide for overcoming the sterility of the concept: their doctrines of creation and revelation, and, in the Christian case, the theology of the Trinity, the incarnation, and the sacraments.

There are moments, however, when James vividly appreciates what religious people have meant when they call God absolute. God is a name, James says in his second Gifford lecture, for "whatever ... were most primal and enveloping and deeply true." This is what is meant religiously by the absolute. In *Pragmatism*, James acknowledges that the absolute has a certain experiential "cash-value;" conveying a deep sense of security and the "right to take moral holidays." There is a tinge of the religious sense of God as absolute in the following passage from his concluding Gifford lecture:

God's existence is the guarantee of an ideal order that shall be permanently preserved. This world may indeed, as science assures us, some day burn up or freeze; but if it is part of his order, the old ideals are sure to be brought elsewhere to fruition, so that where God is, tragedy is only provisional and partial, and shipwreck and dissolution are not the absolutely final things (VRE: 407).[2]

James would like us to think of God as ultimate, rather than absolute; but this passage does suggest something more than the mere *chance* of salvation which is the closing note sounded by *The Varieties*.

We must remember, however, that the aim of *The Varieties* is not to construct a complete theology, but to defend the rational and moral soundness of diverse forms of religious engagement. As an apologetic work, *The Varieties* is obliged to appeal solely to authority—sources recognized by all who make up its intended audience (see Griffiths 1988: 403). Even if James were personally inclined to do so, the rules of his apologetic craft would forbid him to draw upon any particular deposit of faith. James is hardly a multi-culturalist, but his apology does have multiple targets: outright skeptics; religiously-inclined people who have come to believe that the prestige of science weighs in against their own fragile religious impulses; and theologians whose professionalism has put them out of touch with ordinary religious life.

There is only one authority to which James can appeal while addressing simultaneously his whole audience; namely, the problematic but nonetheless commonly intelligible authority of experience.

If we grant the validity of this apologetic concern, then all we have the right to require of James is that he pay greater attention to the ways in which the concept of God (including God as absolute) has shaped individuals' experience of God. Wayne Proudfoot makes this point with regard to James's treatment of conversion: "James does not recognize that the subject's attribution of the change in her life to divine activity is itself part of the experience" (Proudfoot 1989: 165).

James does not recognize this, but we may do so without ceasing to be Jamesian; for nothing in his argument essentially precludes enriching the phenomenological description of conversion so as to do greater justice to the subject's sense of divine agency.

JAMES'S "HERMENEUTICAL TURN"

An ingenious essay by Gerald L. Bruns seems at first to be lodging the familiar complaints: James's pluralism, pragmatism, and preference for private feelings combine to undermine the public character of philosophical discourse (Bruns 1984). In the Gifford Lectures, Bruns observes, James sounds now like a psychologist and now like a theologian, without committing himself to either camp: "The language of psychology, as James uses it, never acquires the status or authority of a philosophical language; it remains a rhetoric" (p. 305); so, too, for theology.

James's brand of empiricism is similarly capacious and hence un-philosophical, according to Bruns, for James's criteria for what counts as experience are so broadly ethical as to be unrecognizable to most children of Locke:

Experience, for James, is not just what occurs in sensation but what goes on in

---

2. James repeats this passage, with minor changes, in "Some Metaphysical Problems Pragmatically Considered": "The notion of God ... guarantees an ideal order that shall be permanently preserved. A world with God in it to say the last word, may indeed burn up or freeze, but then we think of him as still mindful of the old ideals and sure to bring them elsewhere to fruition; so that, where he is, tragedy is only provisional and partial, and shipwreck and dissolution not the absolutely final things," *Pragmatism* (197: 55).

human life; even mystical experiences, for example, although they tend to obliterate sensation and so pose every sort of difficulty as to what they are experiences of, still count as real experiences because they are, after all, experiences that human beings keep having (Bruns 1984: 301).

To the "loose universe" conjured by James's pluralism, James thus matches a corresponding looseness in speech, licensed by his pragmatism (see Ruf 1991; also Seigfried 1978). Religious experience is just a case in point, and Bruns suggests that "what attracted James to religious feelings was just the difficulty of knowing what to call them" (Bruns 1984: 305). He characterizes James as "a nominalist as against a metaphysical realist" (this is a controversial point), and then as a near-skeptic: "... we are on the threshold of that traditional skepticism which, from Pyrrho of Elis to Jacques Derrida, has always threatened to be the undoing not only of philosophical statements but of human talk itself" (pp. 299, 305).

How odd that James, whose own letters and the abundant testimony of his colleagues, adversaries, and correspondents, speak to his genius for philosophical friendship, should be accused of coming close to endangering the arts of human talk. But Bruns's point is not to call James a skeptic or a relativist (a charge that just applies only to a few contemporary neo-pragmatists), but rather to show how James manages at the last instant to redeem himself and his readers from such deadening habits of thought:

It is precisely here, however, at the threshold of skepticism, that James's thinking takes what can only be called a hermeneutical turn—although, of course, the word "hermeneutical" did not belong to any vocabulary James was familiar with, and he himself would have said at this crucial juncture his thinking takes its characteristically pragmatic turn toward the use of hypotheses for the sake of getting on with one's life (Bruns 1984: 306).

If pragmatism is the solution, then is it fair to say that pragmatism created the problem? Perhaps we could have taken James at his word from the beginning, and grant that for him at least, pragmatism bears no kindred relationship to skepticism.

Nonetheless, Bruns's insight about James's "hermeneutical turn" is valuable as a counter-argument to present to James's cultured despisers, for he sees it as rescuing James not only from skepticism but also from privatism.

As Bruns points out, the religious *documents humains* which provide James with his material for the Gifford Lectures are by no means "raw." That is, they are not spontaneous expressions of untutored private feeling; rather, they are intricate texts, often of considerable literary complexity, and texts that are clearly embedded in traditions. James's task is to moderate among interpretations offered by the texts themselves, interpretations which seek to translate those texts into modern idioms, and the host of competing extrinsic interpretations (some claiming explanatory force).

Bruns is among those James interpreters who have emphasized that James's understanding of philosophical truth-seeking is fundamentally a social and a sociable one (Besides Levinson and Cotkin, already cited, see McDermott 1976, 1986). Unlike the Cartesian thinker who philosophizes in radical solitude, the Jamesian pragmatist philosophizes always in a "climate," in conversation with others, and on the basis of historically shaped experience. As Bruns puts it, "the world of pragmatism is received as well as made; it is an ongoing and continuously transforming construction. James recognized the claims of tradition, but what he recognizes in particular is that these claims are not logically fixed but historically contingent" (Bruns 1984: 309). Similarly, Bennett Ramsey has argued recently that by the time James composed his Gifford Lectures, he had decisively moved away from romantic forms of self-definition and self-assertion, towards a vision of the self as "incurably involved in a web of relations" (Ramsey 1993: 13).

By these accounts, James is the forerunner of all that is liberating in post-modernism, without any of it nihilistic bravado or despair.

We may conclude, for the moment, by returning to the central paradox of the Gifford Lectures: James says, on the one hand, that "personal religious experience has its root and centre in mystical states of consciousness" and on the other hand, that he is constitutionally incapable of enjoying such states. He tells James Pratt "I can't possibly pray" (Wulff 1991: 474), yet says in *The Varieties* that prayer is "the very soul and essence of religion."

Consider, alongside this, the central paradox of the lecture on Mysticism: after building towards a crescendo of affirmation for the monistic tendencies and apparent unanimity of mystical testimony, James suddenly reverses direction, undermines the authority of mystical states, questions his earlier assumption about unanimity, and uses the facts of mystical experience to support not monism, but pluralism.

These paradoxes are more than an expression of James's personal ambivalence about religion; they tell us something about the central message of *The Varieties*. They show that James does not consider himself to be describing a realm of private, extreme experiences to which the general public can have no access. All it takes is a "mystical germ" (such as James admits to having), to be able to respond to the testimony of religious experience; and this mystical germ is widely disseminated in the human race.[3]

Conversely, it is clear from his conclusions on mysticism, that private experience is not the final arbiter for James. In short, James portrays religious experience (even in its most intense manifestations) as humanly familiar, as arrayed on the spectrum of ordinary modes of experiencing oneself and one's world, as serving social as well as individual well-being, and as capable of being described and adjudicated according to publicly accessible standards. The portrait is clear, but necessarily and diplomatically incomplete. God is in the picture, but remains featureless. If James had ventured to paint in the features he would have usurped the proper role of the theological voices of the concrete religious traditions. A liberal theistic portrait, such as we might have expected James to supply (though he found the Boston Unitarian version anemic), would foreclose upon alternative, more fully realized, conceptions of the divine.

Despite his own distaste for dogma, James's sense of theological fair-play requires him to leave room (under the heading of "over-beliefs") for the development of classical dogmatic theologies. From the perspective of such theologies, of course, the doctrine of God would not be a mere secondary elaboration, but rather an essential starting point (and *telos*) of all theological reflection. Nonetheless, there is no reason why James's description of religious experience, and his apology for its meaningfulness and worth, may not complement a fully realized dogmatic theology. Certainly there is no danger of confusing the two.

One last word of defense to the psychologists among James's cultured despisers:

Some of the critiques of James have focused on his own personal history. The vagaries of James's eclectic educational formation as artist, scientist, and philosopher, the influence of his eccentric father, his personal struggles with melancholy and illness, and the sheer abundance of his talents produced—depending upon how one reads the records of James's life and works—either chronic pathological indecisiveness or a humane and versatile mind, quickened by suffering and capable of seeing beyond conventional academic boundaries. So, too, *The Varieties* can be read (and has been read) either as the abnormal

---

3. "I have no mystical experience of my own," he told Starbuck, "but just enough of the germ of mysticism in me to recognize the region from which their voice comes when I hear it" (H. James 1920, II: 210).

product of a self-absorbed, neurasthenic, and vacillating thinker or as the generous dis-coveries of a genius of empathy. There is far from unanimity on the role played by James's own "passional nature" and personal history in the shaping of his philosophy.

While we are making up our minds about James, we should recall that it was James who kept the door open when the reigning positivisms and skepticisms were slamming it shut in the face of those who sought a scientific blessing for their faith; it was James who kept the door open when the established orthodox traditions were, by dint of their own apologetic and imaginative failures, slamming it shut in the face of countless unchurched aspirants. Given this achievement, is it reasonable to complain of James that he goes on standing, in non-communal fashion, in the door? There is still need of his door-holding services.

That we can imagine a Jamesian understanding of religious experience being corrected by more recent insights, is no sign that his understanding is obsolete. As Bernard of Chartres said, if we can see further than our teachers, it is only that we are dwarves seated on the shoulders of giants. While making the necessary corrections, we will be none the worse for leaning down now and then to give those giant shoulders an appreciative pat.

REFERENCES

Bruns, G.L. (1984). Loose talk about religion from William James. *Critical Inquiry*, 11: 299-316.

Cotkin, G. (1990). *William James, Public Philosopher.* Baltimore, MD: the Johns Hopkins University Press.

Dittes, J.E. (1973). Beyond William James. In C.Y. Glock & P.E. Hammond (Eds.) *Beyond the Classics: Essays in the Scientific Study of Religion.* New York: Harper and Row (pp. 291-354).

Greeley, A.M. (1974). *Ecstasy: A Way of Knowing.* Englewood Cliffs, NJ: Prentice-Hall.

Griffiths, P. (1988). An apology for apologetics. *Faith and Philosophy*, 5: 399-420.

James, H. (Ed.) (1920). *The Letters of William James*, 2 vols. Boston: Atlantic Monthly Press.

James, W. (1975). *Pragmatism.* Cambridge, MA: Harvard University Press.

———(1978). *Essays in Philosophy.* Cambridge, MA: Harvard University Press.

———(1979). *The Will to Believe and Other Essays in Popular Philosophy.* Cambridge, MA: Harvard University Press.

———(1981). *The Principles of Psychology*, 2 vols. Cambridge, MA: Harvard University Press.

———(1985). *The Varieties of Religious Experience* (in "The Works of William James"). F.H. Burkhardt, Bowers, F., & I.K. Skrupskelis (Eds.). Cambridge, MA: Harvard University Press.

Jantzen, G. M. (1989). Mysticism and experience. *Religious Studies*, 25: 295-315.

Lash, N. (1988). *Easter in Ordinary: Reflections on Human Experience and the Knowledge of God.* Charlottesville, VA: University Press of Virginia.

Levinson, H.S. (1981). *The Religious Investigations of William James.* Chapel Hill, NC: The University of North Carolina Press.

———(1984). Religious criticism. *The Journal of Religion*, 64: 37-53.

McDermott, J.J. (1976). *The Culture of Experience: Philosophical Essays in the American Grain.* New York: New York University Press.

———(1986). *Streams of Experience: Reflections on the History and Philosophy of American Culture.* Amherst, MA: The University of Massachusetts Press.

Mouroux, J. (1954). *Christian Experience: An Introduction to a Theology.* George Lamb

(Trans.) New York: Sheed and Ward.

Niebuhr, R.R. (1983). William James's metaphysics of religious experience. In *Streams of Grace: Studies of Jonathan Edwards, Samuel Taylor Coleridge, and William James*. Kyoto, Japan: Doshisha University Press.

Perry, R.B. (1935). *The Thought and Character of William James*, 2 vols. Boston, MA: Little, Brown.

Proudfoot, W. (1985). *Religious Experience*. Berkeley, CA: University of California Press.

——(1989). From theology to a science of religions: Jonathan Edwards and William James on religious affections. *Harvard Theological Review*, 82: 149-168.

Rambo, L.R. (1982). Evolution, community, and the strenuous life: The context of William James's "varieties of religious experience." *Encounter*, 43: 239-253.

Ramsey, B. (1993). *Submitting to Freedom*. New York: Oxford University Press.

Ruf, F.J. (1991). *The Creation of Chaos: William James and the Stylistic Making of a Disorderly World*. Albany, NY: State University of New York Press.

Seigfried, C.H. (1978). *Chaos and Context: A Study in William James*. Athens, OH: Ohio University Press.

——(1981). James's reconstruction of ordinary experience. *The Southern Journal of Philosophy*, 19: 499-516.

Smith, J.E. (1985). Introduction to W. James, *The Varieties of Religious Experience*. Cambridge, MA: Harvard University Press.

Wainwright, W.J. (1991). James, rationality and religious belief. *Religious Studies*, 27: 223-238.

Wulff, D.M. (1991). *Psychology of Religion: Classic and Contemporary Views*. New York: John Wiley and Sons.

BLOWING ALTERNATELY HOT AND COLD: WILLIAM JAMES AND THE COMPLEX STRATEGIES OF *THE VARIETIES*

TROELS NØRAGER

After almost a century of commentary and criticism, *The Varieties* seems to be generally recognized as a psycho-religious evergreen earning its author his rightful place—alongside Edwards and Emerson—in a distinguished tradition of American religious thought. Furthermore, James is praised as the pioneering psychologist of religion who managed to give an unbiased, nuanced, almost empathic presentation of the religious life. At the same time, the truth is that modern psychology of religion has displayed ambivalent reactions to James. By those emphasizing the need to distinguish between 'psychology of religion' and 'religious psychology', James has been somewhat contemptuously placed in the latter category, whereas others have tended to regard him as a continuing source of inspiration but, alas, too unsystematic to transform into a paradigm.

In what follows, I shall attempt to question some of these taken for granted views. I am doing this out of a conviction that *The Varieties*—in spite of its readable and immediately fascinating character—is the most complex, almost enigmatic, but perhaps also the most important text within modern psychology of religion. It goes without saying that I am definitely not pretending to be the first one to 'see through' the veils of this text, although I do believe that it has been all too often misunderstood or misrepresented, perhaps especially in America. Proudfoot's (1985) distinction between hermeneutics and pragmatism as constitutive of Continental versus American philosophic tradition gives us a clue as to why this has been the case. Following from pragmatism's approach to religious experience as perception, a great many American psychologists of religion have been almost obsessed with the idea of scientific, empirical research as collecting 'religious experiences' and putting them into a computer for factor analysis.

Pragmatist as James was, quantification and statistics were not exactly his idea of how to study religious experience. Instead, he did exactly what any lay person would expect from a psychological approach to 'religion': he tried to understand the nature of religious experience on the basis of relevant accounts. James, in other words, is sticking to the heart of the matter and showing us what psychology of religion is about. A truism as this may seem, the curious fact is that most of his successors in the field have concentrated their efforts on much more peripheral matters. So the reason we should pay real homage and not only lip service to James is that his agenda for a 'psychology of religion' was basically correct. Whether he was entirely successful in handling the issues connected with this agenda is, however, another matter. Perhaps James the pragmatist did never fully realize the extent to which he was engaged in hermeneutics and interpretation, dealing with *texts* as he was.

Why is *The Varieties* such a fascinating work? Why does each new re-reading lead us to discover new facets of this remarkable and rich text? I believe this has to do with three closely interrelated reasons: 1) the composition of the book, i. e. the interesting mixture of accounts of religious experience (*documents humains*) and James's commentaries, 2) James's exceptional rhetorical skills, and 3) his complex strategies of interpreting and explaining individual religion. Before elaborating on these points, however, I would like to raise the issue of the book's continuing power to engage and inspire us. Why, how, and in what specific sense am I being spoken to and involved by reading *The Varieties*? A clue to answering this question may be found in the three points just mentioned, namely in the often overlooked fact that the text displays a *tension* between the heart-language of traditional religion (the examples) and James's psychological language as well as his espousal of a new religious vision. Without going into the intricacies of James's biography and his personal religious background, my guess is that this tension reflects his personal as well as intellectual struggle to strike a balance between an 'old' and a 'new' scenario of individual religion. The way this struggle is subtly dramatized in the text of *The Varieties* speaks strongly to many readers (at least it does to me), because the same struggle is to some extent going on in all of us. Lured by the prospects of becoming pioneers of a new discipline, or even prophets of a new religious vision, we are turned into the prodigal sons and daughters of our own religious heritage.

THE MATTER OF DISCOURSE

The audience was extraordinarily attentive and reactive - I never had an audience so keen to catch every point. I flatter myself that by blowing alternately hot and cold on their Christian prejudices I succeeded in baffling them completely till the final quarter-hour, when I satisfied their curiosity by showing more plainly my hand. Then, I think, I permanently dissatisfied both extremes, and pleased a mean numerically quite small.[1]

The fact that *The Varieties* is composed with the purpose of being delivered (1901/02) in the setting of the prestigious Gifford Lectures in Edinburgh, is in itself significant. The presence of 'the audience' with its 'Christian prejudices' (Scottish presbyterianism!) not only calls forth James's masterful rhetoric, but also forces him to develop complex strategies for 'handling the crowd' before he can get to the point of 'showing more plainly his hand'. In the author's own words he was *blowing alternately hot and cold*, but what does that mean? Is James the only one to be above 'Christian prejudices', and if so, what exactly is he getting at? With these and the many other questions that could be added we are placed in the midst of the riddles that make up the enigmatic character of *The Varieties*. Although in what follows I'll try to unpack some of these riddles, I obviously do not claim to be solving all the mysteries surrounding James's rightly famous lectures. I do claim, however, that most commentators so far have been led astray by attempting to extract the contents, the Jamesian doctrine, as it were, of religious experience. These attempts are misguided, I believe, because the real drama of *The Varieties* is enacted on the level of discourse, and this drama is far more interesting than the elements of 'theory' related to James's treatment of conversion, mysticism, saintliness, etc. In other words, *The Varieties* is a text where you need to 'listen' very carefully to the way things are said. You need to be attentive to different types of discourse, rhetorical strategies, and generative metaphors, because part of James's greatness is that he was – as was Freud – well aware that 'mapping the inner world' is a matter of *metapsychology* and *discourse* alike. In this fundamental respect James the psychologist shares the problems of the religious individual: religious experience is a complex phenomenon arising in a continuum delineated by the poles of 'metapsychology' (what is 'behind' consciousness) and 'discourse' (the effects of linguistic practices, including culture), and any researcher of religious experience is faced with the task of adequately representing this in his own metapsychology and discourse. In the case of James and *The Varieties*, we shall see that this leads to interesting tensions between the 'heart-language' of the religious tradition and the language of the 'new' psychology.

---

1. Letter from William James to Charles Eliot Norton, quoted from Bowers (1985: 544).

THE "HEART-LANGUAGE" OF RELIGIOUS TRADITION

The examples of *The Varieties*, comprising more than half of the entire text, have often been acknowledged for adding a great deal to the 'charm' of the book.[2] And no doubt James has been well aware that these extracts of religious biography would play a decisive role in 'keeping the customers satisfied'. On closer scrutiny, however, much more is at stake. Originally in the lectures (and now in the text itself) the examples play the decisive role of constantly negotiating with the audience the nature of religion and religious experience, and at the same time creating a sense that we are actually 'there'. Therefore, we should not be misled by James's rhetoric when he almost apologizes for having selected his examples among the extreme, abnormal, or even insane conditions of the religious life. This characterization serves, as I shall show later, a different purpose on James's agenda. In other words, James may have his own reasons for thinking (or wishing) that the examples are peculiar, extreme, and 'bathed in sentiment', but if that were really the whole truth, the audience would be as if in a zoo getting a kick out of observing strange and dangerous species at a safe distance. Of course this is not the case. On the contrary, James agrees with his audience that the "religious experience which we are studying is that which lives itself out within the private breast" (VRE: 269). This accords with his definition of religion as well as with the intuitions of his audience. For the sake of brevity I shall only offer a few examples to demonstrate that James's purportedly 'bizarre' cases are simply expressing the metapsychology and discourse of religious tradition; i.e. they are referring to the heart:

- "But never since has there come quite the same stirring of the heart. Then, if ever, I believe, I stood face to face with God, and was born anew of his spirit" (VRE: 62).
- "This life is the real seeking of the kingdom of God, the desire for His supremacy in our hearts" (VRE: 90).
- "My heart kept languishing with another pining emotion. I can call this by no other name than that of a thirst for God" (VRE: 131).
- "This made a strange seizure upon my spirit; it brought light with it, and commanded a silence in my heart" (VRE: 155).
- "My heart seemed as if it would burst, but it did not stop until I felt as if I was unutterably full of the love and grace of God" (VRE: 159).
- "Although up to that moment my soul had been filled with indescribable gloom, I felt the glorious brightness of the noon-day shine into my heart" (VRE: 167).
- "The first condition of a Sufi is to purge his heart entirely of all that is not God. The next key of the contemplative life consists in humble prayers which escape from the fervent soul, and in the meditations on God in which the heart is swallowed up entirely" (VRE: 320).
- "Jesus has come to take up his abode in my heart" (VRE: 332).

In light of the overall importance James attributes to the examples, the reader is surprised to discover that only in two instances does he make a direct commentary or attempts an analysis. One case is the quotation from Augustine's *Confessions* describing the two 'wills' at war with each other (VRE: 143f); and the other is an extract from the diary of David Brainerd (VRE: 175f), where James has emphasized the particular lines he wishes to comment upon. In both cases it is noteworthy that James must interpret the

---

2. But they are also in a more fundamental sense the core and starting point of the book. Thus, when a translator of *The Varieties* suggested shortening the book by omitting some of the examples, James opposed the idea for the following reason: "The book was written round the documents. I got them first, and poured in my connective remarks like a sort of *galantine* jelly to enclose them, and I confess that I should dislike to have any of them sacrificed" (quoted from Bowers, 1985: 553).

examples against their professed self-understanding in order to reach his favored conclusion that "often there seems little doubt that both conditions - subconscious ripening of the one affection and exhaustion of the other - must simultaneously have conspired, in order to produce the result" (VRE: 176).

In this connection one of the examples in *The Varieties* is particularly interesting. From his colleague, Professor Flournoy of Geneva, James has received a statement from a woman who is apparently to some extent versed in psychology. The example is unique for the woman explicitly opposes a psychological interpretation to what is a more heart-felt experience:

> Whenever I practice automatic writing, what makes me feel that it is *not* due to a *subconscious self* is the feeling I always have of a foreign presence, external to my body. It is sometimes so definitely characterized that I could point to its exact position. This impression of presence is impossible to describe. It varies in intensity and clearness according to the personality from whom the writing professes to come. If it is some one whom I love, I feel it immediately, before any writing has come. My *heart* seems to recognize it (VRE: 58, emphasis added).

James uses this example to illustrate the sense of real presence commonly forming an integral part of religious experiencing. Has he not seen that the woman explicitly distances herself from the theory of a 'subconscious self' and instead refers to the heart as a phenomenologically more adequate description? I think it is generally true of *The Varieties* that James does not take the religious language and its perspective seriously, in fact he does not take language itself seriously: "The plain truth is that to interpret religion one must in the end look at the immediate content of the religious consciousness" (VRE: 19). It is difficult to see how this interpretive approach is compatible with James's more explanatory commitment to the 'subconscious self'. More importantly, however, although this statement can be read as proclaiming a sound, phenomenological principle, James is definitely not dealing with the immediate content of the religious consciousness. On the contrary, his examples are religious experiences in the sense of texts or discourse describing 'religious experience'. Thus, in spite of the impressive 'feel' for rhetoric reflected in his own textual practice, James remains trapped in a philosophy of consciousness. This effectively cuts him off from dealing with that which from a contemporary point of view stands out as the systematic core issue: the relation between the discourse of the examples (religious folk psychology, if you like) and the interpretive and explanatory discourse of a supposedly scientific psychology. And yet, at a different level, James has intuitively felt the impossibility of introducing the psychological perspective directly. Instead, he employs a number of what I would call mediating strategies. Before blowing 'cold' he thinks it wise to blow 'hot'.

RELIGIOUS AND SCIENTIFIC DISCOURSE: MEDIATING STRATEGIES

First among these strategies is James's distancing himself from the crude reductionism of 'medical materialism'. This move obviously serves to appease the audience, and up to this day James has commonly been heralded as the anti-reductionist per se. The matter is far more complex, however. In a sense, you might even say that James's polemical attitude towards medical materialism is just a way of anticipating the resistance on the part of the audience. Of course James holds that this type of materialism is too crude a reductionism, but the important thing which has generally been overlooked is that James's alleged anti-reductionism is tempered by the following statement: "Modern psychology, finding definite psycho-physical connections to hold good, assumes as a convenient hypothesis that the dependence of mental states upon bodily conditions must be thorough going and complete. If we adopt the assumption, then of course *what medical materialism insists on must be true in a general way, if not in every detail"* (VRE: 20, emphasis added). James does not explicitly say that he himself adopts this assumption, but since it comprises nothing less than "the general postulate of psychology" (ibid.) no other implication seems possible. Indeed, rejecting it would be the equivalent of excluding himself from the halls of respectable science. Thus, instead of solving the problem by a non-reductionist approach, James only bypasses the problem when he introduces the distinction between the descriptive task ('existential judgment') and the task of normative evaluation ('spiritual judgment').

The difficulty of grasping what exactly is going on in *The Varieties* is a consequence of the fact that James "is speaking to us in a plurality of voices" (Wulff 1991: 479). Wulff distinguishes "James the sensitive artist and pioneering phenomenologist" from "James the empirical scientist and explanatory psychologist", and finally "James the liberal Protestant and pragmatic philosopher" (p. 479). Following this important clue, we might say that in terms of approaching the religious phenomena James is operating on three different levels. First, James is faced with the difficult task of preparing the audience for viewing religion from an objective, dispassionately observing perspective. This obviously relates to James's self-understanding as a scientific psychologist looking for an explanation for the common features of the '*varieties*' of religious experience. Second, and quite contrary to the first approach, James advances the hermeneutic perspective of a 'verstehende Psychologie' pointing out that to really understand the religious life you must view it, as it were, from the inside. Thus, he states that one "can never fathom an emotion or divine its dictates by standing outside of it" (VRE: 261). Further, this approach accounts for his rhetorical apologies for lacking religious experiences himself. Finally, there is James the liberal Protestant who constructs what amounts to an apologetic 'defense' of religion by pragmatically judging its 'best fruits' to be among the best products of mankind (VRE: 49, 210).

The implication here is not that these three levels are necessarily mutually exclusive. Rather, the critical point is that James does not sufficiently distinguish between them nor does he attempt to account for their internal relations. The resulting 'polyphony' may well contribute to the fascination of reading *The Varieties*; as a research strategy for psychology of religion, however, it is unsatisfactory. Nonetheless, James does entertain an explanatory ambition related to the notion of the subliminal or subconscious. But apparently he has been aware of the impossibility of introducing this overall explanation in a direct fashion. Instead, as yet another mediating strategy, he is 'blowing hot' by recurrently speaking the language of the heart or 'the language of devotion' (VRE: 168). In *The Varieties* there are surprisingly many examples of this; here I shall only mention a few of them to illustrate the point (emphasis added by me):

- By a reductionist approach to religion we feel "menaced and negated *in the springs of our innermost life"*, because it threatens to "undo *our soul's vital secrets"* (VRE: 17).
- "All of our *raptures* and our *drynesses*, our longings and pantings" (VRE: 21).
- "The relation goes direct from *heart to heart*, from soul to soul, between man and his maker" (VRE: 32).
- "The believer alternates between *warmth* and *coldness* in his faith" (VRE: 59).
- "If we are in search of *a broken and contrite heart"* (VRE: 83).
- Of Tolstoy and Bunyan as examples of a gradual conversion James notes that "it must be confessed at the outset that it is hard to follow these *windings of the hearts* of others" (VRE: 153).

- Of the person who seems to be religiously 'indisposed' it may happen later in life that "some bolt be shot back in *the barrenest breast,* and the man's *hard heart may soften* and break into religious feeling" (VRE: 169).
- Further, James introduces the very apt expression *'melting moods'* for ways of experiencing that we normally (for good phenomenological reasons) relate to the heart. Especially when we weep, it is "as if our tears broke through an inveterate inner dam, and let all sorts of ancient peccancies and moral stagnancies drain away, leaving us now washed and *soft of heart* and open to every nobler leading. With most of us the customary *hardness* quickly returns, but not so with saintly persons" (VRE: 216).
- Finally, an interesting clash between psychological language and heart-language occurs when James is trying to convince his audience that "it is difficult not to believe that subliminal influences play the decisive part in these abrupt *changes of heart"* (VRE: 218).

Thus, we can see how James—by speaking the heart-language of religious tradition—evokes a religious folk model of the mind. Closely connected to this layer of rhetorical discourse, we find James occasionally allowing himself to step back into the vocabulary of traditional faculty psychology speaking of temperaments, 'animal spirits', conscience, higher affections, will, and 'our instinctive springs of actions'. Why does James make use of expressions which modern psychology has allegedly rendered obsolete? I believe that one reason is to be found in his rhetorical investment of mediating strategies, but it should also be noted that James was not exactly a mainline psychologist. On the contrary, like Freud he was painfully aware of the difficulties arising from any ambition of 'mapping the inner world'. He knows that we can only speak metaphorically about the psyche[3] by applying analogies such as viewing the mind via "the hackneyed symbolism of a mechanical equilibrium" (VRE: 163). In fact, one of the reasons *The Varieties* is so fascinating to read is James's impressive ability to render a nuanced description of the inner world, and he succeeds in this by employing linguistic resources from different domains and traditions. Thus, rhetorical skills form an integral part of James's greatness as a 'psychologist' who was too philosophically minded to be impressed by standard objectivisit versions of the new scientific psychology.

THE EXPLANATORY POWER OF THE SUBCONSCIOUS

What he *was* impressed by, however, was the more heretical notion of the subconscious:

> I cannot but think that the most important step forward that has occurred in psychology since I have been a student of that science is the discovery, first made in 1886, that, in certain subjects at least, there is not only the consciousness of the ordinary field, with its usual centre and margin, but an addition thereto in the shape of a set of memories, thoughts, and feelings which are extra-marginal and outside of the primary consciousness altogether, but yet must be classed as conscious facts of some sort, able to reveal their presence by unmistakable signs. I call this the most important step forward because, unlike the other advances which psychology has made, this discovery has revealed to us an entirely unsuspected peculiarity in the

---

3. I am using the notion of 'metaphor' in the wide sense introduced by Lakoff & Johnson (1980). See also Leary (1990).

constitution of human nature. No other step forward which psychology has made can proffer any such claim as this (VRE: 190).

The fact that James is so fascinated by the discovery of this 'unsuspected peculiarity in the constitution of human nature' is directly related to the sub-title of *The Varieties* as being *A Study in Human Nature*. This reveals something important about James's attitude towards psychology, namely that it primarily deserves our interest when it tells us something about human nature that we did not already know. That this is the case with the notion of the subconscious can hardly be disputed. But how can James apply this concept to the study of religious experiences? Before answering this question, let us take a look at the context from which psychologists inferred the existence of a subconscious region of the psyche.

Whereas on the Continent researchers like Janet and Freud found unconscious and repressed wishes to cause symptoms of neurosis, in England and America experiments with the subconscious region were mainly confined to the less respectable societies of 'psychical research' which James actively supported, risking his scientific respectability. Using hypnosis, psychical research studied curious phenomena such as split personalities, automatic writing, and clairvoyance. As is evident from *The Varieties* James saw these phenomena as casting a whole new light on human nature, but the important thing is that he himself wished to contribute to this overall endeavor by explaining religious experiencing as caused by 'eruptions' or 'incursions' from the subconscious. For, in the subconscious, says James, "lies the mechanism logically to be assumed—but the assumption involved a vast program of work to be done in the way of verification *in which the religious experiences of man must play their part*" (VRE: 192, emphasis added).

Having reached, in a sense, the heart of the matter, let's take a closer look at what James is telling us here. He subscribes to a hypothesis in need of verification, and 'the religious experiences of man' must play their part in this respect. But what if the nature of religious experience instead amounts to a *falsification* or at least modification of this hypothesis? James does not consider this possibility, although two of the three voices in which he speaks in *The Varieties* would seem to point in this direction. Why is James so convinced of the explanatory power of the subconscious? I believe there is a personal background for this in his own experiences with nitrous oxide. This artificially induced 'mysticism' which James succinctly calls 'the anaesthetic revelation' left him with an enduring conviction both personal and intellectual:

One conclusion was forced upon my mind at that time, and my impression of its truth has ever since remained unshaken. It is that our normal waking consciousness, rational consciousness as we call it, is but one special type of consciousness, whilst all about it, parted from it by the filmiest of screens, there lie potential forms of consciousness entirely different. ... No account of the universe in its totality can be final which leaves these other forms of consciousness quite disregarded. ... Looking back on my own experiences, they all converge towards a kind of insight to which I cannot help ascribing some metaphysical significance. The keynote of it is invariably a reconciliation (VRE: 307ff).

The James who complained that he was personally unfamiliar with the religious life has apparently had his own 'artificial' variety of religious experience, where psychology, metaphysics and religion are somehow suffused. This experience which later acquired theoretical support from his psychological investigation of exceptional mental states, is what James gives a more philosophic interpretation in the final lectures of *The Varieties*.

Thus, when he states his opinion on the positive content of religious experiences as point-ing to *"the fact that the conscious person is continuous with a wider self through which saving experiences come"* (VRE: 405) this is based on his experience of nitrous oxide. Two impor-tant conclusions emerge from this. The 'psychology' lying behind *The Varieties* is not the theories outlined in James's famous *Principles* from 1890. Instead, as Taylor (1982) has con-vincingly argued, it is his "Lowell Lectures" of 1896 on exceptional mental states that form the 'missing conceptual link' between *The Principles* and *The Varieties*. Second, as we shall see shortly, having experienced this 'anaesthetic revelation' puts James in a privileged position for trying to reconcile 'religion' and 'science', because he has to some extent dis-tanced himself from both.

But still, how can James justifiably relate exceptional mental states and religious expe-riences? Basically because he was so infatuated by the notion of the subconscious that he was willing to overlook otherwise salient differences. But why was this notion so impor-tant to him? Here, I think we must take into account the fact that James shared with his time the notion that explaining something means explaining its *origins* and *genesis*, and in this respect nothing compared to the subconscious as the region where 'seraph and snake abide side by side' (VRE: 338). Once we are familiar with the 'context of discovery' of the subconscious and once we know why James so eagerly wished to promote it, we can begin to see the subtle strategy he employs for encouraging his audience to contemplate , even find plausible, the idea that religious individuals are possessed by the subconscious.

I am thinking here of what is sometimes referred to as James's method of the 'extreme' cases, i.e. his belief that a phenomenon like religion is best understood if you study the pronounced cases, the religious genius or virtuoso. But just how extreme are the cases that appear in the almost two hundred excerpts contained in *The Varieties*? Granted that some of them might be labeled 'extreme', could it be that it is only from a modern, secu-larized perspective that they appear 'weird'? If so, another factor contributing to this impression is that James treats his 'cases' without reference to dogma, tradition, and reli-gious community. Viewed from a different angle, the examples of *The Varieties* are not so exceptional at all; indeed, as I have tried to demonstrate, they simply speak the heart-lan-guage of our religious tradition. It is apparent, therefore, James has his own reasons for highlighting the allegedly pathological character of his religious informants. According to him they are "subject to abnormal psychical visitations", "liable to obsessions and fixed ideas", and he attributes to them "symptoms of nervous instability", "exalted emotional sensibility", "discordant inner life", and taken together they manifest "all sorts of pecu-liarities which are ordinarily classed as pathological" (VRE: 15). In other words, his 'pathological programme' (VRE: 26) or his 'blowing cold' consists in viewing his religious subjects as cranky cases for psychical research. This is not a very plausible approach to religious experience, and while it is not the only one represented in *The Varieties*, it is, in my view, the dominating one in terms of a causal explanation of the 'nature' of religious experience.

THE IMPORTANCE OF TRADITION FOR PSYCHOLOGY OF RELIGION

As Wulff (1991) has shown, doing psychology of religion is very much a personal pro-ject deeply embedded in the religious background, academic training, and personal val-ues and preferences of the particular researcher. James is an exemplary illustration of this, but we should add that his position vis-a-vis religion is unusual. With his somewhat dis-tant, Protestant background he can regard the traditional language of devotion with a cer-tain amount of sympathy. At the same time, however, the combination of his interest in psychical research and his own 'anaesthetic revelation' prompts him to search for a way of reconciling the differing perspectives of 'religion' and 'science'. This ambition is reflected in *The Varieties* in different ways. On one level it is reflected in James's obvious sympathy for the 'mind cure' movement; on another level it is displayed in his philosophy of religion; and finally, on a third level, it is reflected in his sketchy idea of an unbiased 'science of religions' with the task of summarizing the 'core' of religion "in formulas upon which everybody may agree" (VRE: 342).

This bizarre idea of creating as it were the esperanto language of religion highlights a serious drawback of James's exclusive focus on 'individual men in their solitude' (VRE: 34); in other words, James fails to recognize the formative power of religious tradition, culture, and community. And of course, as one might have predicted, his idea of this kind of a science of religions has never been influential or even taken seriously. Apparently, James badly wanted religion and science to exist in a harmonious relation, because such a balance formed the basis of his own intended 'objectivity' towards religion. Contrary to this, however, what we are witnessing in James's Gifford Lectures is the collapse of intended objectivity. In this sense one might say that the tragedy of *The Varieties* is that the ideal of a harmonious balance between science and 'religion' is illusory or, indeed, only possible as an individual, New Age type of religion which James may be said to have anticipated. A 'religion' totally disconnected from tradition.

Nonetheless, 'tradition' is a far more important subject for psychology of religion than has generally been recognized. The reason for this is that 'secularization' in the sense of experiencing the loss of a normative religious tradition is the precondition for the emergence of psychology and indeed for the idea of a 'scientific' psychology of religion. As Homans (1989) has demonstrated in his interesting study of the social origins of psychoanalysis, this experience of a loss produces a crisis of disillusionment which in turn is overcome by turning inward ('analytic access') and creating new meaning via a process of individuation. It is difficult to ascertain to what extent James passed through a similar process of creative mourning, but the optimistic religious vision of *The Varieties* is that of a pluralistic universe where the gods are basically friendly to the aspirations of mankind.

It is an interesting general lesson for psychology of religion, I believe, that *The Varieties* can make us sensitive to the close internal connections between the religious vision (or anti-vision) of a researcher and his or her interpretive and explanatory approach to religious experience. In the case of James, we find in both respects a tendency to underestimate the influence of tradition and its inherent 'religious psychology'. Although this influence is very much present in the discourse of *The Varieties* and stands in a tension to the language of psychology, neither James nor his many commentators have seen that this problem of differing discourses is also the systematic core issue.

Let us think a little closer about what kind of problem it is that we have here. If we think of metaphors along the lines of Lakoff & Johnson (1980), it becomes obvious that part of the drama going on in *The Varieties* has to do with the fact that James and his informants are reasoning about religious experience on the basis of different metaphors resulting in different conceptual systems. The examples are univocally referring to the heart as the 'seat' of religious experience, whereas James talks about the subconscious and introduces metaphors like 'threshold', 'field', 'energy', etc. A very good (and truly Jamesian) question to ask would be 'What difference does it make?' Trying to answer this question would involve a lot of things such as 1) understanding the nature of metaphors for the self, 2) understanding the differing status of conceptual metaphors in religion and science, and 3) reflecting upon the relation between folk psychology and scientific psychology. Most importantly, however, reflecting upon these issues would amount to the beginnings of a new conception and self-understanding of psychology of religion which has barely begun to ponder the consequences of cognitive semantics and the 'discursive turn' within psychology.[4]

One way to take this seriously would be to dispel the vagueness inherent in the notion of 'religious experience' by introducing a distinction between religious *experiencing* and religious *experience*. This would result in the following idea of a research strategy for psychology of religion: taking his 'material', namely religious experiences in the sense of discursive accounts (oral or written), as a starting-point, the psychologist of religion should be interested in uncovering the religious *experiencing* behind a given experience (account). How is this possible? It is possible, because, according to cognitive semantics, the 'metaphors we live by' are phenomenologically and psychologically grounded in bodily experience consisting of image-schematic gestalts. Note that whereas we ordinarily have tried to focus on inner consciousness and seen 'language' as a very inadequate rendering of this, here the order of things is reversed: language—discourse—is where we must begin, but the goal is 1) an understanding of the underlying experiencing, and 2) formulating a more general theory on the nature (i.e., elements, constraints, and influencing factors) of this kind of experiencing, and 3) explaining why these particular metaphors and concepts have been used. Presumably, such a theory would tend to regard religious experiencing as arising in a dialectic between metapsychology and discourse, but being irreducible to either one.

CONCLUSION

The drama of *The Varieties* and the reason we find it so fascinating and relevant to our confused identities, is the ongoing struggle between religion and science. James must master all his rhetorical skills and employ complex strategies to conceal this and to convince his audience as well of most of his subsequent commentators that he is an unbiased and sympathetic observer, a trustworthy guide in the terrain of religious experiences. Perhaps we should get used to the idea that he very much has his own agenda and thus may be less dependable than we would like to think. By transferring the depths of the heart to the depths of the subconscious he is presenting us with a fairly idiosyncratic and not very plausible picture of religious experiencing. Why, then, does this idiosyncratic treatment refuse to die? One reason may be that it has been backed up by similar approaches to religion like Jungianism. But the most important reason seems to me to lie in James's instinctive 'feel' for metapsychology and discourse, in his unmatched ability to map the inner world via not only one but many metaphors. In this creative respect, psychology of religion (and theology, for that matter) will continuously have much to learn from *The Varieties*.

---

4. See Wulff (1992) for a rare example of one who has recognized the importance of the notion of metaphor for psychology of religion.

REFERENCES

Bowers, F. (1985). The text of *The Varieties of Religious Experience*. In F.H. Burkhardt, Bowers, F. & I.K. Skrupskelis (Eds.) *The Varieties of Religious Experience* by William James. Cambridge; MA: Harvard University Press (pp. 520-587).

Homans, P. (1989). *The Ability to Mourn: Disillusionment and the Social Origins of Psychoanalysis*. Chicago: The University of Chicago Press.

James, W. (1985). *The Varieties of Religious Experience*. In *The Works of William James*. H. Burkhardt, Bowers, F. & I.K. Skrupskelis (Eds.). Cambridge, MA: Harvard University Press.

Lakoff, G. & M. Johnson (1980). *Metaphors We Live By*. Chicago: The University of Chicago Press.

Leary, D.E. (Ed.) (1990). *Metaphors in the History of Psychology*. Cambridge: Cambridge University Press.

Proudfoot, W. (1985). *Religious Experience*. Berkeley, CA: University of California Press.

Taylor, E. (1982). *William James on Exceptional Mental States*. New York: Scribner's Sons.

Wulff, D.M. (1991). *Psychology of Religion: Classic and Contemporary Views*. New York: John Wiley & sons.

——————— (1992). Reality, illusion, or metaphor? Reflections on the conduct and object of the psychology of religion. *Journal of the Psychology of Religion*, 1: 25-51.

II. THE REGENERATED SELF:
THE STRUGGLE TO BE WHOLE

"THAT SHAPE AM I": THE BEARING OF MELANCHOLY ON JAMES'S STRUGGLE WITH RELIGION

DONALD CAPPS

While it was written by an American, most Americans experience *The Varieties of Religious Experience* (1982; hereafter VRE) as foreign to them. For one thing, it is concerned with a lot of issues that are simply not very current today. The subject matter of the very first chapter, "Religion and Neurology," is often enough to turn off the would-be reader, as the question of whether religion is physiologically based is not one that interests us very much these days. The following passage, in which James cites examples of this association of religion and physiology, seems quaint and oddly foreign to readers today:

Perhaps the commonest expression of this assumption that spiritual value is undone if lowly origin be asserted is seen in those comments which unsentimental people so often pass on their more sentimental acquaintances. Alfred believes in immortality so strongly because his temperament is so emotional. Fanny's extra-ordinary conscientiousness is merely a matter of over-instigated nerves. William's melancholy about the universe is due to bad digestion—probably his liver is torpid. Eliza's delight in her church is a symptom of her hysterical condition. Peter would be less troubled about his soul if he would take more exercise in the open air, etc. (VRE: 10).

Today's reader may believe that William should improve his diet and that Peter should exercise more, but we are not very likely to make a connection between diet and melancholy, exercise and soul worries. If this particular passage attracts our attention at all, this is likely because the author gives his own name—William—to the man who suffers from melancholy. Perhaps James is being playful here: "The alert reader will recognize that I have casually but significantly introduced myself into my text. The others will miss it, but they, after all, are not the ones I would expect to convince or persuade anyway."

The foreignness of James's text continues in the second chapter, but the reason for its foreignness in this case is that it seems so out of sync with what religion in America is all about. Here, in the chapter entitled "Circumscription of the Topic," James states the working definition of religion that he will apply throughout the text, and it is a definition which excludes the "institutional branch" of religion altogether (VRE: 28-31). This might not seem so foreign to our usual ways of thinking about the nature of religion if it meant only that he was uninterested in matters of church polity and administration, but he goes much further than this, as he includes within the excluded "institutional branch" such activities as worship and sacrifice, ceremony and theology (including ideas about God), and so forth. The alert reader is likely to say, "This doesn't leave very much of what I've taken religion to be." James agrees, as he emphasizes that his working definition of religion is "for the purpose of these lectures," and asks his listener/reader to accept its "arbitrariness" (VRE: 28, 31). What remains after the institutional branch is "stripped away"? The feelings, acts, and experiences of individual men [and women] in their solitude, so far as they apprehend themselves to stand in relation to whatever they may consider the divine" (VRE: 31). This is his definition of religion, the definition that he asks his listener/reader to accept as valid for this particular enterprise.

To our modern ears, this definition of religion strikes two jarring notes. One is that religion is defined as individualistic and noncommunal. ("individuals in their solitude").[1] The other is that the author of the definition seems rather unconcerned about what it is that these individuals actually "apprehend," so long as they themselves consider it divine. The definition seems quite limited and limiting on the one hand, and rather loose on the other. In anticipation that his listeners/readers may object to this "circumscription of the topic," James imagines what they may be thinking:

> To some of you personal religion, thus nakedly considered, will no doubt seem too incomplete a thing to wear the general name. "It is a part of religion," you will say, "but only its unorganized rudiment .... The name 'religion' should be reserved for the fully organized system of feeling, thought, and institution, for the Church, in short, of which this personal religion so called, is but a fractional element" (VRE: 29).

In responding to this imagined objection, James promises to say something about "the theologies and ecclesiasticisms" in his last lecture, and then notes that at least in one respect personal religion is more fundamental than either theology or ecclesiasticism, for the *founders* of every church owed their power originally to the fact of their direct personal communion with the divine" (VRE: 30). However, James is not really interested in the institutionalization of these personal religious experiences, and the final lecture does not in fact make good on his promise to deal with the relation between personal religious experience and "the theologies and ecclesiasticisms." Instead, he discusses the subconscious self—"a well-accredited psychological entity"—as the "field" through which apprehensions of the divine occur (VRE: 511-513), and he presents these conclusions not in order to initiate a dialogue between psychology of religion and systematic or doctrinal theology, but as a contribution to the emerging field of "the science of religion" (VRE: 488-490). A concluding postscript, added after the final lecture, is concerned to clarify certain philosophical issues left hanging in the final lecture, and it too fails to make good on this promise to discuss the relationship of personal to "ecclesiastical" religion.

What is the contemporary reader to make of this "circumscription of the topic," this exclusive focus on personal religion, on religion as the experiences of individuals in their solitude? In a country where being religious is usually defined as "church-going," and where the growth and decline of religion is measured by the percentage of Americans who belong to churches, James's "circumscription of the topic" seems more than arbitrary. It is downright perverse. He has put forward a definition of religion that excludes the social, participatory aspect of religion, and one that also excludes its theological and ethical preoccupations.

The question is whether personal religion can be "thus nakedly considered"? Some readers of James's text have astutely pointed out that the very language that individuals use to describe their experiences of "apprehending" God is itself derived from the ecclesiastical and theological traditions which James has "arbitrarily" excluded (see Nørager, this volume). They note that the religious experiences recorded in *The Varieties* itself illus-

---

1. Some would say that this "individualistic" and "noncommunal" definition of religion is not jarring at all, for this is precisely how they understand themselves to be religious ("I am not a churchgoer, and I am certainly not into theology, but I have a personal relationship with God"). However, I am taking note here of the many critiques that have been written in recent years of "privatistic" religion by theologians and sociologists of religion. Perhaps the best known is Robert N. Bellah, et al., *Habits of the Heart* (1985).

trates this very fact. For example, the conversion account by Stephen H. Bradley which comes at the very beginning of James's initial lecture on "Conversion" is replete with Christian theological terms (Saviour, Holy Spirit, etc.) and is understood by Bradley himself to be similar to the experience of the first apostles on the Day of Pentecost. Furthermore, while Bradley's experience occurred in solitude, it was triggered by his having attended church earlier that evening (VRE: 189-193). As Proudfoot and Shaver point out in their application of attribution theory to religious experience:

> Bradley, like so many prospective devotees before and since, could not understand his feelings in naturalistic terms. Religious symbols offered him an explanation that was compatible with both his experience and his former beliefs. He did not consider explanations involving Krishna, Zeus, or the Koran. The content of the scripture and the experience of being moved or physiologically aroused were confidently linked together. These are the two components of emotion described by [attribution theorist] Schachter. It seems likely that religious symbols and doctrines often serve as labels for experiences of arousal which initially appear to be anomalous. As in Schachter's experiments, individuals seek plausible explanations for their feelings among whatever explanations are available in the environment (1975: 323).

Thus, for Bradley, the experience derives its meaning from a specific theological and ecclesiastical context, and cannot be understood apart from it. If James separates the personal and the institutional branches of religion, the Bradleys, Bunyans, Luthers and Saint Teresas who populate his own text decidedly do not. Without the institutional branch, they have no way of attributing meaning or significance to their religious experiences. There is no other way for them to authenticate their experiences.

What is the contemporary reader of James's text to make of this objection to James's whole project? The contemporary reader may do one of two things: On the one hand, we may take the view that what James has tried to keep separate—the personal and the institutional—cannot be treated separately from one another; in taking this view, we may actually claim James's own ostensible support for it, as he himself says that his division of the two aspects of religion is an arbitrary one, for the purpose of these lectures only. On the other hand, we may take the view that James seems to have taken in his own life, that an individual may be able to be "religious" in the purely personal sense of the term, and do so without the assistance of the institutional branch of religion. In his discussion of the attacks of melancholy that James and his father experienced, Erikson refers to the "extreme individualism" of each man's religious "life style" (1968: 153). James himself, in challenging the view so common to the sciences of his day that the experiences of individuals are of no concern, that only the aggregate matters, says that

> Religion makes no such blunder. The individual's religion may be egotistic, and those private realities which it keeps in touch with may be narrow enough; but at any rate it always remains infinitely less hollow and abstract, as far as it goes, than a science which prides itself on taking no account of anything private at all .... By being religious we establish ourselves in possession of ultimate reality at the only points at which reality is given us to guard. Our responsible concern is with our private destiny, after all (VRE: 500-501).

To be "privately religious" assumes that one is not a church-goer (which James was not), and therefore that one's personal religious experiences will have no connection to any ecclesiastical context. It also means that one does not use theological language, or the language of any religious tradition, to describe and interpret the personal experiences that one takes to be "religious." The question, then, is whether religion may, in fact, be an entirely individual matter, unrelated to and disconnected from any and all religious traditions?

The illustrations that James employs in *The Varieties* provide overwhelming evidence against this idea. Virtually every account of personal religious experience included in his own book supports the counter thesis, that there is no purely personal religious experience, that all religious experiences are related in one way or another to religious traditions, drawing on their systems of ideas and beliefs, their social and communal aspects, or both. The only experiences in *The Varieties* that might challenge this overwhelming evidence are James's own experiences, and it is to these that I now wish to turn.

THE POSSIBILITY OF PURELY PERSONAL RELIGION

Two years after the publication of *The Varieties*, James (in 1904) responded to a questionnaire sent out by Professor James B. Pratt of Williams College (Brown 1973: 123-125). In response to the question, "Is God very real to you, as real as an earthly friend, though different?," James replied, "Dimly (real); not (as an earthly friend)." When next asked, "Do you feel that you have experienced His presence? If so, please describe what you mean by such an experience," James wrote simply, "never." Addressing those respondents who answered this question in the negative, Pratt asked whether they "accept the testimony of others who claim to have felt God's presence directly?" James answered affirmatively: "Yes! The whole line of testimony on this point is so strong that I am unable to pooh-pooh it away. No doubt there is a germ in me of something similar that makes response." To Pratt's open-ended question, "What do you mean a 'religious experience'?," James answered, "Any moment of life that brings the reality of spiritual things more 'home' to one."

If we take James's response to Pratt's questionnaire at face value, we must conclude that he does not feel that he has ever experienced the presence of God. He is, however, sympathetic toward the testimony of others who claim to have felt God's presence directly. This sympathy is elaborated in his response to another question in the survey:

I suppose that the chief premise for my hospitality towards the religious testimony of others is my conviction that 'normal' or 'sane' consciousness is so small a part of actual experience .... The other kinds of consciousness bear witness to a much wider universe of experiences, from which our belief selects and emphasizes such parts as best satisfy our needs (Brown 1973: 124).

If he has not "experienced" God, does this mean that he does not believe in God? In response to Pratt's question, "Why do you believe in God," for which Pratt offers a list of possible "whys," James indicates that his belief is not based on any rational or intellectual argument for the existence of God ("emphatically, no"), nor on personal experience, nor on biblical authority or the preachings or writings of "a prophetic person." However, he adds to his negative response to the "personal experience" option that he believes "because I need it so that it 'must' be true," and to his negative response to the "biblical authority" option that he does make "admiring response" to "the whole tradition of religious people."

In this response to Pratt's questionnaire, James comes across as a religious outsider, as one who does not belong to the ranks of those who have experienced the presence of God and who are able to articulate these experiences in the language of the religious tradition with which they identify. To say that one makes "admiring response" to those who claim experiences of God is to present oneself as a spectator, as one who watches the others but for one reason or another cannot or will not participate.

In an essay on James's brother Henry, the novelist, Eakin (1985) tells of how Henry was *not* a participant in the Civil War (William and Henry's two younger brothers were), yet viewed his experience of being psychologically immobilized as a result of fighting a fire in his hometown of Newport as simultaneously an acknowledgment of his having "missed out on life" and an imaginative identification of himself as "a member of the elect company of the experienced" (p. 125). A similar ambiguity occurs in the case of William James, as he cannot claim to be numbered among the truly religious—any more than Henry can claim to have fought in the Civil War—and yet he can identify with the religious in an imaginative sort of way because he has had experiences that are similar to religious ones. Another response to Pratt's questionnaire captures some of this ambiguity. On the one hand, he asserts, there is more to "spiritual reality" than God: "God, to me, is not the only spiritual reality to believe in. Religion means primarily a universe of spiritual relations surrounding the earthly practical ones, not merely relations of 'value,' but agencies and their activities." On the other hand, science takes a far too narrow view of what is or is not true: "What e'er be true, it is not true exclusively, as philistine scientific opinion assumes." It is true, but not exclusively true, that Henry was not an active participant in the Civil War, for he was, in some true sense, a casualty of it. William has not had experience of God, but he has had experience of the "spiritual reality" that surrounds the "earthly" reality. The term "religious outsider" captures the ambiguity of his association with "the elect company of the experienced."

While James had a lifelong interest in (and experimented with) psychic phenomena and altered states of consciousness, his most significant experiences that bordered on the religious were his experiences of "mental disease" (James 1950, II: 416), and, more specifically, his struggles with melancholia, which continued throughout his life, and from which he sought temporary relief through various practical remedies, including baths and hydrotherapy treatments, medication, diet, exercise, and hypnotism (or "mind cure"). In a letter to his young daughter, Margaret, written prior to his delivery of the Gifford lectures from the baths of Bad-Nauheim in Germany, where he was receiving treatment for his chronic melancholy, James describes what it is like to suffer from melancholy:

> Among other things there will be waves of terrible sadness, which sometimes lasts for days; and dissatisfactions with one's self, and irritation at others, and anger at circumstances and stoney insensibility, etc., etc., which taken together form a melancholy (Rubin 1994: 20).

He adds by way of encouragement: "Now, painful as it is, this is sent to us for an enlightenment" (p.20).

Gerald E. Myers (1986) points out that James suffered from a variety of psychosomatic illnesses throughout his life, including angina, backaches, fatigue, and depression, and that he was willing to try any practical remedy that might alleviate the suffering. Yet, while he felt that his melancholia, like his other conflicts, had some physical roots, he felt that melancholia "is more philosophical and less medical than angina. Certain kinds of depression intensify or diminish simply in response to the ideas or beliefs which happen to occupy the mind" (p. 51). He seems, according to Myers, to have reasoned that his "despondency was a state of mind that ... would evaporate if he were somehow able to reject philosophical pessimism" (p. 51). Myers also notes that James made little effort to determine the cause or causes of his melancholy (its psychological origins), and even points out James was not especially good at self-analysis, and that his introspective powers were in one sense quite limited:

> James was skillful in rendering his feelings into words or in recording his habits and mannerisms, but he was oddly uninterested in self-analysis. He could be aware

of his tendency to be silent in his father's presence, to feel relief when away from his wife, to dread being alone, to be assertive toward younger siblings, to dislike exact disciplines such as formal logic, to escape whenever he became a parent, to be endlessly neurotic—yet he was not motivated even to speculate about the psychological causes of these phenomena, much less to seek those causes out introspectively. This feature of James's personality is undoubtedly what some scholars mean when discussing his innocence of himself or his lack of interest in self-analysis (Myers 1986: 49).

As far as his depressions were concerned, the challenge in alleviating them was "less finding the nexus of causes underlying them as they appear. It is less important to diagnose their origins than it is to vanquish them through creating future-oriented incentives. James fought his battles largely through what he called acts of thought" (Myers 1986: 52).

I will return later to James's inability or reluctance to trace the psychological origins of his melancholy. For the moment, I want simply to make the point that his lifelong struggle with melancholia was the primary basis for his belief that he had something in common with those of religious temperament. William Styron's (1990) account of his own devastating descent into melancholia supports James's belief, as he speaks of the "pain that crushes the soul" (p. 62) and the "anxiety and incipient dread that I had hidden away for so long somewhere in the dungeons of my spirit" (p. 40). Words like "soul" and "spirit" have an unmistakable religious bearing.[2]

The Diagnostic and Statistical Manual of Mental Disorders (1987) is rather helpful for determining the severity of James's struggles with melancholia. It actually represents melancholy as a somewhat milder form of the major depressive episode, as melancholy, according to the manual, includes loss of interest or pleasure in activities, lack of reactivity to pleasurable stimuli, early morning awakening, psychomotor agitation or retardation, complete or nearly complete recovery from a previous major depressive episode, and previous good response to anti-depressant therapy (p. 224). What is not included in the "melancholic type" but present in the full scale major depressive episode are, in addition to all the above (usually in more severe or exaggerated form), feelings of worthlessness or inappropriate guilt; diminished ability to think or concentrate, or indecisiveness; and recurrent thoughts of death (which may include suicidal thoughts without a specific plan, an actual attempt, or a specific plan for committing suicide) (p. 222). Given this character-

---

2. Styron also offers a passionate argument against our tendency to refer to this sickness as "depression," preferring the traditional term that James himself uses, "melancholy":

> When I was first aware that I had been laid low by the disease, I felt a need, among other things, to register a strong protest against the word "depression." Depression, most people know, used to be termed "melancholia," a word which appears in English as early as the year 1303 and crops up more than once in Chaucer, who in his usage seemed to be aware of its pathological nuances. "Melancholia" would still appear to be a far more apt and evocative word for the blacker forms of the disorder, but it was usurped by a noun with a bland tonality and lacking any magisterial presence, used indifferently to describe an economic decline or a rut in the ground, a true wimp of a word for such a major illness. It may be that the scientist generally held responsible for its currency in modern times, a Johns Hopkins Medical School faculty member justly venerated—the Swiss-born psychiatrist Adolf Meyer—had a tin ear for the finer rhythms of English and therefore was unaware of the semantic damage he had inflicted by offering "depression" as a descriptive noun for such a dreadful and raging disease. Nonetheless, for over seventy-five years the word has slithered innocuously through the language like a slug, leaving little trace of its intrinsic malevolence and preventing, by its very insipidity, a general awareness of the horrible intensity of the disease when out of control (1990: 36-37).

ization of the melancholic type as a somewhat milder form of major depressive episode, it seems that James suffered from the more severe forms of "major depression." Myers alludes to his "suicidal tendencies" (1986: 47), though it would appear that he never actually planned a suicide attempt, and he also mentions that letters written by students of James were critical of his habit of suddenly dismissing his classes, saying, "I can't think today. We had better not go on with class" (p. 487). James's personal sense of worthlessness and guilt for behavior he seemed unable to alter is especially illustrated in his habit of leaving his wife to care for the family. According to Myers, "He was often absent, if only as far away as Newport, on holidays such as Christmas, New Year's Day, and birthdays. Although he must have appreciated the difficulties his absence caused for his family, he seems to have been powerless to alter the habit" (pp. 36-37).

This personal inadequacy was related to his irritability, another indication of his struggle with the more severe forms of depression. As Myers also notes, James "often apologized to his wife for outbursts of temper before a parting, reiterated his love for her and his appreciation of her care and devotion, and expressed the hope that the trip was improving his nerves so that he would be easier to live with when he returned" (1986: 37). He also complained of being "interrupted every moment by students come to fight about their marks" (p. 35), and "when money was involved and he felt unfairly treated, James could become extremely angry and aggressive" (Myers 1986: 29). The DSM-III lists as the first criterion for a major depressive episode a "depressed mood (or can be irritable mood in children and adolescents)" (1987: 222). On James's own testimony, the irritability that the DSM-III especially ascribes to children (perhaps because, for them, the irritability disguises the deeper depression) is an important aspect of adults' depression as well. While Myers suggests that there was "something impish in his manner [that] suggested an eternal boyishness" (p. 41), he also shared with severely depressed children an irritable mood that made close or demanding personal relationships difficult and tense.

What James himself emphasizes in his accounts of his melancholic or depressive episodes is his sense of profound sadness and awareness of the reality of death. In an account of a particularly distressing period in his life, a trip to the Amazon in 1865 (he was 23 years old at that time), he wrote, "To me the peculiar feature which at all times of the day and everywhere made itself felt was the sadness and solemnity produced by the flood of sun and the inextricable variety of vegetable forms, elements which one would suspect beforehand to have a gay and cheerful effect on the observer" (Myers, 1986: 48). This description of his mood during his Amazon trip puts us in mind of his contention that "There must be something solemn, serious, and tender about any attitude which we denominate religious. If glad, it must not snicker; if sad, it must not scream or curse. It is precisely as being *solemn* experiences that I wish to interest you in religious experiences" (VRE: 38).

In his essay, "Is Life Worth Living? (1986) he notes that the question in his title would never arise if our optimistic moods could be made permanent and if the optimistic constitution that some persons exhibit all the time could be made universal:

But we are not magicians to make the optimistic temperament universal; and alongside of the deliverances of temperamental optimism concerning life, those of temperamental pessimism always exist, and oppose to them a standing refutation. In what is called "circular insanity," phases of melancholy succeed phases of mania, with no outward cause that we can discover; and often enough to one and the same well person life will present incarnate radiance to-day and incarnate dreariness to-morrow .... (p. 34).

He then proceeds to quote a poem by James Thomson from the book *The City of Dreadful Night*, which portrays a preacher speaking to a congregation gathered in a great unillumined cathedral at night. The lines from which James quotes begin, "O Brothers of sad lives! they are so brief," and contain this strange word of comfort:

> But if you would not this poor life fulfil,
> Lo, you are free to end it when you will,
> Without the fear of waking after death.

In commenting on these lines, James says that these words "flow truthfully from the melancholy Thomson's pen, and are in truth a consolation for all to whom, as to him, the world is far more like a steady den of fear than a continual fountain of delight. That life is not worth living the whole army of suicides declare" and "We, too, as we sit here in our comfort, must 'ponder these things' also, for we are of one substance with these suicides, and their life is the life we share" (p. 37).

Suicide is a desperately lonely act, but is the outcome of the depressive or melancholic condition if other factors do not intervene (cf. Styron 1990: 65-67). Thus, if James viewed his melancholia as the basis on which he could claim his own "imaginative identification" with the religious, we can understand why the religious experiences would have to be ones that occur in solitude, when an individual is alone and without any social supports whatever, and why such experiences would need to be solemn. His point is not that all melancholic episodes are religious, or that all religious experiences are melancholia-based, but rather that there is sufficient similarity between the two that the one sheds light on the other. To explore this point further, I now want to direct our attention to James's early writings on melancholy, using these as background for his discussion of "religious melancholy" in *The Varieties*.

MELANCHOLY AS MENTAL PATHOLOGY

James discusses melancholy in the second volume of his *The Principles of Psychology* (1950) in a chapter entitled "The Perception of Reality" (pp. 283-384). This chapter is an expansion of an article published in the philosophical journal *Mind* in 1869 when James was just 27 years old. It begins with a consideration of the nature of belief and, specifically, with his assertion that belief is the "sense of the reality" of that which is believed. It is thus "the mental state or function of cognizing reality" (p. 283). This means that doubt and inquiry, not disbelief, are the true opposites of belief, because in doubt and inquiry, the "content of our mind is in unrest"—we do not yet know whether the object is real or not—whereas in disbelief we have settled the issue by declaring to ourselves that the object does not exist in the real world. He then suggests that belief, on the one hand, and doubt and inquiry, on the other, are emotions that may be "pathologically exalted." Belief, for example, is typically "exalted" in states of drunkenness, especially in nitrous oxide intoxication, and doubt is pathologically exalted in what has been called "the questioning mania" (individuals who seem condemned to think about such questions as "Why is a glass a glass, a chair a chair?" "Why are humans the size of humans, and not as big as houses?," etc., etc.).

But then James adds that there is "another pathological state which is as far removed from doubt as from belief, and which some may prefer to consider the proper contrary of the latter state of mind. I refer to the feeling that everything is hollow, unreal, dead" (p. 285). This is melancholy, and James returns to it later in the chapter, after having first discussed what makes something real *for us*:

The mere fact of appearing as an object at all is not enough to constitute reality. That may be metaphysical reality, reality for God; but what we need is practical reality, reality for ourselves; and, to have that, an object must not only appear, but it must appear both *interesting* and *important* .... Whenever an object so appeals to us that we turn to it, accept it, fill our mind with it, or practically take account of it, so far it is real for us, and we believe it. Whenever, on the contrary, we ignore it, fail to consider it or act upon it, despise it, reject it, forget it, so far it is unreal for us and disbelieved (James, 1950, II: 295).

In short, "Whatever things have intimate and continuous connection with my life are things of whose reality I cannot doubt" (p. 298).

What happens in melancholy, or, at least, certain forms of it, is that "nothing touches us intimately, rouses us, or wakens natural feeling. The consequence is the complaint so often heard from melancholic patients, that nothing is believed in by them as it used to be, and that all sense of reality is fled from life. They are sheathed in india-rubber; nothing penetrates to the quick or draws blood, as it were" (p. 298).

James continues with his analysis of melancholy by quoting Wilhelm Griesinger, author of a major text entitled *Mental Pathology and Therapeutics*, who noted that such patients will say, "I see, I hear, but the objects do not reach me, it is as if there were a wall between me and the outer world!" James goes on to quote Griesinger at length:

In childhood we feel ourselves to be closer to the world of sensible phenomena, we live immediately with them and in them; an intimately vital tie binds us and them together. But with the ripening of reflection this tie is loosened, the warmth of our interest cools, things look differently to us, and we act more as foreigners to the outer world, even though we know it a great deal better. Joy and expansive emotions in general draw in nearer to us again. Everything makes a more lively impression, and with the quick immediate return of this warm receptivity for sense-impressions, joy makes us feel young again. In depressing emotions it is the other way. Outer things, whether living or inorganic, suddenly grow cold and foreign to us, and even our favorite objects of interest feel as if they belonged to us no more. Under these circumstances, receiving no longer from anything a lively impression, we cease to turn towards outer things, and the sense of inward loneliness grows upon us .... Where there is no strong intelligence to control this *blasé* condition, this psychic coldness and lack of interest, the issue of these states in which all seems so cold and hollow, the heart dried up, the world grown dead and empty, is often suicide or the deeper forms of insanity (In James 1950, II: 298).

James does not discuss the matter of melancholy any further in this chapter, but toward the end of the chapter he takes up the role played by imagination in making unreal things seem real: "Who does not 'realize' more the fact of a dead or distant friend's existence, at the moment when a portrait, letter, garment or other material reminder of him is found? The whole notion of him then grows pungent and speaks to us and shakes us, in a manner unknown at other times" (1950, II: 303). This illustration implies that melancholy has to do with absence and loss, and the desire to regain the lost object in some form or other, a point to which we will return later when discussing James's own melancholic episodes.[3]

---

3. William Styron confirms the state of indifference that James here describes, and also provides a dramatic illustration of the melancholic's desperate need to be "knifed," as it were, so as to be brought out of this state of indifference. He was watching the tape of a movie set in late nineteenth-

In *Melancholia and Depression* (1986), Stanley W. Jackson has a chapter on views of melancholia in the 19th Century, in which he discusses Griesinger's book, "a work that had a tremendous influence on his contemporaries and on their nineteenth-century successors" (p. 160). According to Jackson, Griesinger's basic thesis was that there are successive states of mental depression in melancholia. The initial melancholic stage, which he termed "stadium melancholicum," and described as "a state of profound emotional perversion, of a depressing and sorrowful character," is "the direct continuation of some painful emotion dependent upon some objective cause [e.g., grief, jealousy] and it is distinguished from the mental pain experienced by healthy persons by its excessive degree, by its more than ordinary protraction, by its becoming more and more independent of external influences" (p. 161). The next stage is hypochondriasis, where the bodily sensations are real but somatically unfounded, and the intellect functions soundly but starts from false premises. The third stage is melancholia proper, in which "the mental pain consists in a profound feeling of *ill-being*, of inability to do anything, of suppression of the physical powers, of depression and sadness, and of total abasement of self-consciousness" (p. 162). Also typical of this third stage, as summarized by Jackson, is "a tendency toward increased unhappiness and dejection, irritability, either discontent or withdrawal from others, preoccupation with self, sometimes hatred of others, and sometimes contrariness. And a tendency toward indecisiveness and inactivity [reflecting] a worsening of the disorder of the will" (p. 162). More serious manifestations of third-stage melancholy are the appearance of false ideas and judgments "corresponding to the actual disposition of the patient" (p. 162).

Griesinger states that the course of melancholia is usually chronic, with remissions. Intermissions of the disease for extended periods of time are rare. If the melancholia worsens, it may be transformed from melancholia into mania, which may in turn result in violent actions, or extreme excitations of the will. As far as predisposing factors are concerned, Griesinger cites influences in one's upbringing as well as hereditary factors. Precipitating causes might include some subtle, as yet unidentified cerebral pathology; subtle physiological changes, perhaps from simple nervous irritation or slight nutritional changes; and circulatory problems. But more important, in his judgment, are psychological factors, especially painful emotional states:

> In individual cases these painful emotional states may vary very much in their nature and in their causes: sometimes it is sudden anger—shock or grief excited by injury, loss of fortune, a rude interference with the modesty, a sudden death, etc; sometimes it is the result of the slow gnawings of disappointed ambition on the mind, regret on account of certain unjust actions, domestic affliction, unfortunate love, jealousy, error, forced sojourn in inadequate circumstances, or any other injured sentiment. In every case there are influences which, through intense disturbance of the mass of ideas of the *ego*, cause a mournful division in consciousness, and we always see the most powerful effects where the wishes and hopes have

---

century Boston. The characters were moving down the hallway of a music conservatory, beyond the walls of which, from unseen musicians, came a contralto voice, "a sudden soaring passage from the Brahms Alto Rhapsody." Styron, who was on the verge of committing suicide, was literally "struck" by the sound: "This sound, which like all music—indeed, like all pleasure—I had been numbly unresponsive to for months, *pierced my heart like a dagger* ...." (1990: 66, my emphasis). Later, Styron informs the reader that his mother, who had died when he was thirteen, had sung the Alto Rhapsody in his own hearing (p. 81). The sound "drew blood," and Styron realized that he could not "commit this desecration on myself" and on "those, so close to me, with whom [his] memories were bound" (p. 67).

been for a long time concentrated upon a certain object. Where the individual has made certain things indispensable to his life, and when these are forcibly withdrawn, the passage of the ideas into efforts is cut off, and accordingly a gap in the *ego* and a violent internal strife results (In Jackson 1986: 164-165).

Griesinger also considers "mixed" causes (physical and psychological combined), and especially notes drunkenness, masturbation, and sexual deprivation (p. 165).

As far as therapeutic interventions are concerned, Griesinger argues that hospitalization is called for only where the condition is at least of moderate severity and has continued unchanged for some months, and instead recommends careful regulation of diet, rest and activity, fresh air, and exercise. He advises distracting the patient from his preoccupations by means of "mild, cheering external influences," and urges that "the topics of melancholics' preoccupations and delusions be avoided." Also, a moderately severe manner is often more helpful than consolation (In Jackson 1986: 166).

We do not know the degree to which James agreed with Griesinger's views either on the nature of the disease or on the treatment for it, but Jackson's summary of Griesinger's views provide us a general idea of what James would have understood his affliction to be, what causes he might have considered responsible for it, and what he judged the long-term prognosis to be. We may assume that James would not have envisioned being eventually cured of his affliction, that he understood that he would need to learn to live with it. The very fact that Griesinger recommends various ameliorative strategies (excluding only bloodletting) underscores the sheer tenacity of melancholia. In reading Griesinger, James could not have missed this point. Jane Kenyon (1993) prefaces her set of poems entitled "Having It Out With Melancholy" with the following quotation from Anton Chekhov's *The Cherry Orchard*: "If many remedies are prescribed for an illness, you may be certain that the illness has no cure" (p. 21). It is hard to imagine James *not* coming to the same conclusion. If he tried many different remedies, this would not have been because he was seeking some magical cure, but was intent on keeping his affliction within the pain threshold that he felt he could endure (1982: 134-135).

Let us now return to *The Varieties* and to James's discussion of melancholy and its relationship to religion.

THE RELIGIOUS ATTITUDE AND THE MELANCHOLY TEMPERAMENT

The chapter of *The Varieties* that relates most directly to melancholy is Chapter 5, "The Sick Soul," which comprises Lectures VI and VII of the Gifford Lectures (VRE: 127-165). This chapter is typically discussed in relation to the chapter that immediately precedes it, "The Religion of Healthy-Mindedness." James, of course, invites this discussion, as he himself sets up "healthy-mindedness" and "sick-soulness" as two general ways in which individuals are religious. Yet, there is much to be gained by relating "The Sick Soul" chapter to Chapter 3, "The Reality of the Unseen," which immediately precedes "The Religion of Healthy-Mindedness" chapter. This chapter enables James to point out a rather different typology, that between "the life of religion" and "the melancholic temperament."

He begins this chapter on "the reality of the unseen" with the statement: "Were one asked to characterize the life of religion in the broadest and most general terms possible, one might say that it consists of the belief that there is an unseen order, and that our supreme good lies in harmoniously adjusting ourselves thereto. This belief and this adjustment are the religious attitude in the soul" (p. 53). He adds that his task in this lecture is "to call attention to some of the psychological peculiarities of such an attitude as this, of belief in an object which we cannot see" (p. 53). In other words, the religious attitude and the melancholic temperament are polar opposites: The religious attitude involves belief in an unseen order whereas melancholy is an inability to take interest in, or give one's attention to, the world that is seen. For the melancholic, the seen world is *unreal*, as it does not appear interesting or important; it is not "believed" in. For the religious individual, the *unseen* world is real, as it is judged to be both interesting and important; it is "believed" in.

We can see from this how the religious attitude and the melancholic temperament, rather than remaining mere polar opposites, might become conjoined, and why melancholic personalities might find themselves peculiarly attracted to the life of religion. For, if the seen world loses interest and importance for them, perhaps the unseen world can assume the place previously held by the seen world. Moreover, the melancholic would find justification for this lack of interest in the seen world from many religious writings, as these writings testify to the belief that only the unseen world ultimately matters. This means that the religious attitude and the melancholy temperament have a complex, not simple, relation to one another, as they are, in one sense, polar opposites, but, in another sense, the mirror image of one another. Thus, James's use of melancholia as a means of exploring religious psychologically is not as arbitrary or self-indulgent as it may first appear.

In his chapter on the reality of the unseen world, James suggests that the "objects" in the unseen realm may be present to our senses or may be present in our thoughts only. But, in either case, these objects

> elicit from us a *reaction*; and the reaction due to things of thought is notoriously in many cases as strong as that due to sensible presences. It may even be stronger. The memory of an insult may make us angrier than the insult did when we received it. We are frequently more ashamed of our blunders afterwards than we were at the moment of making them (VRE: 53).

This is also the case in religion. Very few Christian believers have had a "sensible vision" of their Saviour: "The whole force of the Christian religion, therefore, so far as belief in the divine personages determines the prevalent attitude of the believer, is in general exerted by the instrumentality of pure ideas, of which nothing in the individual's past experiences directly serves as a model" (p. 54). Yet, in addition to the "sensible vision" and the "pure idea," there is another experience that falls somewhere in-between. This is "a sense of reality, a feeling of objective presence, a perception of what we may call 'something there,' more deep and more general than any of the special and particular 'senses' by which the current psychology supposes existent realities to be originally revealed" (p. 58). James suggests that these "vague and remote" senses of "something there" may be "excited" by our senses, but they may also be excited by an idea. Hallucinatory experiences provide proof "of such an undifferentiated sense of reality," as it often happens that an hallucination is imperfectly developed: "The person affected will feel a 'presence' in the room, definitely localized, facing in one particular way, real in the most emphatic sense of the word, often coming suddenly, and as suddenly gone; and yet neither seen, heard, touched, nor cognized in any of the usual 'sensible' ways" (p. 59).

THE CASE OF THE INTIMATE FRIEND

James then offers an illustration of this hallucinatory experience, judging that it will help to clarify what he has in mind before passing "to the objects with whose presence religion is more peculiarly concerned" (p. 59). Which is to say that the experience he is about to consider has relevance for religion but is not itself a religious experience. The experience, he tells us, is that of "an intimate friend of mine, one of the keenest intellects I know" and written "in the response to my inquiries" (VRE: 59). Due to its length, I will excerpt parts of it.

The friend begins his account by noting that several times in the past few years he has felt the so-called "consciousness of a presence." The particular experience that he is about to reveal occurred about September, 1884. The previous night he had had "a vivid tactile hallucination of being grasped by the arm, which made me get up and search the room for an intruder" (p. 59). But the "sense of presence" properly so called came on the following night:

> After I had got into bed and blown out the candle, I lay awake while thinking on the previous night's experience, when suddenly I felt something come into the room and stay close to my bed. It remained only a minute or two. I did not recognize it by any ordinary sense, and yet there was a horribly unpleasant "sensation" connected with it. It stirred something more at the roots of my being than any ordinary perception. The feeling had something of the quality of a very large tearing vital pain spreading chiefly over the chest, but within the organism—and yet the feeling was not *pain* so much as *abhorrence*. At all events, something was present with me, and I know its presence far more surely than I have ever known the presence of any fleshly living creature. I was conscious of its departure as of its coming: an almost instantaneously swift going through the door, and the "horrible sensation" disappeared (VRE: 59-60).

The following night, when his mind was absorbed in some lectures he was preparing, he felt once again the presence of "the thing that was there the night before," and was again aware of the previous night's "horrible sensation." He then "mentally concentrated all my effort ... to charge this 'thing,' if it was evil, to depart, if it was *not* evil, to tell me who or what it was, and if it could not explain itself, to go, and that I would compel it to go." He reports that it left immediately, just as "on the previous night, and my body quickly recovered its normal state" (p. 60).

Noting that he had had precisely the same "horrible sensation" on two previous occasions (once lasting a full quarter of an hour), he observes that

> In all three instances the certainty that there in outward space there stood *something* was indescribably *stronger* than the ordinary certainty of companionship when we are in the close presence of ordinary living people. The something seemed close to me, and intensely more real than any ordinary perception. Although I felt it to be like unto myself, so to speak, or finite, small, and distressful, as it were, I didn't recognize it as any individual being or person (VRE: 60).

James quickly adds the disclaimer: "Of course such an experience as this does not connect itself with the religious sphere" (p. 60). As far as James is concerned, this was an hallucinatory experience, not a religious one. Yet, he adds, this kind of experience may "upon occasion" so connect itself with the religious sphere. In fact, "the same correspondent informs me that at more than one other conjuncture he had the sense of presence developed with equal intensity and abruptness, only then it was filled with a quality of joy." On these occasions, he felt (and here James is quoting him) "the sure knowledge of the close presence of a sort of mighty person, and after it went, the memory persisted as the one perception of reality. Everything else might be a dream, but not that" (pp. 60-61). But, James notes, "My friend, as it oddly happens, does not interpret these latter experiences theistically, as signifying the presence of God. But it would clearly not have been unnatural to interpret them as a revelation of the deity's existence" (p. 61) After all, in this instance, the friend had felt "the close presence of a sort of mighty person." If it was not someone he knew, what would prohibit or inhibit him for determining that this "mighty person" was God? James concludes that he will have more to say about these experiences of what his friend called "a startling awareness of some ineffable good" when he address-es the subject of mysticism (Chapter 11 of *The Varieties*). The balance of the chapter on the reality of the unseen is taken up, for the most part, with accounts of similar experiences in which the individuals did interpret them theistically.

I have centered on this particular account and at some length, however, because I have a strong suspicion that the experiencer in this case is James himself. We know for a cer-tainty that he has included an account of his own experience of "the worst kind of melan-choly" in his chapter on "The Sick Soul," and that he sought to disguise the fact that he was the author of this account by pretending that it was written by a Frenchman with whom he had been in correspondence (VRE: 159-161). So we know that he was not above using his own experiences to illustrate and support the points he wanted to make, nor was he reluctant to devise a false identity for the supposed "author" of the account. As there is a rather "impish" quality to his observation that the Frenchman "was evidently in a bad nervous condition at the time of which he writes" (p. 160), so there is also an impish quality to his observation that his "intimate friend" is "one of the keenest intellects I know" (p. 59). There are various stylistic features to the account that are reflective of James's own style, such as the tendency to underline single words and phrases, to place technical words within quotation marks, and to make frequent use of semi-colons and dashes, etc. We also know that James was a strong proponent of the introspective method of psychology, and this means that he was in the habit of writing detailed accounts of what was going on in his mind. As he stated in his chapter on "The Methods and Sources of Psychology" in *The Principles of Psychology*, "Introspective observation is what we have to rely on first and foremost and always. The word introspection need hardly be defined—it means, of course, the looking into our own minds and reporting what we there discover" (1950, I: 185). He goes on to assert that introspection should include both feelings and thoughts, not thoughts exclusively, for the word "thought" tends to exclude physical sen-sations, and he believes these should not be omitted from the introspective process. The case of the "intimate friend" is replete with allusions to feelings and physical sensations.

An even more significant textual clue, however, is provided by the "French Sufferer" case in the chapter on "The Sick Soul." In that case, James placed a significant clue to his identity in a footnote to the account which cited "another case of fear equally sudden" in a book written by his father (VRE: 161). In the case of the "intimate friend of mine," there is a rather similar clue. The friend reports that, in the course of the second night's experience, he had a very unpleasant sensation, the feeling of which "had something of the quality of *a very large tearing vital pain spreading chiefly over the chest, but within the organism*" [emphasis added]. In the "French Sufferer" case, the author (whom we know to be James) states that he awoke each morning "with a horrible dread at the pit of my stomach" and then, in another footnote, cites John Bunyan's account of a similar experience of his in which Bunyan felt "such clogging and heat at my stomach." But then the Bunyan quotation con-tinues, adding, "by reason of this my terror, [I felt] that I was, especially at some times, as if *my breast-bone would have split asunder*" [emphasis added]. While the sensation of a "tearing" in the chest region does *not* occur in the "French Sufferer" account, it clearly does so in the "intimate friend" account, and is a very important aspect of the "horribly unpleasant 'sen-sation' connected with" the felt presence of something in the room. A letter to his wife is also relevant. In it, he spoke of "a characteristic attitude in me" that always involves an element of active tension, of holding my own, as it were, and trusting outward things to perform their part so as to make it a full harmony, but without any *guaranty* that they will. Make it a guaranty—and the attitude immediately becomes to my consciousness stagnant and stingless. Take away the guaranty, and I feel ... a sort of enthusiastic bliss, of bitter willingness to do and suffer anything, which translates itself physically by a kind of *stinging pain inside by breastbone* (don't smile at this—it is to me an essential element of the whole thing!)" (In Myers 1986: 49, emphasis added).

While these textual clues offer much support for the view that the "intimate friend" account is James's own, the most telling evidence is provided by a comparison of the content of this and the "French Sufferer" account. However, before we turn to that, I want to draw some conclusions from the "intimate friend" account for James's understanding of himself as a religious outsider. Note that he prefaces this account with the disclaimer that it is not a religious experience as such, and then follows the account with a similar disclaimer. His reason for including it in the chapter on "the reality of the unseen" world was not because it was a religious experience, but because it was an hallucinatory experience, and hallucinatory experiences, in his view, give credence to the claims that are made for religious experiences. Key here is the "intimate friend's" observation that in all three instances "the certainty that there in outward space there stood *something* was indescribably *stronger* than the ordinary certainty of companionship when we are in the close presence of ordinary living people (VRE: 60). Which is to say that we should not pooh-pooh the claims of religious persons when they testify to having experienced the presence of God or of some other divine or quasi-divine person, and to having experienced this presence as *stronger* than the presence of persons who belong to the "seen" world. Hallucinatory experiences should make us more receptive to the testimony of individuals who offer personal accounts of *feeling* the presence of God and of having absolutely no doubt that God was there, *in the room*, as it were. This hallucinatory experience, if it was in fact James's own, would therefore support his "hospitality towards the religious testimony of others" while at the same time making no claim to having had a religious experience himself.

But then what are we to make of the "intimate friend's" other experiences, those in which he had "the sure knowledge of the close presence of a sort of mighty person"? Could this have been a religious experience? James says no, because for some unaccountable reason his friend did "not interpret these latter experiences theistically, as signifying the presence of God," though he adds that "it would clearly not have been unnatural to interpret them as a revelation of the deity's existence" (VRE: 61). Evidently, the "intimate friend" did not offer an alternative interpretation (e.g., that the "mighty person" was a human being he had known, perhaps his father), so the theistic interpretation was not thereby foreclosed. He simply did not make the interpretive leap that religious individuals are prepared to make by saying that this "mighty person" was God or some divine or quasi-divine figure. In his response to Pratt's question about God in the questionnaire discussed earlier, James hedged between two of Pratt's options: "Is He a person?" or "Is God an attitude of the Universe toward you?" In response to the former option, James answered, "He must be cognizant and responsive in some way," and in response to the second option, he answered, "Yes, but more conscious." These responses, taken together, suggest that for James God was more than an "attitude" but something less than a "person" as normally construed (i.e., as having a discernible character, personality, or selfhood). Perhaps Pratt's third option—"Or is he only a Force?"—comes closest to the mark, as James answers, "He *must* do." For James, then, the idea of God as a "mighty person" is too static. It fails to capture what he might call the "restless quality" of God.

In "Is Life Worth Living?" (1956), James asks how our faith in the unseen world might be verified, and suggests that it may in fact be *self*-verifying:

I confess that I do not see why the very existence of an invisible world may not in part depend on the personal response which any of us may make to the religious appeal. God himself, in short, may draw vital strength and increase of very being from our fidelity. For my own part, I do not know what the sweat and blood and tragedy of this life mean, if they mean anything short of this. If this life be not a real fight, in which something is eternally gained for the universe by success, it is no better than a game of private theatricals from which one may withdraw at will (p. 61).

Given this understanding of God, we should perhaps not be surprised that the "intimate friend" would be unable to ascribe a "theistic" meaning to the experience of "the close presence of a sort of mighty person," even if this person could not be recognized as any other individual being or person. Nor, if I am correct that James is the "intimate friend," should we be surprised that he has such secure knowledge that no theistic interpretation was ever made by this close "friend" of his.

EXAMPLES OF RELIGIOUS MELANCHOLY

As noted above, the chapter on "The Reality of the Unseen" sets the stage for the chapter on "The Sick Soul." However, the chapter on "The Religion of Healthy-Mindedness" intervenes, and the first several pages of the sick soul chapter continue the discussion of the healthy-minded temperament of the previous chapter. These pages center on the issue of evil, and distinguishes the healthy-minded and the sick soul according to their views of evil. The healthy-minded do not ignore evil or pretend that it does not exist, but they define evil in such manner as to propose that it is curable. For them, evil means a "maladjustment" between the self and the external world, so that "by modifying either the self or the things, or both at once, the two terms may be made to fit" (VRE: 134). But sick souls experience evil differently. They are those "for whom evil is no mere relation of the subject to particular outer things, but something more radical and general, a wrongness or vice in [one's] essential nature, which no alteration of the environment, or any rearrangement of the inner self, can cure, and which requires a supernatural remedy" (p. 134). Such persons have a more pessimistic nature, as they believe that the problem is internal and is very resistant to any lasting cure.

After considering two major pessimistic philosophies (Stoic insensibility and Epicurean resignation), James moves into the psychological themes of the chapter, noting that melancholy lies at the extremity of pessimism: "There is a pitch of unhappiness so great that the goods of nature may be entirely forgotten, and all sentiment of their existence vanish from the mental field .... As the healthy-minded enthusiast succeeds in ignoring evil's very existence, so the subject of melancholy is forced in spite of himself to ignore that of all good whatever: *for him it may no longer have the least reality*" (VRE: 144-145, emphasis added).

Personal accounts of melancholy become James's primary resource for exploring the phenomenon of the sick soul, as they disclose various stages in the evolution of the perception of the universe as evil, devoid of any ultimate good. The first stage of "pathological depression" is "mere joylessness and dreariness, discouragement, dejection, lack of taste and zest and spring" (p. 145) It is usually temporary, owing to circumstances that *can* be altered, though "some persons are affected with [it] permanently," and if it is prolonged, it may result in suicide (p. 147). A worse form of melancholy is a "positive and active anguish, a sort of psychical neuralgia wholly unknown to healthy life" (p. 147). It may take various forms, "having sometimes more the quality of loathing; sometimes that of irritation and exasperation; or again of self-mistrust and self-despair; or of suspicion, anxiety, trepidation, fear" (p. 147). It may involve self-accusations or accusations of others. As in the previous type, it is usually not considered by the sufferer to have any relation to "the religious sphere of experience" (p. 148). James provides an account of this form of melancholy, one in which the sufferer is in fact French, and who rails against the injustice of his having been afflicted with this "horrible misery of mine." James contends that the patient's "querulous temper" (i.e., his excessive complaining and self-lamentation) "keeps his mind from taking a religious direction" (p. 149), a comment that reminds us of his observation on the Amazon trip that a religious attitude "if glad, it must not snicker; if sad, it must not scream or curse." The Frenchman cannot submit to any outside influence, but instead continues to lament his situation and hold at distant remove any thought that there may be some relief for his condition.

James next takes up several examples of "religious melancholy," cases in which the perception of evil is every bit as strong as in the case of the French mental patient, but where there is "a religious solution" (p. 152). His first case is Leo Tolstoy, a man whose "sense that life had any meaning whatever was for a time wholly withdrawn" (p. 151). In contrast to those who have experienced a religious conversion, where there is often "a transfiguration of the face of nature," in melancholiacs

> there is usually a similar change, only it is in the reverse direction. The world now looks remote, strange, sinister, uncanny. Its color is gone, its breath is cold, there is no speculation in the eyes it glares with. "It is as if I lived in another century," says one asylum patient.—"I see everything through a cloud," says another, "things are not as they were, and I am changed."—"I see," says a third, "I touch, but the things do not come near me, a thick veil alters the hue and look of everything."—"Persons move like shadows, and sounds seem to come from a distant world."—"There is no longer any past for me; people appear so strange; it is as if I could not see any reality, as if I were in a theatre; as if people were actors, and everything were scenery; I can no longer find myself; I walk, but why? Everything floats before my eyes, but leaves no impression."—"I weep false tears, I have unreal hands: the things I see are not real things."—Such are expressions that naturally rise to the lips of melancholy subjects describing their changed state (VRE: 151-152).

Life was this way for Tolstoy: "It was now flat sober, more than sober, dead. Things were meaningless whose meaning had always been self-evident" (pp. 152-153). He considered suicide. Yet, all the while that he was overwhelmed by the sheer meaninglessness of his existence, feeling as though he was being devoured from without and within, and asking himself how he might but an end to his misery, his heart, he writes,

> kept languishing with another pining emotion. I can call this by no other name than that of a thirst for God. This craving for God had nothing to do with the movement of my ideas,—in fact, it was the direct contrary of that movement,—but it came from my heart. It was like a feeling of dread that made me seem like an orphan and isolated in the midst of all these things that were so foreign. And this feeling of dread was mitigated by the hope of finding the assistance of some one (VRE: 156).

As James notes, when Tolstoy came out of his state of "absolute disenchantment with ordinary life," there was not a total restitution, for Tolstoy had experienced an evil that he would never, ever forget. But he did find a new special form of happiness:

> The happiness that comes, when any does come,—and often enough it fails to return in an acute form, though its form is sometimes very acute,—is not the simple ignorance of ill, but something vastly more complex, including natural evil as one of its elements, but finding natural evil no such stumbling-block and terror because it now sees it swallowed up in supernatural good. The process is one of redemption, not of mere reversion to natural health, and the sufferer, when saved, is saved by what seems to him a second birth, a deeper kind of conscious being than he could enjoy before (VRE: 156-157).

James's second example is John Bunyan, who differs from Tolstoy in one important respect. Where Tolstoy's preoccupations were largely objective, related to the purpose and meaning of life in general, Bunyan's troubles "were over the condition of his own personal self" (p. 157). James views Bunyan as a typical case of

> the psychopathic temperament, sensitive of conscience to a diseased degree, beset by doubts, fears, and insistent ideas, and a victim of verbal automatisms, both motor and sensory. These were usually texts of Scripture which, sometimes damnatory and sometimes favorable, would come in a half-hallucinatory form as if they were voices, and fasten on his mind and buffet it between them like a shuttlecock. Added to this were a fearful melancholy self-contempt and despair (VRE: 157).

Because he intends to discuss Bunyan's religious recovery in the next chapter ("The Divided Self, and the Process of its Unification"), James does not present it here. Instead, he cites briefly the case of another sufferer, Henry Alline, an evangelist who worked in Nova Scotia a hundred years earlier. These accounts set the stage of his final illustration of melancholy, the case of the anonymous "French sufferer" who, as noted earlier, is himself (see, on this point, Lewis 1991: 202-204; also Erikson 1968: 152).

THE CASE OF THE FRENCH SUFFERER

James prefaces the account of the "French Sufferer" with the assertion, "The worst kind of melancholy is that which takes the form of panic fear" (VRE: 159-160). Here is the full account of the episode:

> Whilst in this state of philosophical pessimism and general depression of spirits about my prospects, I went one evening into a dressing-room in the twilight to procure some article that was there; when suddenly there fell upon me without any warning, just as if it came out of the darkness, a horrible fear of my own existence. Simultaneously there arose in my mind the image of an epileptic patient whom I had seen in the asylum, a black-haired youth with greenish skin, entirely idiotic, who used to sit all day on one of the benches, or rather shelves against the wall, with his knees drawn up against his chin, and the coarse gray undershirt, which was his only garment, drawn over them inclosing his entire figure. He sat there like a sort of sculptured Egyptian cat or Peruvian mummy, moving nothing but his black eyes and looking absolutely non-human. This image and my fear entered into a species of combination with each other. *That shape am I,* I felt, potentially. Nothing that I possess can defend me against that fate, if the hour for it should strike for me as it struck for him. There was such a horror of him, and such a perception of my

own merely momentary discrepancy from him, that it was as if something hitherto solid within my breast gave way entirely, and I became a mass of quivering fear. After this the universe was changed for me altogether. I awoke morning after morning with a horrible dread at the pit of my stomach, and with a sense of the insecurity of life that I never knew before, and that I have never felt since. It was like a revelation; and although the immediate feelings passed away, the experience has made me sympathetic with the morbid feelings of others ever since. It gradually faded, but for months I was unable to go out into the dark alone. In general I dreaded to be left alone. I remember wondering how other people could live, how I myself had ever lived, so unconscious of that pit of insecurity beneath the surface of life. My mother in particular, a very cheerful person, seemed to me a perfect paradox in her unconsciousness of danger, which you may well believe I was very careful not to disturb by revelations of my own state of mind. I have always thought that this experience of melancholia of mine had a religious bearing (VRE: 160-161).

James, as author of *The Varieties*, pretends to have asked "this correspondent to explain more fully what he meant by these last words" (i.e., about the experience having "a religious bearing"), and he replied:

I mean that the fear was so invasive and powerful that if I had not clung to scripture-texts like "The eternal God is my refuge," etc., "Come unto me, all ye that labor and are heavy-laden," etc., "I am the resurrection and the life," etc., I think I should have grown really insane (VRE: 161).

James then declares that there is no need to provide further examples of religious melancholy, as he has given one which emphasizes the vanity of mortal things (Tolstoy), another the sense of sin (Bunyan), and the third the fear of the universe (James).

His footnote reference to his father's experience of fear "equally sudden" does not include the account itself, but the following excerpt from his father's book makes his point that a melancholic episode can come upon a person without any forewarning whatsoever. It happened to his father when the Jameses were in London in 1844. William, the eldest son, was two-and-a-half; Henry his younger brother, had just turned one. His father writes:

One day, however, towards the close of May, having eaten a comfortable dinner, I remained sitting at the table after the family had dispersed, idly gazing at the embers in the grate, thinking of nothing, and feeling only the exhilaration incident to a good digestion, when suddenly—in a lightning-flash as it were—"fear came upon me, and trembling, which made all my bones to shake." To all appearance it was a perfectly insane and abject terror, without ostensible cause, and only to be accounted for, to my perplexed imagination, by some damned shape squatting invisible to me within the precincts of the room, and raying out from his fetid personality influences fatal to life. The thing had not lasted ten seconds before I felt myself a wreck; that is, reduced from a state of firm, vigorous, joyful manhood to one of almost helpless infancy. The only self-control I was capable of exerting was to keep my seat. I felt the greatest desire to run incontinently to the foot of the stairs and shout for help to my wife,—to run to the roadside even, and appeal to the public to protect me; but by an immense effort I controlled these frenzied impulses, and determined not to budge from my chair till I had recovered my lost self-possession (In Lewis 1991: 51).

After a few days had passed, he consulted several physicians, all of whom said he had simply overworked his brain (he had been engaged in exegetical work on the book of Genesis), and they recommended the water cure at a nearby resort (Lewis 1991: 52). While there, he complained about having to listen to the "endless 'strife of tongues' about diet, regimen, disease, politics, etc., etc.," and imagined "How sweet it would be to find oneself no longer man, but one of those innocent and ignorant sheep pasturing upon that placid hillside, and drinking in eternal dew and freshness from Nature's lavish bosom!" (In Erikson 1969: 151-152). In discussing the cases of Bunyan and Alline in *The Varieties*, James remarks that "Envy of the placid beasts seems to be a very widespread affection in this type of sadness" (1982: 159). Each chose a different species to envy. For Bunyan, it was dogs and toads, for Alline it was the birds flying overhead, and for Henry James Senior, it was the sheep pasturing on the placid hillside. Perhaps, for all three, this attention to the placid beasts, even if born of envy, reflected some interest in the visible world, and some sense that, however bad it was for them, it could be pleasant enough for at least some of its inhabitants.

But we are concerned here with James's own melancholic episode, the one attributed to the Frenchman with whom he was ostensibly in correspondence. As his opening statement about his "general depression of spirits about my prospects" indicates, he was young at the time of this experience. The breakdown occurred when he was 28 years old (in 1870). He had received his medical degree the previous June and had spent the next six months reading and lying about as he considered his prospects, as he had decided that he did not want to become a medical doctor. His mother complained to his younger brother Henry, who was in Europe at that time, that Williams was resting too much. In late December he confessed in his journal to being unfitted "for any affectionate relations with other individuals," which appears to have applied especially to young women, as he did not marry until he was 36, a match that his father had vigorously promoted from the outset. A month later, around January 10, he suffered a collapse, evidently more severe than anything he had previously experienced. After three weeks of agony, he wrote in his diary on February 1 that he had arrived at the moment of crisis: "Today, I about touched bottom, and perceive plainly that I must face the choice with open eyes: shall I *frankly* throw the moral business overboard, as one unsuited to my innate aptitudes, or shall I follow it, and it alone, making everything else merely stuff for it?" In the same diary entry he noted that he had not previously given any trial to "the moral interest," but had deployed it mainly to hold certain bad habits in check (Lewis 1991: 201). As he refers in this passage to tendencies to "moral degradation," Lewis speculates that this was probably an allusion to auto-eroticism (p. 201). If so, he may have suspected that this was a physiological cause of his depressive state, and perhaps also a causal factor in the fate of the "epileptic patient" described in his account of his hallucinatory experience, as epilepsy was commonly believed to be caused by auto-erotic self-masturbatory acts. His hesitancy to tell his mother the story of his melancholic episode may also have been due, in part, to this feature of the experience.

In any event, the experience recounted in *The Varieties* occurred sometime around this time (the exact date is not given). In late Spring, he began to improve. The turning point occurred in late April when, in the course of reading the second in a series of philosophical essays by French philosopher Charles Renouvier, he found a basis for taking a new approach to life. Renouvier had defined free will as "the sustaining of a thought *because I choose* to when I might have other thoughts." Instead of assuming that this is the definition of an illusion, James decided that he would believe Renouvier's definition of free will. In effect, "My first act of free will shall be to believe in free will. For the remainder of the year, I will abstain from the mere speculative and contemplative *Grübelei* in which my nature takes most delight, and voluntarily cultivate the feeling of moral freedom, by reading books favorable to it, as well as by acting" (Lewis 1991: 204-205). By "Grübelei," James means the "questioning mania" to which he refers in *The Principles of Psychology*, a state of interminable doubt and inquiry (James 1950, II: 284). This, then, will be his new approach to life:

> Hitherto, when I have felt like taking a free initiative, like daring to act originally, without carefully waiting for contemplation of the external world to determine all for me, suicide seemed the most manly form to put my daring into; now, I will go a step further with my will, not only act with it, but believe as well; believe in my individual reality and creative power. My belief, to be sure, *can't* be optimistic—but I will posit life (the real, the good) in the self-governing *resistance* of the ego to the world. Life shall [be built in] doing and suffering and creating (Lewis 1991: 205).

According to his father, William commented sometime thereafter on the marked difference between himself then and a year earlier, and attributed this positive change to the fact that he no longer believed that "all mental disorder requires to have a physical basis" (Erikson 1968: 154). Erikson suggests that James's first insight, that he could exercise choice over the thoughts that he would allow himself to think, was directly related to the second insight, "the abandonment of physiological factors as fatalistic arguments against a neurotic person's continued self-determination. Together they [i.e. these two insights] are the basis of psychotherapy, which, no matter how it is described and conceptualized, aims at the restoration of the patient's power of choice" (p. 155). Perhaps James thereby severed the casual link between his habit of auto-eroticism and mental disorder.

Significantly, James has nothing to say in *The Varieties* about the role played by the affirmation of "will" in the resolution of a melancholic crisis such as that experienced by the "French Sufferer." Perhaps he assumed that to do so would reveal the true identity of this afflicted individual, for he had written a great deal about the will not only in *The Principles of Psychology* (1950 II: 486-592) but also in his well-known essays in popular philosophy published in 1896, the lead essay of which was entitled "The Will to Believe" (1956: 1-31). Another possible explanation is that at the time of writing *The Varieties* he no longer believed that he could lift himself from the depths by his own act of will. In the summer of 1900, writing despondently to his wife from Bad-Nauheim, he said that he had *"no strength at all,"* and though he had tried to summon up a "will to believe ... it is no go. The Will to Believe won't work (Lewis 1991: 511). Lewis suggests that James "was now inclined to locate the source of psychic renewal, not in a conscious act of will, but much rather in the activities of the subconscious .... If *The Principles of Psychology* can be seen as William James's autobiography into the 1880s and the hard-won victory over the 'obstructed will,' *The Varieties* carries the personal story through the breakdown of energy at the turn of the century and the new alertness to the under-consciousness" (p. 511).

Thus, in explaining why he thought "this experience of melancholia of mine had a religious bearing," the "French Sufferer" says that he kept from going really insane by clinging to scripture-texts like "The eternal God is my refuge," "Come unto me, all ye that labor and are heavy-laden," and so forth. In other words, it was not an act of will but something working in him at the subliminal level that kept him sane. Like Bunyan, he was the yielding recipient of verbal automatisms, but unlike Bunyan, the scripture texts were overwhelmingly favorable. Instead of buffeting his mind between damnatory and favorable scriptural voices, he heard only favorable ones (1982: 157). These verses played a role similar to Styron's hearing of the Brahm's *Alto Rhapsody* that he recalled his mother having sung before her untimely death.

Because he found himself relying on scriptural texts, James now feels that "this experience of melancholia of mine had a religious bearing." Its religious bearing is sufficient, at least, to justify placing it alongside those of Tolstoy and Bunyan. He even uses religious language to describe it: "It was like a revelation" (1982: 160). Still, unlike Tolstoy's experience, his does not include a thirst or craving for God, and unlike Bunyan's, there is no "relief in his salvation through the blood of Christ" (pp. 156, 186). The most that he can or will claim for it is that, as he wrote his daughter from Bad-Nauheim, such experiences, painful as they are, are "sent to us for an enlightenment" (Rubin, 1994: 20). By this, I take James to mean that, through such experiences, we gain insights into ourselves that we may not gain in any other way. Thus, the "French Sufferer" is presented with a mental image of his "potential self." He sees the epileptic patient in the asylum, a black haired youth with greenish skin, knees drawn up against his chin, and sitting there like a sort of sculptured Egyptian cat or Peruvian mummy, "moving nothing but his blank eyes and looking absolutely non-human": "This image and my fear entered into a species of combination with each other. *That shape am I*, I felt, potentially. No thing that I possess can defend me against that fate ...." (p. 160). The moment of enlightenment: That shape am I, potentially, and against this fate I am utterly defenseless. With this horrible moment of self-recognition the world underwent a similar change: "The universe was changed for me altogether" (p. 160). If the potential self "moved nothing but his black eyes," the universe was similarly catatonic: "The world now looks remote, strange, sinister, uncanny. Its color is gone, its breath is cold, there is no speculation in the eyes it glares with" (p. 151). The picture is one of indescribable deadness.

The "intimate friend" experience is similar to the "French Sufferer" episode in the sense that it, too, is *self*-revelatory. The first night the intimate friend felt himself being grasped by the arm. The next night he felt something come into the room and stay close to his bed. It remained only a minute or two, but long enough to stir "something more at the roots of my being than any ordinary perception" (p. 59). As in the "French Sufferer" episode, "there was a horribly unpleasant 'sensation' connected with it" (p. 59). And then it left, as swiftly as it had come. The third night it returned, and James now concentrated all his mental effort on charging it to go away if it was evil and to explain itself if it was not. Wordlessly, it departed as swiftly as it had come.

What was this "something" that was "indescribably stronger" than the presence of ordinary living people? As in the "French Sufferer" episode, it was intimately connected with himself: "*Although I felt it to be like unto myself*, so to speak, or finite, small, and distressful, as it were, I didn't recognize it as any individual being or person" (p. 60). An invaluable clue to "who" this intruder was is Erikson's view that the effort to "form" one's identity in late adolescence and early young adulthood involves more than deciding what one will become. It also involves deciding what one will not become, and thus relinquishing or abandoning whole "parts" of oneself. His term for this is the "negative identity," and it is negative not because there is anything intrinsically wrong with it or immoral about it, but simply because it proves to be the "self" that is eventually abandoned (Erikson 1968: 172-176). Significantly, Erikson gives James credit for his own emphasis on the pain and even the self-violence that is often associated with this identity struggle (1968: 22). Writing of Freud's "negative identity," Erikson says that "It is in Freud's dreams, incidentally, that we have a superb record of his suppressed (or what James called 'abandoned,' or even 'murdered') selves—for our 'negative identity' haunts us at night (p. 22). Later, in his chapter on identity confusion, in a section entitled "The Confusion Returns—Psychopathology of Every Night" (a play on Freud's book, *Psychopathology of Everyday Life*), Erikson analyzes a series of dreams that James reports having had in San Francisco in 1906, the effect of which was to cause him to feel that he "was losing hold of my 'self,' and making acquaintance with a quality of mental distress that I had never known before" (In Erikson 1968: 206).

Erikson's citation for this reference to James's discussion of "abandoned" or "murdered" selves reads "The Will to Believe, New World, V" (1968: 326). No page numbers are provided. However, I believe it refers to the fifth essay in *The Will to Believe and Other Essays in Popular Philosophy* (James 1956), which is the essay entitled "The Dilemma of Determinism." In this essay, James is arguing against the determinists the case that life is filled with "alternative possibilities," that "any one of several things may come to pass," some of which do come about, and some of which do not (1956: 153). Having argued this point, he wants to reassure his audience that this does not mean that life is merely random, totally left to chance, as determinists allege to be the logical outcome of this position:

> For what are the alternatives which, in point of fact, offer themselves to human volition? What are those futures that now seem matters of chance? ... Are they not all of them kinds of things already here and based in the existing frame of nature? .... Do not all the motives that assail us, all the futures that offer themselves to our choice, spring equally from the soil of the past; and would not either one of them, whether realized through chance or through necessity, the moment it was realized, seem to us to fit that past, and in the completest and most continuous manner to interdigitate with the phenomena already there? (1956: 157).

The implication of this view that there are genuine alternatives and that we do in fact make real choices among them is that we live in "a world in which we constantly have to make what I shall, with your permission, call judgments of regret. Hardly an hour passes in which we do not wish that something might be otherwise" (1956: 159-160).

James does not use the words "abandoned" or "murdered" selves in these passages, but Erikson is right, I believe, to "sense" these darker, more ominous realities as hovering about the text, and James does seem to be preoccupied with abandonment and murder at the time this essay is being written, the possible precipitating event for these darker ruminations being his reading in the newspapers of the "self-satisfied" confession of "the murderer at Brockton the other day," an unusually violent instance of wife murder. In a footnote to the above quotation about genuine alternatives, he anticipates the favorite argument of determinists that, if free-will is true, "a man's murderer may as probably be his best friend as his worst enemy, a mother may be as likely to strangle as to suckle her first born, and all of us to be as ready to jump from fourth-story windows as to go out of the front doors, etc." But this is a spurious argument, he counters, because "'free-will' does not say that everything that is physically conceivable is also morally possible. It merely says that of alternatives that *really* tempt our will more than one is really possible." Then he adds, "Of course, the alternatives that do thus tempt our will are vastly fewer than the physical possibilities we can coldly fancy. Persons really tempted often do murder their best friends, mothers do strangle their first-born, people do jump out of fourth-story windows, etc." (1956: 157). The serious, almost depressing tone of these remarks in an essay concerned to advance the case for the *freedom* of the will, and especially the specific references to temptation (mothers murdering their first-borns and persons committing suicide), clearly justify Erikson's clinician's inference that James here is speaking of "abandoned" and even "murdered" selves.

Returning, then, to the "intimate friend" case in *The Varieties*: I do not think it to be at all far-fetched to view the "intruder" in this case to be James's own "murdered self," the self that was "killed" when he resolved his identity struggles in his late twenties, the struggles that were central to the "French Sufferer" episode, which, as we recall, occurred when he was in "general depression of spirits about my prospects" (VRE: 160). This "murdered self," which was "like unto myself" and "finite, small, and distressful" (p. 60), may have been the artist self that he had nourished in his late teens and early twenties before being persuaded by his father to follow a more respectable career in the sciences. Myers suggests that it was William's conflicts with his father over his desire to study art that inaugurated his chronic depression. As Myers explains, "Because William's first neurotic symptoms, such as inexplicable eye and digestive problems and anxiety, occurred at this time, it can be argued that father-son tensions were a critical factor in making William chronically depressed" (1986: 20). In any event, it seems important that the "intruder" appeared when James's mind was "absorbed in some lectures which I was preparing" (VRE: 60), an activity that he would most certainly not have been engaging in had he followed his original intention to be an artist. Furthermore, if the "intruder" is a "murdered self" who has come back almost literally to "haunt" James, then there is a very real sense in which suicide, an act of self-murder, did occur. He is his own victim, which makes all the more "horrible" the sight of this "finite, small and distressful" being, a being destroyed as he was just beginning to come into his own. Jane Kenyon's observation that melancholy is an "unholy ghost" who is "certain to come again" could not be more apt, at least as regards melancholy's sense of sadness and loss (Kenyon, 1993: 25).[4]

In short, if the "French Sufferer" episode revealed to James a "potential self" which he decidedly *did not want to become*, the "intimate friend" account reveals a self that he *could have become but chose another course instead*. Perhaps, for the adult James, there was some consolation in the fact that he was able to form the science of psychology into art, both by insisting on the primacy of the individual over the aggregate (cf. his essay "The Importance of Individuals," 1956: 225-262), and by "illustrating" his points and arguments by means of individual "portraits," such as those we have been discussing in this essay, as "portraiture" was the art form in which he clearly excelled (cf. Miller 1992: 68-73, for a discussion of the relation between illustration and text in his brother's novels).

Before we leave the "intimate friend" case and the theme of the "murdered self," I want to anticipate the final section of this essay ("Metaphysical Anxiety and the Devouring Will"), and to note that the father-son conflict in the matter of James's decision for science over art has been so emphasized by James's biographers that the mother-son conflict has been almost totally ignored. That his father exhibited far greater interest in his son's scientific than his artistic skills there can be no doubt (Lewis 1991: 80-82). But a more subtle, subversive role was played by James's mother, if only because she strongly encouraged James's brother Henry's artistic interests (praising the stories he was writing at the time) and did nothing to encourage William's interests in painting. A possible clue as to why she did not encourage William's artistic interests is provided by Henry, who would accompany William to John La Farge's art studio in Newport, but work on copying plaster casts while William and La Farge worked close by one another painting. One day Henry wandered up to the second floor where William was working. To his shock and astonishment,

---

4. William Styron also emphasizes the fundamental role that loss plays in the progress of depression and also its origins:

> Despite the still-faltering methods of treatment, psychiatry has, on an analytical and philosophical level, contributed a lot to an understanding of the origins of depression. Much obviously remains to be learned (and a great deal will doubtless continue to be a mystery, owing to the disease's idiopathic nature, its constant interchangeability of factors), but certainly one psychological element has been established beyond reasonable doubt, and that is the concept of loss. Loss in all of its manifestations is the touchstone of depression—in the progress of the disease and, most likely, in its origin (1990: 56).

he found his slender, red-headed, and much-liked young cousin Gus Barker, who was on a flying visit to Newport during a Harvard vacation, standing naked on a pedestal, modeling for William's pencil drawing of him. It was Henry's first vision of a life model, and he remembered all his days how his personal artistic ambitions collapsed in an instant: "so forced was I to recognize ... that I might niggle for months over plaster casts and not come within miles of any such point of attack. The bravery of my brother's own in especial dazzled me out of every presumption." Then and there, Henry tells us, he put away his drawing pencil forever (Lewis 1991: 110-111).

What Henry leaves the reader to infer—what goes unspoken here—is that his brother's "bravery" was in the very act of daring to behold the naked body of another young man. As Henry was his mother's confidante, we may assume that he told her why he would no longer be going to the art studio. Perhaps it was this episode that "inspired" their father to write a friend, inquiring as to how he might find a microscope to give his son William for Christmas, a none-too-subtle pressure on William to consider a scientific career instead. Yet, Lewis cautions that there is no hard evidence that Henry Senior actually pressured William to abandon his artistic interests, for, as Henry Junior recalls, their father's role was to caution against making any final choices and always to keep alternatives open (Lewis 1991: 112). William's precipitous abandonment of all plans for a career in art, just as he was "beginning to show real promise as a portrait painter" (p. 111) points, instead, to the influence of James's mother, and to her concerns about the moral temptations to which her son was exposed in an artist's studio. I realize that I, too, lack "hard evidence" that his mother was the key player in the "murder" of his artist self, but, in the final section of the essay, I will offer evidence that gives this view considerable plausibility.

THE PARABLE OF THE PREHISTORIC REPTILES

I also realize that my suspicion that James is himself the "intimate friend" might be mistaken. But, if this were so, it would not affect my basic argument that his hallucinatory experiences, with their decidedly melancholic overtones, are *self*-revelatory, and genuinely so. The "French Sufferer" account, which we know to be his own, makes this sufficiently clear. Nor would this affect James's own argument that such experiences reveal the radical evil that inheres in the universe, and therefore they involve a deeper apprehension of reality than the religion of healthy-mindedness acknowledges. We may protest either against this view of the universe as possessing a radical evil, or against the use of hallucinatory experiences in support of it, but, in *The Principles of Psychology*, James is quick to defend hallucinatory experiences, noting that they are not delusions, for a delusion is a false opinion about a matter of fact, whereas an hallucination "is a strictly sensational form of consciousness, as good and true a sensation as if there were a real object there" (1950, II: 115). They are, in fact, not much different from dreams, which are "our real world whilst we are sleeping, because our attention then lapses from the sensible world .... But if a dream haunts us and compels our attention during the day it is very apt to remain figuring in our consciousness as a sort of subuniverse alongside of the waking world" (1950, II: 294). If dreams are potential sources of enlightenment, then hallucinatory experiences are too. And the enlightenment in the "French Sufferer" case is that in this world the individual self is terribly, horribly vulnerable! "Nothing that I possess can defend me against that fate, if the hour for it should strike for me as it struck for him" (VRE: 160). The corollary of this enlightenment is that, as the "intimate friend" case reveals, we are also fated to be a danger to ourselves, that partial-suicide is an inescapable feature of our life in a world in which we cannot avoid making fateful choices.

James's chapter on the "Sick Soul" does not, however, end with his account of the "French Sufferer." Instead, it goes on to note that he purposely avoided the examples of really insane melancholia in which there *are* "delusions about matters of fact." Had he presented such cases, "it would be a worse story still—desperation absolute and complete, the whole universe coagulating about the sufferer into a material of overwhelming horror, surrounding him without opening or end" (VRE: 162). Here, the evil would not be a matter of "intellectual perception" (enlightenment), "but the grisly blood-freezing heart-palsying sensation of it close upon one, and no other conception or sensation able to live for a moment in its presence" (p. 162). In such cases,

> How irrelevantly remote seem all our usual refined optimisms and intellectual and moral consolations in presence of a need of help like this! Here is the real core of the religious problem: Help! help! No prophet can claim to bring a final message unless he says things that will have a sound of reality in the ears of victims such as these (VRE: 162).

And this, James suggests, is why we may expect that the "coarser religions, revivalistic, orgiastic, with blood and miracles and supernatural operations, may possibly never be displaced. Some constitutions need them too much." The deliverance, it would appear, "must come in as strong a form as the complaints" (p. 162).

In the final paragraphs of the chapter, therefore, James is especially concerned with the melancholic temperament's true apprehension of the evil of the universe, an evil that they know themselves to be among its potential victims. The healthy-minded may dismiss this insight and may argue that, even if it is true, one may avert one's attention from it and live "simply in the light of good" (p. 163). But, while this may be a successful "religious solution," it

> breaks down impotently as soon as melancholy comes; and even though one be quite free from melancholy one's self, there is no doubt that healthy-mindedness is inadequate as a philosophical doctrine, because the evil facts which it refuses positively to account for are a genuine portion of reality; and they may after all be the best key to life's significance, and possibly the only openers of our eyes to the deepest levels of truth (VRE: 163).

One need not be possessed by "insane melancholy" to realize that the normal process of life has moments of "radical evil." After all, "The lunatic's visions of horror are all drawn from the material of daily fact" (p. 163). Consider, for example, the "carnivorous reptiles of geologic times" who are now museum specimens and no longer any threat to anything: "Yet there is no tooth in any one of those museum skulls that did not daily through long years of the foretime hold fast to the body struggling in despair of some fated living victim" (p. 164). Forms of horror just as dreadful to their victims, if on a smaller scale, fill our world today:

> Here on our very hearths and in our gardens the infernal cat plays with the panting mouse, or holds the hot bird fluttering in her jaws. Crocodiles and rattlesnakes and pythons are at this moment vessels of life as real as we are; their loathsome existence fills every minute of every day that drags its length along; and whenever they or other wild beasts clutch their living prey, the deadly horror which an agitated melancholic feels is the literally right reaction on the situation (VRE: 164).

These are no placid beasts: His father, frustrated by talk about diet, regimen, and politics, could envision himself as a sheep grazing on a quiet hillside, Bunyan could envy the dog and toad because they have no fear for the fate of their souls, and Alline could think of himself as a bird flying away from his danger and distress. But James uses the image of prehistoric reptiles and modern-day cats, crocodiles, rattlesnakes and pythons to make the sober point that there is no escape from the evil that the melancholic sees with unusually clearsighted keenness. And perhaps most horrific of all is the randomness of evil, the way it selects one victim and lets the other, temporarily, escape. In a footnote to this passage, James cites the case of a group of travellers who suddenly hear a cracking sound in the bushes and the next instant a tiger has pounced upon one of their party and carried him off (VRE: 164). The "French Sufferer" knows that he is potentially the black-haired youth with greenish skin, entirely idiotic: *That shape am I*, I felt, potentially. Nothing that I possess can defend me against that fate, if the hour for it should strike for me as it struck for him." It makes one wonder "how other people could live, how I myself had ever lived, so unconscious of that pit of insecurity beneath the surface of life" (pp. 160-161).[5]

Exploration of James's recommendations for combatting a world of which radical evil is part would be the next logical step for us to take. His essay, "Is Life Worth Living?" (James 1956: 32-62) is perhaps his most deeply personal reflection on this struggle, and may be viewed as his own "confession of faith." But this is not the time to introduce new issues and themes, but to bring the present discussion to a point of closure. For this purpose, the text I will turn to instead is Erik H. Erikson's *Young Man Luther* (1958), and, specifically, to his own analysis of the last several paragraphs of James's chapter in *The Varieties* on "The Sick Soul."

METAPHYSICAL ANXIETY AND THE DEVOURING WILL

Just prior to introducing these paragraphs, Erikson has been discussing the role that religion plays in reaffirming the basic trust that must develop if the infants are to survive in the world into which they have recently been cast:

In situations in which such basic trust cannot develop in early infancy because of a defect in the child or in the maternal environment, children die mentally. They do not respond nor learn; they do not assimilate their food and fail to defend themselves against infection, and often they die physically as well as mentally (1958: 118).

Even in the most fortunate of situations, however, there will take root "a lifelong mistrust-

---

5. If James uses the beasts in support of the melancholics' vision of the world that *is* seen, he uses them as well to support the religious vision of the world that is *unseen*. In "Is Life Worth Living?" (1956: 32-62) he suggests that the idea "that our whole physical life may lie soaking in the spiritual atmosphere, a dimension of being that we at present have no organ for apprehending, is vividly suggested to us by the analogy of the life of our domestic animals. Our dogs, for example, are in our human life but not of it. They witness hourly the outward body of events whose inner meaning cannot, by any possible operation, be revealed to their intelligence,—events in which they themselves often play the cardinal part. My terrier bites a teasing boy, for example, and the father demands damages. The dog may be present at every step of the negotiations, and see the money paid, without an inkling of what it all means, without a suspicion that it has anything to do with *him*; and he never can know in his natural dog's life" (p. 58). The insights we gain from viewing human existence on analogy with the life of animals seem so important to him that it strikes him as significant and perhaps puzzling "that scarce a word of sympathy with brutes should have survived from the teachings of Jesus of Nazareth"! ("The Importance of Individuals," 1956: 261).

ful remembrance of that truly metaphysical anxiety; meta—'behind,' 'beyond'—here means 'before,' 'way back,' 'at the beginning'" (p. 119). It is the task of religion to address such anxiety.

But Erikson asks: What caused this anxiety to take root? What made it happen? "All religions and most philosophers agree it is *will*—the mere will to live, thoughtless and cruel self-will" (p. 120). Then he quotes the passage in "The Sick Soul" chapter where James describes the prehistoric reptiles, specifically James's assertion that "there is no tooth in any of those museum-skulls that did not daily ... hold fast to the body struggling in despair of some fated living victim." Erikson comments that "the tenor of this mood is immediately convincing. It is the mood of severe melancholy, intensified tristitia, one would almost say tristitia with teeth in it," and then observes that

> James is clinically and genetically correct, when he connects the horror of the *devouring* will to live with the content and the disposition of melancholia. For in melancholia, it is the human being's horror of his own avaricious and sadistic orality which he tires of, withdraws from, wishes often to end even by putting an end to himself. This is not the orality of the first, the toothless and dependent, stage; it is the orality of the tooth-stage and all that develops within it, especially the prestages of what later becomes "biting" human conscience (1958: 121).

Erikson then notes that Luther reversed the picture, and saw "God himself as a devourer, as if the wilful sinner could expect to find in God's demeanor a mirror of his own avarice, just as the uplifted face of the believer [also] finds a countenance inclined and full of grace" (p. 121). Such images of the deity, or of the devil for that matter, are mirror images of "man's own rapacious orality which destroys the innocent trust of that first symbiotic orality when mouth and breast, glance and face, are one" (p. 122).

Here, Erikson traces the desire for a will of one's own to the *penultimate* stage of infancy—the tooth-stage, as it were—and links this desire to James's account of the deadly fight for survival that characterizes all sentient life on this planet. Melancholy, at least melancholy with teeth in it, is about the threat of losing that which has made life so palpably worthwhile. We feel we are losing it, or have already lost it, and somehow, some way, we must gain it back, using whatever means we have to regain it. The one with whom this struggle is originally carried out and forever remembered as our first combatant is the very one who embodies the "maternal environment." Which is to say that our original fight for life is with and against the very one who gave life in the first place. No wonder there is so much feeling of mutual betrayal, of mutual victimization.

"Armed" with Erikson's view of melancholy as having "teeth in it," I want to take a final look at the "French Sufferer" episode, and to explore the suspicions this view raises regarding the role of the mother-son relationship in James's fears for his own sanity. If I have argued that his mother had a hand in the "murdering" of the self he imagined he could be, I now want to propose that she was the key player in his fear that he might become a self that he truly dreaded becoming, but knew to be a genuine possibility. Surely there is more to the story of the "French Sufferer" than James has been able or willing to tell. Conceivably, as Myers suggests, James simply was not very self-analytical (1986: 49), and that the "French Sufferer" case as we have it in *The Varieties* is either an illustration of this fact, or of the limits of introspection as a method of self-analysis. Maybe so, but I think it has more to do with reserve, a reluctance to speak negatively about his parents, especially his mother, and to the fact that he has been asked to give a series of lectures, not a personal life history. To engage in any more personal disclosure than he has already done would be self-indulgent, and an affront to his audience, who came for something else.

Yet, as we have seen, he provides the reader a clue that all was not well in his relationship to his mother when, in the "French Sufferer" account, he presents her as being strangely oblivious to what her son was going through: "My mother in particular, a very cheerful person, seemed to me a perfect paradox in her unconsciousness of danger, which you may well believe I was very careful not to disturb by revelations of my own state of mind" (VRE: 161). Commentators on this passage have drawn the conclusion that James's intent here was to present his mother as a perfect example of the "healthy-minded" temperament, and therefore as one who was constitutionally unable to appreciate what horrible pain and suffering her son was experiencing. As Erikson himself observes, James's assurance "that he did not want to disturb his unaccountably cheerful mother makes one wonder how much anxiety it took for the self-made man of that day to turn to the refuge of woman" (1968: 153).

This may be true as far as it goes. But we have to remember that the story of the "French Sufferer" is the reconstruction of the experience by a man in his late fifties, for whom the mother is no longer objectively present. For a truer account of the feelings of the young man of twenty-eight, for whom his mother is very much alive, I suggest that the story of the *real* French sufferer, the story of the French mental patient who has been hospitalized against his will (VRE: 148-149), hits closer to the mark. Why does James choose to make himself a "French" sufferer if not to draw the reader's attention to the first French sufferer, who is in every respect like himself: young, philosophically minded (and thus also subject to "philosophical pessimism"), and able to speak of his mother and "abuse of power" in one and the same breath? Moreover, the real French sufferer is also suffering from the "worst kind of melancholy," that of panic fear. As the *real* French sufferer writes his *real* correspondent, "Besides the burnings and the sleeplessness, fear, atrocious fear, presses me down, holds me without respite, never lets me go" (VRE: 148). Then the accusation, the biting sarcasm, directed against his mother: "Eat, drink, lie awake all night, suffer without interruption—such is the fine legacy I have received from my mother!" (p. 148). Then the note of uncomprehendingness: Why is this happening to me?

> What I fail to understand is this abuse of power. There are limits to everything, there is a middle way. But God knows neither middle way nor limits. I say God, but why? All I have known so far has been the devil. After all, I am afraid of God as much as of the devil, so I drift along, thinking of nothing but suicide, but with neither courage nor means here to execute the act (VRE: 148).

Finally, the self-pity and consuming rage of the final lines in which he goes back in thought to the beginning of his life:

> But I stop. I have raved to you long enough. I say raved, for I can write no otherwise, having neither brain nor thoughts left. O God! What a misfortune to be born! Born, like a mushroom, doubtless between an evening and a morning; and how true and right I was when in our philosophy-year in college I chewed the cud of bitterness with the pessimists. Yes, indeed, there is more pain in life than gladness—it is one long agony until the grave. Think how gay it makes me to remember that this horrible misery of mine, coupled with this unspeakable fear, may last fifty, one hundred, who knows how many more years! (VRE: 149).

Conceivably, James's "panic fear" for his very existence was not as severe as that of the real Frenchman. Yet, he, too, was contemplating suicide, and he, too, felt "defenseless against the invisible enemy who is tightening his coils around me" (VRE: 148). I also believe that he was no less angry at his mother, the one whom the real French sufferer wants to blame, ultimately, for his hopeless condition. For even twenty years after the "French Sufferer" experience, James at least allows himself a criticism of his mother's "cheerful" demeanor and her "unconsciousness of danger," which is to say that he believes that she was living in denial. He was not the only family member who was experiencing deep psychological pain and anguish at the same time, and whose condition was similarly unacknowledged by the mother. Just prior to William's breakdown, while he was in Germany, his younger sister Alice was also stricken, and, as Lewis points out, their mother's analysis of Alice's difficulties (in a letter to their younger brother Wilkerson) "reflected a wistful incomprehension: Alice's mind was untouched by the disturbance; she did not dread the attacks in advance, was 'perfectly happy when they are over,' and was patient and affectionate throughout" (Lewis 1991: 196-197). In her own commentary on James's essay "The Hidden Self," published in 1890, in which James *does* refer to the "abandoned" self, Alice recalled that, at the time she was having her attacks, "the only difference between me and the insane was that I had not only all the horrors and suffering of insanity but the duties of doctor, nurse, and straitjacket imposed upon me, too" (Lewis 1991: 197). What she means is that she had to "hold herself together" because insanity was forbidden. The problem with their mother's "healthy-mindedness" is that it was a refusal to acknowledge that something was wrong, terribly wrong, with the James family.

Lewis traces the family dysfunctions to the fact that Henry Senior had considered marrying both Walsh sisters, finally settling on Mary, the oldest. Yet the youngest, Catherine ("Aunt Kate"), accompanied the young James family to England, serving as the nurse for little William and Henry (Lewis 1991: 77). William, for his part, seemed to take especially well to Aunt Kate, as she would take him on walks through London. Later, he wrote of the "sort of sub-antagonism" that prevailed between Kate and his father, owing, Lewis suspects, to the fact that Kate was spurned by Henry Senior in favor of her older sister (Lewis 1991: 75). In any event, there were certainly ample reasons for tension and conflict in this arrangement, and one would not be surprised but what Henry Senior's breakdown was more the result of this domestic situation than of his having overworked himself in his exegetical labors. Of special interest to us here, however, is the fact that William was much in the care of his aunt while his mother was occupied with Henry, and that this emotional separation occurred when William was developing a will of his own. In an emotional sense, he was talking about himself in "The Dilemma of Determinism" lecture (1956: 157) when he said that some mothers *do* strangle their first-borns. And no doubt Aunt Kate, the spurned sister, would not have minded it at all if her sister's first-born had a desire to "bite" his mother back for having spurned him in favor of her beloved second-born son?

These family problems were never really resolved. Aunt Kate eventually married (when William was thirteen) but it lasted only three years, and then she was back with the James's for good. When she left, Henry Senior wrote a friend that Aunt kate had been "a most loving and provident husband to Mary, a most considerate and devoted wife to me, and an incomparable father and mother to our children" (Lewis 1991: 76). He is, of course, using these familial names—wife, husband, father, mother—metaphorically, but, just the same, it is quite evident that Aunt Kate had made herself indispensable. Does this mean, however, that William's mother was weak and impotent, her power usurped by her younger sister? This is not how a young visitor to the James family home experienced it. No, she found it "stiff and stupid ... its 'pokey banality' ruled over by Mrs. James," while Mr. James came and went, and "never seemed to 'belong' to his wife or Miss Walsh, large stupid-looking ladies, or to his clever but coldly self-absorbed daughter" (Lewis 1991: 199). If this account is to be believed, it was Mr. James, William's father, who was without much power or influence in the James family, no match, it seems, for the Walsh sisters.

I suspect, then, that William James, like the real French sufferer, held his mother more accountable than his father for his troubles. Living in the house over which his mother ruled, he was a victim, as the real French sufferer put it, of "an abuse of power." This was not the power of coercion and threat, but of denial, the refusal to see reality for what it is, and the determination to see only what she wanted to see. Of the two forms of healthy-mindedness set forth in the chapter in *The Varieties* on "The Religion of Healthy-Mindedness," hers was not the involuntary but the systematic type:

> In its involuntary variety, healthy-mindedness is a way of feeling happy about things immediately. In its systematical variety, it is an abstract way of conceiving things as good. Every abstract way of conceiving things selects some one aspect of them as their essence for the time being, and disregards the other aspects. Systematic healthy-mindedness, conceiving good as the essential and universal aspect of being, deliberately excludes evil from its field of vision (VRE: 87–88).

The systematic type is, of course, the most maddening, precisely because it is a *refusal* to acknowledge that a problem exists, that something is wrong, that someone else may be suffering and, most importantly, that one just *may* be the cause of the suffering of the other.

In short, James understood that his mother was indeed capable of driving him into insanity, of making him "that Shape" that he so much dreaded. If she had a hand in the "murdering" of his artistic self—as I suspect she did—she played a controlling role in the "panic fear" he suffered several years later, when he came face to face with his "potential" self, the self that he knew was horribly possible. With her, he was always locked in a struggle for survival, and the result was a melancholy with teeth in it. She could not or would not give what he wanted and needed, and so he fought back: He wrote home from Germany, saying that he had fallen in love with an actress of Bohemian origin, knowing that this would cause *her* to *fear* that he would marry a bad woman (Lewis 1991: 187).[6] Also, he exhibited little interest in pursuing the medical career for which he had been training, again causing *her* to *fear* that he might never find himself. If he was lacking in any self-analytical skills, as Myers suggests, this was probably where the deficiencies lay: He was depressed about his prospects, but his indecision was serving deeper psychological needs: to get back at his mother for failing to meet *his* needs for a mother who could assuage a child's fears.

Yet, James's parable of the "carnivorous reptiles of geologic times" is the older man's effort to arrive at a more balanced perspective, and it represents a significant step toward a more "religious" view of his lifelong affliction. The "evil," he suggests, is not in the one individual or the other, but in the situation. All are fighting for their lives, and in this fight, all will play both roles—now victim, now victimizer—and there is no way for this "perfect paradox" to be avoided. To come to this enlightenment, however small the consolation that it may give, is to take a major step beyond what James calls the "querulous temper" of the real French sufferer, a temper that "keeps his mind from taking a religious

---

6. Lewis also mentions that, while in Dresden, James had the habit of "peering through a telescope from his room on Christianstrasse at the young girls in a boarding school across the street, among them a ravishing Jewish female" (1991: 187). Was this simply another example of his artistic interests (a pencil sketch with the notation "The lovely young Jewess looking at the large end of the telescope" is reproduced in Myers 1986: 306ff), or is it another instance of being attracted to women of whom his mother would disapprove? (For a similar example of his father's voyeuristic interest in women, see Davis, this volume).

direction," that "tends in fact rather toward irreligion" (VRE: 149). The point, finally, is not to assign blame, to attribute one's troubles to this or that person, but rather to recognize that the universe is so constructed that all of us are engaged in a struggle for our very existence. We are all endangered selves, and this was no less true for his mother as it was, and is, for himself.

If he parts company with the real French sufferer, it is in deciding that there is finally nothing to be gained by assigning blame, for to do so locks us into the very deterministic thinking that will eventually undermine the struggle for life itself. And, when we engage in the struggle for life, we see the real world and its evil—for there is no denying it—but we also see another world, the "more" that the religious temperament enables us to see (VRE: 512-514). As he declares in his essay, "Is Life Worth Living?" (1956), the essay that I have called his "confession of faith":

I confess that I do not see why the very existence of an invisible world may not in part depend on the personal response which any one of us may make to the religious appeal. God himself, in short, may draw vital strength and increase of very being from our fidelity. For my own part, I do not know what the sweat and blood and tragedy of this life mean, if they mean anything short of this. If this life be not a real fight, in which something is eternally gained for the universe by success, it is no better than a game of private theatricals from which one may withdraw at will. But it *feels* like a real fight,—as if there were something really wild in the universe which we, with all our idealities and faithfulnesses are needed to redeem; and first of all to redeem our own hearts from atheisms and fears. *For such a half-wild, half-saved universe our nature is adapted* (1956: 61, my emphasis).

In his psychobiographical study of James, Cushing Strout refers to him as a "twice-born sick soul" (1968). I would rather say that he is "half-wild, half-saved." Pratt asks in his questionnaire whether the respondent believes in personal immortality and if so why? James replies, "Never keenly, but more strongly as I grow older." Why? "Because I am just getting fit to live" (Brown 1973: 125). Six years later (August 26, 1910), he went out into the dark alone, to face the final religious experience that awaits us all, when the fight has gone out of us and our part in the battle is over. This experience is all the evidence we need, and perhaps more than we want, that religious experiences are ultimately—metaphysically, if you will—a solitary solemn affair: They are finally between ourselves and whatever we may consider the divine.

CONCLUSION

I began this essay with the question of whether religion may, in fact, be an entirely individual matter, unrelated to and disconnected from any and all religious traditions. By focusing on the "intimate friend" and "French Sufferer" cases, and comparing them with other cases in *The Varieties*, I have shown that James himself believed that religious experiences are those in which the experiencer interprets the experience in the language and symbols of a religious tradition. And, therefore, James does not believe that his own experiences qualify as religious experiences as he does not so interpret them.

But we have also seen that these experiences reveal the degree to which his own self was endangered, with the "intimate friend" episode revealing that he was haunted throughout his life with remorse over his own "self-murder" (or "murdered self"), and the "French Sufferer" episode revealing how he struggled with, and gained a victory over, the "potential self" that he was in danger of becoming, a victory, however, that left him permanently wounded (i.e., a lifelong melancholic). He did not claim that either experience was religious. Instead of interpreting them in light of any religious tradition, he preferred to see them as powerful psychical experiences (i.e., visual hallucination in the case of the "intimate friend" and verbal automatism in the case of the "French Sufferer"). The most he will claim is that the second experience had "a religious bearing" because the automatisms were consoling scripture texts.[7]

His own reluctance to interpret these experiences as religious leaves *us*, his readers, with an interesting dilemma: We *could*, if we chose to, declare that in our own judgment these were religious experiences, as they may readily be so interpreted. We might call this the Pfister Argument, after Oskar Pfister, the Lutheran pastor who was fond of telling Freud, a self-proclaimed atheist, that Freud was more religious than his believer friends. *Or*, alternatively, we may decide that James is the one who must judge whether or not his experiences are religious ones. If we take this approach, then we also take a giant step toward the view that religious experience is, ultimately, a personal matter, that only the experiencer can say, finally, whether the experience is religious or not.

My own inclination is to take the latter position, even if it means that James's own experiences cannot then be used in support of the thesis that there may be purely personal religious experiences this side of death itself. But, then, we may also imagine that James himself would not have been content to conclude the investigation on this ironic note, but would have wanted to probe further into why James was so reticent about interpreting his experiences religiously when others, in similar circumstances, had no difficulty in doing so. My own introspections into this question yield the possible explanation that for James to have interpreted these experiences religiously would have given others certain satisfactions of which he wished to deprive them, beginning, I would suppose, with his anxious mother. Thus, to refuse to interpret his experiences as religious ones was his revenge for the fact that, as a young man, he believed he had no choice but to commit an act of self-murder. The "teeth" in James's melancholy is that he will *not* give the religious community what it wants, i.e., the right to call him one of their own, a circumstance that it is likely to find the more frustrating in light of the fact that, for his own personal reasons (as a lifelong sufferer from melancholia) he vigorously defended religion against the philistine scientific opinion of his day.[8]

REFERENCES

American Psychiatric Association (1987). *Diagnostic and Statistical Manual of Mental Disorders* (DSM-III-R). Washington, D.C.: American Psychiatric Association.

Bellah, R.N., et al. (1985). *Habits of the Heart: Individualism and Commitment in American Life.* Berkeley, CA: University of California Press.

Brown, L. B. (Ed.) (1973). *Psychology and Religion: Selected Readings.* Baltimore, MD: Penguin Books.

Carroll, M. P. (1985). The Virgin Mary at LaSalette and Lourdes: Whom did the children see? *Journal for the Scientific Study of Religion*, 24: 56-74.

---

7. For a compelling example of how a powerful psychical experience was *not* interpreted by its experiencer as religious until the religious community insisted on so viewing it, see Michael P. Carroll's "The Virgin Mary at LaSalette and Lourdes: Whom Did the Children See?," *Journal for the Scientific Study of Religion*, 24 (1985): 56-74.

8. In my second essay in this volume entitled "Prayer, Melancholy, and the Vivified Face of the World," I discuss further the role that his melancholy played in his defense of religion against philistine science.

Eakin, P. J. (1985). *Fictions in Autobiography: Studies in the Art of Self-Invention.* Princeton, NJ: Princeton University Press.

Erikson, E.H. (1958). *Young Man Luther: A Study in Psychoanalysis and History.* New York: W. W. Norton.

——(1968). *Identity: Youth and Crisis.* New York: W.W. Norton.

Jackson, S. W. (1986). *Melancholia and Depression: From Hippocratic Times to Modern Times.* New Haven, CT: Yale University Press.

James, W. (1950). *The Principles of Psychology,* 2 vols. New York: Dover Publications.

——(1982). *The Varieties of Religious Experience.* New York: Penguin Books.

——(1986). *The Will to Believe and Other Essays in Popular Philosophy.* New York: Dover Publications.

Kenyon, J. (1993). *Constance.* Saint Paul, MN: Graywolf Press.

Lewis, R. W. B. (1991). *The Jameses: A Family Narrative.* New York: Farrar, Straus and Giroux.

Miller, J. H. (1992). *Illustration.* Cambridge, MA: Harvard University Press.

Myers, G. E. (1986). *William James: His Life and Thought.* New Haven, CT: Yale University Press.

Proudfoot, W. & P. Shaver (1975). Attribution theory and the psychology of religion. *Journal for the Scientific Study of Religion,* 14: 317-330.

Rubin, J. H. (1994). *Religious Melancholy and Protestant Experience in America.* New York: Oxford University Press.

Strout, C. (1968). William James and the twice-born sick soul. *Philosophers and Kings:* Studies in Leadership. Vol. 97, No. 3 of the *Proceedings of the American Academy of Religion.*

Styron, W. (1990). *Darkness Visible: A Memoir of Madness.* New York: Random House.

APPENDIX

JAMES'S ANSWERS TO PRATT'S QUESTIONNAIRE

The following document is a series of answers to a questionnaire upon the subject of religious belief, which was sent out in 1904 by Professor James B. Pratt of Williams College, and to which William James filled out a reply at an unascertained date in the autumn of that year.

Questionnaire (James's answers are printed in italics)

It is being realized as never before that religion, as one of the most important things in the life both of the community and of the individual, deserves close and extended study. Such study can be of value only if based upon the personal experiences of many individuals. If you are in sympathy with such study and are willing to assist in it, will you kindly write out the answers to the following questions and return them with this questionnaire, as soon as you conveniently can, to James B. Pratt, 20 Shepard Street, Cambridge, Mass.

Please answer the questions at length and in detail. Do not give philosophical generalizations, but your own personal experience.

1. What does religion mean to you personally? Is it

    (1) A belief that something exists? *Yes.*

    (2) An emotional experience? *Not powerfully so, yet a social reality.*

    (3) A general attitude of the will toward God or toward righteousness? *It involves these.*

    (4) Or something else?

If it has several elements, which is for you the most important? *The social appeal for corroboration, consolation, etc., when things are going wrong with my causes (my truth denied),* etc.

2. What do you mean by God? *A combination of Ideality and (final) efficacy.*

    (1) Is He a person—if so, what do you mean by His being a person? *He must be cognizant and responsive in some way.*

    (2) Or is He only a Force? *He must do.*

    (3) Or is God an attitude of the Universe toward you? *Yes but more conscious. 'God' to me, is not the only spiritual reality to believe in. Religion means primarily a universe of spiritual relations surrounding the earthly practical ones, not merely relations of 'value', but agencies and their activities. I suppose*

that the chief premise for my hospitality towards the religious testimony of others is my conviction that 'normal' or 'sane' consciousness is so small a part of actual experience. What e'er be true, it is not true exclusively, as philistine scientific opinion assumes. The other kinds of consciousness bear witness to a much wider universe of experiences, from which our belief selects and emphasizes such parts as best satisfy our needs.

How do you apprehend his relation to mankind and to you personally?
If your position on any of these matters is uncertain, please state the fact.   { *Uncertain.*

3. Why do you believe in God? Is it
   (1) From some argument? *Emphatically, no.*
   Or (2) Because you have experienced His presence? *No, but rather because I need it so that it 'must' be true.*
   Or (3) From authority, such as that of the Bible or of some prophetic person? *Only the whole tradition or religious people, to which something in me makes admiring response.*
   Or (4) From any other reason? *Only for the social reasons.*
   If from several of these responses, please indicate carefully the order of their importance.
4. Or do you not so much believe in God as want to *use* Him?
   I can't use him very definitely, yet I believe. Do you accept Him not so much as a real existent Being, but rather as an ideal to live by? *More as a more powerful ally of my own ideals.* If you should become thoroughly convinced that there was no God, would it make any great difference in your life—either in happiness, morality, or in other respects? *Hard to say. It would surely make some difference.*
5. Is God very real to you, as real as an earthly friend, though different? *Dimly (real); not (as an earthly friend).*
   Do you feel that you have experienced His presence? If so, please describe what you mean by such an experience. *Never.*
   How vague or how distinct is it? How does it affect you mentally and physically?
   If you have had no such experience, do you accept the testimony of others who claim to have felt God's presence directly? Please answer this question with special care and in as great detail as possible. *Yes! The whole line of testimony on this point is so strong that I am unable to pooh-pooh it away. No doubt there is a germ in me of something similar that makes response.*
6. Do you pray, and if so, why? That is, is it purely from habit, and social custom, or do you really believe that God hears your prayers? *I can't possibly pray–I feel foolish and artificial.*
   Is prayer with you one-sided or two-sided—i.e., do you sometimes feel that in prayer you receive something—such as strength or the divine spirit—from God? Is it a real communion?
7. What do you men by 'spirituality'? *Susceptibility to ideals, but with a certain freedom to indulge in imagination about them. A certain amount of 'other worldly' fancy. Otherwise you have mere mortality, or 'taste'.*
   Describe a typical spiritual person. *Phillips Brooks.*
8. Do you believe in personal immortality? *Never keenly; but more strongly as I grow older.* If so, why? *Because I am just getting fit to live.*
9. Do you accept the Bible as *authority* in religious matters? Are your religious faith and your religious life based on it? If so, how would your belief in God and your life toward Him and your fellow men be affected by loss of faith in the *authority* of the Bible? *No. No. No. It is so human a book that I don't see how belief in its divine authorship can survive the reading of it.*
10. What do you mean by a 'religious experience'? *Any moment of life that brings the reality of spiritual things more 'home' to one.*

VARIETIES OF HELPLESSNESS
AND RELIGIOUS EXPERIENCE

ROGER A. JOHNSON

"To suggest personal will and effort to one 'all sicklied o'er' with the sense of irremediable impotence is to suggest the most impossible of things. What he craves is to be consoled in his very powerlessness, to feel that the spirit of the universe recognizes and secures him, all decaying and failing as he is. Well, we are all such helpless failures in the last resort. The sanest and best of us are of one clay with lunatics and prison inmates."
William James, *The Varieties of Religious Experience* (1902)

"To suggest personal will and effort to one 'all sicklied o'er' with the sense of weakness, of helpless failure, and of fear is to suggest the most horrible of things to him. What he craves is to be consoled in his very impotence, to feel that the Powers of the Universe recognize and secure him, all passive and failing as he is. Well, we are all *potentially* such sick men. The sanest and best of us are of one clay with lunatics and prison inmates."
William James, "Introduction," *The Literary Remains of the late Henry James* (1884)[1]

It is exceptional for an author to repeat himself almost verbatim after the passage of two decades. That James did so testifies to the strength of his conviction that the sense of helplessness is the source of religious need.

INTRODUCTION

Most of us live most of our lives feeling that we are in control—not, as gods, with unlimited control—but with that blundering competence characteristic of our species. We make choices and initiate actions. We respond to other people in ways appropriate to our needs and sense of self. Such activities may not bring us the exalted self-confidence of William Henley's "Invictus"—"I am the captain of my soul, the master of my fate"—but they are sufficient for confidently navigating our way through life. With any luck, most of us come to take for granted such a state of mind.

Despite such a mind-set, events sometimes break in to undermine our usual sense of confidence. We may become ill, overpowered by an infection, with our survival in jeopardy. We may lose our job, and find that our work experience has become obsolete. The people we love and need the most may die, or simply leave us. And finally, we may become so anxious, guilt-ridden, or depressed as to destroy every remnant of our normal sense of self. Suddenly or slowly, we who had been in charge of our lives begin to feel like victims. We become helpless.

In William James's judgment, such experiences of needing help are an essential ingredient of religious experience.

That attitude which the individual finds himself impelled to take up towards what he apprehends to be the divine...will prove to be both a helpless and a sacrificial attitude (VRE: 51).

---

1. William James, *The Varieties of Religious Experience* (1985: 46; hereafter VRE); William James, introduction to *The Literary Remains of the Late Henry James* (1884: 117-118).

...in the presence of (such) a need for help...is the real core of the religious problem: Help! Help! (VRE: 162).

...just as of yore, the devout man tells you that in the solitude of his room or of the fields he still feels the divine presence, that inflowing of help come in reply to his prayers (VRE: 498).

This theme of helplessness was also prominent in the many narratives of religious conversion which James quoted.

Dear Jesus, can you help me? (S.H. Hadley, pp. 202-3).
I saw that it was forever impossible for me to do anything towards helping or delivering myself (David Brainerd, p. 213).
O help me, help, thou redeemer of souls, and save me, or I am gone forever (Henry Alline, p. 218).

For James, only "the sentiment of human helplessness [could] open a profounder view and put into our hands a more complicated key to the meaning of the [human] situation" (p. 136).

My purpose in this essay is to examine several types of helplessness and their religious consequences, in order to identify the singularity of William James's personal experience of helplessness and his model of religion. I will first report several experiences of helplessness which lead to religious outcomes quite different from those projected by James. Near the conclusion of the essay, I will focus on the distinctive form of helplessness experienced by William James and his father, Henry James.

Experiences of helplessness are not the same for all people, but reflect the many factors that shape individual lives: social and economic class, race and gender, family origins and cultural context, personal history and psychological condition.

Experiences of helplessness thus come in all shapes and sizes. Sometimes experiences from our past will be decisive for making us feel helpless in the present; sometimes it is the fear of living through certain situations again that provoke our panic. Other people may play significant roles in triggering such experiences, or resolving them; at other times, such experiences may be private, rooted in our internal struggle to sustain our sense of self against subjective or objective threats. Sometimes our bodies provide the locus for such experiences; sometimes it is our self-esteem. In brief, helplessness is not a uniform experience common to all people.

William James, however, did not offer his readers a variety of experiences of helplessness, but consistently relied on one very specific type of helplessness. Because it was the only model he offered, it acquired a normative role in his account of religious experiences. While I do not wish to dismiss the kind of helplessness James has described—for it is too powerful a force in human life to be taken lightly—I do want to loosen its hold upon the imagination of students of religion. Experiences of helplessness come in as many varieties as do religious experiences; by acknowledging some alternatives, we may better appreciate the very distinctive form of helplessness portrayed by James.

PSYCHOLOGICAL MODELS OF HELPLESSNESS IN RELIGION: WILLIAM JAMES AND SIGMUND FREUD

William James and Sigmund Freud have long been recognized as the co-founders of psychology of religion. On almost every issue, these two disagreed substantially with each other, and the tension created by their fundamental differences has continued to enliven the work of others. On one matter, however, they appear to be in agreement. Both identify helplessness as the decisive antecedent condition for the emergence of religion.

The Future of an Illusion presents Freud's most developed argument concerning the psychological origins of religious belief. Early in that book, Freud noted that

> nature rises up before us, sublime, pitiless, inexorable; thus she brings again to mind our weakness and helplessness (Freud 1957: 23).

Freud believed that humans coped with nature by projecting a supernatural, human-like identity onto these powerful, uncontrollable forces. That way, said Freud, "We are perhaps still defenseless, but no longer helplessly paralyzed; we can at least react "(p. 25). The prototype for this reaction to helplessness is the situation of human infancy.

> For once before one has been in such a state of helplessness: as a little child in one's relationship to one's parents. For one had reason to fear them, especially the father...Similarly man makes the forces of nature not simply in the image of men with whom he can associate as his equals—that would not do justice to the over-powering impression they make on him—but he gives them the characteristics of the father, makes them into gods "(p. 27).

In Freud's view, the very survival of religion depended upon humanity's continuing experience of helplessness. As long as "men's helplessness remains...[so does] their father-longing and the gods," for religion is "born of the need to make tolerable the helplessness of man "(pp. 27, 29).

Although both men's theories of religion relied on a universalized experience of help-lessness, their interpretations of how this experience generates religion differed sharply. First, they assumed quite different models of helplessness. For Freud, the model was developmental: the prototype for adult feelings of helplessness was the genuine vulnera-bility experienced by an infant or toddler who has physical and psychological needs which only an adult can meet. The adult believer, however, has regressed to infantile behavior when he adopts a helpless posture before God, a father-figure. James, by con-trast, located the response of helplessness in his personality theory. According to James's typology of personalities, some people will find themselves caught in long-term situa-tions or repeated experiences of helplessness and others will not. For James, the experi-ence of helplessness is characteristic of one type of personality, not, as with Freud, a child-ish response to an adult situation.

Second, the two authors differed markedly in their theorized consequences of such experiences of helplessness. For Freud, such behavior by adults is not only regressive, but dysfunctional. Like the Stoics before him, Freud admonished his readers to grow up, accept those losses which cannot be avoided, and thereby preserve the strength of their rationality for facing the worst of situations. James, however, found that far from being dysfunctional, the experience of helplessness accurately reflected the actual conditions of human life, including the destructive and evil forces which the culture otherwise denies. For this reason, he sought out testimonies of despair recorded in hymns, diaries, and poet-ry with the intent of reclaiming their witness to the deepest human reality. In his words,

> The normal process of life contains moments as bad as any of those which insane melancholy is filled with, moments in which radical evil gets its innings and takes its solid turn. The lunatic's visions of horror are all drawn from the material of daily fact. Our civilization is founded on the shambles, and every individual existence goes out in a lonely spasm of helpless agony (VRE: 163).

Furthermore, in James's psychology, experiences of helplessness offer decisive therapeutic moments for the religious transformation of individuals. One outcome of such helplessness is a radical surrender of self which James believed was also essential to those kinds of religious experience he found most valuable.

Self-surrender always has been and always must be regarded as the vital turning point of the religious life (VRE: 210).

In any form of religious life—the saint, the mystic, or the convert—the "religious genius" is the person who has not only come in contact with that abject impotence fundamental to the human condition, but has also been released from its burden through a radical surrender of self for the sake of union with some greater power.[2] While James recognized the neurotic element characteristic of such extreme confessions of helplessness and self-surrender, he insisted upon the irreplaceable value of such experiences. Only such a movement of the self—from helplessness to self-surrender—can yield the deepest insights and most profound transformations of the individual.

The agreement between Freud and James on the prominence of helplessness in the origins of religion indicates its importance. In the discussion that follows, I will be concerned only with James's account of helplessness and religion. I have introduced Freud in this preliminary section only to avoid any confusion between him and James.

MY EXPERIENCES OF HELPLESSNESS: WITH OTHERS BUT WITHOUT GOD

When I was younger, and more likely to give authority to what I read in books, William James's texts about being helpless and religious disturbed me. Like most people, I had found myself helpless more than once, but I never found such experiences to be particularly religious. In fact, on occasions when others introduced some religious act into a helpless situation, I found their behavior to be puzzling, if not ridiculous. Perhaps there was something wrong with me. Why should I find such helplessness so devoid of any direct presence of God when the experiences reported by James seemed to lead inevitably to some religious outcome? Perhaps I was one of those people without religious sensibilities. James recognized that such people do exist, and came close to identifying himself with that group. He described such persons as "anaesthetic on the religious side, deficient in that category of sensibility "(VRE: 205).

---

2. For James it was specifically the absence of self that differentiated religious behavior from moral behavior: "This abandonment of self-responsibility seems to be the fundamental act in specifically religious, as distinguished from moral practice" (VRE: 289). In describing traditional forms of saintly behavior, James repeatedly identified self-surrender as the inner power or source of such behavior. For self-denial or asceticism, "the self-surrender may become so passionate as to turn into self-immolation" (p. 273); for charity "the sand and grit of the selfhood incline to disappear, [allowing] tenderness to rule" (p. 279); for obedience, "obedience may spring from the general religious phenomenon of inner softening and self-surrender and throwing oneself on higher powers" (p. 311); for poverty, "over and above the mystery of self-surrender, there are in the cult of poverty other religious mysteries" (p. 323).

Essential to mysticism, in all religious traditions, is the annihilation of the separation between the self and the sacred: "The overcoming of all the usual barriers between the individual and the Absolute is the great mystic achievement. In mystic states we both become one with the Absolute and we become aware of our oneness. This is the everlasting and triumphant mystical tradition, hardly altered by differences of clime or creed" (p. 419).

The nature which is spiritually barren may admire and envy faith in others, but can never compass the enthusiasm and peace which those who are temperamentally qualified for faith enjoy "(p. 205).

However, even such anaesthetic people as James himself became religious when overcome by helplessness. I did not, and I was certain that my own experiences of helplessness did not correspond with his theoretical model or the confessional narratives of his sources. I will recount two such occasions as a potential corrective for the Jamesian model, with the hope that my narratives may trigger recollections of helpless moments experienced by others.

When I was twelve, I was struck by a car on one side of the road and dragged under that car across the street until the car was finally stopped by a grocer's wall. The brakes on this antique Model A had failed, so a grocery store temporarily filled that need. The owner, Mr. Antilla, was not pleased to have his canned goods on the outside wall knocked off their shelves. He raced out of his store to find the culprit, and discovered not only the car, but me underneath it. I had somehow become wedged in a bent-over position under the front axle and was, without qualification, helpless. While I heard things going on around me, I was not able to move, to speak, or even to cry out for help.

The young driver was too scared to get out of the car and check my condition, but I could hear him tell Mr. Antilla that he was going to back off of me. Because I was wedged under the front axle, this most certainly would have killed me, but I still could not scream. I heard Mr. Antilla cursing as, in one motion, he grabbed the driver by his shoulders, threw him out of the car, and lifted up its front end by himself, while ordering my friend to drag my body out from under the axle.

Before the ambulance appeared, my sister arrived, falling to her knees to pray for me. I vividly remember my response to her action: while her love for me made me feel good, it seemed absurd for her to call upon God now. Mr. Antilla, whether acting out of his own self-interest as an injured grocer or as an agent of God, had already saved my life. The drama was over; only the pain and injuries were left.

While this terrifying experience did not bring me closer to God, it did change my view of other people. Mr. Antilla and I had not been friends, to put it mildly. He was on my list of enemies, where my twelve-year-old mind assumed he would remain for all eternity. My buddies and I had repeatedly provoked his wrath by making a nuisance of ourselves in his store. We would rearrange merchandise on his shelves or delay a customer waiting at the cash register while we took our time choosing the perfect penny candy. More than once, he had thrown us out of his store, accompanied by a litany of his curses. He was not the sort of person I would have chosen as a rescuer. His actions on that day made me question my view of human beings as always divided into two camps—friends and enemies. But a new appreciation of my former adversary was not the same as an experience of God.

Other moments of helplessness have been equally devoid of religious sentiment. While looking for a child lost off a mountain trail, I stepped on a sloping rock face with just enough moss under foot to send me rolling. It was too slippery and steep for me to stop my roll, so I went right over the edge. Luckily, a small birch was growing from a ledge fifteen feet below, and I grabbed it. Instead of feeling close to God while rolling down this mountain, I worried about the others who would now have to come searching for me. Would they make the same misstep that I had? How would they get my body out of the ravine into which I was falling, since there were no trails there?

On both of these occasions, I was helpless to alter my fate. Nevertheless, I did not feel myself ensconced within God's almighty care, but entangled with other people in ways that were surprising or foolish. For some time, I used to worry about my response to such experiences. If the movement through helplessness to God was as fundamental to the religious life as James claimed, there must be something fatally wrong in my soul, some profound alienation from God, some radical deficiency of religious sentiment. While I gave up such worries long ago, I did so only as a result of a lengthy reappraisal of William James. In the following, I report two of the turning points in this process.

HELPLESSNESS IN COMMUNITY: WITH GOD THROUGH OTHERS

I first began to make sense of my differences with James while conducting research as part of a study of "effective" religious communities. The purpose of the study was to identify the characteristics of an "effective" congregation as perceived by its lay members. Nine congregations were selected for the study from a broad geographical area of North America and with a diverse mix of racial groups, social classes, and economic conditions.[3]

I began the study by interviewing members of a congregation located in an Appalachian corner of West Virginia. The interview questions I had prepared in advance were designed to let people talk about their individual religious experiences. At the beginning of the project, I had assumed that William James was more or less correct in his definition of religion:

the feelings, acts, and experiences of individual men in their solitude, so far as they apprehend themselves to stand in relation to whatever they may consider the divine (VRE: 31).

However, when I asked people questions about what they experienced "in their solitude" —either physically alone in private devotions and prayer, or psychologically alone before God at worship with others—the answers I received were limited to a few words and no feelings. The tapes of these first interviews consisted of nothing but polite answers given to a visiting authority from up North.

My first break-through occurred while interviewing one of the lay leaders of this congregation. He and I sat in his living room, where he provided more polite answers. His wife was knitting in an adjoining room where she could overhear our conversation. After she had become as frustrated with this dull exchange as I, she interrupted to give me some help. She very kindly told me that I could not be expected to understand the religious life of their community since I was not part of it. She suggested that I ask people about any experiences of God they might have had through their relations with others in that congregation. "Most of us are very simple people, and we meet God in our neighbors, not by ourselves."

Thanks to this woman's interruption, I was delivered from my bondage to William James's invidividualistic model of religion. I threw away my original batch of questions and wrote new ones asking about the interaction of people within this religious community. Instead of brief answers with no affect, my new questions unleashed a torrent of religious experiences, punctuated with many sighs and tears. The answers to these questions also forced me to consider a quite different model of being helpless and being religious.

Here is one example from this Appalachian corner of West Virginia. I was speaking with a man in his eighties. He was a widower who lived by himself and still worked his small farm. His sixty-year old daughter drove me to his farm and, in honor of our visit, he

---

3. The results of this study were published by the commissioning denominations (Johnson, 1979).

had prepared a meal. Sitting at his table, I asked him about any experiences in his life when others in the congregation were particularly important for him. He proceeded to tell me of the time his cow had fallen while he was milking her, breaking his leg in the process. This accident occurred shortly after the death of his wife, and his only help on the farm was his ten year old daughter (the same one then in her sixties). As he remembered the names of the men who, fifty years ago, had come from the church to harvest his crops when he was helpless, the tears flowed from his eyes and he confessed that he has never known God's love so strongly before or since. Indeed, his fifty-year-old tale was so vivid that I sometimes found myself believing that it must have happened the previous day.

After interviewing lay people and clergy from other congregations, I learned that most effective clergy already knew what this old farmer taught me: when people are in a crisis, in situations that make them feel helpless, they often transfer to the minister or helping lay persons the full presence of that God celebrated in the public worship of their community.[4] Sometimes, the objective situation was changed by their help, as in the case of the Appalachian farmer whose harvest was saved. More often, there was nothing anyone could do to remedy the objective situation, but their simple presence could transform the subjective experience of helplessness from despair to hope. What seemed to matter most was the presence of these others who were there, not only in their own right, but also as representatives of a power greater than them all.

The dynamics of helplessness in these religious communities were quite different from those reported by William James. First, the focus of their stories was never upon the disastrous turn of events that led up to the crisis. The fall of the cow upon the farmer's leg was reported in an unemotional way: it was a normal risk of farming life with some bad luck, but not a big surprise. Such a narrative is quite different from the long psychological struggles characteristic of James's sources, which recounted interminable efforts to overcome a problem, such as alcoholism or depression or guilt, and which ended in failure before the moment of conversion.

Second, the source of terror in such experiences was most often social, rooted in a person's bonds with others. Only the social conditions surrounding the cow's fall made that event a source of deep anxiety: the recent death of the farmer's wife who had been his only helpmate for running the farm; the age of his only child who was too young to handle the harvest; the fear of losing a year's crop that would not wait for a broken leg to heal; his economic dependence on the farm to support not only himself, but his child. If one abstracts the farmer from this network of relationships, his broken leg becomes a mere nuisance. The helpless terror triggered by the broken leg was social in its origins and consequences.

Third, when people in religious communities recounted their stories of being helpless in times of crisis, they consistently emphasized the amazing intervention of others. One such story was recounted for me more than a dozen times by different members of a suburban congregation. One of the families of this church had rushed a child to the emergency room only to find their minister already there, waiting for them in his fishing clothes. He had heard the news just as he returned home from his day off, and had not bothered to change into conventional attire before hurrying to the hospital. In the collective memory of this congregation, their minister's fishing garb and prompt arrival became a powerful symbol of the appropriate response to someone in need. He embodied

---

4. In psychoanalytic terms, the stories I heard of God's presence most often resembled a shared transference relationship rather than a private projection.

the caring, loving God who seeks out the one lost sheep, the lost coin, or the prodigal son without regard to the normal rules of propriety and prudent self-interest. By listening to many such stories of spontaneous and selfless care, I learned that religious communities provide effective intervention in moments of helplessness, and a rich symbolic framework for interpreting such experiences.

Fourth, I did not once hear of an episode of helplessness which led to self-surrender and union with a higher power. As long-term members of religious communities, these people had already become accustomed to yielding parts of themselves in order to be united with their community. What they had known of God from the words and symbols of their worship, they now experienced directly from others in their time of need. Therefore, a renewed devotion to their congregation and their faith was the most frequent result I heard from these stories of helplessness.

Such stories dramatically changed my understanding of the dynamics of helplessness. For these people, the experience of moving from helplessness, through salvation, to trust and commitment was always a communal one—very unlike the interiorized, individualized experience of self-surrender and transcendent union reported by James.

HELPLESSNESS FOR WILLIAM JAMES: THE NORM OF MELANCHOLY

For William James, helplessness came in a very specific form, which he knew all too well from his father's life and his own.[5] He chose the term "melancholy" for this condition, and his book on religious experience was in part a vindication of the suffering he and his father had endured. William interpreted their dreadful experience in order to reveal a profound truth of the human condition and to sketch a therapeutic model for self-transformation.

While James referred to melancholy and its significance for religious experience throughout the whole of his book (e.g., pp. 6,10,24,505), he concentrated his most substantive discussion of this mental affliction in the chapter on "The Sick Soul". James began this chapter by citing some of the more common experiences of loss or evil:

> Take the happiest man, the one most envied by the world, and in nine cases out of ten his inmost consciousness is one of failure (VRE: 137). Failure, then failure! so the world stamps us at every turn (VRE: 138).

Perceiving the prominence of failure in one's life is "only the first stage of the world-sickness "(p. 139). Recognizing that all goods are transient, that death alone is final, and that life itself is meaningless constitutes the next step in the transformation of ordinary people into "melancholy metaphysicians" (pp. 139-140).

Yet, even these steps on the road to melancholy are not yet real melancholy.

> For this extremity of pessimism to be reached, something more is needed than observation of life and reflection upon death. The individual must in his own person become the prey of pathological melancholy. [Only then] is the subject of melancholy forced in spite of himself to ignore [the existence] of all good whatever

---

5. William James and his father have become a favorite subject for biographers, historians, and psychohistorians. For a bibliography of such works see King 1983: 385: King devotes the two longest chapters of this work to Henry James the Elder and William James. For a broad if simplified historical sketch of melancholy and its role in Protestantism, see Rubin 1994.

...Such sensitiveness and susceptibility to mental pain is a rare occurrence where the nervous constitution is entirely normal...So we note here the neurotic constitution making its active entrance on our scene, and destined to play a part in much that follows (VRE: 144-145).

Unlike his father, who attributed an acute episode of his own melancholy to God as a gift necessary for his salvation, William James identified such melancholy as a neurosis: a "pathological depression" which could take many different forms (VRE: 145; for Henry James Senior, see footnote 8).

James identified three types of religious melancholy. First was the "subjectively centered form of morbid melancholy" (VRE: 203). In such cases, the depression from which a person suffered had its origins in an overwhelming sense of sin, guilt, or worthlessness. As examples of such a type of melancholy, James quoted extensively from St. Augustine, Martin Luther, John Bunyan, and Henry Alline (a Nova Scotian evangelist). Second were the "objective forms of melancholy in which the lack of rational meaning of the universe...is the burden that weighs upon one " (pp. 203-204). Tolstoy was the most frequently cited source of the radical meaninglessness of life. His third form of melancholy was a "fear of the universe" that was so overpowering as to be a "panic fear" (pp. 160-161). For his source on this "worst kind of melancholy", James quoted an anonymous French text which he personally translated. This French source was later revealed to be James himself.[6]

At the time he experienced his "panic fear", James was in a "state of philosophic pessimism and general depression of spirits about my prospects" (VRE: 160). Upon entering a room at dusk, he was suddenly overcome by "a horrible fear of my own existence" and a mental "image of an epileptic patient ... with greenish skin ... entirely idiotic" observed by him in an asylum.

This image and my fear entered into a species of combination with each other. *That shape am I*, I felt, potentially ... After this the universe was changed for me altogether. I awoke morning after morning with a horrible dread at the pit of my stomach, and with a sense of the insecurity of life that I never knew before ... I have always thought that this experience of melancholia of mine had a religious bearing ... The fear was so invasive and powerful that if I had not clung to scripture-texts like 'The eternal God is my refuge,' etc., 'Come unto me, all ye that labor and are heavy-laden,' etc., 'I am the resurrection and the life,' etc., I think I should have grown really insane "(VRE: 160-161).

In a footnote to his tale, William James also referred his readers to an episode in his father's life which he had recounted in the "Introduction" to *The Literary Remains of the Late Henry James*[7] (James: 1884). As with his own experience, this was "another case of fear

---

6. Henry James III identified his father as the anonymous "French correspondent" quoted in *The Varieties of Religious Experience* (1920, I: 145ff). By comparing the story with diary entries, Henry James III was able to locate this incident in the Spring of 1870, three decades before his father cited that experience. "It was during this period that ... bad health, a feeling of the purposelessness of his own particular existence, his philosophic doubts and his constant preoccupation with them, all these combined to plunge him into a state of morbid depression" (ibid.).

7. In his footnote in *The Varieties of Religious Experience*, William James referred his readers to the original publication (of the Swedenborgian Church) in which his father's story appeared: "Society the Redeemed Form of Man," Boston, 1879. The brief summary of that narrative included here is taken from William James's "Introduction," pp. 58-67.

equally sudden" and associated with a vision of a quasi-human figure (p. 161). In May 1844, Henry James Senior was "suddenly—in a lightning flash as it were"—overcome by a "perfectly insane and abject terror ... only to be accounted for ... by some damned shape squatting invisible to me within the precincts of the room and raying out from his fetid personality influences fatal to life "(James 1884: 59). Both narratives reported the paralyzing consequences of the original experience of fear and helplessness, extending for years for Henry and for months for William. In both cases, help came only through reading and believing a text whose message promised deliverance from depression: Swedenborg's religious writings for Henry James,[8] and Charles Renouvier's essays on Free Will for William.[9]

Melancholy or depression, in any of its types, offers a unique and powerful instance of helplessness. In sharp contrast with the examples of helplessness cited earlier in this essay, other people play a marginal role, if any, in the onset or relief of severe depression. In the case of depressive episodes, James was correct in observing that "these experiences of melancholy are in the first instance absolutely private and individual" (VRE: 145). His definition of religion—"the feelings, acts, and experiences of individual men in their solitude"—is therefore consistent with that particular form of helplessness with which he was most familiar and which became normative for his reflections on religion.

HELPLESSNESS IN PROTESTANT THEOLOGY

Throughout his book on religious experience, James called attention to the congruence between the kind of helplessness experienced in melancholy and Christian theology. Describing experiences of sin or guilt, James noted that

This is the religious melancholy and 'conviction of sin' that have played so large a part in the history of Protestant Christianity (VRE: 170-171).

Later, in commenting on two quotations from Martin Luther, he further emphasized the "admirable congruity" between Protestantism and the helplessness of melancholy:

8. Henry James consulted numerous physicians about his debilitating condition which began in May, 1844. Although he took the best available water-cures, his condition persisted without relief until he chanced to meet a disciple of Swedenborg. She informed him that he was "undergoing what Swedenborg calls a *vastation*," one of the stages through which God gives new birth to men, so that she could only take "an altogether hopeful view of [his] prospects." Mr. James then sought out some books by Swedenborg and found there "the amplest *rationale* I could have desired of my own particular suffering, as inherent in the profound unconscious death I bore about in my *proprium* or selfhood." "[From] a sentiment of death pervading all consciousness, [he was] lifted by a sudden miracle into felt harmony with universal man, and filled to the brim with the sentiment of indestructible life instead" ("Introduction", *The Literary Remains of Henry James*, pp. 64ff).
9. After quoting William James's account of "panic fear," Henry James III cited an entry from his father's diary dated April 30, 1870: "I think that yesterday was a crisis in my life. I finished the first part of Renouvier's second 'Essais' and see no reason why his definition of Free Will—'The sustaining of a thought *because I choose* to when I might have other thoughts'—need be the definition of an illusion. At any rate, I will assume for the present—until next year—that it is no illusion. My first act of free will shall be to believe in free will ... Hitherto, when I have felt like taking a free initiative, like daring to act originally ... suicide seemed the most manly form to put my daring into; now, I will go a step further with my will, not only act with it, but believe as well; believe in my individual reality and creative power. My belief, to be sure, *can't* be optimistic—but I will posit life (the real, the good) in the self-governing *resistance* of the ego to the world" (Henry James, I, pp. 187-188).

It is needless to remind you once more of the admirable congruity of Protestant theology with the structure of the mind as shown in such experiences. In the extreme of melancholy the self that consciously *is* can do absolutely nothing. It is completely bankrupt and without resource, and no works it can accomplish will avail. Redemption from such subjective conditions must be a free gift or nothing, and grace through Christ's accomplished sacrifice is such a gift...Nothing in Catholic theology, I imagine, has ever spoken to sick souls as straight as this message from Luther's personal experience (VRE: 244-246).

There is, however, a wide gap between the very particular and limited role of helplessness in Protestant theology, and its more pervasive role in the thought of William James. For Luther, Calvin, and their followers, the helplessness of humanity is restricted to one specific goal: people are helpless to win their own salvation. That one task, of ultimate significance for each individual, is set outside the boundaries of human capacities. No moral, religious, or intellectual activity will make anyone more acceptable to God. No matter how any of us may conceive of the ultimate, eternal, or infinite, it remains the one realm which human beings cannot reach by their own efforts. Instead, Protestant theology focuses on those promises of God enacted in the work of Christ which have done for all of humanity what no one could do for her or himself.

When the message of divine grace for human helplessness is correctly heard, a person is liberated and empowered to do all the other tasks of this world. Thus, while we may be helpless to contribute to our salvation, we do shape our earthly destiny. For Protestant theology, helplessness is therefore not a fundamental characteristic of the human condition, as James would suggest. To the contrary, we are commissioned to use our talents for the benefit of others.

Contemporary psychiatrists developed the drug Prozac, not to interpret melancholy, but to relieve depression. While pharmacological revolution may be beyond the aspirations of most people, anyone can help a neighbor overcome the despair of a helpless condition: by securing the economic independence of a one parent family, as in the case of the Appalachian farmer; by standing in solidarity with an anxious family in the emergency room, as did the fisherman-minister; or by pulling mad drivers out from behind the wheel of their car, as an angry grocer did for me many years ago.

It may be that all of us become helpless at times, not for the sake of religious experience, but in order to discover the depths of our bonds with others and the purpose of our lives within that finite arena we know as the human family.

REFERENCES

Freud, S. (1957). *The Future of an Illusion*. Garden City, NY: Doubleday Anchor.

James, H. (Ed.) (1920). *The Letters of William James*, 2 vols. Boston: Atlantic Monthly Press.

James, W. (1985). *The Varieties of Religious Experience*. New York: Penguin.

————(Ed.) (1884). *The Literary Remains of the Late Henry James*. Boston: Houghton Mifflin. Republished: Upper Saddle River, NJ: Literature House/Gregg Press, 1970.

Johnson, R.A. (1979). *Congregations as Nurturing Communities*. Philadelphia. PA: Lutheran Church in America.

King, J.O. (1983). *The Iron of Melancholy*. Middletown, CT: Wesleyan University Press.

Rubin, J.H. (1994). *Religious Melancholy and Protestant Experience in America*. New York: Oxford University Press.

DIVIDED SELVES AND THE
"HUE OF RESOLUTION": A COMPARATIVE STUDY
OF WILLIAM JAMES AND MAX SCHELER

MARK RALLS

In the *Principles of Psychology* (1918; hereafter PP), William James identifies three methods of psychological study—introspection, measurement, and comparison. While introspection has the pivotal task of "looking into our own minds and reporting what we there discover," measurement seeks to eliminate the "uncertainty" of this activity through the use of "statistical means" (PP: 185, 192). These methods are then followed by comparison which "supplements" them by tracing "the phenomenon considered through all its possible variations of type and combination" (p. 194).

Despite James's insistence upon the methodological priority of introspection, comparison seems to be his preferred method for the study of religion. In *The Varieties of Religious Experience* (1982; hereafter VRE), James relies upon the comparative method on at least two levels of reflection. At a more abstract level, he compares a variety of types. For example, the healthy-minded are compared with sick souls, the unified self is compared with the self that remains divided, and the religious saint is compared with Nietzsche's ideal type—"the strong man." Within these different types, James considers the even greater variety of religious experience found in the lives of individuals. At this more concrete level, he compares those particular encounters with the divine that elude all attempts to place them into meaningful categories.

By considering the religious experiences of William James and Max Scheler alongside one another, I will be using comparison in a way that is reminiscent of James's own methodological strategies. A comparison of James and another interpreter of religion reveals the relationship between pivotal occurrences in James's own life and his investigations of religious experience. It becomes evident that he drew upon his own encounters with the divine to understand conversion as the resolution of personal crisis. In this way, a new understanding of James's study of religion emerges out of an approach that is, in a sense, prefigured in *The Varieties* itself.

In perhaps the most influential chapter of *The Varieties*, James employs the method of comparison to examine two kinds of religious conversion—the "type by self-surrender" and the "voluntary type" (VRE: 206). He describes the former as a "real, definite, and memorable" event when an "extraneous higher power" has "flooded in and taken possession of the soul" (VRE: 207, 210). James compares this "vital turning point" with a more "gradual" type of development in which "a new set of moral and spiritual habits" are built up "piece by piece" (VRE: 210, 206). While these persons do not experience the "full flood of ecstatic liberation," they gradually achieve a level of cohesion which overcomes their inner division. Through voluntary acts of the will, they slowly and painfully attain the "hue of resolution" (VRE: 188).

As examples of this voluntary type of conversion, James compares the lives of Leo Tolstoy and John Bunyan. He considered Tolstoy to be a "heterogeneous personality" who "slowly" overcame the division between his "inner character" and his "outer activities" by accepting belief in "the idea of God" and "the divinity of the soul" (VRE: 186, 184). By "gradually and imperceptibly" discovering his "genuine habitat and vocation," Tolstoy was able to get "his soul in order," achieve "unity," and restore "energy" to his life (VRE: 185-186). John Bunyan's recovery, on the other hand, was both slower and more "tumultuous." For Bunyan, peace came intermittently with the "guilt and fear" that ran through his soul like the "roar and bellow" of "masterless hell-hounds." He finally experienced resolution in an "ever growing relief" as the "tempest" and "thunder" which fell upon his soul were reduced to "only some drops" (VRE: 186-187).

Despite their different religious experiences, Tolstoy and Bunyan shared this voluntary type of conversion which did not provide them with a complete and final resolution. As James puts it, "they had drunk too deeply of the cup of bitterness ever to forget its taste" (VRE: 187). While the "effective edge" of their sadness was broken, it remained a "minor ingredient" of the very faith which had overcome the intensity of their inner division. Thus, they were not offered the resolved certainty of the "healthy-minded," but rather the "hue of resolution" attained by those have gained the insight that life holds both tragedy and promise. They found themselves along the arduous path of those who struggle toward redemption by stumbling into "a universe two-stories deep" (VRE: 187).

A COMPARISON OF WILLIAM JAMES AND MAX SCHELER

The German sociologist and religious philosopher, Max Scheler, is rarely discussed in connection with William James. In one sense, this neglect is surprising because they shared a strong interest in the study of religion, and they both published works on religious experience in the early twentieth century. In 1902, James's Gifford lectures were published as *The Varieties of Religious Experience*, and in 1916, Scheler's work on the phenomenology of religion entitled, *On the Eternal in Man*, made its appearance in Germany.

Yet, it is also understandable that these two scholars are rarely mentioned in the same breath. They seem as unlikely a pair as Tolstoy and Bunyan. In fact, popular interpretations of William James and Max Scheler place them on opposite poles. James is often understood to be a pure individualist whose pragmatic approach to life extolled the effective as the most worthwhile. Scheler, on the other hand, is viewed as a strict communitarian who placed hope in solidarity and eschewed pragmatism as a seduction of bourgeoisie society which mistakenly confuses the expedient with the most meaningful.

Despite these differences much can be gained by following James's own methodological strategy to consider this unlikely pair alongside one another. A comparison of James and Scheler reveals an important similarity connecting their life experiences with their subsequent studies of religion. Following in the path of Tolstoy and Bunyan, both James and Scheler attained only the "hue of resolution"—never quite leaving the tragic divisions of the past behind while pressing ahead toward the promise of their own redemption. Out of this common experience, they both drew upon the momentous occurrences of division and resolution in their own lives to interpret religious experience as a redemption from personal crisis.

For William James such a pivotal experience occurred as he struggled to discern his life's vocation. As a young man, James was torn between science and art. At the age of eighteen he decided to study painting, but soon changed his mind opting to attend Harvard medical school. This decision was a costly one. For the next few years he agonized over his withdrawal from the aesthetic life. He feared that by choosing science, he had lost the possibility of trusting blindly in something beyond his sensory observations. One year before he graduated from medical school this inner division culminated in a crisis that continued for the next five years (Lasch 1991: 287).

From 1868 to 1872, William James suffered an extended period of depression which brought him to the brink of suicide. In his anonymous memoir which appeared as a part of his 1901 Gifford lectures, he portrays these years as a time of despondency rooted in a paralyzing uncertainty whether life was truly worth the struggle. He describes waking up "morning after morning" with a "horrible dread at the pit of my stomach, and with a sense of the insecurity of life that I never felt before, and that I have never felt since" (VRE: 160).

James credits his ability to avoid suicide to his private prayers in which he quoted words of comfort from the Bible such as "The eternal God is my refuge" and "Come unto me all ye that labor and are heavy laden ..." (VRE: 161). Yet, while these prayers sustained him, a different sort of religious experience lies behind the resolution of this crisis. In 1872, James described in his diary a momentous decision that finally compelled him to break out of his "internal stagnation:"

> My first act of free will shall be to believe in free will ... Not in maxims ... but in accomplished acts of thought lies salvation (Darrow 1988: 217).

With this pronouncement, James apparently "willed" himself out of the depression which was depleting his inner resources. From that time on, he began a very productive career as a psychologist and philosopher living out the "strenuous life" which characterized his own initiative at the age of twenty-eight.

This momentous decision to "believe in free will" was, like those surrendering types of conversion, a "vital turning point" providing new direction for his life. Yet, like more voluntary types of conversion, this "liberation" was neither final nor complete. Throughout his life, James continued to struggle with melancholy. While he undoubtedly experienced a dramatic breakthrough from his "internal stagnation," this experience was not a final culmination or a complete resolution. Rather, it was a new beginning which set James, like Tolstoy before him, on the arduous path toward the cohesion of his "inner character" and his "outer activities."

Twenty-six years later, James experienced a different kind of religious resolution attained not by an act of the will but through surrendering his own initiative to a higher, cosmic power:

> I had a great crisis as I lay in bed ... A sort of moral revolution passed throughout me ... and the dear sacred Switzerland whose mountains, trees and grass and water ... all got mixed up into my mood; and in one torrent of adoration for them, for you, and for virtue, I rose towards the window to look at the scene ... mountain ... milky way ... big stars ... I had one of those moral thunderstorms that go all through you and give you such relief (Myers 1986: 51).

This time relief came not from his own inner resources but from a more mysterious source joining the depths of his being to the world around him. This "revolution" was not the moral initiative of the heroic individual but a flash of recognition of the virtue which encompassed his relationship with his wife and his place in the cosmos. It was a surrender of the self to a different kind of moral power which passed through him like a "thunderstorm."

In a letter of July 9, 1898, three years before he was to give the lectures which became *The Varieties of Religious Experience*, James wrote his wife to describe a strange occurrence while camping in the Adirondack mountains:

> I spent a good deal of [the night] in the woods where the streaming moonlight lit up things in a magical checkered play, and it seemed as if the gods of all the nature-mythologies were holding an indescribable meeting in my breast with the moral gods of the inner life. The two kinds of gods have nothing in common—the Edinburgh lecture made quite a hitch ahead ... the intense significance of some sort, of the whole scene, if one could only *tell* the significance ... I can't find a single word for all that significance, and don't know what it was significant of, so there it remains a boulder of *impression* (Myers 1986: 52).

In this experience, James encountered the most unsettling of spiritual strangers. He was offered the ambiguous assurance of an ineffable significance which is perhaps best described with words he applied to John Bunyan. Like Bunyan, James found himself at that paradoxical spiritual destination which is also a crossroads. He ran aground on a "boulder of impression" encountering here the unsettling presence of the "hue of resolution."

Like James, Max Scheler experienced a period of inner division while he was pursuing a doctorate in medicine. At the age of nineteen, a few months before he was to enter the University of Munich, Scheler had a liaison with a married woman who was eight years his senior. This affair left him in a state of moral confusion. In his studies at the university, Scheler found that at one moment he was able to grasp the most complex academic problem while discovering in the next that he was unable to resist abandoning his studies in favor of pursuing new sexual interests. He soon became too divided to devote himself to the study of medicine (Bershady 1993: 1-6).

While the inability to choose a vocation paralyzed William James with uncertainty, Scheler used his own indecision to galvanize some moral clarity in his life. Ridden with guilt over his breach of the tenets of the Catholic faith, he decided to leave medicine in order to dedicate himself to the study of moral philosophy (Bershady 1993: 1-6). In response to his transgressions, Scheler was compelled to study the religious experiences which he believed lay behind the moral life that had eluded him.

A second pivotal experience in Scheler's life occurred at the height of his academic career. When war was declared in 1914, Scheler responded, along with many other German intellectuals, by glorifying the war as a chance for Germany to fulfill its historical mission to the world (Staude 1967: 63-64). He wrote an essay entitled "The Genius of War" claiming that Germany's penchant for the spirit would guarantee her military success. When the skirmish extended into the first world war, Scheler expanded his brief essay into a book of several hundred pages. This work which celebrated the atoning powers of war was even more emotionally charged than his previous essay. Here Scheler proclaimed the coming of the war to be a "miracle" that opened the way for a new national spirit. He eulogized the war as "fresh air" capable of replacing the "musty fog of peace" (Staude 1967: 66-68, 72).

The patriotic zeal of this work was matched only by its popular appeal. Even though Scheler was completely unknown to most Germans until they read "The Genius of War," it was not long until almost every educated household in Germany owned a copy. By celebrating the German spirit of aggression, duty, and discipline, it quickly rose to the status of a classic, making Scheler famous throughout his country (Staude 1967: 80-81; Bershady 1993: 19-20).

Yet, in the midst of his rapidly increasing fame, Scheler shocked the German populace by abruptly changing his mind. By the end of the war, he was filled with remorse. In little more than a year, he had become thoroughly disillusioned with what he once considered to be the "unifying powers" of war. He no longer celebrated the war as a liberation from the individualism of the bourgeoisie society. At the end of 1915, he was convinced that the war was nothing less than the revelation of a baneful spirit which had the potential to destroy Europe (Staude 1967: 86-87).

Realizing his complicity in encouraging Germany's enthusiasm for war, Scheler retreated to a Benedictine abbey where he confessed his sins and began receiving once more the sacraments of the church. The following year, he published a very different book, entitled *On the Eternal in Man* (1960; hereafter OEM), reversing his earlier stance that had won him great popularity. He depicted war as a destructive force that had no hope for spiritual rebirth. He demanded that Germany bear responsibility for the suffering caused by the conflict, and he concluded that the only hope for a lasting harmony in

Europe was for each nation to repent and to affiliate under a renewed solidarity (Bershady 1993: 19-20).

Scheler, like Bunyan before him, was tormented by the tempest of guilt. Peace came slowly to his soul and, yet, slipped quickly away leaving him once again with the deliberate task of piecing his divided self back together. This tempest was only brought under control as he accepted a new vocational calling and reversed his views on the war. Thus, following in the path of Tolstoy, Scheler struggled toward redemption by building up new moral practices in greater coherence with his religious convictions, gradually attaining the "hue of resolution" through the strength of his own resolve.

William James and Max Scheler relied upon these different experiences of inner division as well as their common pursuit of resolution for their religious interpretations found in *The Varieties* and *On the Eternal in Man*. By extending this comparative study to their portrayals of the divided self, the experience of resolution, and the unified self, it is revealed that James and Scheler offer different interpretations within a single, common perspective.

THE DIVIDED SELF

James and Scheler drew upon their own experiences to describe the self in need of resolution. Out of his struggle with depression, James considered the primary religious problem to be a sickness of the soul characterized by melancholy and pessimism. Scheler, in response to his own moral confusion, viewed the greatest obstacle to the religious life to be the overwhelming power of guilt. Thus, they each turned to pivotal occurrences of division in their own lives to discern what they considered to be the deepest needs of the human soul.

James described the self in need of conversion as a "sick soul" who experiences "absolute disenchantment from ordinary life," "self-contempt," and "despair." Most of all, the sick soul is beset by a "panic fear" which occurs when the self is divided against its own purposes (VRE: 156-157). The sick soul witnesses the tragic roots of life with frightful clarity. In this "extremity of pessimism," melancholy reaches a "pathological" state that renders all of life meaningless. It is this confirmation with the abyss at the center of human existence which reveals the necessity of conversion. For James, only a radical cure of "religious deliverance" can bring resolution out of this recognition of the tragic (VRE: 144-145, 160).

Scheler, on the other hand, portrays the self in need of repentance as being overwhelmed by a "flood-tide of bygone guilt and wickedness." By producing "ever new guilt from old so that the pressure grows like an avalanche," the mistakes of the past divide the self against its present life "sweeping" the promises of its future "relentlessly away" (OEM: 4). For Scheler, the inner turbulence of guilt revealed the necessity of a spiritual power capable of resolving the self that is divided by its own past.

William James once wrote the British liberal L.T. Hobhouse, who strongly opposed American pragmatism, "Your bogey is superstition; my bogey is desiccation" (Lasch 1991: 295). If Max Scheler and William James had corresponded concerning what they believed to be the fundamental religious problem of life, Scheler would have named a bogey out of those inner feelings of guilt which overcome the soul like a powerful flood. James, in turn, would have pointed to an undertow that gradually pulls the life out of the soul leaving nothing but the shallow waters of disenchantment.

Their portrayals of the self in need of deliverance reveal very different interpretations of religious experience while also pointing to an important similarity. As those who attained no more than the "hue of resolution," James and Scheler were able to recognize both the depth of the chasm in the soul and the radical nature of any cure which sought to provide this divided self with resolution.

In response, they were both critical of the popular messages of their day that espoused simple solutions to problems which they knew from their own experience required ultimate answers. In *The Varieties,* James reserves most of his criticism for the remedies of the "healthy-minded" which offered sick souls trite slogans such as "God is well and so are you" or "Cheer up ... you'll be all right ... if only you will drop your morbidness!" (VRE: 108, 139-140). While James is suspicious of the religious optimist, Scheler denounced the easy salvation of the progressive who always looks ahead with the words, "No regrets— but do better in the future" (OEM: 56).

James considered the healthy-minded approach to life as a failure to recognize the underside of human existence. One who subscribes to this doctrine is a death-denying person whose "contentment with the finite incases him like a lobster-shell and shields him from all morbid repining at his distance from the Infinite" (VRE: 93). Religious optimists ignore the "breath of the sepulchre" that "surrounds" all of life. By neglecting the fragile character of human existence, these persons hope to forget that all human beings are "partners of death and the worm is their brother" (VRE: 139, 141).

The healthy-minded do not simply hide from existential questions, they also ignore the "smaller blunders, misdeeds and lost opportunities" that constitute the failures of every day life. James considers such seemingly incidental events to be "pivotal human experiences" that taken together constitute the "inmost consciousness of the self" to create the "subtlest form of suffering known to man." By sheltering themselves from the negatives of life, from the fear of death to the smallest mistake, healthy-minded persons live irreligious lives that respond to their fears by "consecrating" both "forgetfulness and superficiality" (VRE: 138-140).

James despised the insufficiency of popular remedies which offered simple cures to those ills of the soul that had brought him to the brink of suicide. For him, such positive thinking is an affront to the self in need of resolution. It is inadequate to motivate the inner depths of resolve that he discovered in his own decision "to believe in free will" after years of despair and disenchantment.

The religious progressives that Scheler criticizes are so afraid of the guilt that lies in their own past that this fear not only infiltrates their deeds but also contaminates the "schemes and resolutions" which precede their action. For Scheler, those who seek to escape guilt by looking only to the future are "eternal fugitives from their past." They are surprised to discover that such a flight only causes them to "sink deeper and deeper into the dead arms of that very past" which they hope to leave behind (OEM: 56).

Max Scheler could not tolerate such a superficial solution to the guilt that had plagued his own life. As one who had failed time and again to curtail the infidelity that threatened his career and ruined his marriages, he knew that the residue of guilt created chains that were too strong to be broken by those who only looked to the future.

Realizing from their own experience the difficulty of attaining merely the "hue of resolution," both James and Scheler feared the consequences of popular remedies which claimed to resolve the divisions of the self with simple solutions. James is concerned that we would lose sight of those unavoidable failures which plague us in small ways until we ultimately lose all desire for life. Scheler is more concerned that we would forget those failures, which may be equally unavoidable, but ultimately implicate us as immoral agents. James fears that we will lose our proper sense of sadness by ignoring the tragic nature of ordinary life while Scheler fears that we will turn our eyes away from the entanglements of our own culpability by taking flight from the turbulent flood-tides of residual guilt.

THE EXPERIENCE OF RESOLUTION

After portraying the self in need of transformation and denouncing the inadequacy of popular remedies, James and Scheler offered more substantial religious alternatives. In different ways, both expanded the context of religious experience beyond its assumed boundaries in order to explore what they believed to be the true depth and breadth of those encounters with the divine that lead to religious rebirth.

James contended that religious experiences could only be understood through attention to both "an objective and a subjective part" of the self which includes not only what people think and feel but also something deep inside them which cannot be accessed. Thus, to truly investigate religious experiences, one has to pursue "full" facts which include "a conscious field *plus* an attitude towards the object *plus* the sense of a self to whom the attitude belongs" (VRE: 499). Since such a complete understanding of the whole person could not be investigated without reports from the subjects themselves, James provides narratives to explore those private experiences which lie beneath the surface of lived reality.

He views his subjects in light of their experiences of the "extra-marginal" which exists outside the center and margin of ordinary consciousness (VRE: 232). In this realm, which James simply characterizes as the "more," memories, thoughts, and feelings comprise the spiritual attitudes which in turn provide for an "incubation of motives." A person reaches the moment of conversion when these motives mature at the "subconscious" level and break through to the conscious realm in much the same way that a seed "bursts into flower" (VRE: 232-233). Thus, for James, there is not only a variety of religious experiences, but there is also a deep continuity that underlies religious rebirth. For this reason, he asserts that despite the pluralism that characterizes the "whole field of religion" "the feelings...are almost always the same" (VRE: 504).

Scheler sought to go even further beneath this underlying continuity to establish the unity of an a priori essence of religious experience which remains coherent throughout the development of human identity. While James expands the location of religious experience to include ever deeper levels of the self, Scheler offers a linear perspective that holds the experiences of the past, present, and future together in a single moment. For Scheler the temporality of life's experiences cannot be divorced from the permanence of the self. In each moment, the self has the capacity to capture the meaning of its past, discern the character of its present and anticipate the promise of its future.

The radical nature of this view is best seen in the remarkable capacity of human memory. For Scheler, the act of remembrance "re-possesses" the past by not only recalling previous conduct but also by actually encountering the self as it once existed. As "a true incursion into the past sphere of our life" remembrance plays a significant role in repentance. It makes it possible not only to alter future direction but, in fact, to change the meaning of the past (OEM: 39-46). As he puts it, "repenting is equivalent to re-appraising part of one's past life and shaping for it a mint-new worth and significance" (p. 36).

The interpretations offered by James and Scheler point to different ways that spiritual renewal transforms ordinary experience. Rebirth occurs for James in those rare moments when the "more" breaks through into ordinary consciousness. Scheler, on the other hand, views religious rebirth as that experience in which the past, present, and future collapse into a single moment of realization.

These differing interpretations reflect the religious experiences of their own lives. In response to those inner motives which overcame his own spiritual acedia, James conceives of a vertical horizon of religious experience which stretches from the surface level of our thoughts and actions to the inner depths of the human soul. Scheler, who lived a life looking back with remorse over on his previous deeds, found consolation in acts of penance which "repossessed" his past and gave his life renewed worth. He depicts the religious horizon as a horizontal one which unites present experience and future direction with those events of the past that continue to haunt us. Thus, owning to their own experiences of rebirth, James was led to interpret religious experience with metaphors of depth expressing the ability of spiritual attitudes deep within us to penetrate to the surface of our daily lives while Scheler used temporal metaphors to express the power of religious renewal to hold the linear progression of our lives together in a single unifying moment of rebirth.

Despite this difference, James and Scheler share a similar perspective rooted in their common struggle to find redemption. They both agree that true resolution can only occur when a power greater than the self overcomes its division. They both turn to images of water to describe this cleansing force. For James, this power is like a waterspout bursting through the self to restore life. For Scheler, it is more like a flood-tide which washes away the hardened residue of guilt.

James portrays the experience of conversion as single moment when the "ultra-marginal" penetrates into primary consciousness providing a new psychic center so that those ideas that previously existed in a peripheral place become central to the conscious life of the self (VRE: 196, 210, 234). He described this movement as a breaking through to a deeper reality so that for the first time "the real meaning of the thought peals through us" or the avoidance of an act which was previously a part of one's daily routine has "suddenly turned into a moral responsibility." It is at these moments that peripheral ideas which were once "cold and dead" have now become central convictions that are both "hot and live" (p. 197).

He describes the experience of conversion as "floods and waterspouts" that violently breakthrough the undertow of melancholy. In conversion, the "anger, worry, fear [and] despair" of the sick soul is washed away, while new emotions such as "hope, happiness, security [and] resolve" burst through their barriers like a waterspout to overcome this sickness as "a sudden flood" (VRE: 198, 212, 216).

For this past victim of acedia, conversion is not so much the taming of a sinful will but a wake up call for a soul in the midst of a deep slumber. As a result, James uses words such as "cold and dead" to describe the previous state of the self, and words like "hot and live" to describe a conversion to a vital new center (VRE: 197). He contrasts this experience with his own past characterized by "negativity and deadness," a time when the self is so divided that it is "suddenly stripped of all ... emotion" so that life is "without significance, character, expression, or perspective." Out of this personal experience, James celebrates the passions as "gifts" which transcend the logical and persist "beyond our control" (VRE: 150-151). In response, he portrays conversion as an encounter with the living water of the passions that pours in like a waterspout flooding the desiccated terrain of the sick soul.

Finally, James's portrayal of conversion culminates in the relinquishing of the self's will to the violent breakthrough of a higher power which paradoxically establishes an underlying peace amid the turbulence of the soul. This understanding of conversion is reminiscent of James's experience while vacationing in Switzerland. Through this encounter, James glimpsed the insight that resolution is not so much an heroic act of the will but rather a recognition of a cosmic power which encompasses all aspects of life. This "moral thunderstorm" left peaceful waters in its wake, calling James to put aside the inner workings of his despairing soul and to find rest in a greater, cosmic power. In response, he understood the apex of the conversion experience as an act of self-surrender. Ultimately, the will of the self is replaced by a willingness to be—a "willingness to close our mouths and be as nothing in the floods and waterspouts of God" (VRE: 47, 209-210).

Max Scheler viewed the experience of repentance from this same perspective. According to Scheler, repentance reaches its final resolution by "driv[ing] guilt out of the vital core" of the self, wiping away its inner division to make it "whole" (OEM: 54-55). As repentance "annihilates" guilt, the penitent feels a "keen, burning, overwhelming" anguish when the movement of repentance encounters an unyielding flood-tide of guilt that has overpowered the core of the self. Anguish operates like a surgeon's knife to free the soul from guilt which Scheler knew from his own experience could spread with the deadly silence of a cancer through the soul. For one who felt the pains of remorse over his sexual infidelity and his role in enticing a country's thirst for war, the inner transformation of repentance must include the sharp pains of anguish.

Yet, along with anguish there is a "simultaneous peace and contentment which may rise to the height of bliss." This peace goes deeper than anguish and actually increases as feelings of regret gain in force. As a result, repentance is ultimately characterized, not by a tormented despising of the self, but by an inward spirituality that is identified by feelings of "calm, repose and gravity" (OEM: 53-54). Thus, as James portrayed conversion as a waterspout that breaks forth in the soul to establish a new center of energy, Scheler viewed repentance as taming the violent flood-tides of guilt by driving it out of the "vital core" of the self into a peripheral realm where its forces can be contained.

As those who had only attained the "hue of resolution" through voluntary acts of the will, James and Scheler recognized that a complete resolution required a surrender of the will to a greater power. In their struggle toward redemption, they never passed all the way through the turbulent waters of religious experience to reach a final, peaceful destination but, like Tolstoy and Bunyan, they traveled far enough along the way to glimpse the soul's harbor in the distance.

THE UNIFIED SELF

After describing the experience of religious resolution, James and Scheler portrayed the renewed life of the unified self as a life characterized by peace in the midst of turmoil. Following the wisdom of his own experience, rebirth is for James, a birth to the "more," to a new depth as one is initiated into a "universe two stories deep" (VRE: 187, 512). Out of his own experience, Scheler also viewed rebirth as a birth to the more. Yet, for him it was to the new breadth of universally expanded horizons.

For James, the new depth of the unified self offers a new perspective upon life which includes a recognition of the tragic. A renewed willingness to live is gained without losing those tragic insights that once overwhelmed the divided self. Unlike either the sick soul or the healthy-minded, those who are "twice-born" perceive the sanctity of life in the face of suffering. Through being disciplined by the "iron of melancholy," they discover the will to live while retaining the tragic wisdom that lies at the heart of the "strenuous life" of sainthood (VRE: 362).

Religious rebirth culminates in a stalwart decision to live in spite of all that seduces the soul toward death. As James looked back to his own initial step toward inner transformation—his decision to "believe in free will"—he discovered in the clarity of that moment the freedom to believe in the goodness of life in spite of the evil of this world. Twenty-six years later, while camping in the Adirondacks, he discovered in the ambiguity of that moment the freedom to face the evil of this world without turning away from the goodness of life. As these two experiences coalesced, James came to understand life on the far side of resolution as the ability to live comfortably at the crossroads by preserving the insights of the desire to die with the tenacity of the will to live.

Max Scheler viewed the other side of religious renewal as a shared life of solidarity. The expansive power of repentance lies in the entanglements of life-histories. Even though repentance is felt within the hearts of individuals, it is fundamentally a "social" and "collective" phenomenon. Repentance can proceed from its "mighty power of self-regeneration" to "rush" through a generation of people and whole civilizations in order to open "obdurate hearts to compassion" (OEM: 54-58). Thus, the life of redemption points beyond personal renewal to a morally broader world in which the self resonates with "all stirrings of all finite hearts" (p. 57).

As one who found that his own sins of the past implicated others in a life of shared bondage, Scheler believed that true repentance had to go beyond the individual to include the ties that bind human beings in ever widening circles of responsibility. For Scheler, whose own fervor played a role in leading a nation to war, transformation could not be complete unless it not only changed the heart of individuals but also moved whole civilizations to a new life of solidarity. He knew from his own life not only that personal choices carry broad implications, but also that religious transformation must transcend a redeemed self to encompass the ideal hope of a regenerated people.

Their portraits of life on the other side of religious resolution suggests that James and Scheler offer different interpretations of the unified self. Rooted in his experience in the Adirondack mountains, James recognizes the "unsharable" depths, that "boulder of impression," which comprises the "private destiny of each individual" (VRE: 499, 501). In response, he depicts the unified self along a vertical line in which an individual experiences an "inner communion" with the deepest part of the soul (p. 485). As one who struggled to discover renewal from deep within, James stresses the importance of the self's relation with the self. On the other hand, Scheler who sought redemption through participation in a reformed community emphasizes the self's relation to the other. Through his repentance from his own role in inciting a country to war, Scheler realizes the unimaginable complicity of life. As a result, he conceived the unified self along a horizontal line by prioritizing the shared life of an interrelated community.

Yet, underlying these different interpretations is, once again, a similar perspective. Their common struggle to attain the "hue of resolution," allowed both James and Scheler to recognize that the unified life does not leave the divisions of the past behind. Like Tolstoy and Bunyan, they "had drunk too deeply of the cup of bitterness" to forget the tragic insights of the divided self (VRE: 187). James, who recognized the depth of evil in the human soul, viewed redemption as a will to live in the face of a "real wrongness in this world" (VRE: 367). Scheler, who acknowledged the destructive force of life's entanglements, distinguished this new life not so much by a will to live but by a willingness to accept one's own "tragic" participation in the lives of "communities, families, peoples and all humanity" (OEM: 54-55).

Following in the path of Tolstoy and Bunyan, both James and Scheler attained only the "hue of resolution"—never quite leaving the tragic divisions of past behind while pressing ahead toward the promise of their own redemption. Out of this common struggle, they understood religious experience from a single perspective. By viewing redemption as the resolution of personal crisis, both envisioned a new life that transcends the boundaries of the divided self. For James, this redeemed life is a birth to a new depth, to a universe that is "two stories deep." For Scheler, it is an opening to a new breadth, to the expanded horizons of universal solidarity. Thus, both James and Scheler view redemption as an initiation into an existence of previously unimagined dimensions. It is an entry into something beyond the self which James cryptically described in a single word. With the wisdom of those who never achieved a final resolution, they envisioned the redeemed life as a birth to something "more".

Reading their religious interpretations alongside a comparison of their lives implies that the study of religion cannot be divorced from self-reflection. To explore the mystery of religious experience is to encounter a phenomenon of such depth and breadth that the experiences of the investigator are contained within the subject of inquiry. By using a methodological strategy prefigured in James's own study of religion, I have pointed to the strong connection between his life and thought. I have suggested that the religious interpretations of William James, like those of Max Scheler, are rooted in pivotal experiences of division and resolution. Thus, James's life provides an important context for reading *The Varieties*. As this context is considered, it is possible to recognize that behind James's investigations of religious experience lies his own struggle toward redemption.

REFERENCES

Bershady, H.J. (Ed.) (1993). "Introduction" to Max Scheler, *On Feeling, Knowing, and Valuing*. Chicago, IL: The University of Chicago Press (pp. 1-46).

Bjork, D.W. (1988). *William James: The Center of His Vision*. New York: Columbia University Press.

Darrow, W.R. (1988). The Harvard way in the study of religion. *Harvard Theological Review*, 81: 215-239.

James, W. (1918). *The Principles of Psychology*, vol. 1. New York: Dover.

————— (1982). *The Varieties of Religious Experience*. New York: Penguin Books.

Lasch, C. (1991). *The True and Only Heaven: Progress and Its Critics*. New York: W.W. Norton.

Myers, G.E. (1986). *William James: His Life and Thought*. New Haven, CT: Yale University Press.

Scheler, M. (1960). *On the Eternal in Man*. Bernard Noble (Trans.) London: SCM Press.

Staude, J.R. (1967). *Max Scheler: An Intellectual Portrait*. New York: The Free Press.

THE DIVIDED SELF AND ITS REPARATION: A KLEINIAN INTERPRETATION OF JAMES'S THEORY OF THE SELF

RICHARD CHILES

It is commonplace to say that *The Varieties of Religious Experience* (1982; hereafter VRE) is a multi-level work exploring many themes in its study of human nature, which is, in fact, the subtitle that is often overlooked. The attempt to read *The Varieties* apart from the life and other works of William James results in a narrow and limited understanding of the text, and misses the deep richness and complexity of the text itself (Myers 1986: 446-480). *The Varieties* should be read in a kind of dialectic with other works of James. It should also be read in terms of its own socio-cultural context. While it approaches the religious impulse as universal and *sui generis*, James's copious use of illustrations of the religious experiences of individuals locates the religious impulse within the life of the experiencing self and its social-cultural environments. Thus, as presented through autobiographical material, the religious impulse is always encountered within a particular socio-cultural context, not in any pure form.

If this is true of James's illustrations, it is also true of *The Varieties* itself. In this essay, I will be concerned with James's discussion of the divided self, and specifically with the need to say more than James himself has said about the socio-cultural location of the self. An essay on his consideration of the divided self in the eighth chapter of *The Varieties*, however, needs to take particular account first of his discussion of the self in his earlier work, *The Principles of Psychology* (1950; hereafter PP), for there is a direct connection between his earlier writings on the self and his discussion of the divided self in *The Varieties*.

THE SELF IN *THE PRINCIPLES*

In *The Principles of Psychology*, James devotes the whole of chapter 9 to an analysis of "The Stream of Thought." Here he asserts that "the only thing which psychology has a right to postulate at the outset is the fact of thinking itself" (PP, I: 224). His use of the progressive form of the verb in identifying psychology's "first fact" is itself significant, for he insists that thought is a stream or process. He discusses the stream of thought under five assertions:
(1) Every thought tends to be part of a personal consciousness.
(2) Within each personal consciousness thought is always changing.
(3) Within each personal consciousness thought is sensibly continuous.
(4) It always appears to deal with objects independent of itself.
(5) It is interested in some parts of these objects to the exclusion of others, and welcomes or rejects—*chooses* from among them, in a word—all the while (p. 225).

This personal consciousness, "whose meaning we know so long as no one asks us to define it," is taken up in chapter 10, "The Consciousness of Self," as it is the fact of our personal consciousness that enables us to claim that we, indeed, "have" or "are" a self (PP, I: 291-401). Here, in chapter 10, he approaches the self phenomenologically and linguistically, describing the experience of the self and examining the common ways of talking about self, thus making an important distinction between the manner in which the self experiences itself and the way in which the self is talked about or conceptualized. He rejects the common substance psychologies of his day in favor of a process view of consciousness. The self is not an enduring substance but rather a series of new experiences always open to self-expansion as well as to self-diminishment. The categories he uses to render the self intelligible are not meant to suggest that the self is comprised of discrete parts or segments, but to highlight the multiple aspects and dimensions of the self. They include the *material self*, the *social self*, the *spiritual self*, and the *pure ego* (PP, I: 292). The "Me" is constituted of the material, social, and spiritual selves, while the "I" is the pure ego.

The "material me" is the body as well as the extra-corporeal supports and accompaniment of the body. The body is the innermost part of the material self and certain parts of the body seem more intimately ours than the rest. Our possessions and even our family members are also part of the material self, as the material self is not confined to, or even wholly resident within, the envelope of one's skin. It is made up of our instinctive preferences coupled with the most practical interests of life.

The "social me" is the image or set of images that others have of oneself. These images are both organismically internalized in the present and collectively stored as one's historic social me. Our "social me" is the recognition we receive from others, and is rooted in our "innate propensity to get ourselves noticed" (PP, I: 293). Strictly speaking, we have as many social selves as there are individuals who recognize us and carry an image of us in their minds. For this very reason, the social self exhibits the most instability. It is, in effect, our reputation. It is our "image" in the eyes of others. It is what they see in me, or, better, it is what I take the others to be taking me to be. Practically speaking, however, we do not experience ourselves as having as many social selves as there are individuals who recognize us. Since those who have images of us fall naturally into classes, we have as many different social selves as there are distinct groups or persons about whose opinion we care. We generally show a different side of our self to each of these groups. This division among our several social selves may be a "perfectly harmonious division of labor" such as when the various selves and the roles they play, although dramatically different, still somehow fit each other with only a minimum of tension. On the other hand, these various selves and their respective identities can be "discordant" with one another. James refers to this as a "discordant" splitting, as where one is afraid to let one set of his acquaintances know him as he is elsewhere" (PP, I: 294).

The "spiritual me" comprises the entire stream of consciousness with all its faculties, dispositions, and activities, and all that it reveals over a lifetime of being experienced as a dynamic unity. By the spiritual self, James means a person's "inner or subjective being," or one's "psychic faculties or dispositions" (p. 296). These dispositions "are the most enduring and intimate part of the self, that which we most verily seem to be" (p. 296). This spiritual self may be divided into faculties (e.g., our ability to argue and discriminate, our moral sensibility and conscience, our indomitable will, etc.), which is to view the spiritual self abstractly. Or it may be viewed concretely, "and then the spiritual self in us will be either the entire stream of consciousness, or the present 'segment' or 'section' of that stream" (p. 296). But whether we take it abstractly or concretely, "our considering the spiritual self at all is a reflective process, is the result of our abandoning the outward looking point of view, and of our having become able to think of subjectivity, as such, *to think of ourselves as thinkers*" (p. 296, emphasis in original).

The spiritual me is at any moment capable of becoming an object of reflection. In turn, it is characteristic of the spiritual self to attend to the objective world. It is "the *active* element in all consciousness .... It is what welcomes or rejects. It presides over the perception of sensations, and by giving or withholding its assent it influences the movements they tend to arouse. It is the home of interest,—not the pleasant or the painful, not even pleasure or pain, as such, but that within us to which pleasure and pain, the pleasant and the painful, speak. It is the source of effort and attention, and the place from which appear to emanate the fiats of the will (pp. 297-298).

Attempts have been made to define its precise nature: "Some would say that it is a simple active substance, the soul, of which they are conscious; others, that it is nothing but a fiction, the imaginary being denoted by the pronoun I; and between these extremes of opinion all sorts of intermediaries would be found" (p. 298).

On the basis of his own introspective efforts, James believes that the spiritual self is best described as the "Self of selves," as the central active self in the various aspects that make up the total self. Yet, he wants to assert that the spiritual self involves more than "thinking," if "thinking" is thought of as a purely conceptual act, for

> the acts of attending, assenting, negating, making an effort, are felt as movements of something in the head. In many cases it is possible to describe these movements quite exactly. In attending to either an idea or a sensation belonging to a particular sense-sphere, the movement is the adjustment of the sense-organ, felt as it occurs. I cannot think in visual terms, for example, without feeling a fluctuating play of pressures, convergences, divergences, and accommodations of my eyeballs. The direction in which the object is conceived to lie determines the character of these movements, the feeling of which becomes, for my consciousness, identified with the manner in which I make myself ready to receive the visible thing (PP, I: 300).

By identifying the material, social and spiritual selves, James would seem to have separated these "me's" from each other. However, as experiences, the three coalesce, forming one continuous whole which is, furthermore, not discontinuous with the rest of our consciousness's complex objects. These aspects of the self have no absolute demarcation between them, and what they all have in common is that they are objects of reflection. What makes James radical is that he does not begin with thought itself, but with thought's objects, that which is immediately presented to thought or consciousness. Accordingly, he begins his specification of the self from "the outside." Instead of beginning with a notion of thought as an internal psychic existent of some sort, and, from this, developing a view of the self as an internal psychic source or repository of such existents, he begins with the objects of thought. The self, he asserts, is formed by what we choose to attend to, and, conversely, by what we choose to ignore. For example, self-love, which James considers a positive asset to the self, is not a general feeing or attitude toward ourselves, but is related to the field of objects which we love and for which we care. Thus, "To have a self that I can *care for*, nature must first present me with some *object* interesting enough to make me instinctively wish to appropriate it for its *own* sake, and of it to manufacture one of those material, social, or spiritual selves, which we have already passed in review" (PP, I: 319).

Besides the three selves that comprise the "me," James posits the Pure Ego, or the "I." The first—the "me"—may be viewed as the "objective person," while the second—the "I"— is the passing subjective thought or feeling that knows or recognizes the objective person. The conscious self involves a stream of thought each part of which as "I" can remember those I's which went before, and can know the things they knew. Thus, the "Pure Ego" or "I" is a "consciousness of personal sameness" (p. 331), the sense that I am the self that I was yesterday and hope to be tomorrow (p. 332). The sense of "I" is "the sense of our own personal identity" (p. 334). To say, then, that I remember that I thought something is to say that I remember that I once was, and this means that within the present "I" there is given the past "I," which is known as past, but also as my sense of "I" in the present. This perception of myself as an "I" is personal. The sameness I experience is a personal sameness. The thoughts that I had yesterday are recalled as *my* thoughts, not those of another (p. 334). The bodily sensations that were mine yesterday are recalled as mine, not someone else's today (p. 336). It is therefore insufficient to say that I become aware of myself as an instance of the genus animal, species Homo. I am aware of my own particularity, of having this mind and this body. My particularity may appall me, but it is mine, all the same. Moreover, at every moment this particular mind and body means something particular. Even a "blank stare" is not really such, but characterizes me at this given moment. If my face and body do not reveal myself to others, then this lack of revelation is itself a revelation, as I reveal that I am hiding something.

This ever-dying/ever-renewing sense of myself is all the "I" there is in James's theory of the self. The self has no substantial unity with the thoughts that it succeeds as these are irrevocably gone. Yet the "I" is the principle of personal sameness in consciousness, and "the sense of our own personal identity, then, is exactly like any one of our other perceptions of sameness among phenomena. It is a conclusion grounded either on the resemblance in a fundamental respect, or on the continuity before the mind, of the phenomena compared" (p. 334). On the resemblance of warmth and intimacy, and the continuity of time and gradual change, it judges the self of differing moment to be the same self enduring through time. When the self is remembered it is a living body; it is remembered as the same self which now does the remembering, because the body involved so centrally is identified as the same body (p. 334).

James also emphasizes that the self originates in the empirical world, maintains itself or collapses, and then passes away. A narrow, rigid self can be readily achieved with the aid of stable circumstances. But a wide ranging, growing self cannot be developed and maintained without strain and struggle, as it engages with the real world outside itself. He stresses, too, that as the deepest features of reality—its "thickness"—are grasped in "feeling," or immediate or perceptual experience, the self, insofar as it is an identity-in-diversity, a sameness-amidst-differences, a unity-within-plurality, must be "felt." James writes:

> *Resemblances among the parts of a continuum of feelings* (especially bodily feelings) experienced along with things widely different in all other regards, *thus constitutes the real and verifiable 'personal identity' which we feel*. There is no other identity than this in the 'stream' of subjective consciousness .... Its parts differ, but under all their differences they are knit in these two ways; and if either way of knitting disappears, the sense of unity departs. If a man wakes up some fine day unable to recall any of his past experiences, so that he has to learn his biography afresh, or if he only recalls the facts of it in a cold abstract way as things that he is sure once happened; or if, without this loss of memory his bodily and spiritual habits all change during the night, each organ giving a different tone, and the act of thought becoming aware of itself in a different way; he *feels*, and he *says*, that he is a changed person. He disowns his former me, gives himself a new name, identifies his present life with nothing from out of the older time (PP, I: 336).

The sense of "I," then, is something we "feel." It has, as noted above, the quality of warmth and intimacy (p. 333).

In short, James is critical of any essentialist conceptualizations of the self that would imply some static, fixed, or immutable entity. But he does not attempt to strip the self of its past. James's theory of the self might be seen as constituting a "multiplicity of selves," but they are not totally fragmented without vital connections. In fact, James's spiritual self is the connecting link among the various selves.

THE DIVIDED SELF IN *THE VARIETIES*

In chapter 8 of *The Varieties* (VRE: 166-188), James offers a portrayal of the divided self and its process of unification. He views the self here as one that struggles with its own passions as well as forces beyond itself. He rejects, as he does in *The Principles*, the existence of a fixed, inherited self. The self is viewed as a bundle of relations constantly open to new experience. It can never be described without reference to its relations.

I now want to turn to his idea of the divided self, using his descriptive typology of the healthy-minded and the sick-soul, but treating them as not only private and internal, but also as social and relational. My concern here is, in part, to bring his notion of the self into dialogue with postmodern theories of the self. With postmodernism James would affirm individuality, but not in the sense of the a-historicity of the self. He would seem, however, to be in agreement with postmodernism in his rejection of the essentialist or absolute nature of the self (cf. Foucault 1978).

The postmodern critique of the self attempts to free the self from any historical or pre-formed conception of what the self is, and from the power relationships in which it is embedded. However, in its move to free the self from its ideological enslavement, the self of postmodernism is not merely a divided self, for its very existence is one of fragmentation. In the writings of most postmodernists, there is a multiplicity of selves with no connecting links. In contrast, James's self is a self-in-process, but nevertheless a self having "sameness in multiplicity" or "personal identity." Furthermore, his self, at least when elaborated in the way I propose to do here, challenges post-modernist pessimism concerning the future of the self in postmodern society. That there can be a commitment to self-shaping that delivers the self from the tyranny of custom and convention, creating a wider community of selves who create themselves out of their own stories and struggles, is more than post-modernists, especially Foucault, could admit, as he viewed all knowledge and arguments themselves as tools of power. Even the concept of the self itself depends on a particular psychohistorical perspective that is itself derived from an aspect of power relations (Foucault 1978).

While we need to take these cautions seriously, I will be making the case here that James's conception of the self, as presented in *The Principles* and in *The Varieties*, is as invigorating today as when it was first set forth. But I will also be arguing that its implications for relationality and community are underdeveloped. I will employ the motif of "seeing and not seeing" to highlight a particular way in which James's construction of the self has social and cultural implications which are not explicit in *The Varieties*. A central emphasis in James's view of the self is the unexamined and disavowed aspects of the self. Their existence is revealed in the religious experience itself, when one becomes conscious of the presence of evil, with evil referring to those unacceptable, not-seen, hateful, destructive forces which are inherent within the self, but split off from it. As James puts it, "The person's interior is a battleground for what is felt to be two deadly hostile selves, one actual and the other ideal" (VRE: 171).

The motif of "seeing and not seeing" provides a deeper understanding of the two deadly hostile selves, one actual, the other ideal, by illuminating their social and relational aspects which are only implicit in the text. The social and relational reading of James is often overlooked with most of the emphasis placed on his concern for the individual and preserving individuality. "Seeing and not seeing" is a paradoxical way in which the self is both protected and enhanced by its dealing with its splits and divisions. The "not seeing" aspect uses a mode of protective exclusion and denial much like the operation of the healthy-minded, in that whenever an experience is felt to be painful or unpleasant, it is located outside the self, thus maintaining the self's sense of well-being. On the other hand, the "seeing" aspects proceed by the entirely opposite way of expansion and inclusion, much like the sick-soul in its inclusion of the presence of evil.

UNIFICATION AS MOVEMENT TOWARD REPARATION

In his chapter on the sick soul (VRE: 127-165), James focuses on the fact that evil is a pervasive element in the universe. In his chapter on the divided self and its process of unification (pp. 166-168), he centers on the individual's sense of sin and thus considers the evil that is inherent in human nature. What we do not get much sense of in *The Varieties* is the evil that exists between these two, what we may call social or systemic evil. However, a basis for the social view of evil is provided by his recognition of the role that reparation may play in the unification of the self. While James does not use the term "reparation"—a term I have borrowed from Melanie Klein (1937)—the idea of reparation is implicit in his discussion of the unification of the self, i.e., overcoming of the discordancy within itself and between itself and the other. He refers in *The Varieties* to the individual's effort to "repair" the effects of misdemeanors and mistakes (VRE: 169). The fact that Klein's discussion of reparation occurs in her consideration of the psychodynamics of guilt and love is also relevant to James, as, in his consideration of the role that conversion may play in the unification of the self, guilt and love play central roles.

James formulated the "healthy-minded" and the "sick-soul" as attitudes or dispositions which emerge in part as the self encounters the presence of evil. The sense of evil results in a divided self, which in turn activates internal longings for harmony and unity. As the self struggles toward unification, it engages in a process of reparation which may be understood as the desire to make amends, to restore, to repair damage done to others (as well as oneself) as a result of its own inherent destructiveness and hatred. The concept of reparation allows us to envision the social and relational character of the unification process while not losing sight of its more internal, private dimension. The unified self not only has its own self-interest but also a wider, communal interest. Thus, the unification process has social and relational dimensions as well.

In the process of unification, identified here as the movement toward reparation, the sick-soul realizes the good as well as the bad and seeks to preserve the good for its own sake while not denying the bad. In its recognition of the good, the sick soul breaks the edge of its sadness. It does not block it out completely. The sadness remains as a minor ingredient in the heart of faith and love, the means by which it was overcome. James identifies a final something welling up in the inner reaches of the personal consciousness—in the spiritual self—by which such extreme sadness can be overcome (VRE: 187). What is this something? A stimulus, an excitement, a faith, a force that re-infuses the positive urges given to life even in the full presence of the evil perceptions that make life seem unbearable (pg. 187). James is describing here what I have called reparative efforts. On one hand, this involves an internal reparation, involving one's relationship to God. As James explains:

> Now in all of us, however constituted, but to a degree the greater in proportion as we are intense and sensitive and subject to diversified temptations, and to the greatest possible degree if we are decidedly psychopathic, does the normal evolution of character chiefly consist in the straightening out and unifying of the inner self. The higher and the lower feelings, the useful and the erring impulses, begin by being a comparative chaos within us—they must end by forming a stable system of functions in right subordination. Unhappiness is apt to characterize the period of order-making and struggle. If the individual be of tender conscience and religiously quickened, the unhappiness will take the form of moral remorse and compunction, of feeling inwardly vile and wrong, and of standing in false relations to the author of one's being and appointer of one's spiritual fate. This is the religious melancholy and 'conviction of sin' that have played so large a part in the history of Protestant Christianity (VRE: 170-171).

On the other hand, it may also involve reparation in one's relations with the social world. Thus, "Tolstoy came to the settled conviction—he says it took him two years to arrive there—that his trouble had not been with life in general, not with the common life of common men, but with the life of the upper, intellectual, artistic classes, the life which he had personally always led, the cerebral life, the life of conventionality, artificiality, and personal ambition. He had been living wrongly and must change. To work for animal needs, to abjure lies and vanities, to relieve common wants, to be simple, to believe in God, therein lay happiness again" (VRE: 184-185). What was wrong, and required reparation, in Tolstoy's case, was the

> clash between his inner character and his outer activities and aims. Although a literary artist, Tolstoy was one of those primitive oaks of men to whom the superfluities and insincerities, the cupidities, complications, and cruelties of our polite civilization are profoundly unsatisfying, and for whom the eternal veracities lie with more natural and animal things. His crisis was the getting of his soul in order, the discovery of its genuine habitat and vocation, the escape from falsehoods into what for him were ways of truth. It was a case of heterogeneous personality tardily and slowly finding its unity and level. And though not many of us can imitate Tolstoy, not having enough, perhaps, of the aboriginal human marrow in our bones, most of us may at least feel as if it might be better for us if we could (VRE: 185-186).

Thus, in his chapter on the divided self and the process of its unification, James recognizes that reparation is not only between self and God—though it almost always involves putting this relationship to rights—but also between oneself and society, or one or more segments of society. We need to consider the healthy-minded and sick-soul temperaments in the light of this twofold process, and flesh out their social-relational implications, implications which, in my judgment, James does not adequately develop. If *The Varieties* is to make a contribution toward an understanding and possible construction of the self in the postmodern world, a deeper analysis of the social, cultural and even political dimensions of the healthy-minded and sick-soul representations is called for. These representations have socio-cultural implications of which James and many of his interpreters may not be sufficiently aware. This is not because James was deliberately "not seeing," but because the process by which a cultural form produces and reproduces meaning—through developing mental sets for recognizing and ignoring, suppressing or effacing others—is largely hidden from itself. From this perspective, his categories of healthy-minded and sick-soul are at best mental sets or representations, and at worst symptoms of the process by which culture, like language, masks the effects of the ideas that are promoted by it (cf. Said 1961). To understand any representative human action and aspiration is, then, to come to terms with the way they are sedimented, in Wittgenstein's sense, in all the past "forms of life" that went into any given formulation of the principles informing them. It is to see them configured both as products of meaning and also as processes of its creation (Said 1961).

Thus, we need to see any human production within its own sociopolitical and economic site of its production and to chart the cultural forms it might take. Certainly, healthy-minded and sick-soul orientations are expressions of the individual's encounter with evil. However, these expressions are rooted in an historical socio-cultural context and gain expression via cultural form. The healthy-minded consciousness can be viewed, in this light, as a paradigm of the motif of "not seeing," which is a particular style of American culture as it relates to its own inner-sense division. The central question here is what factors come together to create a consciousness that attempts to banish from its awareness all that would be considered evil or bad and seek to build its construction of the self solely on the basis of not seeing what is an integral part of its natural life (Hofstader 1965).

Some of James's own richest reflections on this process of understanding the creation of cultural forms occur in an essay entitled "Humanism and Truth" (James 1955: 229-256). In this essay, James observes that experience comes to us initially in the form of questions that are then digested or assimilated through reference to fundamental categories wrought so long into the structure of human consciousness that at least within specific cultural traditions they seem practically irreversible. This apparent irreversibility in turn allows the categories themselves not only to define "the general frame within which answers must fall" but also "gives the detail of the answers in the shapes most congruous with all our present needs" (1955: 236). But James does not believe that the process is irreversible because we are not necessarily locked into categories we have used for interpreting new experience. As we select cultural categories in which this experience is given expression, we may select other categories if we are sufficiently motivated to do so. In this sense, my reading of the Jamesian notions of healthy-minded and sick-soul as cultural categories would seem to be in continuity with James himself.

James, however, was more interested in relating these orientations to their presumed physiological than to their cultural roots. He kept a sharp eye out for what contributions our physiological constitution might make toward behavior. He believed that, to some extent at least, the difference between the healthy-minded and the sick-soul was physiological, and thus a matter of temperament. Regarding the healthy-minded, he writes:

> Some persons are born with an inner constitution which is harmonious and well-balanced from the outset. Their impulses are consistent with one another, their wills follow without trouble the guidance of their intellect, their passions are not excessive, and their lives are little haunted by regrets (VRE: 168).

But there are others, the sick-souled,

> whose existence is little more than a series of zigzags, as now one tendency and now another gets the upper hand. Their spirits war with their flesh, they wish for incompatibles, wayward impulses interrupt their most deliberate plans, and their lives are one long drama of repentance and of effort to repair misdemeanors and mistakes (VRE: 169).

James notes that these differences have been attributed to inheritance, and that the latter, more heterogenous types, are believed to have inherited "the traits of character of incompatible and antagonistic ancestors ... supposed to be preserved alongside of each other" (p. 169). He does not dispute this claim for inherited traits, but says that they need to be corroborated in each case, and that, in any event, a stronger case can be made for the influence of physiological factors, those discussed in the first lecture in *The Varieties* on religion and neurology.

But even if James was primarily interested in the physiological roots of these two orientations, they are cultural, even as described by him, because they represent ways of seeing and not seeing the world. To see the world through a healthy-minded consciousness is to conceive of the self as a basically rational being that overlooks the presence of the irrational. It is a denial of the unconscious dynamics and forces in the formation of the self. It seeks to fashion a self split off not only from its instinctual basis, although predisposed to some extent by its own constitution, but devoid of those cultural elements that are seen as dark and unacceptable. To see the world through a sick-soul consciousness is to conceive of the self as being pulled apart by irrational forces which are again disavowed but nevertheless cannot be banished from consciousness.

These, then, are two distinctive "cultural selves," involving two different strategies for relating to the cultural world. In the one case, the self is construed—and construes itself—as a rational being, as one who is able to act rationally and to avoid acting on impulse or purely emotionally. Such a self is well-controlled. In the other case, the self is a victim of irrational forces that constantly threaten to destroy it, and these are forces that may be perceived by the individual as either internal (e.g., one's inherent evil) or external (e.g., social and cosmic forces). By linking these two types to Melanie Klein's "paranoic-schizoid" and "depressive" positions (Klein 1946), we are able to explore further how James's healthy-minded and sick-soul orientations are ways of interacting with the social world, and are therefore not only psychological—i.e., temperamental—types, but also cultural types, i.e., reflecting two socially constructed ways of being religious, with each having significant political implications, as each has its own understanding of how one is expected to behave with regard to issues of power and control.

THE HEALTHY-MINDED SELF AND THE PARANOID-SCHIZOID POSITION

I would argue that what keeps the healthy-minded in its state is not only the mechanism of happiness that James describes, but a whole constellation of anxieties and defenses keeping rage and its possible destruction at bay. It evinces a blindness of its own destructive rage and builds a superstructure to keep it from awareness. This superstructure might be seen as the healthy-minded orientation.

I would not go so far as to claim that the healthy-minded orientation is synonymous with the paranoid-schizoid position as described by Melanie Klein (1984: 347-348; 428-438), but it does bear certain similarities. The healthy-minded orientation seeks to avoid completely those sets of anxieties identified as evil within the self by a simple mechanism of "not seeing," whereas in the paranoid-schizoid position evil is encountered, split off, and projected outside the self. On the other hand, the paranoid-schizoid is aware of its fears of retaliation from its projected evil and the evil that remains inside. The healthy-minded orientation attempts to remain completely unaware of its own evil both within as well as without. As described by James, the healthy-minded consciousness utilizes defenses from Klein's paranoid-schizoid position. It shares the same set of basic anxieties regarding its own inherent evil.

Two aspects of the paranoid-schizoid position which are important for us are its use of splitting as a means of separating good from bad, and its paranoid style, which is in constant fear of the irruption of the unconscious and thus the need to maintain constant vigilance. The systematic cultivation of healthy-mindedness requires a vigilant attitude, one that protects the self from danger which lurks just beneath. The healthy-minded orientation seeks to divert attention from disease and death as much as possible. It insists on the dignity rather than on the depravity of humankind. In fact, it is more than mere insistence, as "Systematic healthy-mindedness, conceiving good as the essential and universal aspects of being, deliberately excludes evil from its field of vision .... Evil simply cannot then and there be believed in. He [the healthy-minded] must ignore it; and to the bystander he may then seem perversely to shut his eyes to it and hush it up (VRE: 88).

Although James emphasizes the religious nature of the healthy-minded (i.e., its implications for the self's relation to God), and mainly engages in psychological analysis of the healthy-minded temperament, he is not entirely unaware of its cultural and political implications. He recognizes that it has an immense appeal to the practical turn of character of the American people, as it supports a somewhat shallow approach to continuous progress. By banishing forever the bad or evil forces, good-will prevails, and progress becomes a kind of inevitability for nothing stands in its way. If this view becomes a cultural outlook, what happens to evil? Where will it be banished? What other cultural forms or social groups will have to be invested with the evil for the notion of the all-good to survive? If James did not explore these implications of his theory in any detail, he seems at least to have been aware of what may happen on a cultural level when healthy-minded consciousness prevails.

The cultural implications of a consciousness dominated by healthy-mindedness is a self which has interrupted its dialogue with itself. It is a self that seeks not to see the evil from which it flees. If evil is recognized, it is seen as residing in persons or objects outside the self and hence are viewed as a threat to the self. The self of the healthy-minded is able to deny its own madness and invest it in others. Healthy-mindedness thus provides a rational justification to destroy the other since the other is considered the embodiment of evil and deserving of destruction.

The self as conceived by the healthy-minded orientation is driven by a particular kind of rationality. It ignores the message and utterances of the split-off bad self. It is blind to its own aggression and anxiety. It sees no need for salvation, conversion or reparation. It is a rationality that seeks to banish ambiguity, complexities, and nuance. It seeks to force experience into its own rigid and prefabricated categories, which is a characteristic of the paranoid style. What it cannot completely fit into its categories, it attempts to manipulate and control, and whatever cannot be manipulated and controlled is split off. It is also self-interested only: "It is only concerned with the good to the extent that the good serves its own purposes" (Alford 1989: 169).

James did question how the healthy-minded consciousness could ever be sustained. He asks:

> How can things so unsecure as the successful experience of this world afford a stable anchorage? A chain is no stronger than its weakest link, and life is after all a chain. In the healthiest and most prosperous existence, how many links of illness, danger, and disaster are always interposed? Unsuspectedly from the bottom of every fountain of pleasure, as the old poet said, something bitter rises up: a touch of nausea, a falling dead of the delight, a whiff of melancholy, things that sound a knell, for fugitive as they may be, they bring a feeling of coming from a deeper region and often have an appalling convincingness. The buzz of life ceases at their touch as a piano-string stops sounding when the damper falls upon it (VRE: 136).

He continues: "Of course the music can commence again;—and again and again—at intervals. But with this the healthy-minded consciousness is left with an irremediable sense of precariousness. It is a bell with a crack; it draws its breath on sufferance and by an accident" (p. 136). Again the universality of death, healthy-mindedness can only survive by ignoring it. Thus, James asks the healthy-minded: "Can things whose end is always dust and disappointment be the real gods which our souls require? Back of everything is the great spectre of universal death, the all-encompassing blackness" (p. 139).

I have argued that the healthy-minded consciousness is similar to Klein's paranoid-schizoid position. The paranoid-schizoid position originates as the self attempts to manage the anxieties evoked by its own sense of evil and fears of annihilation. The self responds to this constellation of anxieties by splitting itself into all good and all bad. A particular style of rationality emerges which serves to deny and block out all aspects of the irrational. In my view, this constellation of anxieties and defenses provides a deeper understanding of the psycho-social dynamics and cultural implications of the healthy-minded consciousness. It enables us to see that healthy-mindedness is a particular style of relationality, and, as such, is found in all forms of human community, including family, social institutions, and whole societies. It is an especially dangerous type as it is blind—"not seeing"—to its own aggression and anxiety. It is unaware of its own faults, and therefore sees no need to make reparations in order to restore harmony and unity. It projects the "bad self" onto others (individuals and groups) and views these as the embodiment of evil. As a cultural type, healthy-mindedness either denies the existence of evil (we might call this the sunny type of healthy-mindedness) or attributes evil to others (the darker type of healthy-mindedness). By linking it to Klein's paranoid schizoid position, I am emphasizing its darker side, as this is the type that projects its own evil onto the other, and is therefore especially dangerous. But the sunnier type, even if it does not project evil onto the other, often colludes with the darker forms of healthy-mindedness by choosing to ignore the evil that is perpetrated by the projective process itself.

THE SICK-SOUL AND THE DEPRESSIVE POSITION

Just as healthy-mindedness manifests "shallower and profounder" levels, so also, there are different levels of sick-soulness. On the shallower side are those for whom evil means only a maladjustment with things, a wrong correspondence of one's life with the environment. Such evil as this is curable, in principle at least, by modifying either the environment or oneself. James notes that this quickly passes over into the more profound level of sick-soulness, and it is this latter level that is the more revealing. In this regard the sick-soul consciousness sees "evil as no mere relation of the subject to particular outer things, but something more radical and general, a wrongness or vice in one's essential nature, which no alteration of the environment, or any superficial rearrangement of the inner self, can cure (VRE: 134). The entire consciousness of the sick-soul is choked with feelings of evil, tragedy and being damaged, so the sense of there being any good in the world is threatened altogether. Whatever sense of good is felt is quickly overshadowed by the menacing faces of evil. One distinction between the healthy-minded and the sick-soul is that while the healthy-minded actively seeks to banish evil totally from its awareness, the sick-soul does not seek to banish the good. The good is held to be under threat, however, from the overwhelming presence of evil.

If the healthy-minded consciousness manifests the self in earlier phases of the paranoid-schizoid position in which either all good or all bad predominate, then the sick-soul consciousness represents the beginning of the depressive position in which the self struggles with the presence of both good and bad and the fear that the bad will destroy the good (Klein 1946). Whereas the healthy-minded sees no need for salvation, conversion, or reparation, the sick-soul is seeking a process of redemption, a way to repair what it experiences as its divisions. Thus, if the healthy-minded self projects evil onto the other, the sick-soul internalizes this evil, even that which is projected onto it. In this way, the healthy-minded self exercises a kind of tyranny over the sick-soul, and the sick-soul is helpless to do much about it. This is perhaps why James placed so much emphasis on the will, and attacked determinism, for the sick-soul (of which he was one) is all-too-likely to become depressed, to believe that the situation is hopeless, and to adopt a fatalistic view of life. Reparation—self-reparation in this case—results from making an act of will, from deciding that one will no longer allow the "other" to determine one's fate.

Like healthy-mindedness, sick-soulness is more than a personality type, as it is also a social and cultural type. It is characterized by "seeing," not by "not seeing," but such seeing can be immobilizing if it means that the evil that is seen is so overwhelming that no reparative action seems possible. Also, there is the danger that the reparative efforts, if attempted, will be less than redemptive because they are misdirected (inward rather than outward). The only consolation that the sick-soul may experience for its suffering is in the knowledge that the healthy-minded may eventually suffer the same fate and not be at all prepared for it when it happens. As James writes:

> The method of averting one's attention from evil and living simply in the light of good is splendid as long as it will work. It will work with many persons; it will work far more generally than most of us are ready to suppose; and within the sphere of its successful operation there is nothing to be said against it as a religious solution. But it breaks down impotently as soon as melancholy comes; and even though one be quite free from melancholy one's self, there is no doubt that healthy-mindedness is inadequate as a philosophical doctrine, because the evil facts which it refuses positively to account for are a genuine portion of reality; and they may after all be the best key to life's significance, and possibly the only openers of our eyes to the deepest levels of truth (VRE: 163).

Thus, the sick-soul types have the grim satisfaction of knowing that they are "seeing" reality more clearly than the healthy-minded. Of the two temperaments, the sick-soul is the more perceptive—"seeing"—because it recognizes the evil that the healthy-minded are so invested in ignoring. But the sick-soul is susceptible to depression, or melancholy, and is in danger of succumbing to pessimism. For the sick-soul, the reparation occurs when it recognizes that it is not doomed to repeat the past, and not utterly helpless against the evil that exists in their world. After all, they *can* struggle against the evil that exists in the world and in themselves, and they can being this struggle by making a clear and accurate determination—"seeing"—as to the locus of the evil (i.e., how much of it is "outside" and how much is "inside").

What Klein's categories enable us to see, therefore, is that both the healthy-minded and the sick-soul types have social and cultural implications. I have been especially concerned here with the healthy-minded type because James himself considers it the most inadequate as a religious world view. I have shown that it is also the most inadequate as a social orientation. As noted, James does not provide a systematic analysis of the social dimensions of the healthy-minded consciousness and its use of instrumental reasoning as a tool of power and control. By looking at healthy-mindedness through a Kleinian lens, we provide what is missing in James's analysis. We see that the healthy-minded consciousness has difficulty in locating and naming the pathology in its politics, and that it seeks to banish and control all that does not conform to its predetermined categories. Paranoia is the most obvious manifestation of this self that begins with a conception of self that excludes evil. Evil is not a part of the rational, thinking self.

The concept of a rational self, therefore, capable of pure decision and calculations, without affect, is in itself a kind of fantasy, a formulation (disembodied) that ignores the contingent and unconscious qualities of human experience, that assumes human beings live without any unconscious content. In order to attain the level of rationality necessary to sustain this view, the healthy-minded consciousness requires a social world that is clearly non-conflictual, which means that it has a constant need to block out evil, and to behave as though any evil that does not exist is "out there," i.e., not resident within the self.

JAMES AND THE EVIL OF SLAVERY

It is well known that James identifies himself as the sick-soul type in *The Varieties*. It would not make much sense for him to acclaim that sick-souls are able to see the evil to which healthy-minded selves are oblivious, and then turn around and declare that he is a healthy-minded type. Yet, it is also clear that he was deeply attracted to healthy-minded strategies for dealing with evil (e.g., mind-cure), finding them useful for helping him to cope with the events of everyday life. It might be argued, therefore, that James took a healthy-minded view of certain evils, that he was consciously or unconsciously "not seeing," not out of a desire to project evil on to others, but out of a personal need to cope with the evil in his soul. The social evil that comes immediately to mind is the evil of slavery.

While James includes scores of accounts of religious experience in *The Varieties*, documents describing the religious experiences of African-Americans are curiously lacking. One might argue that written documents were not readily available to James, but this is not, in fact, the case. Many slave narratives, those deeply religious documents detailing conversion experiences and confrontation with evil as experienced in the institution of slavery, were available and part of the social context of the Abolitionist movement, a movement with which James was certainly familiar (what American at the time wasn't?). Also, two of his younger brothers (Williamson and Robert) were officers in the Civil War in charge of Black regiments. Why does James fail to include any of these accounts in *The Varieties*? Is his failure to include them symptomatic of a failure to recognize, as we have argued here, that the orientations of the healthy-minded and sick-soul have profound social and political implications?

Of particular interest here is James's relationship with W.E.B. Dubois, a relationship that clearly had mutual benefits, and enabled both to "see" more than either would have seen had they not encountered one another. His personal relationship with DuBois kept him in touch with social issues and problems wider than those of his own social class. Yet biographers of James have paid scant attention to his relationship with Dubois, and none has explored in any detail Dubois's influence on James's views on the "race" question, or Dubois's role in helping James to see more clearly than those of his generation and class the contradictions within American society (Otto 1943).

Dubois was probably the greatest African-American of the late nineteenth and early twentieth centuries. His role in shaping the discipline of sociology in America was enormous. His sociological studies of *The Philadelphia Negro* originally published in 1899 remain a classic. He was optimistic in the sense that he was convinced that the race problem was essentially one of ignorance (of not-knowing). He was determined to unearth as much evidence as he could, thereby providing the "cure" for color prejudice. On the other hand, he was not so optimistic that he could not see that prejudice has an evil side as well. When he enrolled in Harvard in 1888, James became his academic advisor, supervising the completion of his doctorate. Dubois credited James with having prepared him for a psychoanalytic understanding of the irrational and unconscious roots of racial prejudice (Dubois 1940: 34). Thus, through James, Dubois came to understand that education and knowledge alone would not erase racial prejudice. Racial prejudice was reproduced not only in the individual but in various cultural forms through language itself and had its unconscious dimensions as well, dimensions that partook of the evil in human nature.

Dubois's personal friendship with James is attested in this remark of his in his autobiography: "I was repeatedly a guest in the home of William James; he was my friend and guide to clear thinking" (1968: 133). Margaret Wade Deland was a very popular short-story writer and novelist. In a letter to Dubois written in 1928 she recalls meeting both men:

> I remember with great pleasure meeting you many years ago at the home of my friend, Mrs. Ebons, in Boston. I recall William James was there also, and that we had a delightful time. As I have always been profoundly interested in the political, industrial, and spiritual welfare of the people who were so deeply wronged some three hundred years ago, I am keenly alive to the advancement of Negro Americans today (Dubois 1968: 383).

Dubois's personal relationship with James began in his student days at Harvard and continued until James's death. He attests to the fact that James influenced him on his ideas of "double consciousness," "behind the veil," and other matters. That Dubois fully grasped James's theory of the self is shown in his *The Soul of Black Folks*, where he describes the split within the consciousness of the Negro. One of his central themes is the duality in the life of the African-American, the paradox of being so intimately a part of the national culture and yet so starkly apart from it; or, as he expressed it, "an outcast and a stranger in mine own house" (Dubois 1961: 3-4). Both Dubois and James are haunted by this vision of a divided self at the core of human consciousness. Both are concerned with how one achieves mature self-consciousness or wholeness of self.

Whether and how Dubois influenced James is less clear (Burkhardt 1987). It is not an easy matter to show direct influence where there is no close collaboration between two authors or direct attestation to such influence by the author in question (in this case, James). Since their relationship began as teacher to student, the influence is admittedly greater from the teacher's than the student's side. It is more difficult to demonstrate that a student has influenced the thinking of the teacher in direct and significant ways, and this may be especially difficult to show where the student is African-American and the teacher is a symbol of American originality and intellectual creativity (cf. Chametzky and Kaplan 1969). To chart James's social and political views, showing his agreements and disagreements with those of his social class, would take us too far afield from the core concerns of this essay. Suffice it to say that many of James's most cherished political assumptions were influenced by the New England Mugwump intellectuals, which, from the point of view of this author, is not an altogether appealing one. He appeared to have Mugwump sympathies in his private correspondence when he revealed the class prejudices that were common to the elite who swelled the Mugwump ranks. He referred to the Haymarket Riots in Chicago as little more than the "work of a lot of pathological Germans and Poles." Elsewhere in his correspondence, his language reveals racial and ethnic stereotypes (Garrison and Madden 1977). Yet, as Gerald Myers argues, it was commonplace for American writers of James's time to refer to individuals by their racial or ethnic identity, and the letter to his brother Henry in which his negative comment on pathological Germans and Poles occurs contrasts their "senseless 'anarchist' riot" with the more successful efforts of the Knights of labor in Boston to effect industrial change (Myers 1986: 595-596). Myers also emphasizes James's "ethics of individualism" (p. 427) which led him to take the side of any individual "struggling to hold his [or her] own" (p. 422).

Most importantly, although sharing certain opinions and prejudices held by New England Mugwump intellectuals, James departed from the Mugwumps on the issue of racial prejudice, and it is very possible that this was in large measure due to his personal relationship with Dubois, for, in Dubois, he found an African-American whom he not only respected for his keen intellect but also cherished as a personal friend. Actually, his openness to others brought him into contact with a company of individuals from diverse backgrounds, and this openness in general kept him from the cultivation of prejudices of class, taste and religion (Armstrong 1974). He also departs significantly from the political and social views of his class when he recognizes that since the 1830s the slavery question had been the only question, and by the end of the fifties our land lay sick and shaking with the disease, like a traveler who has thrown himself down at night beside a pestilential swamp, and in the morning finds the fever coursing through the marrow of his bones. James, like Dubois, analyzed the contradiction inherent in American life in regard to race and slavery. Writing in 1897, he exclaimed: "Our great Western Republic had from its origin been a singular anomaly—a land of freedom, boastfully so-called, with human slavery enthroned at the heart of it, and last dictating terms of unconditional life. What was it but a thing of falsehood and horrible self-contradiction?" (James 1987: 42).

It is not my purpose here to assess the impact of James's actions on the moral and political climate of the times. Through his relationship with Dubois, however, he was able to see with greater acuity aspects of his own country that remained hidden to others. That he wrote so eloquently regarding the self-contradiction within American society may also indicate that he was acutely aware of the relationship between the cultural self and its inherent contradictions and the individual self and its dividedness. We should credit Dubois, however, with having taken this insight and applying it with such sociological acuity to the "double consciousness" that exists among those who are the direct victims of the "horrible self-contradiction" that exists in the very marrow of American society.

I maintain, in short, that an adequate reading of the Jamesian text on the divided self cannot limit itself to the typology of healthy-minded and sick-soul as individual orientations, for these orientations also reflect social and cultural anxieties and defenses that not only point to the ways in which the self organizes itself, but also to the ways in which social and cultural forces are organized as well. Melanie Klein's differentiation of two major groupings of anxieties and defenses, the paranoid-schizoid and the depressive, has served as a valuable conceptual model to examine the ways in which the self organizes itself at different levels of development. Even as James cautions against viewing the healthy-minded and the sick-soul temperaments as mutually exclusive, so, in Klein's view, a continuous movement between the two "positions" takes place so that neither dominates with any degree of completeness or permanence. We must be careful, therefore, not to identify too easily these cultural types along racial and ethnic lines, though I would want to argue that "not seeing," which is especially associated with healthy-mindedness, is most likely to occur among those who hold power in society, and "seeing," which is more associated with the sick-soul, is more likely to occur among those who are socially and politically powerless.

THE SAINT AS CULTURAL TYPE

If James's categories of the healthy-minded and sick-soul can be shown to have social and cultural implications, what about conversion? How might its social and cultural implications be more fully articulated? Significantly, both James and Klein envisioned a self beyond its divisions. Klein viewed the self as emerging and splitting into a good and bad self in response to its own inherent destructiveness, but she held that it was not destined to remain locked in its divisions. The self held within itself the possibility of moving toward acceptance of both its good and bad aspects. James understood the division within the self as emerging from its encounter with evil. He described the possibility of overcoming the division—the unification of the self—using the religious concept of conversion.

One of the especially interesting features of *The Varieties* is James's analysis of the religious change in a person's life called "conversion." He analyzes this change through certain psychological principles, some of which he himself had developed in his *Principles of Psychology* and some of which, especially theories of the subconscious, were formulated later. He describes the process of conversion in this way: "To be converted, to be regenerated, to receive grace, to experience religion, to gain an assurance, are so many phrases which denote the process, gradual or sudden, by which a self hitherto divided, and consciously inferior and unhappy, becomes unified and consciously right superior and happy, in consequence of its firmer hold upon religious realities" (VRE: 189). Whether or not divine operation or intervention is needed to bring about this process, James would not commit himself. But he did believe that the religious realities were in contact with or mediated by one's "subliminal consciousness" (VRE: 234-236). What happens in a persons' religious conversion is that religious ideas previously peripheral in consciousness now take central place and form the habitual center of energy. Although psychology can describe the process of change, it cannot really say why the change occurs.

Conversion, then, is the religious name for the sick-soul's recovery. It occurs by a refocusing of the field of consciousness and by the incursions into it of impulses from a subliminal region beyond the margin of consciousness. The spiritual self is the self in the journey toward unification. As we saw earlier, this self is not viewed by James as a substantive self, as composed of inherent characteristics. Rather, it is profoundly relational. Reality is not experienced in an atomized fashion. It is presented to us, even before our selecting process begins, in a whole moving wave or stream. Since the process of experiencing is one of selecting and refocusing of one's attention, what happens in a religious conversion is that religious ideas previously peripheral in consciousness now take central place and form the habitual center of energy (VRE: 230-233). Thus, through conversion, there emerges a wider self that is open to influence from beyond the previous range of consciousness. In conversion, the spiritual self is enlarged, and more of that which was unseen is now seen, and attended to, perhaps for the very first time.

In his chapters on saintliness, James presents the lives of the saints as empirical evidence for the positive effects of the conversion experience. Saints and mystics are the "twice-born" individuals marked by the experience of having "drunk too deeply of the cup of bitterness ever to forget its taste." The memory of this defining experience allows "twice-born" persons to inhabit a "universe two stories deep," where they strenuously confront the problems and predicaments posed for them by evil. Saints therefore embrace a "wider and completer" outlook. The twice-born saintly attitude favored by James allows healthy-mindedness to be merged with the sick-soul or morbid-mindedness into a "higher synthesis" that enables "heroic" and "solemn" energies to be exercised and released (VRE: 266-268). "The strenuous life" that James ascribes to the saintly type is a manifestation of the self no longer split asunder, but unified (VRE: 271ff). James recognized that the strenuous life of the saint was not necessarily without its excesses. It could result in fits of imperial domination and moral inquisition, and he warned against the excesses of saintly moral fervor in pursuit of "paltry ideals" (p. 370; also 345) and condemns "saintliness of character" if not accompanied by superior "intellectual sympathies" (p.346).

Thus, his view of the spiritual self and its expression in saintliness is his effort to envision an orientation to life that transcends the healthy-minded and the sick-soul division that is the condition of the divided self. The spiritual self as expressed in and through saintliness reflects a move toward unification, and this unification in turn exhibits a concern for the other as the other and not solely as an expression of enlightened self-interest. Thus, what emerges from this conversion is the spiritual self expressed in "the strenuous mood" of living. In his description and analysis of the individual's experience of the religious impulse, and its subsequent impact on the emotional and cognitive orientations toward life, James recounts a fundamental split or division within the self. In the process of conversion, he describes how the person refocuses energies which were once almost wholly concerned with personal interests toward a wider community of interest.

When viewed within the social context of James's time, the limitations of "the strenuous mood" of living are apparent, as it tends to mirror the values of a particular social class. On the other hand, James was aware that mediating between the realm of the person and of the philosophical is the public sphere, the realm of culture, and much of his work and its agenda may be viewed as responses to the cultural imperatives as he understood them at the time he was writing. And, in responding to these imperatives, he seems to have recognized, more than others of his social class, his own split-off selves, and to have sought to reclaim them. In doing so, he moved beyond a divided self toward a fuller self in which both good and evil are acknowledged. In this acknowledgment, he realized that good must be fought for strenuously and continually. His metaphor was that virtue must always keep vice's neck beneath its foot. Even though the strenuous life as he articulates it has its limitations—limitations partly owing to the fact that he relies on personal testimonies that are themselves limited in various ways—it is concerned with ideals that transcend the present and its problems. Strenuous morality is relatively rare as it requires wider passions, deeper loves, larger indignations, and involves bigger fears than are possessed by the average individual. Thus, in a very real sense, James has provided his own argument for viewing the unification of the self as a basis for moral action. In his own way, he has himself made the necessary social and cultural connection. We *could* take his efforts here one step further by providing a case study of an African-American "saint," such as Dubois himself, who is certainly exemplary of the reconciliation of the healthy-minded and sick-soul temperaments expressed in a lifetime of energetic, unflagging commitment to issues of justice and freedom. To do so would be a very Jamesian thing to do.

CONCLUSION

This essay has centered on the divided self with its religious representations of healthy-mindedness and sick-soulness. It has suggested that these representations have wider significance than indicated by James in *The Varieties* and that this significance may be illumined by Melanie Klein's paranoid-schizoid and depressive positions. When the latter constructs are examined, they reveal the socio-cultural dimensions of the Jamesian self. To his credit, James developed a theory of the self that stood in sharp contrast to the prevailing psychological theories of his day. He rejected notions of a substantial self or a transcendental ego that supposedly exists behind the self, thus safeguarding the integrity of the self and even making a case for its immortality. His self grows out of the kaleidoscopic nature of experience and consists of the empirical self with its material, social and spiritual components. The Jamesian self is one that suited the nineteenth century spirit of continual evolution and adaptation to one's environment, and this may be its limitation. However, the boundaries of his self are fluid and constantly shifting, depending on the interest toward which one's consciousness directs itself, and is open to the possibilities of reparative and unificative efforts. The innermost spiritual self holds the possibilities of connections to wider realms of consciousness through the subliminal consciousness. If there are unseen powers in the universe that aid the self in its struggles for life, these powers make their impact through their irruption from the subliminal consciousness.

The divided self, then, gives rise to a certain style of experiencing. I have argued that a fundamental aspect of this style is the motif of "seeing and not seeing." This is the mechanism by which the self and society, by means of projection, attempt to maintain their security by splitting off (creating their own division) and denying those unacceptable (evil) parts which are considered bad, dangerous, and fearful. Thus, my basic argument here has been that James's healthy-minded and sick-soul representations are in fact the self's way of dealing with evil, and that its felt divisions get projected into various cultural forms that mirror the division not only within the self but within society as well. In his construction of the self, James was aware of the conflicts to which the self gives rise. He sought to resolve the conflict through "the strenuous life," which involves harnessing the two polarities which the self must constantly mediate. To advocate the strenuous life in this fashion is, in a sense, not to resolve the conflicts but rather to extend them indefinitely, until death finally intervenes. Still, what James has done in *The Varieties* is to have struggled—as courageously as he knew how—with how an individual might be unique and special, yet realistically regard one's limitations, including mortality, and therefore find truer ways of relating to others within a wider community of interests. In this regard, James mirrors contemporary life, and expresses our own struggle to live in a universe in which good and evil coexist.

REFERENCES

Alford, C.F. (1989). *Melanie Klein and Critical Social Theory*. New Haven, CT: Yale University Press.

Armstrong, W. (Ed.) (1974). *The Gilded Age of E.L. Godkin*. Albany, NY: State University of New York Press.

Chametsky, J. & S. Kaplan (1969). *Blacks and Whites in American Culture*. Amherst, MA: University of Massachusetts Press.

Dubois, W.E.B. (1940). *Dusk of Dawn: An Essay Toward an Autobiography of a Race Concept*. New York: Harcourt, Brace.

—— (1961). *The Souls of Black Folks: Essays and Sketches*. New York: Fawcett.

—— (1968). *The Autobiography of W.E.B. Dubois: A Soliloquy on Viewing My Life from the Last Decade of Its First Century*. New York: International Publishers.

Foucault, M. (1978). *The History of Sexuality*, vol. 1. R. Hurley (Trans.). New York: Pantheon Books.

Garrison, G.R. & E.H. Madden (1977). William James—warts and all. *American Quarterly*, 29: 207-221.

Hofstader, R. (1965). *The Paranoid Style in American Politics and Other Essays*. New York: Knopf.

James, W. (1950). *The Principles of Psychology*, 2 vols. New York: Dover Publications.

—— (1955). Humanism and Truth. In *Pragmatism and Four Essays from the Meaning of Truth*. New York: Meridian Books (pps. 229-256).

—— (1982). *The Varieties of Religious Experience*. New York: Penguin Books.

—— (1987). The problem of the Negro. In F.B. Burkhardt, Bowers, F. & I.K. Skrepskelis (Eds.) *The Works of William James: Essays, Comments and Reviews*. Cambridge, MA: Harvard University Press (p. 192).

Klein, M. (1946). Notes on some schizoid mechanisms. *International Journal of Psychoanalysis*, 27: 99-110.

—— (1984). *The Writings of Melanie Klein: Love, Guilt and Reparation and Other Works 1921-1945*, vol. 1. New York: The Free Press.

Myers, G.E. (1986). *William James: His Life and Thought*. New Haven, CT: Yale University Press.

Otto, M.C. (1943). On a certain blindness in William James. *Ethics*, 53: 184-191.

Said, E.W. (1961). *The Word, The Text, and the Critic*. Cambridge, MA: Harvard University Press.

III. SAINTLINESS: THE STRUGGLE TO BE STRONG

OVER MY DEAD BODY:
A "COMMON SENSE" TEST OF SAINTLINESS

RICHARD A. HUTCH

William James (1842-1910) sought, he wrote, "to test saintliness by common sense" (James 1961: 264). He wished to use "human standards" to decide how far the "religious life" commends itself as "an ideal kind of human activity" (James 1961: 264). If the religious life commends itself, then any theological beliefs that may support it stand accredited. Only on such a basis of "human working principles" (James 1961: 264) has religion in the long run supported life as it is, and not misled people about what life ought to be. This paper specifies what two such "human working principles," or "human standards," are in the context of James's life and work, and these are particularly expressed in *The Varieties of Religious Experience: A Study in Human Nature* (1961; hereafter VRE).

I shall argue that these two principles are associated with James's experience of his body (Hutch 1991; 1993; 1994). James always worried about bodily fitness, perhaps as an emblem of his fragile philosophical hope that goodness would triumph over evil, that life would outweigh death. His philosophical hope not withstanding, he was even more powerfully haunted by what his chief biographer, Ralph Barton Perry, called "a ghost or premonition of disability" (Perry 1954: 361): James was declared physically unfit for military service during the Civil War, lost the use of his eyes for two long periods, once as a youth and again in old age, suffered from chronic insomnia, weakness of the back, digestive disorders, grippe, nervous fatigue and, in 1898, not long before giving the Gifford Lectures, severe heart strain.

But it was the death from tuberculosis in 1870 of his beloved cousin, Minny Temple, that so devastated James and had a lasting affect throughout his life. He was twenty-eight years old at the time, and had just taken out his M.D. degree from Harvard the year before. She was twenty-five years old, and had been an orphan who was raised by the Tweedys, neighbors of the James family in Newport, Rhode Island. Young Minny Temple had captivated James as no other woman ever did in his life except, perhaps, his mother-in-law, Eliza Putnam Gibbens, with whom he shared "complete mutual trust" (Allen 1967: 360). James himself had suffered a "nervous collapse" (Allen 1967: 161) late in 1869 just prior to Minny's death. This was in part related to his experimentation with the hypnotic drug, chloral. His physical and emotional disablement set him up to be overwhelmed by the force of circumstances.

Shortly after Minny's death, James revealed a considerable personal engagement with death. In his diary for March 22, 1870 (Holographs in the James Papers, Houghton Library, Harvard University) appeared an entry about the positive value that he associated with death, whilst also obviously engaged emphatically in Minny's life:

By that big part of me that's in the tomb with you, may I realize and believe in the immediacy of death! May I feel that every torment suffered here passes and is as a breath of wind,—every pleasure too. Acts and examples stay. Time is long. One human life is an instant. Is our patience so short-winded, our curiosity so dead or our grit so loose, that one instant snatched out of the endless age should not be cheerfully sat out. Minny, your death makes me feel the nothingness of all our egoistic fury. The inevitable release is sure; wherefore take our turn kindly whatever it contain. Ascend to some sort of partnership with fate, and since tragedy is at the heart of us, go to meet it, work it in to our ends, instead of dodging it all our days, and being run down by it at last. *Use* your death (or your life, it's all one meaning), "tut twam asi." ("Thou art that.")

Evidently, death was a preoccupation that James sought to convert into a constructive moral force for living, or compensation for this "ghost" or "premonition" of disability. The linkage between James's nervous collapse of 1869 and his bereavement in 1870, itself linked to a young woman and her death, created a potent symbolic nexus that would affect his personal and professional life into the new century. Converging in that nexus were the forces of life and death, men and women—the power of beginnings and endings, and sexuality. James's bereavement became a source of spiritual power, or the compelling moral force evident in all of his activities.

He spent the rest of his life trying to negotiate an inner settlement with this traumatic confluence of Minny's death and his own disability, or the frailty of his body. His feelings as a man, his sense of Minny as a woman and their deep empathic connection from childhood served James as a microcosm of a personal drama of life and death combined with a virtual archetypal sense of relations between women and men in general. Men and women at their best share projects based on complementary self-reliance and moral freedom, whilst always on death's door, or sensing the fragility of life. James's grief and feeling of personal devastation were, perhaps, intergenerational counterpoints of his father's "vastation" near Windsor Castle when William was a baby, sometime around 1844 (Edel 1982: 301). Knowledge of the mystical episode of Henry James Sr. in England set a youthful William on a course of curiosity about religious experience, a preoccupation with lived experience and its inherent patterns, rather than with theological beliefs *per se*. Soon after his father's death, James wrote to his wife, "... you must not leave me till I understand a little more of the value and meaning of religion in Father's sense, in the mental life and destiny of men" (letter of January 6, 1883; quoted in Perry 1954: 253). Thus, filial piety also pressed James to undertake the Gifford Lectures on religion.

A turnover of the generations placed a father's spiritual legacy on the agenda of a son's life of self-reliance and moral freedom (Perry 1954: 253-254). This self-conscious legacy floated on the surface of the less than self-conscious powerful current composed of James's persistent sense of disability and grief that was made so poignant for him in 1869-1870. All of this was inserted into his marriage and given form as a shared intellectual project in which reckoning with women figured prominently. But Alice Howe Gibbens, James's wife, fell in second behind her mother, to whom *The Varieties of Religious Experience* is dedicated. His mother-in-law took him to seances, inspired his studies of psychic phenomena and was his constant and reassuring correspondent during his time overseas (1899-1902), when he was recovering from serious heart strain and other illnesses and also preparing to give the Gifford Lectures (1901-1902). James himself often conflated the identities of his wife and her mother, and continually sought their shared maternal support (Allen 1967: 406). Writing to his mother-in-law from London as he was preparing the Gifford Lectures, James said that his wife "had almost come to feeding me .... After you, Dear Mother, she is the blessedest phenomenon I have struck upon this earth ...." (letter of November 14, 1899; quoted in Allen 1967: 406). Although influences mediated to him by parents formed a significant immediate backdrop behind the Gifford Lectures, they were not the most powerful ones. Lingering and unresolved grief over the death of Minny Temple in 1870, though removed in time, conflated with his relationship to his wife and especially with her mother and commanded James most as the Gifford

Lectures neared, this in spite of a current of scholarly thought that lay emphasis on the influence of James's relationship with his father (Strout 1968).

James's nervous collapse of 1869 and his devastation and sustained grief over Minny Temple's death in 1870, together converging as a "bodily grounding of meaning" (Johnson 1993: 413; 1991), are the torments to which his famous "panic fear" vision of the so-called "French sufferer" in *The Varieties of Religious Experience* is attributed (James VRE: 138-139). This anguished portrayal is central to the lecture entitled "The Sick Soul," dare say to all of the Gifford Lectures, and it has attracted wide-ranging scholarly interest (Strout 1971). Also, it has been called an "hallucinatory" experience, and has been directly linked to James's "'Crisis' texts" from his diary of 1870 (McDermott, ed. 1967: 3, 6-8). The "panic fear" vision is recognized by scholars to be thoroughly and characteristically autobiographical (Allen 1967: 165-166), and the personal inner source of the energy conveyed by James's entire lecture series. Thus, disability and death, or the body in decline and dying, formed the undercurrent of James's study of religious experience, and this was associated intimately with women and intergenerational forces. A standard test of saintliness by "common sense," James believed, would eliminate the humanly unfit and promote the survival of the humanly fittest, applied to religious beliefs. But fitness depended on facing disability and death, and wresting value from it.

Although my essay focuses specifically on James's lectures, "Saintliness" and "The Value of Saintliness," it also is evoked by my own readings and re-readings of *The Varieties of Religious Experience* as a devotional text in my pursuit of the truth of life. My project is about how I myself have been reflected in James's text and instructed by it, about how reflection on saintliness and the cultivation of a "saintly character" (VRE: 220) together have become professional and personal endeavors for me, this in spite of postmodern critics who claim that such pursuits are impossible in principle. James calls the fundamental mystery of religious experience "the satisfaction found in absolute surrender to the larger power" (VRE: 256). Such a power, I now foreshadow, gripped me suddenly about twenty-five years ago, and it has held me in awe and fascination ever since. It was nothing short of a religious "vision," and it will be described in Jamesian fashion soon.

As a result, like James, I too find the spectre of disability and death, or the body in decline and dying, to be an affirmation of what he called the "Sick Soul," or that kind of person who accepts all that would put us asunder (what he refers to as "evil"). Such a person accepts evil "not only as incurable but as *essential*," says James, and has "made his peace with the world on terms which evil dictates" (VRE: 116-117). Evil is not just a social condition that, like an injustice, could be eliminated. Rather, it is an ontological faultline, or a condition of human existence that would limit life, and even destroy it (VRE: 119). The opposite temperament, "healthy-mindedness," to my thinking, flies in the face of my personal experience (as also for James) and, hence, pales in contrast (Vasilyuk 1991). If the lectures on "The Divided Self," "Conversion," and "Conversion Concluded" are viewed as elaborations of the lecture, "The Sick Soul," then it is clear that on quantitative grounds alone James himself was much less interested in "The Religion of Healthy-mindedness" than he was in the faultlines and deep rumblings of psychological morbidity as an opportunity to engender saintliness.

Suffering, the emblem of the "Sick Soul," is for James a part of the deeper meaning of life, sublimated into what his chief biographer rightly called the "exaltation of self-sacrifice" (Perry 1954: 359). Death and dying loomed large as a crucible in which the saintly character is formed: "No matter what a man's frailties otherwise may be," writes James about saintly value, "if he be willing to risk death, and still more if he suffer it heroically, in the service he has chosen, the fact consecrates him forever" (VRE: 288). It is a mystery recognized by common sense, he avows, that "he who feeds on death that feeds on men possesses life supereminently and excellently, and meets best the secret demands of the universe" (VRE: 288). Such is saintliness. But this takes place, says James, only insofar as a person is "congenitally fated to suffer from its presence," that is, to suffer from "consciousness of evil," or our complicity in all human suffering, dying and death (VRE: 119).

How such a process works psychologically is to recognize, as Ralph Barton Perry puts it, an "exaltation of self-sacrifice" as a practical Jamesian strategy for living. This is accomplished by means of acceding to the natural trajectory of our bodies toward disability and death, or bodily decline and dying (and aligning our wills with these inexorable forces). As this occurs, certain indicators appear by which saintliness can be compellingly understood, cultivated and tested. The abiding questions for me have become, How might one, indeed, be said to have a saintly character? and, furthermore, How might "human standards," or "human working principles,"—what James called "common sense"—be used to test it for living? A preliminary answer to these questions involved my conviction that saintliness should not be based upon a "forensic metaphor," in which individual and social merit (sin/guilt) is the issue, but, instead, its grounding in human *"mortality"* needs to be recognized—a recognition which calls into question systems of merit themselves (Aden 1994: 92-96).

The keys are our perceptual field and human embodiment, which together compose an intuitive backdrop that emphasizes saintly corporeality (Wyschogrod 1990: 17; Merleau-Ponty 1962). "The body is the storm centre," writes James, "the origin of coordinates, the constant place of stress .... Everything circles round it and is felt from its point of view" (James 1976: 86). Put in other words, the body "as a *whole*" functions as a "sensorium" (Wyschogrod 1990: 17). The extremes of ecstacy and distress express the "organic range of saintly corporeality," quite literally the "systole and diastole of saintly consciousness," in which the body as a whole expresses itself" (Wyschogrod 1990: 18-19); also see Falk 1985; Feher, Naddaff and Tazi, eds. 1990; Johnson 1991; Sullivan 1990). In a Jamesian spirit, I shall propose a common sense test of saintliness based on the body and its inherent potential for disability and death, or the body in decline and dying. This will be *self-sacrifice*, and how lives "exalt" this *bodily* to one degree or another. But first, it is important to set up James's view of saintliness for the purpose of seeing exactly what it is as well as all it is not, and then developing our thought from there.

JAMES ON THE SAINTLY CHARACTER

The "ripe fruits of religion" James calls "Saintliness," or that character for which "spiritual emotions" are the "habitual centre of [ones] personal energy" (VRE: 200). Two matters arise. On the one hand, James identifies and describes at length those "ripe fruits," or outgrowths of "spiritual emotions." Intellectually, these were associated with his father and with his father's imminent death. James called him "ripe," this being a tribute to his "sacred old Father" (James 1920: 220). At first sight, we are led to believe that if a person can be said to evidence all of the spiritual emotions most of the time, then *ipso facto* saintliness is present in that life (see Cunningham 1980; Kieckhefer and Bond, eds. 1988). One could read James as a member of thinkers who constitute a major lineage of American Puritan thought. In this regard, one could well associate James's list of spiritual emotions with Benjamin Franklin's "little book of virtues," in terms of which Franklin assessed his daily success or failure at character building (Franklin 1940: 103-160).

On the other hand, however, James falls short of suggesting just how people might establish such an "habitual centre of [their] personal energy." This methodological shortfall is perhaps characteristic of James's iconoclastic intellectual style and resistance to functional explanations, in favor of the personal autobiographical testimonial and phenomenological descriptions of lived experience. James suggests that the "fruits" of religion appear on the vine of life of certain individuals, but he says little about the dynamic "ripening" of such fruits. Perhaps by failing to take up this matter of the formation of the saintly character, James sustains vicariously (and happily) an aura of mystery about the religious experience beneath the surface of his father's intellectual life. Thus, the process of the "ripening" of the saintly character needs to be addressed lest we end up only with (say) "sour grapes" about religious commitments that may fail, or fruit that "rots on the vine," never finding suitable expression. After all, James's discussion of saintliness, as one major commentator has put it, is "not to describe or endorse" any particular and exclusive *list* of fruits of religion, so much as it is to insist that it is "to the fruits, the pragmatic outcome, that we must look for validation" of an inner process of growth come what may (Dittes 1973: 310). However, unripened fruit is of little use (Kotarba and Fontana, eds.).

What is saintliness, variously ripened in the lives of individuals, for James? The Jamesian view is twofold, with what he calls (A) "fundamental inner conditions" that overide in importance what he suggests are (B) "characteristic practical consequences" that grow from them (James 1961: 221).

Of the former, (A) "fundamental inner conditions," which pertains to the "habitual centre" of a person's self-understanding, four "spiritual emotions," or archetypal affects, are mentioned: (1) "A feeling of being in a wider life than that of this world's selfish little interests; and a conviction, not merely intellectual, but as it were sensible, of the existence of an Ideal Power" (VRE: 220); (2) "A sense of the friendly continuity of the ideal power with our own life, and a willing self-surrender to its control" (VRE: 221); (3) "An immense elation and freedom, as the outlines of the confining selfhood melt down" (VRE: 1961: 221); and (4) "A shifting of the emotional centre towards loving and harmonious affectations, towards 'yes, yes,' and away from 'no,' where the claims of the non-ego are concerned" (VRE: 221). These four internal spiritual emotions constitute the "fundamental mystery of religious experience" (VRE: 256). They yield the more formulaic view, as James put it in his famous definition, that religion as the sum total of "the feelings, acts, and experiences of individual men in their solitude, so far as they apprehend themselves to stand in relation to whatever they may consider the divine" (VRE: 42).

Of the latter, (B) "characteristic practical consequences" of saintliness, or the "ripe fruits" of religion that are said to follow from well established "fundamental inner conditions," James cites four specific lifestyle features that arise and shape the saintly character. Each is an aspect of the overall shift of the emotional centre of the self to the "fundamental mystery of religious experience," the central axis of *homo religiosus*: (1) "Asceticism," which is an idiom of "sacrifice" and a measure of "loyalty to the higher power" (VRE: 221); (2) "Strength of Soul," or a sense of "enlargement of life," one so uplifting that the power of self-interest is denied and "new reaches of patience and fortitude open out" (VRE: 221); (3) "Purity," or an enhancement of sensitivity to "spiritual discords" and an imperative to cleanse from existence "brutal and sensual elements" (VRE: 221); and (4) "Charity," or "tenderness for fellow-creatures," which inhibits "ordinary motives to antipathy" and makes the saint love his enemies and treat "loathsome beggars as his brothers" (VRE: 221). The laudatory nature of James's list loses its otherwise compelling force with the realization that in time it could appear to be dated and neglected, much as Franklin's list of virtues appears to be today. What counts most for James "as a good outcome" of cultivating spiritual emotions depends in large measure "on the culture and expectations and values within which the outcome occurs" (Dittes 1973: 310).

However, although such "characteristic practical consequences" may possibly vary from context to context, presumably, the "fundamental inner conditions," or one's "spiritual emotions," do not. Quite apart from "asceticism," "strength of soul," "purity" and "charity," the inner "spiritual emotions" specify a self-conscious engagement by an individual, as James puts it, in the "fundamental mystery of religious experience," or that basic emotional centre of the self as essentially religious, or dialectically related to "Otherness" as a quality of lived experience. But James never goes into these emotions. The process that ties together the "fundamental inner conditions" remains unelaborated. But this is precisely where the "common sense" test of self-sacrifice and its bodily exaltation in lives comes into play.

I shall argue that an elaboration of the "fundamental inner conditions" of a person's self-understanding will readily be served by focusing on the *human body*, and on the ways in which the body, by necessity, engages in a sacrificial cycle of life. Cultivating an awareness of this natural process, not resisting it, is to engender "spiritual emotions." Certain elements to which the body is responsive during living occasion the "fundamental inner conditions" of the individual. James only partially took up this consideration, and it needs to be developed beyond what he offers.

The "human standards," or "human working principles," soon to be described, form what James profiled as the saintly person, who is beckoned on by the pursuit of an ideal social self that is "at least *worthy* of approving recognition by the highest *possible* judging companion" (James 1890, I: 315). This "sense of an ideal spectator" is an inner tribunal that most men "carry in their breast ... (and) .... Those who have *most* of it are possibly the most *religious* men" (James 1890, I: 316). Here possibly is stated James's understanding of the conscience as a visual modality, based not on a sense of punishment, but literally on *facing* disability and death, or the body in decline and dying, and bearing witness to this, or seeing all of one's life from such an angle of vision. The point is that James "embodied" such witness. For example, his style of embodying mortality made a lasting impression on Sigmund Freud when they met at Clark University in 1909:

> I shall never forget one little scene that occurred as we were on a walk together. He (James) stopped suddenly, handed me a bag he was carrying and asked me to walk on, saying that he would catch me up as soon as he had got through an attack of angina pectoris which was just coming on. He died of that disease a year later; and I have always wished that I might be as fearless as he was in the face of approaching death (Jones 1961: 267-268).

Thus, it is not sufficient to react to a terminal illness only as James suggested it should best be met, namely, by "gentlemanly levity, by high-minded stoicism, or by religious enthusiasm...taking each in turn *pro re nata*" (quoted in Perry 1954: 360). How by facing disability and death, or the body in decline and dying, a list of cultural and/or social values or virtues arises, is not my specific emphasis here.

"THERE WAS SUCH A HORROR OF HIM"

An unconscious conspiracy with the force of evil, in which one unknowingly turns a blind eye towards disability and death, or bodily decline and dying, gives rise to "healthy-mindedness" and the "once-born" type of consciousness, which, says James, bears "no element of morbid compunction or crisis" (VRE: 81). For the "Sick Soul," evil has become a conscious recognition, one that can be evoked repeatedly, thereby becoming a valuable standpoint for strenuous and robust living. When one surveys contemporary culture, a preponderance of the former kind of personality is evident. "Healthy-mindedness" implies an attitude of denial towards death; the "Sick Soul" suggests an obsession with dying.

Two principles contribute to the formation of saintliness as a process of *ongoing human sacrifice*, itself based on a need to embody thought. The two principles to abide if thought is to become embodied and if a lifestyle of self-sacrifice is to command allegiance, are what I call, (I) the *turnover of generations*, that we live not just "now," but also out of past generations and into future ones; and (II) *biological (and gender) complementarity*, that males and females, not just males and not just females, together create generational turnover. Although these two principles are downplayed in many contemporary religious outlooks, increased attention to them will be the foundation on which an expanded worldview, itself based on a new "historical horizon", namely, the *"death event"* (Wyschogrod 1990: xiv), can be established. Like James, who was haunted by the prospect of bodily disability and decline, so too we are invited to think under the spectre of an awareness framed by dying and death. Being human is represented by the body as a biological entity, with an ecological integrity and inherent principles all its own, ones beyond our control. It is James's "fundamental mystery of religious experience," and this compels us to present our bodies as a living sacrifice to life.

The "mystery of religious experience," by means of an emphasis on the body, can be recovered just as James gathered himself together after his nervous collapse of 1869 and amidst his grief over the death of Minny Temple a year later. James embodied the "mystery of religious experience" by means of his "panic fear" vision that is recounted in *The Varieties of Religious Experience* in 1901-1902. In his vision, evil was banished and death squarely faced in bodily form, right on down to the "pit" of his stomach—"a black-haired youth with greenish skin, entirely idiotic ... looking absolutely non-human .... There was such a horror of him ... I became a mass of quivering fear .... I awoke morning after morning with a horrible dread at the pit of my stomach, and with a sense of the insecurity of life ... (that) has made me sympathetic with the morbid feelings of others ever since" (VRE: 138). The "panic fear" vision is a virtual orchestration of the two principles that contribute to the formation of saintliness as a process of ongoing human sacrifice.

Thus, feeling panic and fear in the "pit of my stomach" leads the "French sufferer" (a.k.a. James) to think that most people are "unconscious of that pit of insecurity beneath the surface of life"—a "revelation" from which, curiously, the sufferer sought to shield his "mother," in spite of the "religious bearing" of that insight and his own personal tactic of taking refuge in "scripture and texts" that invoked "God" (James 1961: 138-139). Generations mix in the scenario, along with male and female associations. James then draws out a lesson of disability and death, or bodily decline and dying, from the sufferer's "fear of the universe," namely, "...it always is that man's original optimism and self-satisfaction get leveled with the dust" (VRE: 139). Thus, James implies that the human body is the basis of religious thought. Such thought embodies life-giving death, or generational turnover, and shared sexuality, or biological (and gender) complementarity.

An adherence to such principles of embodied thought leads to primordial associations with the symbolic infrastructure of the world's religions. In regard to the first principle of the turnover of generations, symbolic associations, or traditions of "wisdom," have always been passed down through generations, usually by moral exemplars like respected "tribal elders." "Apostolic succession" and other "lineages" of highly developed individuals in a number of the religions of the world are examples of this. Primordial and symbolic associations that flow from the second principles of biological (and gender) complementarity link women with the earth, the waxing and waning moon, and fertility; and men have been traditionally linked with the sky, the fire of the sun, and tool usage. Such symbolic associations represent life sacrificed, or less than sanguine prospects in the cultural and religious repertoire of humankind for accessing, retrieving and cultivating human meaning. James was clearly on to this.

He thought that the "completest religions" of the world were those in which the "pessimistic elements are best developed," and he cited Christianity and Buddhism as the best known examples (VRE: 141). The motif of the sacrificed life is pointedly illustrated in Christianity by the figure of Jesus (not yet the Christ, the Saviour) being crucified on the cross, and in Buddhism by the emaciated Siddhartha Guatama (not yet the Buddha, the Enlightened One) surrendering his quest for enlightenment beneath the Bo Tree. Both images portend a "sacred marriage" (*hieragamos*), where the sky (male) and the earth (female) are joined by means of axial "trees of life," this connection made available to us as the "birth" of the "wisdom" of the Christ's and Buddha's acts and teachings. Such cultural imagery constitutes an unending reverie that exists as an actuality beneath the moral reflection according to which the human species aims to survive and thrive into the future, and it is linked to nature and to the human body in a principled fashion (Eliade 1958; Cave 1993). Thus, I shall now embody my own thought, and become autobiographical.

STOPPED DEAD IN MY TRACKS: A LESSON

The central Jamesian question throughout *The Varieties of Religious Experience* is, how might one secure an integrated worldview, and then live it out, from moment to moment, always on the brink of a fundamental disintegration and the possibility of death? The process of affirming our "common humanity," its joys but especially its sorrows and horrors, even as we are biologically similar, is for me the source of the saint's "fundamental inner conditions" or "spiritual emotions." Living out this process, which is both moral and biological, engages us in what Christian theologians call "incarnation," the inseparable unity of "flesh" and "spirit," where disintegration and death are more commanding than is the integrated worldview and life itself.

My conviction about the importance of this derives mostly from my spiritual mentor, Martin Luther King, Jr. I volunteered to work in King's American civil rights movement early in the 1960's. Besides advocating political enfranchisement for southern blacks in a segregated (and still racist) society, the movement also represented a spiritual and moral force not seen in the United States since the end of the Civil War in 1865. During my time in the Deep South, I was nearly killed twice by gunfire and once badly assaulted, wounded and hospitalized due to the hostility of my fellow white Americans, albeit southern "rednecks."

This historical engagement with forces beyond my control subsequently had a psychological expression. When King was assassinated in 1968 an acute grief reaction overcame me, one that links me with William James and his own critical personal juncture of 1869-1870. My experience involved a visionary episode, or a temporary psychotic break with reality, in which my body discorporated (horribly) and was then reincorporated (profoundly peacefully). Since becoming an Australian citizen, I look back on this episode and offer the following testimony on behalf of that "American sufferer," who was a person who consciously recognized evil in a way that was similar to James's own "nervous collapse" and devastation over Minny Temple's death:

> News of the assassination came on the radio, and I fell back on my bed listening in disbelief late into the afternoon. But things soon grew strange and began to change horribly. There I stretched out on my bed—no, what?!—a slab of slate on the floor of a desert canyon that was encircled by low rolling hills. Stars in the night sky twinkled overhead. A green/yellow light enveloped my body, at first emanating from my heart, and pulsated from head to toe. Fear overcame me. Then I was seized by panic. It was the *horror* of observing my body fall apart, seeing bones protrude through my flesh and blood vessels spurt like leaking hoses, and then witnessing

my body decay into a puddle of putrid matter and gore. "Dead," I said to myself. However, suddenly I was caught by the realization that it was I myself who was watching my discorporation from above, and reassurance seemed to emanate from the stars overhead. Calmness took hold and I felt a profound trust in the universe, as if my body no longer was needed, as if a lesson was being learned. Nonetheless, the scene then slowly reversed itself: my body reincorporated, the pulsating light diminished, and I found myself back on my bed in the middle of the night with the radio still on, though the station was now off the air. Neither before nor since that day has anything else so powerfully moved me, causing me to doubt all security and trust in the universe, and thereafter shaping my life personally and professionally. You could say that my historical and psychological engagement with Martin Luther King, Jr., truly a religious leader in a worldly sense, continues to fuel most of my vocational activities and preoccupations in one way or another, even to this day. I never mentioned any of it to my parents. It is an understatement for me to say that I can relate personally to the "panic fear" vision of William James, which was presented as the testimony of the "French sufferer" in *The Varieties off Religious Experience*.

Always pursuing a liberating historical cause I, nonetheless, continue to walk through the "valley of the shadow of death," so to speak, itself a powerful and ever-present psychological actuality. But I cannot say comfortably the line that follows (Psalms 23:4), namely, "I fear no evil." More of the evil and horror than the goodness and peace of that powerful personal event remain a memory that has impact on my life each day.

Back then in 1964-1968 I found, and today I keep on finding, myself propelled into an hallucinatory scenario that resolves itself in a most powerful conviction that violence must always precede nonviolence, that spiritual wholeness comes about only by means of the *bodily expenditure of life*, and that wholeness comes in only second to falling apart. Continuing to haunt me from my youth, now for very different reasons, is not only the Old Testament imagery of the "valley of dry bones" (Ezekial 37:1-14), itself also an uncanny representation of my more recent experience of the Australian Outback. But also premonitory and haunting is the New Testament injunction, "I appeal to you brethren, by the mercies of God, to present your bodies as a living sacrifice, holy and acceptable to God, which is your spiritual worship" (Romans 12:1). Perhaps needless to say, this injunction also resonates within the Four Noble Truths of Buddhism, which imply that extinguishing the human desire to make all things permanent (including the body and its extension, the self) is the central soteriological task of the *arhat*, or saint. An implicit theology of lived experience becomes evident, one that suggests to me now accredited theological beliefs that are based on my own (in James's words) "religious life" (VRE: 264).

Such now accredited theological beliefs can be stated. They are extensions of the truth discovered by being "stopped dead in my tracks," so to speak. Thus, what I now call the "god of death," who exacts humility, is more important than the "god of life," who supports human pride, at least when we claim to reckon with saintliness and saintly formation, whatever tradition of religion may from time to time command our interest and personal commitment. All this has propelled me into a life of religious preoccupation and, at the same time, has set me thinking, as academics must, about "human standards" of the "religious life" based on my experience (VRE: 264). Whilst most people are familiar with the "god of life," I argue that, in the end, it is the "god of death," or the harbinger of all sorrow, horror, disintegration and annihilation, with whom we must become acquainted if Jamesian saintliness is to become a living actuality in our lives. Together, both of these gods can be combined and called the *god of destruction*, whose lure is inescapable for those who would seriously engage in saintly formation. It was the god of destruction that touched James irreversibly in 1869-1870, and remained a powerful influence even into his last decade of life. My own historical engagement with Martin Luther King, Jr., and his movement during the summers of 1964 and 1965 drew my intuition to the god of destruction, and laid the foundation for my "vision" of 1968, itself of continuing influence decades later.

James tried to reckon with this god in the fabric of his inner sense of living. "I am getting really anxious lest I be cut off in the bud" (letter to F.C.S. Schiller, April 8, 1903; quoted in Allen 1967: 436), he wrote in 1903. Although James wanted to write "a general system of metaphysics" (letter to H. Bergson, December 14, 1902; quoted in Allen 1967: 435), he embodied his project and called the task of formulating truths a "virulent disease" that he had recently contracted:

> I actually dread to die until I have settled the Universe's hash in one more book, which shall be *epoch-machend* at last, and a title of honor to my children! Childish idiot—as if formulas about the Universe could ruffle its majesty, and as if the common-sense world and its duties were not eternally the really real! (letter to Mrs. H. Whitman, August 2, 1903; quoted in Allen 1967: 437).

Throughout all of James's works, the never-ending dramatic convergence of forces of destruction in the individual is a dominant motif.

Childish vanities though he resists, such motives have driven other people to create otherworldly images by which an individual might feign saintliness. Thus, even though we all can be "cut off in the bud" and may "dread to die," our anxiety can volatize into images of attaining an afterlife, the final human actuality and death, or bodily decline and dying, notwithstanding. James himself occasionally submitted to such a vanity:

> I never felt the *rational* need of immortality ...; but as I grow older I confess that I feel the practical need of it much more than I ever did before; and that combines with reasons ... to give me a growing faith in its reality. (letter to Carl Stumpf, July 17, 1904; quoted in Perry 1954: 268).

Like James alive, but now in death's tightening grip, the urge towards creativity was heightened.

Enjoying spiritual solace was never a Jamesian activity, though seeking it was. He often sifted through the Christian tradition for spiritual mentors. When his sister, Alice, died in 1892, a grief-stricken James selected a passage from Dante's *Divine Comedy* (1300) to be inscribed on her urn: "After long exile and martyrdom comes to this peace" (James 1947: 321). From Dante, James turned to a protestant for consolation when he cited John Bunyan's *The Pilgrims Progress* (1678 and 1684). Although James refers to John Bunyan as "Poor patient Bunyan," a typical case of the "psychopathic temperament" and sensitive of conscience "to a diseased degree" (VRE: 136-137), he uses Bunyan's testimony as confirmation of his own "sense of the insecurity of life," the absolute and horrible nadir of his "panic fear" vision (VRE: 138, footnote 18). Although it may be unusual, James relies very little on Augustine's autobiography in *The Varieties of Religious Experience*, but does say that Augustine illustrated a "discordant personality," in which having a "divided self" continued to be a nagging emotional problem for at least four years after his conversion episode of 386 C.E. (VRE: 146-147; footnote 6, citation about the research of Louis Gourdon on Augustine's "premature" account of conversion). But James himself was not palliated by sifting through the works of would-be spiritual mentors. In being "otherworldly," they were too sanguine; the human potential for devastation, horror and death was neglected. This James realized bodily, deep in the "pit" of his stomach.

To my mind, James's preoccupation with disability and death, or bodily decline and dying, at every turn of thought makes him more responsive to the "god of death" than to the "god of life." Whilst I had a sense of *walking* in the "valley of the shadow of death" during my civil rights engagement in the early 1960's, it was the actual sense of dying during my visionary episode of 1968 that literally "stopped me in my tracks." As James himself realized, the likes of Dante, Bunyan, Augustine and others may offer only limited insight into the necessary connections between saintliness and the mortal body. In other words, James remained more "incarnational" in his views on such matters, perhaps, than his well known Christian theological predecessors, which I myself can well appreciate.

Movement through imaginal time and space, perhaps journeying even to heavens, hells and within reincarnational cycles of rebirth, characterizes the religion of "healthy-mindedness," where growth, personal development and self-actualization are emphasized. But typical of the religion of the "sick soul" is a cessation of movement, a recognition of things at an end. The spiritual journey *as journey* is nothing more than, as Ralph Waldo Emerson once put it about global travel, a "fool's paradise" (Emerson 1964: 165). However, for those travellers who would not finally be fooled, it is a matter of recognizing that the end of life and cessation of "travelling" count most toward saintliness, or that which stops us, so to say, "dead in our tracks" during the course of living.

A "COMMON SENSE" TEST OF SAINTLINESS: LIFE SACRIFICED

A *sacrificed life* (to death) model of religious experience: This I proposed as an elaboration of what James had in mind when he wrote about "human standards," or "human working principles," that lie at the heart of saintliness. The human community itself, *not* individual selves, looms into prominence. The sacrificed life (to death) model accomplishes three things: (a) it allows us to take disability and death, or bodily decline and dying, on board; (b) raise high the body itself (not just thoughts or symbols of the body) as our natural sacrifice ("human sacrifice") to the future (generational turnover); and (c) affirm the inclusivity of the human community (biological and gender complementarity). This leads to a pervasive sense of global human solidarity and to moral vision based on a desire to repeat affirmations of such solidarity wherever and whenever this may be possible.

However, let life sacrificed not be taken naively. The predatory design of nature by which our bodies are determined presents a radical evil the minute our eyes are closed to it. Writes James,

> The lunatic's visions of horror are all drawn from the material of daily fact .... To believe in the carnivorous reptile of geologic time, is hard for our imagination .... Yet there is no tooth in any one of those museum-skulls that did not daily ... hold fast to the body struggling in despair as some fated living victim. Forms of horror just as dreadful to their victims, if on a smaller spatial scale, fill the world about us today .... Crocodiles and rattlesnakes and pythons are at this moment vessels of life just as real as we are; ... and whenever they or other wild beasts clutch their living prey, the deadly horror which an agitated melancholic feels is the literally right reaction on the situation (VRE: 140-141).

It is not only the "literally right reaction" for the melancholic, but also an appropriate reaction that may contribute to building up a "moral community" in the sense described by Emile Durkheim (1915) and, more importantly, by his nephew and most distinguished pupil, Marcel Mauss (1967).

Mauss concluded that human exchange was the key to moral empowerment: a "wise precept that is evident in human evolution" and valuable as an action plan for living, he writes, is that "we should come out of ourselves and regard the duty of giving as a liberty, for in it there lies no risk (Mauss 1967: 69). I suggest that a human "moral community" would be one supported by a vision of an *exchange of bodies* through death, sexuality and birth, a vision that is based on the two principles identified above. Each principle works in concert to foster such an exchange of bodies. Together the principles develop James's thought. My suggestion is that they are elaborations of the "fundamental inner conditions" by which, says James, the "spiritual emotions" of saintliness are formed.

The first principle of the sacrificed life model, as I said, is the turnover of generations. It is activated by what I have called the "god of death." Lived experience becomes moral insofar as present self-understanding is framed by awareness of one's ancestral past as it converges on the present, and how this gives rise to progeny and a future. Generational turnover is marked best by taking seriously the possible role played by mortality in one's life. It is difficult in living to "learn to die," or to give way to the next generation, and obedience to this first standard requires unusual moral courage. French thinker, Georges Bataille, suggests that religious experience is an exercise in cultivating "animality," this being an inner sense of "immediacy and immanence" (Bataille 1973: 23). Animality is the unbroken, unselfconscious continuity between an individual being and its environment. Emblematic of this is that instant, writes Bataille, in which *"one animal eats another"* (Bataille 1973: 23, original emphasis). Thus, the oneness of the animal world is such that violence and death are no disruption to it, but simply stages through which all life passes. Such a view represents the predatory design of nature to which James himself pointed.

The standard of this design is the "sacrificed life," in which death of the body and an annihilation of the self are, at bottom, fundamentals of living. Involved here is a process of exchanging bodies—those of the older generation, albeit ones that do not in themselves get returned, for those of the new generation. In Christianity, it is the metaphor of "crucifixion" writ large, and in Buddhism it is the metaphor of the "extinguished flame" of the human desire for permanence. The prospect of exchanging bodies sets in motion a series of challenging personal interrogations: Are we "death-aware?" Do we look for signs of death-awareness in others? Thus, when I read stories of lives like that of the "French sufferer" and others with mortality management in mind, or tell my own personal story as the "American sufferer," do I find useful instruction in *ars moriendi*, the "art of dying," as a lifestyle amidst my ordinary suffering (Mellor 1991)?[1] One hopes so.

The second principle of the sacrificed life model, also foreshadowed above, is biological (and gender) complementarity. It is activated by what I have called the "god of life," but who is obedient at all times to the first god. Biological production of the future requires women and men to unite sexually. (A genetics of reproduction based on experimental genderless technologies is far from common practice.) Here sexuality leads to natality, but also may lead to horrific sexual perversity and violence (Bataille 1928, 1973, 1985; Irwin 1993; Nehamas 1989), as nature's predatory design implies. But reproduction also must occur socially and culturally. This process would include not only the "front line," so to speak, of heterosexual practice, but also a homosexuality that is responsive to intergenerational realities and responsibilities. Any creative effort on behalf of the future in the face of the god of destruction must take into account not gender exclusivity, but

1. Suffering is a readily available idiom of human mortality. It is an experiential point of embarcation to understanding systems of soteriology (transformation of the self) evident in the history of religions.

inclusivity—that men and women reproduce the best of themselves together, as they also die together as members of their generation (Stevens 1991).[2] Learning to be biologically (as well as socially and culturally) inclusive, perhaps by gaining an initial awareness of this through sensuality and eroticism, implies a moral stance for life.[3] Sexuality in practice, of course, usually implies a pleasurable exchange of bodies, albeit ones that ordinarily get returned in themselves after sexual activity.

However, there is a downside to this sanguine view of sensuality and eroticism. Sexual activity partakes of the idiom of mortality: The self loses, or temporarily "sacrifices," itself to the partner in an exchange process. Nevertheless, in Christianity the metaphor of "resurrection" expresses this second principle of biological (and gender) complementarity on the basis of an erotic and sensual dimension, and this also is played out in some Buddhist traditions (*Tantra*) where erotic and sexual practices become means to "enlightenment." Here, too, challenging personal interrogations arise: Do we embrace inclusive sensuality/sexuality as an idiom of self-understanding, even by means of empathy, perhaps as James approximated in his relationships with Minny Temple and Eliza Putnam Gibbens? Do we view others not only with their sex life in mind, but also with a view to the biologically procreative and culturally creative implications of sexuality? (One could well wonder whether James's Gifford Lectures would ever have eventuated had he not received pampered personal indulgence from his wife in Europe, and professional support by means of correspondence from his mother-in-law at the time.) Thus, when I read stories of lives like that of the "French sufferer" and others with inclusive sensuality/sexuality appreciation in mind, or tell my own story as an "American sufferer" of decades ago and even to this day, do I find useful instruction in how to seek extension and completion of myself whilst affirming the "Other," this on the backdrop of my biologically evident incompleteness, as I am obviously not a woman? One hopes so.

In other words, what I call the god of destruction, or that combination of the "god of death" and the "god of life," with the latter always obedient to the former, has three faces—mortality, sexuality, and natality. These biological forces constitute what can be abstracted and called, "Otherness." This collective force is inherent in each of our bodies. Like a spreading malignancy, it annihilates us in the end, often horribly, as James himself well realized from his personal trials of 1869-1870. A sacrificed life is a style for living that is congruent with disability and death, or bodily decline and dying. A realistic lifestyle strategy would include as a central preoccupation an ongoing consideration of the role played by this force in one's life. Such, then, is a lifestyle of saintliness. James, I trust, would be sympathetic to such a view.

---

2. For example, the "monastic community" implies neither a primary nor an exclusive form of religious vocational commitment amongst many Christian groups. That a "nuptial community" predominates in historical Christianity suggests that gender complementarity, especially the biology inherent in it, forms the basis of a religious vocational commitment that is at least on a par with taking monastic vows.

3. Homosexuality is a cultural epiphenomenon with a biological appearance. It is not directly engaged in biological reproduction but may, of course, contribute a "sensuality of care," on the basis of the erotic dimension of lived experience, that supports the rearing of children and, more broadly, which constructively contributes to the future of the species. (The responsible management of HIV infection by means of insisting on "safe sex" and the compassionate regard and care of AIDS sufferers are examples of this. Not only is this strictly a short term private matter, but it may also become the basis for long term political activism and social policy formation.) In effect, the exclusivity evident in gay and lesbian communities must in the end bow to a species-specific awareness of the necessity of inclusivity, or the requirement to pass up self autonomy and to foster a sensuality of care that favours the future, cultural gender issues notwithstanding.

It is the nature of the universe, says James, that everyone is "drawn and pressed" into "sacrifices and surrenders of some sort" as "permanent positions of repose" (VRE: 57). Unlike non-religious sacrifices, which are viewed as necessary, in the saintly life, on the contrary, "surrender and sacrifice are positively espoused" (VRE: 57). Concludes James, *Religion thus makes easy and felicitous what in any case is necessary*" (VRE: 57, original emphasis). Inseparable from the body, selfhood is a continuously revised narrative of reckonings with the predatory design of nature. Eyes must open to see the "material daily fact" of evil, James wrote; and life must be lived facing the reality that "forms of horror ... fill the world about us today" (VRE: 141-142). Glimmers of insight come particularly when each and every one of the three faces of the god of destruction gains recognition in a life. Saintly formation, as a constructive means of mortality management—one that affirms disability and death, or bodily decline and dying, and does not deny it—will develop insofar as generational turnover and biological (and gender) complementarity are abided in living.[4]

The question of whether these two general principles are affirmed together in a life, even deliberately cultivated by means of some kind of disciplined spiritual practice, provide us with a "common sense" test of saintliness. This test specifies and elaborates upon what James called the "human standards," or "human working principles," by which saintliness can be recognized. The test permits us to understand the connection between the "fundamental inner conditions" of saintliness in individuals, and how these might be said, as James put it, to undergo "ripening" into identifiable "spiritual emotions" that mark the saintly character. The test is based on "common sense," namely, that we are born and die and rehearse each of these dramas together under the banner, "LIFE." However, though it is in the way a "common sense" test of saintliness, the sense of cultivating a saintly character is far from common.

Introspection has allowed me to know the test from experience, or from that uncanny inner connection I continue to feel between James's "French sufferer," my own "American sufferer" and our shared compliance with the exacting demands of the god of destruction. Perhaps specifically because of our similar adversities—James's of 1869-1870 and mine of 1964-1968—this god would propel us both on a road in life that slowly becomes a shared realization of budding sainthood. For me, the ripening of saintliness takes place only "over my dead body," so to speak. Or, at least, with reference to the daily actuality of disability and death, or the body in decline and dying, within the lived experience that holds me, as it clearly held William James, in its ever tightening grip.

---

4. There are instructive case studies of how exemplary individuals comply with the "god of destruction" and begin to engender "saintliness" (Beckett 1957; Bernanos 1937; Frank 1992; Heller 1964; Keenan 1993; Monette 1988; Murphy 1990; Scarry 1986 and Updike 1989).

REFERENCES

Aden, R. (1994). Justification and sanctification: A conversation between Lutheranism and Orthodoxy. *St. Vladimir's Theological Quarterly*, 38: 87-109.

Allen, G. W. (1967). *William James: A Biography*. New York: Viking Press.

Bataille, G. (1928). *The Story of the Eye*. Paris: Gallimard.

_____ (1973). *Theorie de le Religion*. Paris: Gallimard.

_____ (1985). *Visions of Excess: Selected Writings, 1927-1939*. Allan Stoekl (Ed. and Trans.). Minneapolis, MN: University of Minnesota Press.

Beckett, S. (1957). *Murphy*. New York: Grove Press.

Bernanos, G. (1937). *The Diary of a Country Priest*. P. Morris (Trans.). New York: The Macmillan Press.

Cave, D. (1993). *Mircea Eliade's Vision for a New Humanism*. Oxford: Oxford University Press.

Cunningham, L.S. (1980). *The Meaning of Saints*. New York: Harper and Row.

Dittes, J. (1973). Beyond William James. In C.Y. Glock & P.E. Hammond (Eds.). *Beyond the Classics? Essays in the Scientific Study of Religion*. New York: Harper and Row (pp. 291-354).

Durkheim, E. (1915). *The Elementary Forms of the Religious Life*. J.W. Swain (Trans.). London: George Allen and Unwin.

Edel, L. (1982). *Stuff of Sleep and Dreams: Experiments in Literary Psychology*. London: Chatto and Windus.

Eliade, M. (1958). *Patterns in Comparative Religion*. Rosemary Sheed (Trans.). London: Sheed and Ward.

Emerson, R. W. (1964). Self-Reliance. B. Atkinson (Ed.). *The Selected Writings of Ralph Waldo Emerson*. New York: The Modern Library (pp. 145-169).

Falk, P. (1985). Corporeality and its fates in history. *Acta Sociologica*, 28: 115-136.

Feher, M., Naddaff, R. & N. Tazi (Eds.) (1990). *Fragments for a History of the Human Body*. New York: Houghton Mifflin.

Franklin, B. (1940). *The Autobiography of Benjamin Franklin*. New York: Washington Square Press.

Heller, J. (1964). *Catch-22*. London: Corgi Books.

Holographs (n.d.). The James Papers, Houghton Library, Harvard University.

Hutch, R. A. (1991). Mortal body, studying lives: Restoring *eros* to the psychology of religion. *International Journal for the Psychology of Religion*, 1: 193-210.

_____ (1993). Biography as a reliquary. *Soundings: An Interdisciplinary Journal*, 76: 467-485.

_____ (1994) Reading lives to live: Mortality, introspection, and the soteriological impulse. *Biography: An Interdisciplinary Quarterly*, 17: 121-139.

Irwin, A.C. (1993). Ecstasy, sacrifice, communication: Bataille on religion and inner experience. *Soundings: an Interdisciplinary Journal*, 76: 105-128.

James, H. (1947). *The Notebooks of Henry James*. F.O. Mattiessen & K. B. Murdock (Eds.). New York: Oxford University Press.

James, H., III (Ed.) (1920). *The Letters of William James*, 2 vols. Boston: Atlantic Monthly Press.

James, W. (1890). *The Principles of Psychology*, 2 vols. London: Macmillan.

_____ (1961). *The Varieties of Religious Experience: A Study in Human Nature*. London: Collier-Macmillan.

_____ (1976). *Essays in Radical Empiricism*. Cambridge, MA: Harvard University Press.

Johnson, M. (1991). Knowing through the body. *Philosophical Psychology*, 4: 13-18.

_____ (1993). Conceptual metaphor and embodied structures of meaning: A reply to Kennedy and Vervace. *Philosophical Psychology*, 6: 413-422.

Jones, E. (1961). *The Life and Works of Sigmund Freud*. L. Trilling & S. Marmo (Eds.). New York: Basic Books.

Keenan, B. (1992). *An Evil Cradling*. London: Hutchinson.

Kieckhefer, R. & G. D. Bond (Eds.) (1958). *Sainthood: Its Manifestations in World Religions*. Berkeley, CA: University of California Press.

Kotarba, J. & A. Fontana (Eds.) (1984). *The Existential Self in Society*. Chicago, IL: The University of Chicago Press.

McDermott, J. J. (Ed.) (1967). *The Writings of William James: A Comprehensive Edition*. New York: Random House.

Mauss, M. (1967). *The Gift: Forms and Functions of Exchange in Archaic Societies*. Ian Cunnison (Trans.). New York: W. W. Norton.

Mellor, P. A. (1991). Self and suffering: Deconstruction and reflexive definition in Buddhism and Christianity. *Religious Studies*, 27: 51-63.

Merleau-Ponty, M. (1962). *Phenomenology of Perception*. Colin Smith (Trans.). London: Routledge & Kegan Paul.

Monette, P. (1988). *Borrowed Time: An AIDS Memoir*. New York: Avon.

Murphy, R. (1990). *The Body Silent*. New York: W. W. Norton.

Nehamas, A;. (1989). The attraction of repulsion: The deep and ugly thought of Georges Bataille. *The New Republic*, October 23, pp. 31-36.

Perry, R. B. (1935). *The Thought and Character of William James*, 2 vols. London: Oxford University Press.

_____ (1954). *The Thought and Character of William James, Briefer Version*. New York: George Braziller.

Scarry, E. (1986). *The Body in Pain: The Making and Unmaking of the World*. New York: Oxford University Press.

Stevens, C. (1991). The trinitarian roots of the nuptial community. *St. Vladimir's Theological Quarterly*, 4: 351-358.

Strandberg, V. (1981). *Religious Psychology in American Literature: A Study in the Relevance of William James*. Madrid: Jose Porrua, S. A.; Potomac, MD: Studia Humanitatis.

Strout, C. (1968). William James and the twice-born sick soul. *Daedalus*, 97: 1062-1082.

_____ (1971). The pluralistic identity of William James: A psychohistorical reading of *The Varieties of Religious Experience*. *American Quarterly*, 23: 135-152.

Sullivan, L. E. (1990). Body works: Knowledge of the body in the study of religion. *History of Religions*, 30: 86-99.

Updike, J. (1989). *Self-Consciousness: Memoirs*. New York: Fawcett Crest.

Vasilyuk, F. (1992). *The Psychology of Experiencing*. New York: New York University Press.

Wyschogrod, E. (1990). *Saints and Postmodernism: Revisioning Moral Philosophy*. Chicago, IL: The University of Chicago Press.

THE SKY-BLUE SOUL: WOMEN'S RELIGION IN *THE VARIETIES OF RELIGIOUS EXPERIENCE*

PATRICIA H. DAVIS

At a time when women were largely invisible members of American culture, William James recognized the need to include women's voices in *The Varieties*, his study of "the religious propensities of man" (VRE: 4). Indeed, it seems that James distinguished himself as somewhat of a heroic figure toward women in his scholarly work and in his public life. Although he could never be considered a political activist for the burgeoning woman's movement, his writing reveals that he was very impatient with those who tried to dismiss women's moral and intellectual abilities. He was quick, for example, to defend women against two of the major figures of his time, Horace Bushnell and J. S. Mill, when they voiced their views on the "natural" subordination and subjugation of women—views which had wide public appeal and approval (Myers 1986: 424-427).

This paper poses a natural question of *The Varieties*: How are women's religious experiences *actually* represented by James in a text which he hoped would describe the totality of human religiousness? To answer this question onJames's methodology and its effect on his interpretations of women's experience will be examined. In addition, these interpretations themselves will be explored examining James's placement of and use of the women's narratives in his overall text. Several women's lives and writings will be examined in detail, including Mary Baker Eddy's and Saint Teresa's, to show ways in which alternate readings to James may be more appropriate. The paper will ultimately show that while James recognizes women's experience as important enough to reckon with, he is, unhappily, unable to appreciate the complexity or depth of the lives of the women he includes. Most of them tend to be portrayed as having less realistic (and therefore less valuable) religious experiences than the men he also chronicles. *The Varieties* is shown to be, among many other more positive things, a testimony to James's mostly unsuccessful attempts to understand women and their religious experiences.

JAMES'S METHODOLOGY IN *THE VARIETIES*

James's method of investigation in *The Varieties* was designed with the aim of discovering and describing the "religious feelings and the religious impulses" inherent in human experience (VRE: 12). He begins by separating the question of the description of these religious propensities from the question of their philosophical significance. Although his original intention in the Gifford Lectures was to spend equal time on both questions, his final project concentrated mainly on the first. His starting place for uncovering religious experience was not with philosophy, historical origins, or theology, but rather with the testimonies of religious men and women. James M. Edie has described this method which illustrated how to "remain faithful to the uniqueness, the primordiality, and the intrinsic complexity of the experience itself" (1987: 55) as James's unique contribution to the study of religious experience.

James's aim was to remain "experience-near" in his investigation and to elucidate, in as precise and accurate a form as possible, the actual *experiences* of the men and women he studied as distinct from their reflections on or preunderstandings of these, and also as distinct from the theorizing of the scholars and scientists who encounter them. In Lecture III, for example, James goes so far as to suggest that some persons even experience the religious dimensions of their lives on a pre-reflective level—prior to and foundational for belief—in the form of "quasi-sensible realities directly apprehended" (VRE: 59). Their thoughts and ideas about their experiences were second-hand to the actual experiences themselves.

James was not unaware, however, that all understandings are tempered and preformed by "background" ideas and abstractions: "Everything we know is 'what' it is by sharing in the nature of one of these abstractions ... we grasp all other things by their means...". In fact, for James, the "absolute determinability of our mind by abstractions" is one of the fundamental facts of human life (VRE: 53-54). James's phenomenological methodology can be critiqued precisely on this point; along with most other scholars of his time, he believed that a description of the world in which he lived and worked was a more or less complete description of universal reality. To be fair, he, himself, was sensitive to the possibilities of blindspots in "the cleric-academic-scientific type" of which he included himself, and was committed to overcoming the "besetting temptation" of ignoring others who did not fit this category: "... nothing can be more stupid than to bar out phenomena from our notice, merely because we are incapable of taking any part in them ourselves" (p. 95).

Regardless of his care to remain open to all kinds of experience, however, *The Varieties* could not be the systematic exploration of universal religious experience that James hoped it would be. It is rather, for the most part, an exploration of the religious options available to James as a Western man of his era. As most men of his time, he was unaware of his own blindspots when he tried to positively attend to and appreciate much of women's experience. Several important aspects of James's methodology contribute to this blindspot: (1) James's definition of religion which is primarily individualistic, (2) his preference for the religious "genius" which he defines in masculine terms, and (3) his own ambivalence toward women and their religious experience.

First, James was not particularly interested in experiences which had to do with community religion. For the purposes of *The Varieties* James defined religion as "the feelings, acts, and experiences of individual men in their solitude, so far as they apprehend themselves to stand in relation to whatever they may consider the divine" (VRE: 34). He thus intentionally excludes all forms of institutional/ecclesiastical and relational forms of religious experience. For James churches, theologies, and "ecclesiasticism" are relegated to "second-hand" religion; individual religion—the religion of the "founders"—is imbued with power due to "direct personal communion with the divine" (VRE: 33).

The omission of communitarian forms of religious experience is a significant one for anyone concerned with women's spirituality and experience as it has been described time and time again from James's era (Starbuck 1899) onward (Conn 1986; Williams 1993; Broner 1992; Morton 1985; Johnson 1992; Adams 1994; Ruether 1992; Keller 1986; and many others). As these works show, women's spirituality and religious experience tends to be relational: concerned with connection to the divine and also tied to relationships with other humans and with nature.

Keller, in fact, makes the claim that religious experience, when released from the constraints of patriarchal bonds is, at its core, communal: "Religion true to its name activates connection. It 'ties together,' binding up the wounds of breaking worlds. It is the bridging, bonding process at the heart of things." The individualistic kind of religion James describes could be seen, by Keller, as a threat to the process of love (Eros) which "seeks to get things together, no matter what." In fact, "Religion defining holiness as separation has made itself into the bearer of barriers, of disconnection, of exclusion" (1986: 218-219).

In *Women's Psyche, Women's Spirit: The Reality of Relationships* (1987), Mary Lou Randour undertakes a project similar to James's in order to describe and define women's spirituality specifically. In her study ninety-four women subjects from diverse religious, economic, and ethnic backgrounds completed a questionnaire designed to elicit accounts of an "important or memorable spiritual experience." They were instructed to describe the situation and their emotional responses to it as completely as possible (p. 27). Randour's assumption was not that men's and women's spiritual experiences would prove to be totally dichotomous, but rather that there would be certain distinctive and instructive elements in women's experience (p. 13). Her two major findings were that women's religious experience tends to include one or both of the following motifs: a feeling of acceptance by others and the divine, and a feeling of "connection to life and otherness" or "self-in-relation" through which many "apprehend the divine" (pp. 23, 25, 33).

Randour's findings would not be as instructive in terms of a study of James and *The Varieties* if they did not correspond almost exactly with E. D. Starbuck's findings from James's own era, in *The Psychology of Religion: An Empirical Study of the Growth of Religious Consciousness*. Starbuck, whose work centered on conversion experience and gender differences, administered questionnaires to 192 subjects: 120 females and 72 males (p. 24). One of his major findings regarding conversion was that males seemed to be controlled "more from within [i.e., individualistic motivation], while the females are controlled more from without [i.e., are more sensitive to "objective forces" which included teaching, imitation, and social pressure] (p. 53). Starbuck also quotes a study by George Coe entitled *Man and Woman* in which he agrees with Coe's conclusion that men "attain more in solitude" and women "attain less in solitude" (pp. 80-81).[1]

A second possible aspect of James's methodological blindspot in *The Varieties* has to do with his preference for some *kinds* of experience over others. For James, not only was individual religious experience privileged over community or relational experience, but the experience of the religious "genius" was privileged over those whose experience "exists as a dull habit" (VRE: 15) as a part of religious communities. James favored subjects whose experiences were tinged with what he would describe as "manly" strenuousness. Even where he downplays the values of manly athletic attitudes, in the face of the overriding Christian virtue of surrender, he does it grudgingly and admiringly. "A life is manly, stoical, moral, or philosophical, we say, in proportion as it is less swayed by paltry personal considerations and more by objective ends that call for energy, even though that energy bring personal loss and pain." A man who lives this way "lives on his loftiest, largest plane. He is a high-hearted freeman and no pining slave." (VRE: 45).

The religious genius was, for James, an "articulate and fully self-conscious" person (VRE: 13) and was, in addition, more than likely possessed of a "psychopathic" (i.e., extravagant [p. 48] and somewhat unbalanced [p. 27]) temperament in combination with "ardor and excitability of character" and "a superior intellect" (VRE: 26-7). These were, as we shall see, not characteristics he normally attributed to women.

The final aspect of James's methodological blindspot towards women, seems based in his own psychology. James was, it will be shown, unwilling to see women as "completely evolved and perfect"—his criterion for reliable witnesses to religious experience (VRE: 12). This basic mistrust of women's experience was almost surely a reflection of his father's attitudes toward women. James family biographies are full of indications that the women of their households were not often treated with much respect. His father, Henry, who was presumably his mentor in "manliness" (and who apparently used the word quite frequently in their home) was opposed to the education of women, and was (along with William's mother, Mary) against the newly powerful woman's movement of the time. In 1895 in an article on the movement Henry wrote:

---

1. Starbuck had been a student of James at Harvard; *The Psychology of Religion* was first published in 1899. In his preface to Starbuck's volume James notes that he had originally tried to "damn" the whole project with "faint praise" (James: 1915, vii). It is interesting to note that many of the personal testimonies and case histories which James uses in *The Varieties* come directly from Starbuck's research (VRE: 523); a significant number of the cases involving women's experience in *The Varieties* are from Starbuck's document collection.

woman is ... inferior to man ... She is his inferior in passion, his inferior in intellect, and his inferior in physical strength ... Her aim in life is ... simply to love and bless man (Henry James in Strouse 1986: 45).

In spite of this general inferiority, however, Henry believed that women were the spiritual superiors to men, embodying everything that men could not—girls were naturally moral; boys needed to be trained. This innate virtue made women unsuitable for formal learning, but made them natural lawgivers for men:

The very virtue of woman, her practical sense, which leaves her indifferent to past and future alike, and keeps her the busy blessing of the present hour, disqualifies her for all didactic dignity. Learning and wisdom do not become her. Even the ten commandments seem unamiable on her lips, so much should her own pure pleasure form the best outward law for man (1986: 45).

Thus, for Henry, woman is man's inferior at the same time she is his voice of conscience. She is in the unfortunate position of having no role but the demanding and moralistic guard of men's lives—the unbounded superego to his struggling ego. But, of course, she gets no credit for this. As Strouse observes, "Struggle, the essence of manhood, marked the path to divinity. Woman, therefore—mindless, selfless, naturally virtuous—was of no real account" (1980: 46).

In addition to the more formal and public statements by Henry on the issue of women, he also made statements by his lifestyle which certainly did not go unnoticed by William. Henry had a rather undistinguished track record with women in his own home; he placed his wife, Mary, on a moral pedestal; he ignored Alice, his daughter's, abilities; and, he abused the family maids. In a letter to his youngest son, Robertson, Henry described Mary as "the home of all truth and purity" to whose "spotless worth" he abandoned himself when he was, in some way or other tempted by the "clanging rookery" of hell (Henry James in Strouse, p. 13). Toward Alice, Henry was dismissive—he totally underestimated her considerable intellectual abilities and did not allow her to be formally educated (Strouse, P. 57). In addition, according to his memoirs, he liked to "tease" the "good-natured chambermaids" in his home to the point where they "threatened to smother him with hugs and kisses" (Lewis 1991: 45).

The influence of his father's attitude toward women on William can only be guessed at, although as Strouse shows, it probably had considerable impact on William's relationship with Alice.[2] The fact that he included women in *The Varieties* but gave them mostly superficial treatment can, without much stretch of imagination, be seen as a way for William to reflect the influence of his father's gender philosophy: women were spiritually superior (and, therefore, must be accounted for) but were not to be taken extremely seriously, because their moralisms could be too painful. This conclusion is made all the more feasible in light of William's own conscious connection of Henry to the project: a letter to his wife, also named Alice, describes *The Varieties* as his way of trying to understand "the value and meaning of religion in Father's sense" (VRE: xv). Although the issue of women was never an overriding concern for either of the men, William's ambivalence toward women, mirroring his father's, is clearly evident in this work.

---

2. There is ample evidence that William's relationship with Alice was a troubled one. It has been characterized as seductive at best and abusive at worst by biographers of both (Myers 1986: 31-3; Yeazell 1981: 9,21,25; Strouse 1980: 52-55).

JAMES'S USE OF WOMEN'S NARRATIVES

An exploration of James's use of women's narratives in *The Varieties* will be accomplished in four different ways: First, the number of women's passages employed will be compared to the number of men's. Second, the crucial placement of these passages in the overall text will be explored using lectures which most clearly exhibit his feelings about the value of women's religious experience: Lectures IV & V ("The Religion of Healthy-Mindedness") and XIV & XV ("The Value of Saintliness") in which women play a prominent role; and Lectures VI & VII ("The Sick Soul") in which women are almost absent. Third, the ways in which James dealt with these narratives will be explored, especially by examining the ambivalence present in many of his interpretations of them. Finally, James's use of Saint Teresa, the one major woman figure of *The Varieties*, will be explored briefly as an illustration of how James both appreciated and misunderstood women's religious experience.

A NUMERICAL COMPARISON

Numbers, obviously, do not tell the complete story regarding James's use of women's narratives in *The Varieties*, but a numerical comparison between women's and men's narratives is instructive, because it is so dramatic.[3] Of a total of 214 narratives women's narratives account for less than 17% (N=36)[4] of the total of all personal narratives used by James. On a lecture by lecture basis the numbers are even more dramatic. The number of women's narratives equals or comes close to the number of men's in only four lectures: Lectures IV and V, "The Religion of Healthy-Mindedness" (women's narratives=6; men's=9; unknown=2); and Lectures XIV and XV, "The Value of Saintliness" (women's narratives=5; men's=6). Women's narratives are almost completely absent from Lectures VI & VII, "The Sick Soul" and VII, "The Divided Self and the Process of its Unification," lectures in which he lays the foundation for what he considers the most adequate form of religious experience. (See Appendix I).

WOMEN'S RELIGIOUS EXPERIENCE IN LECTURES IV & V

Lectures IV & V are devoted to the study of the religion of the "healthy minded" character: those in whom "happiness is congenital and irreclaimable" (VRE: 72). The healthy-minded "positively refuse to feel" unhappiness or evil even when it is thrust upon them "in spite of the hardship of their own condition, and in spite of the sinister theologies into which they may be born." The mark of the healthy-minded is the sense of unity with the divine (VRE: 72). Women, and the young, according to James, have a special predilection for this kind of consciousness:

It is to be hoped that we all have some friend, perhaps more often feminine than

---

3. For the purposes of comparison, narratives were counted according to the following guidelines: (1) All passages in which the subject relates something of his or her own religious experience are counted whether they are found in the main text or in the footnotes. (2) Those passages in which the author is making a purely theological or philosophical point (e.g., Cardinal Newman in Lecture XVIII) were not counted. (3) Names in lists were not counted. (4) If James uses one person's narratives more than once in one chapter it is counted as one passage. If he uses one person's narratives in several chapters, they are counted once for each chapter. (5) If the gender of a subject is unrecognizable by name or circumstance, the passage is categorized as "unknown."

4. Or 22% if all the narratives of which there is not indication of whether the author was male or female are counted.

masculine, and young than old, whose soul is of this sky-blue tint, whose affinities are rather with flowers and birds and all enchanting innocencies than with dark human passions, who can think no ill of man or God, and in whom religious gladness, being in possession from the outset, needs not deliverance from any antecedent burden (VRE: 73).

These are the hallmarks of women's religion for James: affinities with innocent pastimes and objects, little concern with deep passion, little need of spiritual struggle, and a "kind of congenital anaesthesia." James uses six women's narratives to illustrate this naturally happy and oblivious soul-type.

A closer reading of the texts James employ tends to undermine his characterization for these women, however. Although James does not seem cognizant of it, each of the women's narratives he employs in these lectures expresses the author's deep suffering— from depression, to chronic physical distress, to other forms of mental illness. Each woman also seems to have resolved the suffering (or at least coped with it) by negating it, through psychological mechanisms, especially cognitive distancing—refusing to allow it to have final authority in her life. Most of the women make allusion to a sense of unity with either the divine or with nature/the cosmos which allows them to do this distancing. None of these women seem to have blithely or superficially avoided questions of evil, suffering, or death as James seems to imply.

The first passage James employs is from the *Diary of Marie Bashkirtseff*, a Ukrainian artist and writer who died at age 24. She writes about her suffering and how she has learned to "love life" in spite of it:

In this depression and dreadful uninterrupted suffering, I don't condemn life. On the contrary, I like it and find it good ...I enjoy weeping, I enjoy my despair. I enjoy being exasperated and sad. I feel as if these were so many diversions, and I love life in spite of them all ... It is not I who undergo all this—my body weeps and cries; but something inside of me which is above me is glad of it all (VRE: 75).

In this passage James finds an expression of adolescent "luxury in woe." Modern thought might instead see evidence of two of the most common forms of reaction to overwhelming negative life circumstances (be they chronic illness, trauma, neglect, or abuse): depression and dissociation ("not I ... but something inside"). She seems to cope with her suffering by waging her own kind of struggle with a divided self; a part of herself is separated from the pain and, thus, can continue to be "glad of it all." Where James attributes adolescent dramatic carryings-on, a careful reader can discern an intense psychological drama.

The second through sixth women's narratives are from women who were disciples of one of the branches of the mind-cure movement, a movement which intrigued James with its vigorous attacks on scientific method and philosophy. A puzzling feature of his use of these women and their religious thought and experience is that he does not seem to realize the deep struggle involved in their affirmations of faith. All of these women experienced what sound like serious physical illness and depression before their self-proclaimed enlightenments. On careful reading none of them seem to embody the "sky-blue soul" that James attributes to them.

The second woman James uses here, a correspondent and personal friend of his, writes of her feeling of continuity and unity with the Divine Energy and the ways this connection has empowered her (VRE: 89).

I have worked as a healer unceasingly for fourteen years without a vacation, and can truthfully assert that I have never known a moment of fatigue or pain... For how can a conscious part of Deity be sick? Since "Greater is he that is *with* us than all that can strive against us."

This woman makes it clear that she did not come to this intellectual or psychological position lightly or without suffering. Her earlier life was full of serious physical and probably emotional illness including years of confinement to her bed:

The first underlying cause of all sickness, weakness, or depression is the *human sense of separateness* from that Divine Energy which we call God ... [The] possibility of annulling forever the law of fatigue has been abundantly proven in my own case; for my earlier life bears a record of many, many years of bedridden invalidism, with spine and lower limbs paralyzed. My thoughts were no more impure than they are today, although my belief in the necessity of illness was dense and unenlightened...(VRE: 89, emphasis hers).

By affirming her continuity with the Divine and identifying her own relationship to God with that of Jesus she resisted the impure belief in the power of disease—"The soul which can feel and affirm in serene but jubilant confidence, as did the Nazarene: 'I and the Father are one,' has no further need of healer or of healing" (VRE: 89).

The third woman James uses writes of her belief that she must remain in constant "relation or mental touch" with the "essence of life which permeates all and which we call God" in order to remain healthy (VRE: 90). She relates that earlier in her life, before "the New Thought took possession" of her, she had been afflicted with various serious physical and emotional diseases:

Life seemed difficult to me at one time. I was always breaking down, and had several attacks of what is called nervous prostration, with terrible insomnia, being on the verge of insanity; besides having many other troubles, especially of the digestive organs.

She had tried many physicians and had taken dangerous drugs in an attempt to cure herself. Nothing had helped her until she came to the realization life should be a "constant turning to the very innermost, deepest consciousness of our real selves or of God in us, for illumination from within, just as we turn to the sun for light, warmth, and illumination from without" (VRE: 90). This realization was not a superficial one for her, but rather an intense struggle for self and God-knowledge.

The fourth woman, who it seems may have suffered from some form of eating disorder, details her struggle to resist an image of herself which separated her from "God's Perfect Thought." This woman apparently gave details of her physical struggle to James, but he chose to delete them. Nevertheless, he includes her introductory remark that she had been "a sufferer" from her childhood until she was forty years old when she visited a "mental healer." At the time of her visit she could not accept everything that the healer taught her, so she translated the healer's words for herself:

There is nothing but God; I am created by Him, and am totally dependent upon Him; mind is given me to use; and by just so much of it as I will put upon the thought of right action in body I shall be lifted out of bondage to my ignorance and fear and past experience (VRE: 91).

The day she made this translation for herself, she began to feel better, and to eat food that was offered to her (signaling a breakthrough for someone suffering from an eating disorder). Again she writes of food when she indicates that within ten days of her enlightenment she was able to eat whatever was "provided for others."

She reveals that she was tempted by a dream to revert back to her old way of thinking. Her former negative body image, represented as a "four-footed beast with a protuberance on every part of my body where I had suffering," begged her several times to "acknowledge it" as being herself. She refused to do this and ultimately was given the "inner conviction" that she was "perfectly well" (VRE: 91-92). By aligning herself with the good/Soul/God's Perfect Thought within her she was able to reject and separate from that part of herself which was potentially unhealthy and dangerous, the part that desired her death. This again was not a casual or superficial change for her. She writes that she had learned to trust in the "Truth" through trial and error, had "learned the simplicity and trustfulness of the little child," and had continued healthy since that time for nineteen years (VRE: 92).

The fifth woman is Mary Baker Eddy, the founder of Christian Science, who according to James resists evil by calling it "a lie" (VRE: 93). Although James does not give much description of Eddy's life, we know from her autobiography and from biographies that her "discovery" in 1866 at age 45 of Christian Science came in the midst of intense personal struggle: her first husband dead, her second marriage falling apart; chronic illnesses since childhood; and a recent near fatal fall on ice. She had her spiritual breakthrough as she was lying in bed, reading the Bible. Jesus's words, "I am the way, the truth, and the life: no man cometh unto the Father, but by me," suddenly made new sense to her, and she realized that "her life was in God—that God was the only Life" and was healed (Peel 1966: 197).

Her spiritual struggles had been present in her life since early childhood originating in the religions of her father and mother. Her father, Mark Baker, was a strict Calvinist with a "strong intellect and an iron will" (Eddy 1920: 5). Eddy later wrote that her father's theology was very difficult for her to bear; she found it especially hard to reconcile a loving God with the eternal damnation that Mark Baker and her minister threatened. There is evidence that many of her "spells" and illnesses, including protracted periods of unconsciousness, were preceded by arguments with her father relating to his theology and the theology of the Congregational Church of which she became a member at age twelve (Peel 1966: 22-23; Eddy 1920: 13).

Her mother, Abigail's, religion was of a much gentler sort. In fact, after Mary's pitched battles with her father, Abigail often would come to her and talk about God's lovingkindness and gentleness. According to Mary's autobiography, Abigail was the first to introduce her to the principles of healing to which she would return in later life. She writes that after one particular battle with her father over the doctrine of predestination ("belief in a final judgment-day, in the danger of endless punishment, and in a Jehovah merciless towards unbelievers") she was "stricken with fever." Her mother, in caring for her, brought her to a healing through reminding her of God's love:

My mother, as she bathed my burning temples, bade me lean on God's love, which would give me rest, if I went to Him in prayer, as I was wont to do, seeking His guidance. I prayed; and a soft glow of ineffable joy came over me. The fever was gone, and I rose and dressed myself, in a normal condition of health. Mother saw this and was glad.

At this point, she states, "the 'horrible decree' of predestination ... forever lost its power over me." (Eddy 1920: 13-14). In a very real way Mary's parents can be seen as fighting their theological (and other?) battles through Mary, at the cost of Mary's health. Mark would threaten and fight; Abilgail would reconcile and sooth. Mary Baker Eddy's eventual discovery of Christian Science can be viewed as the final triumph of her mother over her father. The battle which had consumed much of her life, was finally resolved with her "discovery" that her mother was right. Her father's religion was thoroughly renounced. Her pronunciation that evil is a "lie" was not the result of a "congenital anesthesia" as James would have it, but rather the conclusion of a lifelong battle with her father's "relentless theology" (Eddy 1920: 13).

Finally, James's sixth example is a woman who details a shopping trip in which she resisted becoming ill by submitting herself to "the stream of life" and becoming "the handmaid of the Lord." "There was no place in my mind for a jarring body. I had no consciousness of time or space or persons; but only of love and happiness and faith" (VRE: 103-4).

A skeptical reader of these texts may point out that (1) it was common and very socially acceptable for women of this time to complain of and be afflicted with what came to be known in psychoanalytic circles as "hysterical" illnesses; and that (2) most of these women may have had even more reason than others to exaggerate, to prove the claims of mental healing. Nevertheless, even with these suspicions in mind, the very real suffering and struggle behind the women's narratives James uses are clear if the texts are read sensitively and especially if the women's social contexts are kept in mind.

James did not seem able to recognize that the healthy-minded attitudes and beliefs of these women were anything but evidence of their simple mindedness. He was, for instance, tremendously interested in the *results* which the mind cure movement produced, but ultimately dismissed the teaching as a "savage and primitive philosophy" effective only for "a certain class of persons."[5] James ultimately disparages healthy-mindedness by pointing to its shallow nature:

[Healthy-mindedness] will work with many persons... But it breaks down impotently as soon as melancholy comes; and though one be quite free from melancholy one's self, there is no doubt that healthy-mindedness is inadequate as a philosophical doctrine, because the evil facts which it refuses positively to account for are a genuine portion of reality (VRE: 136).

Healthy-mindedness would be unable to sustain, he believed, a real encounter with the evil present in every individual's life. For James, the healthy-minded person's eyes were either blinded to reality, kept shut, or averted from evil and pain. He had no conception that healthy-mindedness could be the result of struggle—could be a means of survival in a harsh world.

---

5. Examples of male healthy-mindedness took an entirely different tone. Aside from Walt Whitman (who he describes as "the supreme contemporary example of [the] inability to feel evil,") the men he quotes in these lectures tend to write in more *philosophical* prose. "A Swiss writer," for example, writes about the proof of God's existence (being the "feeling of happiness" which is connected with the nearness of God's spirit) (VRE: 72). Another man writes about "consciousness of sin," and a third writes about the characteristics of "religious struggles" and the knowledge of God's love (VRE: 74-5). The five men he quotes from the mind-cure movement all write more about abstract notions (fear, mind control, concentration) and less about personal experience than their female counterparts.

WOMEN'S EXPERIENCE IN LECTURES XIV & XV

Lectures XIV & XV, "The Value of Saintliness" are the other major lectures in which the number of women's narratives employed are close to equal the number of men's, thus signaling again that in this realm James takes women's religious experience seriously. In these lectures he endeavors to evaluate the "fruits of other men's religion," (VRE: 265) admitting that in doing so he is, in fact, taking on the role of "theologian" (VRE: 263) along with the pragmatic philosopher. He proposes to "test saintliness by common sense, to use human standards to help us decide how far the religious life commends itself as an ideal kind of human activity" (VRE: 266). He explores the less immediately attractive phenomena of saintliness by attending to what he terms its more extravagant and excessive examples: "all the saintly attributes ... devout love of God, purity, charity, [and] asceticism" which "may lead astray" when attended to at the expense of other interests (VRE: 273).

These lectures (along with portions of the previous ones on saintliness) are filled with examples of what James considers pathological saintliness: fanaticism, and excesses of purity, tenderness, charity, and asceticism. They might be considered the carnival sideshow of *The Varieties*. And, it must be admitted, here men's and women's religion are put into equally bad light.

James doesn't seem sure exactly how to value the experiences he describes here. At one point he agrees with Nietzsche that a real man, "the carnivorous-minded 'strong man,' the adult male and cannibal" could see nothing but "mouldiness and morbidness" in the saint's lifestyle and would regard the saint with "pure loathing." Yet, he also writes with seeming alarm at the "unmanly" way in which members of the "so-called better classes" are afraid of the kind of affliction which the "saints" he describes encountered and lived with on a daily basis:

> ... we are scared as men were never scared in history at material ugliness and hardship; when we put off marriage until our house can be artistic, and quake at the thought of having a child without a bank-account and doomed to manual labor, it is time for thinking men to protest against so *unmanly* and irreligious a state of opinion (VRE: 293, emphasis mine).

The women of these lectures suffer, for the most part, from an excess of what James portrays as the less arduous virtues: devoutness and purity. The most dramatic of the characters afflicted by these is termed "theopathic," distinguished by the excess love of God: "When the love of God takes possession of such a mind, it expels all human loves and human uses" (VRE: 275). James provides three examples of theopathic women: "the blessed Margaret Mary Alacoque;" Saint Gertrude, a Benedictine nun of the thirteenth century; and Saint Teresa who will be discussed in more detail below.

Margaret Mary Alacoque received the revelation of the Sacred Heart in which Jesus told her that his love for humanity would be expanded through her discipleship. Christ provided her with hallucinations of "sight, touch, and hearing" and called her "the well-beloved disciple of my Sacred Heart" (VRE: 275). James comments on her: "...what were its good fruits for Margaret Mary's life? Apparently little else but sufferings and prayers and absences of mind and swoons and ecstasies." According to James she became little more than a useless burden to those around her (VRE: 276).

According to him, Saint Gertrude's gifts were even less useful than Margaret Mary's. She received proofs of God's love toward her alone: Her major work, *Revelations*, was filled with "... assurances of [Christ's] love, intimacies and caresses and compliments of the most absurd and puerile sort addressed by Christ to Gertrude as an individual" (VRE: 276). James terms these "worthless fruits" formed by "inferior intellectual sympathies" (VRE: 277).[6]

Thus, on the matter of religious excess, just as on the matter of healthy-mindedness, women were important models. Their excesses tended to be, not surprisingly, of the relational sort—they were so devoted to the love of God that they could only make insignificant contributions to those around them. Indeed, they often seemed to be burdensome.

WOMEN'S ABSENCE FROM LECTURES VI & VII

Except for two minor examples, women are absent from the extremely important lectures on the sick soul, where James sets the kinds of religious experiences which he seems to favor above all others. The sick soul is the one which "maximizes" evil based on "the persuasion that the evil aspects of our life are its very essence, and that the world's meaning most comes home to us when we lay them most to heart" (VRE: 112). This is the soul that struggles mightily to exist because of its awareness of death, decay, and morbidity on all sides. Where the healthy-minded Marie Bashkirtseff luxuriated in her melancholy, sick-souled individuals are depressed in their joys. James quotes a friend of his: "The trouble with me is that I believe too much in common happiness and goodness ... and nothing can console me for their transiency" (VRE: 119).

The lectures on the sick soul are filled with heroes of the faith. Here we meet Luther, Tolstoy, and John Bunyan as they struggle (manfully) to reconcile sin and grace, a fear of life with the will to continue to live, and a personal self-contempt and despair with assurance of Christ's love. It is here we also meet those most afflicted with depression and fear. The sick souled person who is also afflicted with melancholy "is forced to ignore that of all good whatever: for him it may no longer have the least reality" (VRE: 122). And, although James claims not to judge between forms of religious experience (VRE: 122), it is obvious that he finds this form of religion the most convincing. It is probably no accident that this corresponds most closely to his own kinds of experience.

The narrative in which he describes the *most* painful form of sick-souledness—that which is associated with "panic fear"—was later revealed in a letter to Frank Abauzit (VRE: 447) to be his own story. Ostensibly quoting a frenchman, he writes of his feeling of terror that he could be identified in his own imagination with a madman:

> I awoke morning after morning with a horrible dread at the pit of my stomach, and with a sense of the insecurity of life that I never knew before ... I remember wondering how other people could live, how I myself had ever lived, so unconscious of that pit of insecurity beneath the surface of life" (VRE: 134-5).

It is extremely informative that precisely at the point of revealing his own sick-souledness and pain, he also reveals the insensitivity of a woman—his mother—to it. In this narrative he describes his mother as a typical healthy-minded woman who could see no evil or pain, and who thus was of no use to him:

---

6. The men in these lectures suffer from excesses of these kinds of virtues as well as the more strenuous excesses of tenderness and charity (his example is John G. Paton, a missionary who faced "brutish Melanesian cannibals" armed with no more than the gospel) and asceticism (his example is St. Peter of Alcantara who "passed forty years without ever sleeping more than an hour and a half a day" (VRE: 286-7). For these examples James has more kindly comments, in fact, crediting asceticism with representing "nothing less than...the essence of twice-born philosophy" (VRE: 289).

My mother in particular, a very cheerful person, seemed to me a perfect paradox in her unconsciousness of danger, which you may well believe I was very careful not to disturb by revelations of my own state of mind (VRE: 135).

One might even imagine that her seeming unawareness (or denial) of his terror exacerbated the problem for James.[7]

JAMES'S PORTRAYAL OF SAINT TERESA OF AVILA

Saint Teresa emerges as perhaps the only female "hero" of faith of *The Varieties*. She is by far the most quoted woman, and appears in lectures I ("Religion and Neurology"); XI, XII, & XIII ("Saintliness"); XIV & XV ("the Value of Saintliness"); and XVI & XVII ("Mysticism"). James's ambivalence toward her is revealed in striking fashion in the lectures on saintliness. The aspects of her character which he valued in her most were those which reveal her strenuous or "energetic" nature (VRE: 216). He quotes her own affirmation of masculine qualities from *Vie de Sainte Terese* when she describes the overwhelming good effects of her mystical spiritual life which filled her with "masculine courage and other virtues" (VRE: 26). The aspects of her character he valued least were the more "feminine" ones (VRE: 20,23). These, he adjures, should not detract from her theology however:

> ...if her theology can stand these other tests [logic and experiment], it will make no difference how hysterically or nervously off her balance Saint Teresa may have been when she was with us here below (VRE: 23).

In his lectures on mysticism James describes Teresa as the "expert of experts" (VRE: 324) on the values and uses of mystical revelation, especially the "orison of union" in which as she explains it, the soul is "asleep as regards things of this world and in respect of herself" but "fully awake as regards God" (Teresa, VRE: 324). His admiration for her detailed writing on mystical experience culminates in a declaration that nowhere in literature is there a more "evidently veracious account of the formation of a new centre of spiritual energy" (VRE: 328).

James's longest description of her is found in his lectures on the value of saintliness; it begins with what seems like exorbitant praise.

> ... Saint Teresa ... [was] one of the ablest women, in many respects, of whose life we have the record. She had a powerful intellect of the practical order. She wrote admirable descriptive psychology, possessed a will equal to any emergency, great talent for politics and business, a buoyant disposition, and a first-rate literary style (VRE: 277).

But even this remarkable woman doesn't escape his ultimate dismissal. She is, as mentioned earlier, one of three women who exemplify, for James, the unfortunate state of "theopathy," the excess of devotion which renders one's life unuseful to the human community (VRE: 275). He continues the above paragraph with his evaluation of her work:

---

7. In his massive biography of the James family R. W. B. Lewis notes that Mary James, William's mother, had a hard time being patient with her son's mental states. He writes: "'Morbid' was her recurring word for him. She remarked, with a curious lack of approval, that William had 'a morbid sympathy' for any form of privation or trouble" (1991: 233).

... She was tenaciously aspiring, and put her whole life at the service of her religious ideals. Yet so paltry were these, according to our present way of thinking, that ... I confess that my only feeling in reading her has been pity that so much vitality of soul should have found such poor employment (VRE: 277).

This is surprising censure for someone who he, in other respects, seemed to consider so remarkable. Her shortcoming was that she expressed her religious sentiments in ways which were too paltry (feminine?) for James's tastes. His distaste for her experience was not only that it seemed "superficial." To him she seemed not to be truly contrite in the way he believed true religious geniuses should be; she seemed not to grasp the idea of "radical bad being," but rather to concentrate on "faults" and "imperfections" in the plural. Most damning, for James, was that her idea of religion seemed to have been "that of an endless amatory flirtation...between the devotee and the deity," which had little public value apart from "helping younger nuns" (VRE: 278).

In her seeming disinterest in "radical bad being" and total devotion to relationship with the deity (which James interprets as superficial flirtatiousness) she seems to align herself with "feminine" and "sky-blue" healthy-mindedness he had previously found inadequate. Thus, despite her keen intellect and genius in other aspects of her religious life, her religion could not measure up on the Jamesian scale.

CONCLUSION

Readers will have to decide for themselves whether or not to trust James and *The Varieties* to interpret women's religious experience. My own conclusions follow the lines of feminist biblical scholars who have taken on the immense task of trying to both recover and critique the Bible, to uncover positive women's experience and to reveal the many layers of patriarchal oppression. These scholars along with feminist literary critics have shown that we can no longer afford to read any text naively, no matter how interesting, important, or even classic. And, while it is somewhat anachronistic to hold James accountable for his misunderstanding of women's texts, it is crucial that we hold ourselves accountable for our own readings of and use of the text in our present situation.

Is there anything of value (apart from historical) for feminist social scientists in *The Varieties*? I believe the answer is yes. First, we must acknowledge James's efforts in recognizing women's experience as important enough to include in his volume; as noted above, women were all but invisible in his social milieu. We may credit Starbuck and Coe with bringing women's religious experience to James's attention, but ultimately he made his own choices of subject material.

Second, James valued diversity of experience, even though he evidenced considerable blindspots when it came to appreciating women's experience. Yet, he seemed to be striving toward openness to all, even the most bizarre, religious phenomena. This analysis of *The Varieties* can be a reminder to ourselves to keep cleaning our own glasses—both to avoid making groups and individuals invisible to our sight, and also to avoid a distorted view of them. Recent critiques of anglo-feminist theology from women of color makes this point all the more forceful and personal.

Finally, I believe that for all of his negativity about women's religious experience (expressed both covertly and overtly in the text) James understood something very important. Although he did not acknowledge that he was describing two separate categories of religiosity—male and female—he aptly reflected the research he was aware of by Starbuck and Coe, and he enhanced it with reference to other documents and religious classics. As modern feminist scholarship has shown repeatedly, women do express spirituality in different ways (but not totally different) than men. Questions of *why* this is so are hotly debated—Is this an essential fact of women's biology and nature, or a sociocultural artifact, or a result of the combination of both? Nevertheless, James as a scientist appreciated the *fact* of difference in women's and men's religious experiences.

James's problem seems to have been that he could not appreciate the actual *struggles* involved in operating out what he saw as a feminine religious perspective, and thus could not give the perspective full credence. Modern readers may choose to give more value to the healthy-minded viewpoint than James did, whether encountered in women or men. This appreciation would entail recognizing that most healthy-mindedness, even that which seems to be grounded in denial, is rooted (at least as much as sick-souledness) in personal struggle to survive and make sense of life. The choice, whether it is made consciously or unconsciously, in the midst of a quest for meaning and survival, must be honored and respected for the struggle it represents—whether that choice is to give final authority to the blue sky, health, happiness and unity, or to give it to illness, evil, and death.

REFERENCES

Adams, C.J. (1994). *Ecofeminism and the Sacred.* New York: Continuum.

Eroner, E.M. (1993). *The Telling.* San Francisco, CA: Harper, San Francisco.

Conn, J.W. (1986). *Women's Spirituality: Resources for Christian Development.* New York: Paulist Press.

Eddy, M.B. ([1891]1920). *Retrospection and Introspection.* Boston: Trustees of the First Church of Christ, Scientist.

Edie, J.M. (1987). *William James and Phenomenology.* Bloomington, IN: Indiana University Press.

James, W. ([1899]1915). Preface to E.D. Starbuck, *The Psychology of Religion: An Empirical Study of the Growth of Religious Consciousness.* New York: Walter Scott.

———— ([1902]1985). *The Varieties of Religious Experience,* Vol. 15. In F.H. Burkhardt, Bowers, F. & I.K. Skrupskelis (Eds.) *The Works of William James.* Cambridge, MA: Harvard University Press.

Johnson, E.A. (1992). *She Who Is: The Mystery of God in Feminist Theological Discourse.* New York: Crossroad.

Keller, C. (1986). *From a Broken Web: Separation, Sexism, and Self.* Boston, MA: Beacon Press.

Lewis, R.W.B. (1991). *The Jameses: A Family Narrative.* New York: Farrar, Straus and Giroux.

Morton, N. (1985). *The Journey is Home.* Boston: Beacon Press.

Myers, G.E. (1986). *William James: His Life and Thought.* New Haven, CT: Yale University Press.

Peel, R. (1966). *Mary Baker Eddy: The Years of Discovery.* New York: Holt, Rinehart and Winston.

Randour, M.L. (1987). *Women's Psyche, Women's Spirit: The Reality of Relationships.* New York: Columbia University Press.

Ruether, R.R. (1992). *Gaia & God: An Ecofeminist Theology of Earth Healing.* San Francisco, CA: Harper, San Francisco.

Starbuck, E.D. ([1899]1915). *The Psychology of Religion: An Empirical Study of the Growth of Religious Consciousness.* New York: Walter Scott.

Strouse, J. (1980). *Alice James: A Biography.* Boston, MA: Houghton Mifflin.

Williams, D.S. (1993). *Sisters in the Wilderness: The Challenge of Womanist God-Talk.* Maryknoll, NY: Orbis.

Yeazell, R.B. (1981). *The Death and Letters of Alice James.* Berkeley, CA: University of California Press.

APPENDIX

Total Narratives in *The Varieties*	214		
Total Women	36		
Total Men	167		
Total Unknown	11		

Lecture	Female	Male	Unknown
I - Religion and Neurology	1	2	
II - Circumscription of the Topic	1	8	
III - The Reality of the Unseen	3	12	3
IV & V - The Religion of Healthy-Mindedness	6	9	2
VI & VII - The Sick Soul	2	13	
VIII - The Divided Self	2	12	
IX - Conversion	0	8	
X - Conversion— Concluded	1	15	6
XI, XII,& XIII - Saintliness	10	36	
XIV & XV - The Value of Saintliness	5	6	
XVI & XVII - Mysticism	5	28	
XVIII - Philosophy	0	0	
XIX - Other Characteristics	0	13	
XX - Conclusions	0	5	
Postscript	0	0	

FEAR FOR LIFE ITSELF: WORLD WAR I AND THE VARIETIES OF FRENCH RELIGIOUS EXPERIENCE

JOSEPH F. BYRNES

In the past fifteen years only one title has imposed itself as appropriate to a collection of my studies of French national and religious identity in the nineteenth and early twentieth centuries: "The Varieties of French Religious Experience." William James is still such a presence that no other title really suits me. To be sure, I have not referred explicitly to James's basic text in my work thus far. Permit me to cite without reference studies of the Revolutionary Festivals, the polarities of religious and ideological expression at the beginning of the nineteenth century, the revival of monasticism, the revival of pilgrimage, the positive religious influence of linguistic isolation, and the reappropriation of the Catholic religious patrimony by the secular Third Republic (these studies have appeared or will appear separately). When this work is revised for my French "*Varieties*," James will no longer remain anonymous behind the interpretations. But in this and other work on the religious and national identity of soldiers in World War I—my final topic—I give James his due the first time around.

WILLIAM JAMES, GORDON ALLPORT, AND WORLD WAR I

To do psychology of religion with William James (1961) is to do psychology with Gordon Allport (1950, 1955; also 1942, 1965). Allport said that his own convictions about the uniqueness of the personality and the dynamic role of religion in the construction of each personality were in the direct line of James: "William James perceived this point [the centrality of religion] when fifty years ago he wrote his incomparable *The Varieties of Religious Experience*." To be sure, Allport believed that he himself had something to add. "I should not presume to restate his thesis if I did not feel that the progress of dynamic psychology in the past two generations has been great enough to warrant its sharpening and reinforcement. James did not have access to modern theories of personality. It is a tribute to his genius that in most respects these theories readily accommodate his earlier findings and interpretations" (1950: xiii). To say that James can be accommodated by contemporary theories, is, if not faint praise, at least a neutral observation. I would say that James's *The Varieties* is the grounding of Allport's religious psychology and is itself incomplete without Allport. I would further say that James and Allport are the grounding—can only be the grounding—of our own psychological interpretation of historical data. Today we treat the psychological theories of the past as hypotheses: they must be confirmed in their own right and they must bring precision to our interpretation of the historical record—enabling us to sort out and label the data.[1]

"Veterans" is the title of a central section of Gordon Allport's chapter on "The Religion of Youth" in *The Individual and His Religion*. Having in hand a collection of "sincere and candid" reports of veterans (in this case World War II veterans), Allport wrote, "The diversity of these statements speaks for itself. As so often happens in the development of personality, the crises of existence tend merely to intensify the style of life which was in any case developing" (1950: 53-54). The statistics indicated that 55% of the veterans found

---

1. For me the foundation texts are Runyan (1984) and T. Kohut (1986). For a criticism of the inconsistent use of psychological theory in historical reconstruction see my review of a study of French national celebrations (Byrnes 1989).

no religious change in themselves because of their war experience; 26% believed that they had become more religious; 19%, that they had become less religious. Allport draws a single conclusion from this data: "The war created a few more anti-religious attitudes than are present among non-veterans, but in those retaining a religious sentiment the effect was to intensify its prominence" (p. 54). This was Protestant-Catholic-Jewish America in mid-century, a far cry from the France of 1914, where there were two interpretations of France, one Catholic and conservative (the old royalist and imperial traditions), and the other anti-clerical and Republican (the old revolutionary tradition). It is legitimate, though, to take Allport's single conclusion and make it a thesis to be tested in the study of French soldiers: "Crises of existence tend merely to intensify the style of life, which was in any case developing" (p.54).

In the France of 1914, the challenge was to unite the two Frances. For more than a decade the government had been formally secular—even more, anti-church—in reaction to the nineteenth-century clerical attempts to dictate government policy. The solution was to form a *union sacrée*. President Poincaré introduced the term as an expression of a unified France. The Prime Minister, Georges Clemenceau, even boasted that monks, expelled by the government only a few years before, had returned (Fontana 1990: 126). The Jesuit religious review *Etudes* reported, "The foreign invasion has provoked in France a surge of patriotic revolt, an élan of national solidarity that genuinely surpasses the most optimistic hopes" (cited in Fontana 1990: 126). We cannot say that differences were resolved; but only that antagonisms were submerged. Some of them were never permitted to surface again, probably losing their importance and identifiability in the great leveling experience of war. I do not have evidence that the war changed the religious habits of the French population or brought the indifferent to thier knees. But, given the present state of my research, I can present evidence that the experience of war gave a specific religious and nationalist coloring to both the religious soldier and the secular soldier, effectively uniting the two Frances of the preceding century.[2] The psychologies of James and his successors will be an integral part of my presentation.

Psychological Interpretation

In my psychological interpretation, I will consider three factors: 1) over-all influence of the basic temperament or personality orientation; 2) the function of religious experience in the development of the whole personality; 3) personal mysticism and devotion (here privileged moments in the direct experience of the agony, fear, and despair, as well as the exaltation, of war). Then, reviewing the evidence, I will sketch a psychological profile of the religious and nationalist dimensions of the war experience, contributing thereby to the developing literature on soldiers' personal experience of World War I (Hanak 1970; J.J. Becker 1985; Winter 1989; Mosse 1990; Smith 1994).[3]

Personality Orientation, Structure, and Development

The broadest possible personality orientations are optimism and pessimism. As we well know, James (1961) sketched out healthy, sick, and twice-born personality types. If I

---

2. Giving greater specificity to Maurice Barrés (1917) who saw a flourishing of religion and ideological reconciliation within the *union sacrée*.
3. I suggest Robbins (1984) for a useful survey of the war on all fronts and Miquel (1983) for a survey of the war in France.

may so put it, conversion was for him the core of developmental experience; types of saint-liness, the specifically religious elements of the personality as he understood it. Healthy souls are happy, enthusiastic, and convinced of the goodness of people; sick souls see and feel evil, despairingly. And divided souls move back and forth between the optimism-pessimism poles. By conversion—or submission to perceived reality—the divided self is stabilized. The types of saintliness are asceticism, strength of soul, purity, and charity; the interior basis for this saintliness is a feeling of elated self surrender to a wider world. Allport (1950), building on James, set religious experience in the context of personality structure and development. The religious intention dynamically moves people toward ultimate goals and is based on a fundamental sentiment or disposition in the personality. The conscience decides on behaviors that integrate the personality for the attainment of the ultimate goals. I propose to employ and adapt these James/Allport labels and descriptions to interpret the soldiers' accounts and interpretations of the experience of war.

The Functioning Personality

The isolated religious moments in history—here, World War I—must be understood as part of a broader evolution and development. Faith and conscience—holiness, as James would say—do not develop on the basic level of opportunistic functioning where the biological needs and the survival of the organism are the only concern (Allport 1955). Rather religion takes form on the higher level of propriate functioning (the *proprium* is Allport's term for the unique individual). Bodily sense is the fundamental way in which individuals are positive or negative on themselves. Self-identity, marking oneself off from the surrounding environment with increasing awareness of one's own developing personality, subsumes experiences of God, beauty, evil into the self. In ego-enhancement religion is promoted for personal ends, and ego-extension makes possessions, home, region, nation, and most broadly religion a part of the identity. Rational agency is a more philosophical synthesizing of inner needs and external reality; here a personal way of thinking about religious experience is developed. Self image is aspiration combining past religious experiences with projected religious goals. Propriate striving is therefore the effort to unify the personality and pursue long-range goals—including religious goals of understanding, equilibrium, and charity. At their best individuals know themselves existentially; this is self-awareness of humanness and responsibility in truth.

The Allportian categories put James's discussion of orientations and holiness on a developmental scale of increasing personal achievement and tie them into distinctive personality theory. Bodily sense is perception of reality in optimistic or pessimistic colors—or in the alternation between the two poles. Self-identity functioning forces the divided selves to decide; and on that basis their ego-enhancement and ego-extension appropriates the elements of faith and conscience in a positive or negative way. To live with one's self image requires a distinctive movement away from negativity or dividedness. Propriate striving and self-knowledge function religiously to move individuals toward those areas that James has labelled "saintliness." We are, then, back to James's productive asceticism, strength of soul, purity, and charity.

Personal Religious Experience: Mystical, Philosophical, and Devotional

In the setting of fundamental orientation and personality development, then, the religious experiences (Let us call them privileged moments) take place. James isolated four qualities of the all-preoccupying religious moment, which is to say the mystical experience. We know them well: ineffable, noetic, transient, and passive. Mystical experiences cannot be described; they are perceived, they quickly pass, and they cannot be actively induced. To step back and analyze is to lose the intensity, even the reality, of the religious experience. When one steps back, one produces religious thought, which is not a direct experience, but a philosophical one. In addition, one may isolate from among James's examples of the mystical experience a more ordinary sort of religious experience that can properly be called devotional. The believer believes in God, pictures God, and talks to God—with greater or lesser intellectual certainty, with greater or lesser emotional involvement; though noetic like the mystical experience, devotion is describable, long-term or frequent, and active. I suggest then, that James really gave us three types of religious experience: mystical, philosophical, and devotional. (Byrnes 1984: 33-40).

I want to go beyond James in these matters of mystical, philosophical and devotional religion. I believe that the mystical moment does not have to be explicitly religious in content, and philosophical religion can have a pragmatic turn that James, surprisingly, did not deal with. Furthermore, the case can be made that the psychophysical foundations of devotional experience are the same as for other emotional experiences. Let me explain.

Only the thoughts and emotions that come before and the interpretations that come after give the mystical moment its definition as religious or not (Spilka, et al. 1985). Changes in the brain and nervous system may have a religious attribution or not. A movement toward calmness and a movement toward energy are the general qualities of the sympathetic nervous system, brain waves, eye movements, the relation of sensory to motor and apposition to proposition—of felt meaning to expressed meaning (Fischer 1971, 1986). In a war setting the existential moment can be mystical in the religious sense or can be an indescribable moment of fear or can be (and probably most often is) a combination of both. In battle, in the lives of soldiers at war, there are the mystical moments that must be studied in the light of what the soldiers say about the antecedent and subsequent moments. The soldiers' last word on these moments occurs during the formal interpretation necessary to write up or otherwise explain it all, hours, weeks, months, or years later.

Of course, the religious experience may lack a defining mystical moment. In ordinary devotion the normal range of interpersonal thoughts and feelings are turned toward heavenly personalities in the imagination. Christ, Mary, the saints, the "larger world" of which one might be a part can enter the imagination—or slip from consciousness. Among the most religiously tenacious, devotion is alive at even the most stressing moments. To understand these events, the historian needs to know the "data of experience," the literal thoughts and feelings and their symbolic—heavenly, if you will—counterparts. Paul Pruyser (1968)[4] examined at length perceptual, intellectual, and emotional processes, the linguistic and motor-system functions, and the relational attitudes that served as the basis for religious (and here, I believe, primarily) devotional experience. He illustrates religious behaviors that depend upon the experiences of the five senses: the functions of reasoning and memory; the selection of appropriate emotions of dread and love; myth, ritual, and sacred language. There are special psychomotor processes and attitudes towards authority, loved ones, and, of course, one's own body. For my own part, I want to understand how these experiences were integrated with the war experience: religious men died fighting both because of their devotional lives and in spite of their devotional lives.

---

4. For a recent appreciation of the continuing applicability of Pruyser's work see Malony and Spilka (1990).

ON INTERPRETING WORLD WAR I:
THE CHALLENGE OF JEAN NORTON CRU

The real war experience is restricted to the existential (let us call it mystical) moment by Jean Norton Cru in his definitive study of French war literature.[5] Cru was himself a longtime professor of French literature at Williams College and a veteran of the French army. He reviewed everything from letters and diaries through bestselling fiction. His principal criticism:

> Military history up to now has been written only on the basis of documents origi-
> nating with those who were in no position to see, to hear or to feel, mentally and
> physically, the direct effects of the struggle (1988: 16).

For Cru, the worthy testimonies came from the front, where he had himself witnessed the truth of war, the reality of war in soldiers' lives.

> The testimonies from the front will teach the specialist two lessons, which the pub-
> lic itself will be able to comprehend. They will teach the historian that all military
> history viewed from the top conceived in terms of a chess match, written on the
> basis of staff documents and without the testimony of the true protagonists, of
> those who give and take the blows, such history is an agreeable illusion leading us
> to believe in our ability to construct a whole, itself a mass of details, without know-
> ing the essential nature of these details (pp. 18-19).

Cru insisted that it was "impossible for the psychologist to reproduce the conditions of battle in his laboratory" (p. 54). The only solution, then, is to attend to testimony from the center of the battle.

> Due to the great number and the variety of the spontaneous notes jotted down at
> the front, the war books make available to the psychologist of today and tomorrow
> an ample harvest of facts or of cases which he can turn to account, which he *must*
> turn to account since there is no other way to set about surveying such facts or to
> bring about their repetition at will (pp. 54-55).

The challenge is difficult because Cru opposes virtually all *interpretation*. War is existential fear, suffering, and senselessness; nothing more. Soldiers at the front or rear, whether they be military professionals, chaplains, intellectuals, more or less educated farmers, cannot think out or voice anything beyond life and death self-concern—when the shells are falling on all sides and the order comes to go "over the top" and begin the advance on enemy trenches.

For me there is great similarity between the ur-experience of the soldier and ur-experi-ence labelled mystical by James and his successors. I have no trouble concurring with the fundamental insight of Jean Norton Cru that there is a moment of horrible existential truth for the soldier, a moment that cannot be adequately expressed by any interpretation,

---

5. Cru's encyclopedic study of the recollection and literature of World War I ([1929] 1993) is a fundamental tool for social historians of the French experience of the war. Later he published a much shorter work
([1931] 1988)—more quotation but much less analysis—that I quote from extensively in the pages that
follow. In his major study of Catholics in France during the First World War, Jacques Fontana (1990) lists
Cru's two works in the bibliography as his only "instruments de travail" before laying out the full list of
sources. See for comparison Edmund Wilson's study of the literature of the American Civil War (1962).

religious or otherwise. But I hasten to add that the minutes, hours, days, or weeks that lead up to, and away from these moments of truth can be explained by the soldiers themselves and by those who seek to understand them.

Let us look more closely at the documents on the psychology of the combatant collected by Cru. In his moment of truth the soldier longs to live:

> I did not think there could be such joy in breathing, in opening your eyes to the light, in letting it permeate you, in being warm, in being cold, in suffering even (p. 127, citing Paul Lintier, *Ma Piéce*).[6]

Qualities of the fundamental experience depend upon the personality structure of the soldier.

> The gamut of personalities diversifies the aspects of fear. They vary according to the time and the place, from irritation to madness, from depression to flight, sometimes comical, sometimes terrible, often repugnant, but always glaringly sincere; that is the only state about which you cannot deceive yourself nor deceive others (p. 131, citing Jean Marot, *Ceux qui vivent*).

For soldiers, abstractions are of little account; only self and extensions of self really count.

> What does the man from Brest, born to the sea, care about Metz? And then who still believes that Europe is on fire for that gob of land?... Are they fighting for fatherland? They do not know what fatherland is. General ideas remain inaccessible to the masses (p. 132, citing Louis Mairet, *Carnets d'un combattant*).

The natural tendency of the historian is to deform the inexpressible moments by describing or explaining them.

> The historians certainly have an easy time of it. When they describe an epoch they rely upon official documents, and we know what these are worth, because we have seen some drawn up... We are all workers of falsehood. We relate badly or falsely what we have seen. This is the inevitable result of our conceit and our incompetence. Whatever we failed to engrave immediately on enduring metal, dies out of our memory. Whatever we fix, is deformed the very instant it enters the rigid mold of words (p. 105, citing Max Deauville, *La Boue des Flandres*).

We cannot remember the war disasters of earlier generations.

> Who will rescue from the shadows which encompass it, the savagery of the unceasing struggles we are waging? All that is irretrievably lost, and it is too bad (p. 108, citing André Maillet, *Sous le fouet de destin*).

Take, for example, the Napoleonic wars, the millions who slaughtered one another "for his [the Emperor's] sole vainglory" in what was "a boundless folly." These men were "our ancestors," long gone, and we now have only the data and not the feelings (p. 108).

---

6. In this author-date text citation system, there is no provision for quotation from, in effect, anthologized texts. I therefore place the author and book quoted in Cru ([1931] 1988) in parenthesis.

Cru and his favorite authors rejected all romanticizing and all dramatization, because it merely panders to readers' curiosity and emotional needs.

> Never having led the life many people picture it as they would like it to be. They build, in good faith, a romance that pleases them. They let no personal reminiscences stand in their way. And unconsciously, out of the accounts you give them, they keep only what fits in with their plan. They are sincere. They believe they have sought the truth, and even that they have found it, but they have found only themselves in the heart of their dream (p. 92, citing Max Buteau, *Tenir*).

Cru would have us examine the historical record for the soldiers' moments of truth, not our own. Accordingly, let us look at recent studies of religious and national identity: mystical moments, devotional movements, theological and practical interpretations of the war.

Studies of French Religious and National Identity

In February 1994 a review in the principal Paris newspaper *Le Monde* evaluated the renewal of interest in and research on world War One. Jean Pierre Riout (1994) favorably reviewed Annette Becker's study (1994) and a collection of essays edited by Nadine-Josette Chaline (1993). At the same time he questioned—more tentatively than Jean Norton Cru before him—the possibility of understanding the horror that provided the context of religion. He wondered if "the apt investigation of archives and of unpublished vestiges" of soldiers' religion would help any more that the "flag-waving pieties [les bondieuseries tricolores]" of certain writers of the period. In effect, he was asking how a person could understand the part (religion) without understanding the whole (the total war experience). Yet the writings of Becker and Chaline represent a new step in the study of soldiers' religion in World War I, work more specific than Jacques Fontana's recent and fundamental *Les Catholiques francais pendant la grande querre* (1990).

Mystical Religion

Mystics (their number was miniscule among the millions of nominally Catholic soldiers) experienced union in total sacrifice (A. Becker, 1993, p. 26). Teilhard de Chardin, for example, wrote that he marvelled at the "clinging and definitive perfume of exaltation of initiation, as if one had passed into the absolute." War tore open "the crust of banalities and conventions" and "a 'window' was opened on the secret mechanisms and profound levels of human becoming" (p. 29, citing Teilhard de Chardin, *La Nostalgie du front*). Pascal's themes of misery and the grandeur of the human being spiritually nourished intellectual readers in the trenches (p. 29).

A handful of intellectuals,[7] including the writers Ernest Psichari and Henri Ghéon, converted to Catholicism during the war period (p. 46). This was part of a decades-long phenomenon in France, where those who were raised in the Catholic religion and later on rejected it returned to the religion of their culture. Having allowed a divided France to divide their inner selves, they converted, "twice born," to Catholicism. Others resisted conversion and waited until after the war because they believed conversion under pressure and fear to be dishonest. For example, this testimony:

---

7. For a discussion of the war roles of French intellectuals see J.-F. Sirinelli (1990).

Since the beginning of the war, I have had the thought and intuition to set myself straight with God, to go to confession, to live completely as a Christian. I have not done it because I have been held back by a scruple. I thought that it would not be loyal or honest to seek out God now that I have the need under the threat of danger (cited on p. 47).

This officer did return to Catholicism after several battles, having proved to himself that he would not convert for base reasons. Other similar conversions took some of their principal qualities from the war. Becker believes that "the reality of the front imposed itself" on the soldiers' conversions. The soldier could not avoid suffering and was deeply aware of his own need for assistance in vital areas of life. Still others postponed conversion until after the war. The philosopher Gabriel Marcel said,

I think that superficially the war certainly retarded my approach to Christianity considered in its confessional aspect. I was profoundly shocked to see how the adversaries each claimed the support of God (cited on p. 50).

Though scandalized that each side proclaimed Holy War, he says that the war made an existentialist thinker out of him: he had to approach the "religious problem" more directly.

Some saw the war as an obstacle to religious consciousness: "The military life has become for all of us soldiers a slow burial of our faculties ... These conditions of existence constitute an obstacle to any kind of life, however incomplete it be" (cited on p. 51). When Pierre Villard wrote this to the philosopher Jacques Maritain, Maritain responded with a spiritual interpretation of the experience, likening it to a dark night of the soul, thereby making the war integral to the mystical experience, and, for that reason, conducive to conversion. In war a soul is even more likely to be sick and twice born. The conversion is just as real whether the sickness is congenital or comes from without. The essence is that this takes place at the center of one's existence.

Devotional Religion at the Front

A genuine "spirituality of the front" existed (p. 7); to what extent we cannot say. But "dolorism"—a spirituality of suffering—suffused expressions of love of France and of Christ. The soldiers repeated in their suffering the sufferings of Christ. As such, they were redeemed by Christ and were redemptive in turn. One chaplain said, "During this war there is no sad death" (cited on p. 34). The writer and social reformer Léon Bloy, however, raged against those who valued dolorism in others while not suffering themselves. His special target was the writer and ultra nationalist Maurice Barrés: "The professionals of devotional journalism absolutely want to open to them [the soldiers] the paradise of the Martyrs. To hear them, each [soldier] has given his love for the love of God, with a supernatural detachment from every earthly concern" (p. 35).

Of course the Sacred Heart was the principal image. One observer cites "a million pennants" of the Sacred Heart on the breasts of the soldiers. One hundred thousand soldiers and officers belonged to a "Guard of the Sacred Heart." There were special reviews such as *L' Écho mensuel des Sanctuaires du Sacré-Coeur* and *Le Pèlerin de Paray-le-Monial*—which contained a section "The Sacred Heart at the Front" (pp. 79-80). One fanatic wrote to President Poincaré echoing the French rightist notion of a Masonic plot against France, eternal and Catholic (pp. 82-83).

Because the Virgin wept at LaSalette she became a powerful image for those suffering in war. Jacques Maritain insisted on the Virgin's strange ability to suffer (cited on p. 59). The sanctuaries of the Virgin were well frequented by soldiers: Rue du Bac, LaSalette, Lourdes, Pontmain; and the less renowned shrines at Lyon and Dunkerque. A hundred thousand soldiers inscribed themselves in a Living Rosary society, constituting small groups for rosary recitation everywhere. Naturally, some injured soldiers went to Lourdes; this was in addition to the soldiers already recuperating in the hospital there. Ex votos pictured the Virgin surrounded by the usual rays and by cannon explosions (pp. 59-60).

Soldiers' religious practice also included the standard Catholic list: masses, communions, prayers, rosaries, the Blessed Sacrament, Joan of Arc, and Saint Thérésé of Lisieux were the popular intercessors—along with Marguérite-Marie Alacoque, the Sacred Heart visionary of the seventeenth century (pp. 72-73). The reports on "superstitions" center primarily on fetishes, prayers and objects; naturally the clergy of the day were concerned to sort out the truth from the superstition. Although sometimes a fetish object, the Bible was read in the trenches (pp. 89-90). And prayer books were published specifically for the soldiers. In 1916, fifty thousand copies of Father Lenoir's *Livre de priéres du soldat catholique* were sold. Part one presented the standard prayers—Our Father, Hail Mary; Acts of Faith, Hope, and Charity. Procedures for Confession and Communion, services for the dead, and advice on assistance for the dying were, naturally, highlighted. The second part consisted in a brief explanation of the Catholic religion, a discussion of the obligations of a soldier; there were extracts from the gospels and a selection of Catholic hymns (Chaline 1993: 119). The *Missel du Miracle de la Marne*, however, was much less successful since it was published in 1916 when the war had slowed to a deadly stalemate. The 1914 victory had been taken literally as miracle, accomplished with the help of Joan of Arc and the Blessed Virgin, especially the Virgin of LaSalette (A. Becker 1994: 70-71).

The other side of this devotionalism could be anti-Protestant and anti-government sentiments. Hatred for Germany magnified an already existing anti-Lutheranism:

> Our soldiers, penetrating into a cemetery in Flanders, found themselves in the presence of a large cross. In place of the Christ, which had been torn off, a man had been crucified by the Germans ... That can only be explained by a kind of collective possession of the whole German army ... It is the Lutheran abcess, growing for four centuries, that has finally burst ..." (p. 22, citing Leon Bloy).

And there was the penchant, proper to the anti-government Catholic right, to see the war as a chastisement for the wickedness of the religion-destroying France of revolutionary traditions. This was the basis for the belief that Catholics wished the defeat of France, divine chastisement, as a salutary lesson (p. 33).

In sum, everyday personal, social, and political relationships were transferred to the effective levels of religious devotion. Heavenly figures were imagined to complete the tasks that believers wanted fulfilled in their own history.

Rational Religion: A Conscious Apostolate

Both chaplains and priests under arms are probably our best witnesses to the theological reasoning required to kill for France and love for God. Dolorism took on a specifically sacerdotal cast. A priest wrote, "My death will be my final Mass, and I unite my blood to that which Jesus shed on the cross, and which so many times by my sacerdotal hands I have made to flow on the altar" (pp. 39-40). Priests engaged in a discussion of practical ministry, though, in fact, the vast majority of them were ordinary soldiers rather than chaplains. Not exempt from the draft, and desiring to prove to the anti-clerical government that they were the most loyal of French citizens, they entered the armed forces in great numbers. In all, 32,699 priests, religious, and seminarians were mobilized. Only 1,500 of these were official military chaplains. The rest were simple soldiers or officers; of these, half worked in the medical corps and half carried guns. This placed the Catholic clergy in a bizarre situation, because according to Canon Law priests are not permitted to bear arms. But Rome made an exception for the French clergy because of that tenuous relationship with the anti-clerical government (Fontana 1990, ch. 8; Mayeur 1979). Much of the literature—memoirs, letters, directives—was produced by chaplains, obviously a small percentage of the priests who were in the armed forces. French soldiers' contact with a priest was most likely to be the medic, the stretcher bearer, or the companion in arms next to him.

In the army, priests mixed with the general population as they never had before. And the future Cardinal Liénart reported an ecumenism "lived everyday among the men" (A. Becker, 1994: 43). Becker says of this, "For numerous Catholic observers the 'Union sacree' meant above encounters, improbable before the war, which multiplied under the particular conditions of the front" (p. 443). These encounters included agnostics and freethinkers. Dealing with their own Catholics, priests could complain about the profound ignorance of the men. Nadine-Josette Chaline records that "Father Aucler [was] struck by the tabula rasa on religious matters that is evidenced by numerous soldiers" (1993: 115). They also complained about the minimal communions among medics and stretcher bearers, the few confessions; the colonial soldiers seem even to have little idea of a future life.

The return to religious practice was then, as it is now, difficult to assess. Geoffroy de Grandmaison wrote for a number of chaplains—"We are too quickly called back to reality above all at Easter. We have only to compare the number of Easter Communions (the number of hosts distributed—so as not to exaggerate) with the number of those assigned to the battalion. In my section, one hundred out of twelve hundred made their Easter Duty in the space of four to five weeks" (A. Becker, 1994: 98). This estimate was confirmed by the prefect of the Marne: "The religious sentiment that showed itself in the first months of the war has considerably diminished, the association with death has bred indifference, and the uncertainty of life has given to many of those who fight the desire to have pleasure, without any obstacle and immediately" (p. 98).

Their roles no longer trivial or peripheral, the French priests of World War I intellectualized the existence they shared with the other soldiers. Their theology was inflected, intoned, after the manner of William James's Cardinal Newman, who could make theology and philosophy emotionally alive for the sake of rational goals (1961: 357).

Nation, God, and Personality Structure

National sentiment intrudes itself here, because it can serve as a substitute for, or overlap with, religious sentiment. Both sentiments have been recently examined by Stephane Audouin-Rouzeau (1992), in his study of the trench newspapers of World War I. Here we find evidence of the experiences of soldier journalists, some of them with professional and intellectual connections. Audouin-Rouzeau provides broad summaries of expressions of "national sentiment" and "religious sensibility" from these journals.

To begin with, trench newspapers "disregarded both national and international news, the soldiers concerning themselves above all with individual and immediate problems": "The poilu thinks quite simply about his house, his bit of land, the retrospective delights of his pre-war life" (p. 156, citing *Le Périscope*).[8] Though it was important, even Verdun was not analyzed in any way as strategically central to France's interests. Summing up the response to French national news, Ardouin-Rouzeau says,

---

8. Once again with the author-date style of documentation, materials cited by the author must be given in the text itself.

Despite their more or less extensive reading of national newspapers, the men in the ranks remained psychologically cut off from current affairs because life in the trenches largely deprived them of any wish to know, to be interested, or to understand. Even middle-class townsmen, more cultivated and of broader vision than the rural soldiers, do not appear to have escaped this attitude: "If you only knew how little it [the news] concerns us and how little we think about it" (p. 160, citing *L'Explosif*).

War was an atrocity, there was a strain of pacifism even in these newspapers.

War was therefore devoid of meaning—or justification—unless it was to lead to peace. From the first outbreak of hostilities the theme of the "war on war" is solidly established ... "Everyone must concentrate on fighting wholeheartedly, according to his ability and without weakening. And in the end we will establish a peace which nothing will break" (p. 161, citing *Le Poilu*).

Clearly the fundamental first step in propriate functioning was necessitated by battle, life-threatening in essence and at every turn. To the extent the men could think at all, they had to focus on their own persons. Fellow combatants were valued inasmuch as they were necessary for one's own survival.

French propagandists were especially successful in demonizing the Germans to keep up fighting spirit. But according to the trench newspapers "it was the leaders who bore the responsibility, in particular the military aristocracy and the businessmen of the middle classes" (p. 164). Infrequently there were reports of sympathy between French and Germans; incidents of comradery were more played up only after the war. Audouin-Rouzeau says that, "the image of the adversary improved steadily in the trench press between 1914 and 1918. The papers appeared much less harsh at the end of the war than at the beginning, but despite this moderation it was anegative image of the enemy that prevailed until the end of the conflict" (p. 169). The soldiers were concerned lest contempt for the enemy make him into an unworthy adversary, thus demeaning their own battle prowess: "It is not the cause of the Boche that I am pleading, but that of the poilu who is appalled by the systematic disparaging of the enemy" (p. 170, citing *Le Crapouillot*).

Finally, Audouin-Rouzeau tries to interpret the French soldiers' understanding of Germans as, let us just say, "other." "What separated the French from these Germans marching past them? Was it not the impression—unspoken and inexpressible—of not being of the same blood? Between the former and the latter there appeared to be an impassable mental barrier—or passable only with difficulty" (pp. 172-173). Solidarity could help many soldiers to the ego-extension and ego-enchancement that included fellow soldiers. But it could not help them to an existential knowledge of themselves as part of a humanity that included enemies. At most they were able to deepen their existential awareness of their own participation in a chain of French being based upon a self-awareness of their pasts and futures.

Patriotism and loyalty waxed and waned over the four years of the war, alternating within a range of "unsophisticated certainty" and doubt/discouragement. The most important component of French patriotism, as Audouin-Rouzeau sees it, was defense of the soil: "Poor French soil, of which every mound had been turned over, crushed, ground down by steel" (p. 177, citing *Sans tabac*); "Every fragment [of this land is] soaked with the blood of our brothers, is a sort of sacred clay" (p. 177, citing *L'Argonnaute*). This was closely allied to defense of "one's own": "We fought because we could not do otherwise ... We were forced to make war and to fight by all the social ties which bind us; by the dependence and the subjection in which the individual exists in relation to the State within modern societies; by the thousand threads which attach him to the soil, to the very atmosphere of his land, and which form morally binding attitudes more powerful than any physical shackles" (p. 181, citing *Le Tord-Boyau*). In Audouin-Rouzeau's view, then, "More or less consciously, the soldiers appear firmly *forced* into national feeling: this feeling obtrudes on them at the death of their comrades, the acclaim of the local people, at a front-line advance or retreat ..." (p. 182). In this context, the fundamental concept and feeling of duty becomes totally understandable.

There was less expression of religious sensibility in the trench newspapers—surprisingly, given the constant presence and possibility of death. For Audoin-Rouzeau, the soldiers' behavior (confidence in religious medals, etc.) represents "invasive superstition" (p. 85). Nevertheless, religious faith could serve as a "shield" against discouragement and despair: "I cannot believe, I shall always refuse to believe, that so much youth, so much ardour, so much strength cut down and broken, could be lost forever and ever in space and time" (p. 85, citing *L'Horizon*). Again, the image of the crucifix as the embodiment of human suffering: "At the center of the cemetery stands a large wooden figure of Christ...the face, dripping with rain, appears to reflect an infinity of suffering and sadness" (p. 85, citing *La Saucisse*). Isolated reports describe prayer, special Mass celebrations, and even on occasion widespread participation in Holy Communion: "A few terrified men suggest that we pray together" (p. 86, citing *Le Crapouillot*); "the mystery of Christmas, the mystery of love and of sacrifice, was reborn" (p. 86, citing *Le Poilu marmité*); Masses for the dead at the front were the most moving of all ... the whole regiment took communion in the same distress" (p. 86, citing *La Marmite*).

Nationalism, then, was a "more profound experience than formal religion," although trench journalists might have said that talking about religion represented "a failure to meet the demands of neutrality"—like talking about politics (p. 87). In any case, according to Audoin-Rouzeau, the trend was away from religion, after an initial increase of public manifestation.[9] But I believe that we can set up an agenda to find out more about the roles of religious and national sentiments in the lives of World War I soldiers.

THE NEW AGENDA

We do not have airtight categories for the varieties of religious—and national—experience in normal times. In war these experiences interpenetrate and become all-embracing. And they are themselves subsumed by the existential experience of mortal danger. For each soldier, religion and nation are experienced as elements of the structure and development of his own personality. But historians cannot study each soldier individually; nor should they. Such work would be methodologically impossible and totally resistant to historical narrative. In the actuality of war individual personalities are subsumed by the group effort. The only reasonable procedure, then, is to study select individuals as part of the larger group. Here the orientations and categories of James (VRE) would be modified in application—with greater refinement than I have managed thus far. In the study of individuals, the orientations and categories of Allport (1950, 1955; also 1942, 1965) serve some precision as a completion of James. And both James and Allport must be modified in each use or reference to these categories and orientations. In fact, in a historical narrative they belong in the footnotes.

I propose, then, a study of both reflective writings and attitude surveys. It is clear to me that the most generally reflective of the professionals who actually fought during the

---

9. Audouin-Rouzeau says that there was more religion talk in 1915, but all his quotes come from 1916/1917.

war were the medical doctors and the clergy (Grandmaison 1916). Systematic annotated bibliographies of letters and diaries have already been made.[10] And there exists one formidable general survey of soldiers' attitudes: the archives of the army's bureau of postal censorship. From 1916 to the end of the war a cross-section of soldiers' letters were read by a host of censors, carefully trained to record the morale of the soldiers—the physical and mental states expressed in the letters (Jeanneney 1968).

As a first step, I have chosen some suggestive excerpts from the writings of a doctor and a priest, followed by a cross-section of the postal censors' report for the French First Army (SHAT 1916). The two personalities I wish to introduce here are Dr. Ferdinand Belmont and Rev. Pierre Leliévre. Belmont, according to Annette Becker, is the soldier who "in all English speaking lands ... has become the symbol of the French Catholic soldier of the First World War" (1994: 20. n. 17); at least we are justified in using him as an example. As for Leliévre, Jean Norton Cru considers his book "the most solid, the most sincere of the war books by ecclesiastics" ([1929] 1993: 173).

The young Doctor Ferdinand Belmont engaged himself as a fighting officer rather than as a member of the medical corps. His letters to family and friends were published in 1916, within a year of his death in battle. Piety, resignation to the point, I would say, of mystical union characterize his language about the war. There is little reference to religious history and theology, little reference to national history and political tradition: themes that dominated the language of Leliévre.

All Saints Day was the occasion of thoughts on faith, prayer, duty, and God, "It is one of the feasts I prefer, because it is among those that best recall to us all the force, all the profound peace that one can find in the faith" (Belmont 1916: 79). One needs to, "seek out the courage, the resignation, the hope that are necessary to all of us to go all the way without weakening in the trial that God requires of us." God challenges; this is a trial. It will be an occasion to "unite us more closely by prayer, which does not know separation."

> He said that the heights of spirituality could be found in the trenches. I will pass my Feast of All Saints in my trench; our good God hears our prayers, whatever the place from which they are addressed.

The war should not shake one's trust in God.

> We need only avoid anxiety, and submit ourselves to Him who loves us and takes care of us at every second (pp. 79-81).

Submission brings rewards, because life can bring us nothing "more consoling and more sure than this blind submission to the will of God." The evil that we see is not the real evil, that is to say, God has to demand this suffering for his greater purposes: "The sorrow that it pleases him to demand from us is a mysterious ransom of more authentic misfortune that our veiled eyes cannot see" (pp. 83-84).

God is compared to a sculptor with war as one of his tools for sculpting.

> Each cut of the chisel little by little makes us less grand, purifies us, separates us from our original encasement [gaine] and leads us towards perfection. Ah! If we only knew how to let ourselves be carved by the cool of the heights and make more abundant the first flows of Spring (pp. 161-162).

---

10. But Jean Norton Cru ([1929] 1993) has not been surpassed.

Full happiness comes only through total and perfect submission: "We must desire neither life nor death, since we know neither what awaits us in this world nor what is reserved for us in the next" (p. 199).

Though Belmont values the joys of Catholic liturgy, he fights no apologetic or theological battles. True, he was writing to his own family—simple people of deep faith, it would seem. But on the other hand, French Catholics were just coming out of a period of great national controversy over religion; it would have been natural to defend official Catholicism. Yet, on tradition, on confessional identity, there is this single, isolated comment::.

It does us good, across the inevitable monotony of our earthly existence, to find again in such a peculiar setting, the old practices of that religion that, as little children, we learned to love—before penetrating the meaning of it and feeling the benefits of it (p. 269).

Expressions of national identity are virtually never explicit and always subordinated to nostalgia for family and home ground. Germany is simply "them"—"les boches," as they are for everyone—although I note one reference to geography: "Certainly in our admirable élan at the beginning, we promised ourselves ahead of time a triumphal march across the Rhine into the heart of Prussia" (p. 109). But he did label as "fine discourse" (p. 109) one official government declaration. Of pure national expression, of love for the fatherland, he had little regard. Not that he formally rejected it; he simply did not see it in the soldiers.

The words, "Fatherland," "ideal," and even "duty" themselves designate only abstractions. It is good to concretize them by colors and forms; one should speak to the men of their church tower or their own roofs when dealing with the fatherland, speak of the flag when symbolizing honor and military duty. For the rest, one must not try to give them the cult of an ideal when their own turn of mind and their own formation does not put them in a position to conceive (p. 233).

Greatest respect was reserved for the comrades with whom one lives and dies. Belmont was touched by the reverence for the bodies of slain comrades, often nothing more than "a mass of decay" (p. 274). Burial of the dead was more than a health measure:

There is a simple, profound faith that comes out of an ancestral soul. There is an evangelical tenderness of mortal man for his own kind; there is also perhaps a vague awareness of the silent mediating role [délégation] that is established between the men and the families of their comrades (p. 274).

This was a bond sealed by the immediacy of shared existence.

It is not inaccurate to say that this reunion of men grouped in front of the enemy and danger forms an authentic family and binds one another together by the same duties as brothers; they are brothers in arms (p. 275).

The one embodiment of France that I found in Belmont's writing was not grounded in a metaphor of greatness of immortality. Rather "France is an eternal child; one can neither wish nor hope that the lesson of the events she traverses transform her in her tastes or her affinities; it is sufficient that she orient and discipline them" (p. 280).

Ferdinand Belmont expresses classical resignation to the will of God with encourage-ment to generosity and greatness of soul: a healthy personality who never seemed to experience any inclinations to dividedness. The faith of the family and the faith derived from the cultures were essential elements of his identity. But he felt that each trial was the hand of God fashioning his self and his existence. Unlikely, then, that his religion remained on the level of ego-enchancement; war had driven an already "original" spirit to a recognition of goals beyond the surrounding violence. Nature, the liturgy, and memo-ries of his Catholic youth were experiences that nourished his devotional life. His self-knowledge does appear to have led to the domain of personal strength that James labeled "saintliness": pristine moments of asceticism, strength of soul, purity and charity. These virtues did not lead to negativity, harsh judgments about others, or taboo-like renuncia-tion of human affection.

Father Pierre Leliévre, an army chaplain, was more conscious than Belmont of both Catholic and French identity, though probably no more intense in his love of God and the land. In his notes and impressions of war he described the military action in and about the city of Reims with interpretation of the cannonading of the cathedral—Reims, where the Church crowned the kings of France. Leliévre gave voice to the French Catholic com-monplace that the cathedral was an incarnation of France.

> The baptism of Clovis by St. Rémi after [the battle] of Tolbiac [took place here]. The cathedral was [also] where Charles VII was crowned under the victorious standard of Joan, the Maid [of Orleans]. Two unforgettable dates in the history of a France that stubbornly wants to forget in these latter times all of our formal history. Without the victory of Clovis over the Germans, the Ile de France would not have become the gentle cradle of the our race; and without Clothilde and Rémi, the Church would not have leaned over this crib, so like a region of violence. Without Joan the Maid finally, what would have become of French unity, saved at that time by a daughter of the people, incarnating the fatherland and inclining her King before God (pp. 76-77)?

Of course, the worshippers inside count the most; the cathedral served them by giving them a liturgy to live by; the liturgy animated their souls: "Yes, this people once had a soul, and they lived out of the eternal" (p. 77). The liturgy was of a piece with the art and architecture; the symbolism, naturally, pointed beyond itself to the mystical life:

> How much I would like to linger however, to study the marvels and the symbolism of each detail and of the whole: the figures of the apostles and those of the Virtues around the Virgin! How much I would like to control my education and my reli-gious faith, so positive and dry in comparison to the faith so mystical and loving of those former ages (p. 79).

Yet, though he waxed so eloquent on official religion, Leliévre was not a defensive cleric. He looked for faith rather than hierarchical standing. Here is his criticism of another chaplain.

> Useless to open myself up to my colleague, the official chaplain. He thinks only of his title, which gives him officially the rank of captain. Happily there are several priests among the stretcher bearers. Little by little I make their acquaintance, and little by little also I make the acquaintance of the young medical students, happy and open companions (p. 83).

It came as no surprise to Leliévre when the cathedral was shelled. Men around cursed the barbarity that ended in the cannonading of one of the great masterpieces of world architecture. He said, "I admit that I did not share their surprise. I expected at each hour, so logical and inevitable did the disaster appear to me" (p. 87). Such a breakdown in humanity was not to be blamed solely on Germany. This cathedral that animated and symbolized the soul of the French people was often appreciated more by non-French. As he lamented the war as a breakdown of civilization, he lamented the French loss of their true identity.

> Nothing is more French in France than our cathedrals, and the cathedral of Reims most of all. But we did not understand this. We had become so strange to our national religion and history that we needed a German Baedeker to explain the cathedral of Reims, the purest masterpiece of the French soul (p. 88).

Even so, Leliévre was more appreciative than many clerics of the simple, powerful human forces at work in the War; his humanity was broader than that of the self-interested priests who peddled religion with the enthusiasm and the attitudes of salespeople.

In self-image and propriate striving Leliévre differs from Belmont. His self-image is composed more of the past history of France and a priest's understanding of his contemporaries' humanity (Belmont emphasized family more than nation, cosmos more than humanity). Leliévre's propriate striving was less ambitious, if not less worthy, than Belmont's. Leliévre's understanding of equilibrium and charity did not have such a heroic cast; he would appear to be here more honest than Belmont, were it not for Belmont's self-transcending simplicity. In sum, the two of them, the doctor and the priest, achieved, to all appearances, a high level of existential knowing: individuals responsibly producing justice and love to contradict a Europe plunged into hate and destruction. Mystical, devotional, and rational religion had reinforced one another in the lives of these men.

The morale of the French soldier during the long stalemate of trench warfare was cause for official concern. A Commission of Postal Control was established, with sufficient personnel to systematically sift through all of the soldiers' letters. Letters were selected, opened, and quoted in a massive operation involving more than a hundred full-time censors. The commission established a grid of selected issues to look for in the content of the letters. Censors looked for remarks on hygiene, the war, external affairs, and the home front; and these four were divided into subheadings. As a result, the military and government administrations could get a good idea of what the ranks thought on one hand, about food, sanitation, and state of the trenches; and on the other hand, the quality of material, officers, the enemy, and the future (optimism and pessimism). Hundreds of thousands of letters were examined in an effort that would be worthy of a modern survey of opinion. This collection of censors' reports at the French Army archives at the Chateau de Vincennes on the outskirts of Paris is a valuable witness to the state of mind of the French soldier during World War One. Over the past generation, Jean-Noël Jeanneney (1968) and Anick Cochet (1983) published general analyses of this documentation. Jeanneney in particular studied national sentiment—producing results similar to the studies of formal publications (Cru [1929] 1993) and trench journals (Audouin-Rouzeau, 1992). When it came to *expression* of national—or religious—sentiment, the soldiers did not differ from their published (or eventually published) confreres. I have sampled the many cartons, each carton containing thousands of typed pages of systematic reports. Expressions of religious sentiment/identity or national sentiment/identity, while few and far between, were revealing.

I found one combination of French Catholic identity and cultural militancy: a perfect sense of the other territory and culture being "them."

Joan of Arc inspires in our leaders an excellent strategy. You see, everything tells me to hope and have confidence. If we go over to their land, woe to their humble dwellings. We will make them tremble before our tricolor; we will rid the world of that vermin, of those enemies of letters, arts, and of all that is good and noble. Let us hope that the conclusion of this frightful struggle will take place this year. Pray to God for that and for all the allied soldiers who are going to fall (10th Inf.)[11] (SHAT 1916).

Mention of the Sacred Heart follows out the official Catholic line of nineteenth- and twentieth-century France.

The war will finally have its hunger satisfied. All are firmly convinced of it. May the Sacred Heart take pity on France and bless our arms and our soldiers (SHAT 1916).

The belief that Christ revealed himself centuries before as Sacred Heart to a French nun made this image a special sign of God's love for the French. Another writer sees events in the context of the Church liturgical year. One wonders, since he belonged to the medical corps, if he were a priest or seminarian.

Many make the case that everything will be ended in October, and may God hear them. For my part, I extend it a little further and I will be very happy if everything is ended by All Saints Day. And after that, God willing, may we enjoy the benefits of peace (Ambulance 2/7 Neuchâteau), (SHAT 1916).

Again from the medical corps, an expression of faith and resignation:

You must be reasonable. I have never had a scratch. I certainly think that I will not be killed before having seen you. And then afterward, God will protect me always as he has done in the past, which is what makes me so confident (Medic 4/66) (SHAT 1916).

Perhaps this letter, too, comes from a priest, but one cannot be sure.

I must emphasize that these quotations are virtually the only ones to be found after a review of the censors' reports of many months. One can take the twenty odd pages of any weekly report for any one of the twelve armies and find no real expression of religious sentiment or self-conscious nationalism. The solution here may be to choose a set of terms for content analysis—as has been done in a study of the American Civil War (Goodman 1981)—and see the merit of isolating the language of religious and national expression used in a broad range of letters. We could say, "When expression of religious and national identity is found, here is the language used." An important problem would still remain, however: the language might only be used by clergy and very self-conscious Catholics, or by very self-conscious secularized Republicans.

In conclusion, I must bring us back to William James. We have used Allport to situate the religious experience in a theory of personality structure and development, and contemporary studies of physiological phenomena to broaden the categories of mystical and devotional experience (e.g., Fischer 1971, 1986; Pruyser 1969). But this must not obscure the terminology of James—eclectic, idiosyncratic, but, I believe, right on the mark. As historians of the War, we cannot insert a large number of personal lives into a coherent nar-

---

11. Censors often noted the military assignment and sometimes the rank of the letter writer.

rative. But we can classify the personality orientation expressed in a remark or judgment; we can classify the type of interior and exterior dedication manifest in reported behavior; and we can classify the nuances of mystical, devotional, and rational religion. For this we have William James to thank. We need only, on occasion, insert the developmental story of selected individuals within the narrative, and, in general, broaden the experiential categories. In particular, we should include within the mystical experience within the broader awareness of mortality-grounded existential fear.

It was an American chaplain who once said of the troops: "There was more religion in the trenches than anywhere else in the world. Before the attack, many read their Bible and prayed ... This war has given a sense of dependence upon God ... It is not that these men were Christian or affiliated with a Church. It was a sort of unitary mystical experience" (A. Becker 1994: 99, citing Emmet Shipler, *War Work in the Diocese of New York*). At the end of the war, an observer wrote in the *Atlantic Monthly*, "After decades of materialism, a new mysticism is born ... This mysticism is conscious. We have attained a wisdom of maturity by experiencing the abyss and returning voluntarily to the confidence of a child" (A. Becker 1994: 99, citing Winifred Kirkland, "The New Death"). Could it be that through common experience of the horrors of war in face of the eternal mystery of death, the French soldiers while possessing opposing ideologies or no ideology at all, recognized one another as sharers of a common French experience? Perhaps, too, the war taught them to tolerate, among their compatriots, both greater and lesser degrees of specifically religious and confessional awareness. I believe that "the varieties of religious"—and national—"experience," having a common mystical base, effected the transformation of France into a unified nation, one of the few in the world today. The *union sacrée* was a reality after all.

REFERENCES

Audoin-Rouzeau, S. (1992). *Men at War, 1914-1918: National Sentiment and Trench Journalism in France during the First World War.* Helen McPhail (Trans.). Providence, R. I.: Berg.

Allport. G. (1942). *The Use of Personal Documents in Psychological Science.* New York: Social Science Research Council.

———— (1950). *The Individual and His Religion: A Psychological Interpretation.* New York: Macmillan Company.

———— (1955). *Becoming: Basic Considerations for a Psychology of Personality.* New Haven, CT: Yale.

———— (1965). *Letters for Jenny.* New York: Harcourt Brace.

Barton, M. (1981). *Goodmen: The Character of Civil War Soldiers.* University Park, PA: Pennsylvania State University Press.

Becker, A. (1994). *La Guerre et la foi: De la mort á la mémoire, 1914-1930.* Paris: Armand Colin.

Becker, J.J. (1985). *The Great War and the French People. Translated by Arnold Pomeràns.* New York: Berg, 1985.

Belmont, F. (1916). *Lettres d'un officer de Chasseurs alpins (2 août 1914-28 décembre 1915.* Paris: Plon.

Byrnes, J.F. (1984). *The Psychology of Religion.* New York: Free Press.

———— (1989). Review of *Festivals and the French Revolution* by Mona Ozouf, *History and Theory*, 28: 112-125.

Chaline, N.–J. (Ed.) (1993). *Chrétiens dans la première querre mondiale.* Paris: Cerf.

Cochet, A. (1983). Les Paysans sur le front en 1916. *Bulletin du Centre d'histoire de la France contemporaine*, no. 3: 37-48.

Cru, J.N. ([1929] 1993). *Témoins: Essai d' analyse et de critique des souvenirs de combattants édités en francais de 1915 á 1928.* Nancy: Presses Universitaires de Nancy.

———— ([1931] 1988). *War Books: A Study in Historical Criticism.* E. Marchand and S. J. Pincetl, Jr. San Diego, CA: San Diego State University Press.

Fischer, R. (1971). A cartography of the ecstatic and meditative states: *Science,* 174: 897-904.

———— (1986). Toward a neuroscience of self-experience and states of self-awareness and interpreting interpretations. B. Wolman and M. Vilman (Eds.), in *Handbook of States of Conscousness,* New York: Van Nostrand Reinhold (pp. 3-30).

Fontana, J. (1990). *Les Catholiques francais pendant la grande guerre.* Paris: Cerf.

Grandmaison, L. de (Ed.)(1916), *Impressions de guerre de pretres soldats.* Paris: Plon.

Hanak, P. (1970), De Volksmeinung wahrend des letzten Kriegsjahres in Osterreich-Ungarn. R. G. Plaschka and K. Mack (Eds.). *Die Auflösung des Habsburgerreiches: Zusammenbruch und Neuorientierung im Donauraum.* Vienna: Verlag fur Geschichte un Politik.

James, W. (1961). *The Varieties of Religious Experience: A Study of Human Nature.* New York: Collier Books.

Jeanneney, J-N. (1968). Les Archives des commissions de Controle postal aux armees (1916-1918): Une source précieuse pour l'histoire contemporaine de l'opinion et des mentalites, *Revue d'histoire moderne et contemporaine,* 15: 209-233.

Kohut, T.A. (1986). Psychohistory as history. The American Historical Review, 91:336-354.

Lelièvre, P. (N.d). *Le Flèau de Dieu (notes et impressions de guerre).* 2me èdition. Paris: Paul Ollendorff.

Malony, H. N. and B. Spilka (1991). *Religion in Psychodynamic Perspective: The Contributions of Paul W. Pruyser.* New York: Oxford University Press.

Mayeur, J.M. (1979), La Vie religieuse en France pendant la première guerre mondiale. *Histoire vécue du peuple chrétien,* 2 vols. Toulouse: Privat.

Miquel, P. (1983), *La Grande guerre.* Paris: Fayard.

Mosse, G. (1990). *Fallen Soldiers: Reshaping the Memory of the World Wars.* New York: Oxford University Press.

Pruyser, P.W. (1968). *A Dynamic Psychology of Religion.* New York: Harper & Row.

Rioux, J-P. (1994). L'histoire: 'Tous ceux qui pieusement ...'. *Le Monde (des livres),* 18 fevrier, p. 7. On A. Becker, *La Guerre et la foi;* and *Chrétiens dans la premiére guerre mondiale.* N-J. Chaline (Ed.).

Robbins, K. (1984), *The First World War.* New York: Oxford University Press.

Runyan, W.M. (1982), *Life Histories and Psychobiography: Explorations in Theory and Method.* New York: Oxford University Press.

Service historique de l'Armee de terre (SHAT)(1916), Carton 16N 1388. *Rapports de commission de contrôle postal de lre armée, mars 1916-juin 1917.*

Sirinelli, J-F. (1990). Les intellectuels français et la guerre, *Les Sociétés européennes et la guerre de 1914-1918: Actes du colloque organisé à Nanterre et à Amiens du 8 au 11 dècembre 1988.* Publié sou la direction de J.J. Becker et S. Audoin-Rouzeau. Paris: Publications de l'Université de Nanterre.

Smith, L. V. (1994). *Between Mutiny and Obedience: The Case of the French Fifth Infantry Division During World War I.* Princeton, NJ: Princeton University Press.

Spilka, B., Shaver, P., and L. Kirkpatrick, (1985), A general attribution theory for the psychology of religion. *Journal for the Scientific Study of Religion;* 24: 1-20.

Wilson, E. (1962), *Patriotic Gore: Studies in the Literature of the American Civil War.* New York: Oxford University Press.

Winter, J.M. *The Experience of World War One.* New York: Oxford, 1989.

IV. MYSTICISM: YIELDING TO THE "MORE" OF LIFE

THE FORCE OF EMOTION: JAMES'S REORIENTATION OF RELIGION AND THE CONTEMPORARY REDISCOVERY OF THE BODY, SPIRITUALITY, AND THE "FEELING SELF"

WADE CLARK ROOF AND SARAH MCFARLAND TAYLOR

The rapid growth and attraction of contemporary drumming groups, "neo-tribal" ritual, charismatic religious experience and even the "dance trance" of Techno-Hippie "Rave" culture all bespeak a movement toward physically active modes of spirituality that express a powerful desire to "embody the body." This effort to "make the body matter" as a locus for spirituality ironically, but not surprisingly, comes at a time when telecommunications and now cyberspace have made "bodilessness" more of a reality than ever before. The ability to "surf" the Internet and various virtual worlds, not as a disembodied telephone voice or even as the flattened human surface conveyed by television, but rather as a pure transmutable electronic intelligence, now coincides with movements to resacrilize the body and consequently make it the center of religious experience.

In the Religious Studies field, scholars have begun to address this movement to decenter normative notions of religion and to look to the body as a more nuanced and too-often ignored interpretive lens through which to investigate religion. In her 1989 Presidential Address to the Society for the Scientific Study of Religion, Meredith McGuire posed the key, and yet almost perversely obvious, question: "What if people—the subjects of our research and theorizing—had material bodies?" (1990). Her question marks a comprehensive shift in the way the study of religion approaches, and thus defines, religion itself.

Before what is now being called the "body craze," however, and some eighty-eight years prior to McGuire's speech calling for the "rediscovery of the body," William James's own Gifford Lectures, later compiled in *The Varieties of Religious Experience* (1985; hereafter VRE); called for a similar decentering and reorientation of the study of religion.

By taking as his subject of study not creed or religious philosophy but rather the emotion and feeling of religious experience, James decenters the location of religion away from the realm of the intellectual and the philosophical and places it instead in the physicality of the senses. He clearly describes his purpose in giving these lectures as being "bent on rehabilitating the element of feeling in religion and subordinating its intellectual part" (389).

James likens the then current study of religion, which was grounded almost totally in the study of religious philosophy, to looking at a picture of a moving express train. One sees the size and shape of the train and its details, "But where," asks James, "is the energy or the fifty miles an hour?" (389). For James, "the energy" of this express train of religion is religious emotion:

> If religion is to mean anything definite for us, it seems to me that we ought to take it
> as meaning this added dimension of emotion, this enthusiastic temper of espousal, in
> regions where morality so called can at best bow its head and acquiesce" (VRE: 55).

That "energy"—the force of emotion—is located in the body. He identifies the powerful emotions associated with narratives of conversion and saintliness as indicative of a "biological as well as psychological condition" (VRE: 391). By omitting or marginalizing this body-based ("biological") manifestation of religion, argues James, one is presenting merely a picture of a train without the motion or steam that gives it life or power.

James's ideas about body, emotion and religious experience presented in *The Varieties* are informed by his *theory of apperception*, in which he posits the thesis that emotional experiences follow from bodily changes. In his attention to perception and senses in *The Varieties*, we can see that, for James, religious experience likewise has a bodily counterpart. He establishes, in his discussion of mystical experience and New Thought movements, an immediacy between bodily experience and mental and emotional states—a link that connects his theory of "What is an emotion?" (1884) with his reorientation of "What is religion?"

The Varieties is often dismissed as an apologetic for the "necessity" of religion to the existence of humanity. (James says he agrees with Tolstoy that faith "is among the forces by which men live" and says that "The total absence of it, anhedonia, means collapse" [VRE: 391]). However, analyzing James's theories of body and religion at the beginning of this century and the way his approach seeks to decenter the study of religion away from the philosophical and intellectual and toward the experiential and physical provide us with a valuable American grounding for current exporations of body and spirituality, as well as its contemporary cultural expressions.

James's interpretations also raise a series of provocative questions that will be addressed in this article. What are the linkages between body, emotions or feelings, and religious experience? Is there evidence from the contemporary religious culture that supports James's thinking or perspectives on the body as it relates to emotion? Have mainstream religious institutions become a gallery of "express train pictures?" And by seeking more physically active, more body-oriented alternatives, are New Agers, New Charismatics and even Techno-Hippies merely asking "Where's the energy or the fifty miles an hour?" The theories of religion and emotion expressed in *The Varieties* provide valuable perspectives and possible frameworks relevant to this discussion.

REORIENTING RELIGION TOWARD THE SENSES

James's emphasis on feelings and experiences was, and still is, a singularly important contribution to the study of religion. For James, it is important to recognize that religion consists of a set of psychological processes and actions—"feelings, acts, and experiences"—which he took to be primary and necessary to consider rather than to rely on the "overbeliefs" by which they are labeled. Because he set for himself the task of rescuing the study of religion from philosophy and reorienting it around feelings and experiences, James tends to minimize the role of ideas and culture. He did not seriously consider as a perspective what today would pass as "labeling theory" or "constructivist" interpretations. His concern at the time was more fundamental, more practical—to get back to the religious experience itself. Social scientific study of religion still does not fully appreciate his concern for what he described as the "blooming, buzzing, confusion" of experience in all its richness, considering that psychologists of religion continue to be more concerned with beliefs and ideas and sociologists of religion with institutions and culture.

James recognizes in *The Varieties* that feeling and thought are both key components of religion, but he privileges feeling over thought, locating the source of religion in the senses. "I do believe that feeling is the deeper source of religion," says James, "and that philosophic and theological formulas are secondary products, like translations of a text into another tongue" (VRE: 337). For James, before the existence of a theological narrative, there is a narrative of experience and emotion which is subsequently and imperfectly translated into words.

We are thinking beings, and we cannot exclude the intellect from participating in any of our functions. Even in soliloquizing with ourselves, we construe our feelings intellectually. Both our personal ideals and our religious and mystical experiences must be interpreted congruously with the kind of scenery which our thinking mind inhabits... But all these intellectual operations, whether they be constructive or comparative or critical, presuppose immediate experiences as their subject matter. They are interpretive and inductive operations, operations after the fact, consequent upon religious feeling, not coordinate with it, not independent of what it ascertains" (VRE: 338-339).

James therefore does not deny the realm of the intellectual and the philosophical, but rather says that it has received too much emphasis and has wrongly been made to be the center of the study of religion.

By focusing on the varieties of religious *experience*, on *"feeling* or *emotion* as the deeper source of religion," James, in effect, is also asking the question, "What if people—subjects of our research and theorizing—had material bodies?" Focusing on feeling specifically reorients the study of religion toward the body in the James text because, for James, feeling and emotion have a body source.

In an earlier work called "What is an Emotion?" (1884), James puts forth his *theory of apperception,* in which he posits that emotions are "feelings of bodily changes" and argues for a biological manifestation of emotion. He explains that:

Our natural way of thinking about these standard emotions is that the mental perception of some fact excites the mental affection called the emotion, and that this latter state of mind gives rise to the bodily expression. My thesis on the contrary is that *the bodily changes follow directly the* PERCEPTION *of the exciting fact, and that our feeling of the same changes as they occur* IS *the emotion.* Common sense says, we lose our fortune, are sorry and weep; we meet a bear; are frightened and run; we are insulted by a rival, are angry and strike. The hypothesis here to be defended says that this order of sequence is incorrect, that the one mental state is not immediately induced by the other, that the bodily manifestations must first be interposed between, and that the more rational statement is that we feel sorry because we cry, angry because we strike, afraid because we tremble ... Without the bodily states following the perception, the latter would be purely cognitive in form, pale colourless, destitute of emotion (1884: 247).

What James is getting at in his thesis is what recent studies in the psychology and physiology of emotion have come to support—that physical action produces real emotional response and that emotional response can produce real physical change (see Laird and Bressler 1990). Research findings show, for example, that manipulations of facial expressions do, in fact, produce changes in emotional experience. At least 28 separate studies have demonstrated an inductive physical-emotional relationship, just as James proposed. People feel the emotions their faces try to express, whether they are fear, anger, sadness, humor, pain or happiness. James was careful to mention several differing kinds of emotional behaviors for which this relationship should hold, and recent experimental evidence shows this as well.

Other studies point to a similar conclusion. Subjects who adopt certain physical postures report feeling emotions appropriate to their posture (Duclos et al. 1989; Riskind 1983; and Riskind and Gotay 1982). When people are led to walk in emotionally expressive ways, they report feelings in keeping with their behavior (Snodgrass, Higgins, and

Todisco 1986). When opposite-sex pairs act as if they are "in love" by gazing into each other's eyes, as opposed to simply gazing at each other's hands, those gazing into each other's eyes report greater romantic feelings (Kellerman, Lewis, and Laird 1989).

Schachter's work on autonomic arousal, which differs in some ways from James, still shares the same core assumption that bodily changes precede and generate emotional feeling. Research stemming from Schachter's earlier work suggests that autonomic arousal contributes to the experiences of fear, anger, and romantic love, though perhaps not happiness. Laboratory experiments using electric shock treatments demonstrate that when people perform actions that represent emotions, they *feel* the corresponding emotion (Laird and Bressler 1990).These recent empirical studies and others support the kind of mind/body connection that James first put forth in his essay "What Is an Emotion?"

A review of James's theory of apperception is key to understanding and exploring the way he deals with feelings and emotions in *The Varieties* because it is this theory that informs his treatment of religion. James centers discussion of religion on feeling and then locates that feeling within the realm of the body. In his discussion of mystical experience, for instance, he says that "our immediate feelings have no content but what the five senses supply" (VRE: 318). James even classifies religion as something not merely cultural or psychological but as something *biological*.

> Taking creeds and faith-states together, as forming "religions," and treating these as purely subjective phenomena, without question of their "truth," we are obliged, on account of their extraordinary influence upon action and endurance, to class them amongst the most important biological functions of mankind. (VRE: 391).

It is important to note that, when James speaks of the physicality and biology of religious experience, he not only speaks as a philosopher and a scholar of religion in the most phenomenological sense, but also as one who has received a degree in physiology at Harvard, where he later taught courses on anatomy. As one who literally "taught the body," James sees religious emotion as inexorably body linked. Although James adamantly criticizes those who would *reduce* religious experience to nervous disorders or physical ailments, in his discussion of ecstatic religious feeling, James again asserts that the "faith state" is both biological and psychological:

> [W]e have seen how this emotion overcomes temperamental melancholy and imparts endurance to the Subject, or a zest, or meaning or an enchantment and glory to the common objects of life. The name "faith-state," by which Professor Leuba designates it, is a good one. It is a biological as well as psychological condition ... (VRE: 391).

Some of his examples of this biological condition are "sudden raptures of the divine presence" and "mystical seizures." James's point is that with religion, no less than other experiential realms, behavior has effects upon experience and certainly upon the body. This is seen most effectively in his treatment of mystical experience.

Particularly intriguing is his discussion of the *transport*. The transport is the mechanism by which an individual achieves the mystical state—that is, some sort of action, practice or exercise that "brings you there." To get "there" involves mental and bodily exercises that trigger the experience, a catalyst for the emotion. The very idea of "transport" is itself interesting, since one of its dictionary meanings is "to carry away by strong emotions," or to be moved by powerful feelings. The actual term "transport" James adopts from the Persian philosopher and theologian Al-Ghazzali, who uses it to refer to "whirling dervishes" or to the mystical spinning practices of the Sufi. The bodily performance of spinning becomes a physical means to bring body, mind and spirit as a whole to a transformed and mystical state. James does not deny that the attainment of the mystical state involves thought, but it is the sensory experience that is central to the process.

James's pragmatism is evident here: That which produces the desired religious results is deemed worthy of practice. At the same time, James says that the transport is incommunicable, that mystical truth and how it is arrived at defy logic or explanation. Implied as well is psychic distance, or the necessity of movement from one mental state to another. If the pinnacle of religious experience is, as James describes it, "joyful ecstasy," then its achievement rests at least in part upon such a transport.

Although the oncoming of mystical states may be facilitated by preliminary voluntary operations, as by fixing the attention, or going through certain bodily performances, or in other ways which manuals of mysticism prescribe; yet when the characteristic sort of consciousness once has set in, the mystic feels as if his own will were in abeyance, and indeed sometimes as if he were grasped and held by a superior power" (VRE: 300).

In this passage, we see that efforts at producing a religious experience must be distinguished from the overwhelming power of the experience itself. Bodily performances and mental concentrations are, in some sense, "preliminary," beyond which the individual's relation to the religious experience undergoes a fundamental change. There is a point one reaches in mystical experience, James observes, where one surrenders and gives oneself over to it, thus bringing out the tensions in the relationship between actively directing the spiritual experience and releasing one's control.

In his discussion of mystical experience, James mostly concentrates on Eastern religious practices, some of which strive to go beyond the body and the realm of the senses into pure consciousness but, in effect, manipulate the body itself as a catalyst for achieving this end. Echoing his comments that religion cannot be reasoned and cannot be reached in an "*a priori* way," James locates the transport, and ultimately the mystical experience itself, in the physicality of the senses: "[I]t resembles the knowledge given to us in the sensations more than that given to us by conceptual thought" (VRE: 318).

He observes two types of mystical experiences—the "sporadic" and the "cultivated." The former is a random occurrence, the latter is more deliberate and planned. The mystical state can thus be produced through a variety of means. His discussion of both the sporadic and the cultivated mystical experience deals with mind-body reciprocity and communicates a biological component to religious emotion. His examples of "transports" to the sporadic mystical experience, for example, include drugs that induce some sort of chemical bodily transformation. James talks of alcohol as a mind-expanding drug and about nitrous oxide dreams as bringing upon the inhaler what he perceives to be a "genuine mystical revelation" (VRE: 305). He relates his own experiments with nitrous oxide and his observations of how, when taken into the body, this gas can induce transformed physical/emotional states. Just as he finds that religious emotion can "overcome temperamental melancholy," he finds drugs able to produce similar chemical mood-changing effects to his own severe "melancholia" or manic depression.

A "transport" to the sporadic mystical state, however, can also be something as simple as a sensory experience with nature. James cites passages from Walt Whitman and others describing their mystical experiences induced by their physical communion with nature (VRE: 311). One such illustration is a passage from J. Trevor's autobiography, in which he tells of leaving his wife and children to attend church one morning while he takes a walk in the hills with his dog:

In the loveliness of the morning, and the beauty of the hills and valleys, I soon lost my sense of sadness and regret ... On the way back, suddenly, without warning, I felt that I was in Heaven—an inward state of peace and joy and assurance inscrutably intense, accompanied with a sense of being bathed in a warm glow of light, as though the external condition had brought about an internal effect—a feeling of having passed beyond the body, through the scene around me" (VRE: 312).

This kind of chance mystical experience is "sporadic," for James, because it occurs randomly and is not sustainable. "The Vedandists," he points out, "say that one may stumble into superconsciousness sporadically, without previous discipline, but then it is impure" (VRE: 315).

The "cultivated mystical experience," on the other hand, involves *methodical practice* and training and raises the issue of religious learning—one must learn and then practice how consciously to manipulate the senses to "get there." Here, James cites the example of Yoga, in which the "transport" consists of "persevering exercise," "diet," "posture, breathing, intellectual concentration, and moral discipline" (VRE: 314). The "transport" involves some sort of body-related activity, whether it be feeding the body certain foods, placing the body in certain positions or causing the body to inhale and exhale in controlled ways. Even the meditation or "intellectual concentration" component requires a specific body position and can involve the repetition of a mantra.

Although James does not address learning *per se*, it is important to note that each of these performative activities crucial for "transportation" to the "cultivated" mystical experience is learned. James's discussion of the "cultivated" mystical experience communicates that religious experience can arise out of practice and that people have the capacity to learn to have religious experiences. Or to put it more accurately, they can learn how to create their own brain-states, which are defined or labeled as religious. But such learning involves more than just "learning about" religion; it has to do with learning (and language) that flows forth from the religious life itself.

James V. Spickard echoes James's notions of "cultivation" of experience through learning, practice and the notion of a body component to this cultivation, when he argues that:

Like learning to play the piano, one studies with teachers and reads books, then one practices (see Sudnow 1978). As he or she masters the first exercises, the piano teacher monitors progress, gives new instructions or guidance, and sets the student to practicing again. Guidance consists not so much in labeling what is occurring as in suggesting technical changes: a different posture, a different mantra, and so on. Gradually one learns to focus one's attention in the right way and attains the proper state of consciousness (1993: 117).

Likewise, David Preston (1988) emphasizes that learning Zen follows essentially from meditative practice, and not from ideas or even rules about the practice of Zen. the teacher may guide the student, but the "Zen reality" comes as a result of the student's extended practice.

Although James's discussion emphasizes the emotions or feelings that result from performative activity, he does not *reduce* the mind/body connection to a one-way street. Just as he recognizes the intellectual component of religion but chooses not to emphasize it, preferring rather to reorient the study toward religion's more neglected feeling side, James also recognizes the mind's ability to produce real bodily change. He praises Mind-Cure, for instance—a practice that effects body results through mental effort and "hypnotic practice"—for recapturing what the Christian mystic tradition once had but has since lost. For James, Protestant

Christianity is no longer "therapeutic" in the way of mystic tradition. As a "train," it has abandoned its "energy." James says that in this absence, "It has been left to our mindcurers to reintroduce methodical meditation into our religious life" (VRE: 319).

Therefore, while James by no means reduces all to the body, his discussion of mystical religious experience still communicates an immediacy between bodily experience and religious emotional states—an immediacy that makes James's *The Varieties of Religious Experience* particularly germane to the discussion of contemporary spirituality and its rediscovery of the body, spirituality and what we will call the "feeling self."

CONTEMPORARY RELIGIOUS CULTURE

Turning to contemporary American life, the question arises: What significance does James's approach have for us today? His concern with religious experience, as opposed to belief, creeds or institutions, has given *The Varieties* an abiding relevance ever since it was written. But beyond this, what more might be said about James's insights?

The present authors have recently been engaged in research on contemporary religion, particularly among younger generations looking at baby boomer spirituality, women's spirituality, and twentysomething Rave culture. In our judgment, and in that of many others, there is a renewed and genuine interest in religious experience today. Since the 1960s, we have witnessed a number of religious and spiritual movements which have privileged the role and significance of experience—as evident in earlier countercultural religious movements, the rediscovery of Eastern spirituality, the Pentecostal, charismatic and born-again evangelical movements of the late 1970s and 1980s, and, more recently, the many forms of New Age spirituality, Goddess Worship, neo-paganism, eco-spirituality, and even the latest craze of all-night "Gen X" raves. We would go further to suggest that there is a strong affinity between James's insights and several important developments in our own time. Let us look at these developments with an eye toward how James's approach can further their better understanding.

Rediscovery of the Body

James's reorientation of religion away from the institutional and philosophical (he says his aim is to "discredit the intellectualism of religion") and toward the personal and sensory experience of "spirituality" provides an ideal framework for the discussion of current movements in spirituality, emotion and body narrative. For James, philosophy, theology and creed are always a necessarily flawed way of translating the biology of the religious emotion into language. His claim is "that philosophic and theological formulas are secondary products, like the translations of a text into another tongue" (VRE: 337). Movements toward more active body involvement and toward the exalting of sensory experience in contemporary spirituality also seek a return to the primacy of body narrative or body text as opposed to reliance on a derivative, and thereby less authentic, "translation." Instead of dealing with the translation, these contemporary movements go to the "origin" or source of religion, and the body is seen as being that source. Body-centered spiritual practices aim to enable participants to go back to a non-discursive form of religion, one that is so "pure" that it cannot be expressed in words, only experienced.

Like James's "express train" analogy, the body movement in contemporary spirituality looks at the outline and external details of the "train" of mainstream organized religion and asks, "where's the energy?" They, as does James, find that missing "energy" in the primacy of emotion and the ecstasy of religious experience—emotion and energy which, as in his theory of apperception, are by their very nature centered in the body.

New Age, neo-tribal, and neo-shamanic movements have discovered that engaging in a physically active spirituality can be a powerful tool for invoking spiritual emotion. Much of the counterculture spirituality of the 1960s achieved this biological/spiritual transformation through drugs (the "sporadic"), but more recent New Age spirituality focuses more on a "sustainable spirituality" than on a "quick high." "Transports" for intense spiritual experience take the form of drum rhythms, ecstatic dance, ritual psychodrama, candles and incense to please and excite the senses, and highly active performative ritual—all ways of celebrating the "embodiment of the body" to a spiritual end.

The importance and centrality of the experiential, the sensual and the physical in contemporary spirituality challenge what Ann Taves refers to as "the assumption that a true religion (or authentic religious experience) is unique and thus incomparable and the assumption that true religion is spiritual and rational as opposed to sensual and material" (1993: 220). This, in turn, gives rise to a shift away from the Calvinistic centrality, the all-importance of the "word" and the Enlightenment exaltation of intellect and reason over "superstition," to a more material experience which Taves terms "knowing through the body."

Among theorists (see Butler 1993; Scarry 1985; Mellor and Shilling 1994), as well as within the realm of popular religion, "knowing through the body" has marked the recognition and rediscovery of the body's spatio-temporal contribution to spiritual reality. To talk about religious emotion, to say that the self "feels," is also to affirm something that is obvious, yet fundamental: It is through our bodies that we experience our selves, the world and our topic at hand, religion. Bodies are the intersection of self and society. Meredith McGuire expresses the point well:

Through our bodies, we see, feel, hear, perceive, touch, smell, and we hold our everyday worlds. While each individual is uniquely embodied, the experience is also profoundly social. For example, our experience with our bodies is mediated by learned roles and other expectations; it is shaped by the immediate social context, as well as by historical antecedents of which the individual may not even be aware; and it is apprehended and communicated indirectly through language and other cultural symbols (1990: 285).

James speaks of how our "mental life is knit up with our corporeal frame" (1884: 266), arguing against a philosophical dualism of mind versus body. The human body is both a biological and a cultural entity, both an active agent and an object of social conditioning. The notion of a "mindful body" captures this sense of a unitary phenomenon (Schepper-Hughes and Lock 1987). Such a notion seems in keeping with James's outlook.

The notion also illuminates a wide range of contemporary religious phenomena: in ritual forms of healing, where healing groups use body ritual as a means of transforming themselves (McGuire 1988); in pilgrimage rituals, involving a bodily transition in time and space (Frankenberg 1986); and in trances, in which body postures affect an altered state of consciousness (Goodman 1986). The summer 1994 schedule alone for the Omega Institute, a nationally popular "spiritual growth center," lists workshops in the following areas: "Mind-body Medicine," "Movement and Bodycare," "the Mind-Body-Spirit Connection," "Body Ecology: The Art of Touch," "Bodysound and Text," "Somatic Therapy: Touching Mind and Emotion Through the Body," "Bodystories," "Dancing on the Body," an "Introduction to Body-Mind Centering" and something called "Be Body Smart."

The "Rave" scene of the Techno-Hippies, or what has been termed "Zippie" culture, has also centralized the body to spiritual experience. Zippies are "hippies with zip," those who have "balanced their hemisphere to achieve a fusion of the technological and the spiritual" (Marshall 1994: 80). Not dissimilar to Al-Ghazzali's spinning Sufis, Zippies engage in prolonged ecstatic "dance trance" to the fast and hypnotic beat of "Acid House" music in neo-tribal gatherings called "Raves." This fusion of body and spirituality in the form of dance and trance-music has become so popular amongst those in the twentysomething generation that some churches in England and now in the United States have begun to incorporate them into church activities. Mathew Fox, for instance, at San Francisco's Grace Cathedral, has imported from England the "Rave in the Nave" concept, in which twentysomethings and other Rave culture Zippies dance ecstatically in the cathedral, while giant video monitors project various earth and body images along with messages such as, "Eat God"—the ultimate consumption of the divine body projected into a body-centered ritual of ecstatic worship.

In these contemporary examples we see a reorientation of spirituality toward the primacy of the body. We see that, for these groups, religion is not so much about creed and philosophy as it is about emotion and performance, an immediacy between bodily experience and religious emotion. We see, therefore, that the movement toward centering religion in the space of the body becomes linked to a movement toward "spirituality" or rather a movement toward James's redefinition of "religion." Religion, in the body-centered context, draws the focus away from ecclesiastic institutions and theology and toward a more autonomous, more personal, more immediate "spirituality."

Rediscovery of the Spiritual

For many middle-aged Americans, this distinction between "religious" and "spiritual" is very real. Many of them dropped out of organized religion when they were growing up and still have little to do with it. They grew up questioning authority and still have less confidence in social institutions than did, say, their parents' generation. Not surprisingly, a great number of them feel some distance from most churches, synagogues, mosques and temples, and they experience the world within them as far removed from anything they have known in everyday life.

Today, some are shopping around for an inspiring faith, and if successful, they most often find it within an evangelical or charismatic church. Others explore new spiritualities and cultivate their own inner resources (see Roof 1993). Contrasting the yeasty growth of these new spiritualities to the mainstream religious scene conjures up James's picture of an express train lacking the energy that gives it the life or power to move forward. We observe a strong yearning on the part of many for some kind of spiritual experience, some new source of "energy" they can claim as their own. Both inside and outside the religious establishment, we find there are signs of considerable spiritual ferment. This yearning for a richer, more immediate and all-encompassing type of experience is expressed in many ways, in both traditional and non-traditional religious languages: centering one's life, knowing God, getting in touch with oneself, exploring the higher self, finding it.

By making individual experience and feeling central, and by codifying theological, moral and dogmatic formulas as "secondary products" (VRE: 338), James redefines "religion" in terms of what we might now call "spirituality" instead of religion. He says in *The Varieties* that "the word 'religion,' as ordinarily used is equivocal" because it has been used to signify the organizations and ecclesiastic institutions that grow up around religious leaders and eventually fall prey to "the spirit of politics and the lust for dogmatic rule" (VRE: 267). He points out, in a timely fashion for current discussion, that:

When we hear the word "religion" nowadays, we think inevitably of some "church" or other; and to some persons the word "church" suggests so much hypocrisy and tyranny and meanness and tenacity of superstition that in a whole-sale undiscerning way they glory in saying they are "down" on religion altogether ... But in this course of lectures ecclesiastical institutions hardly concern us at all. The religious experience which we are studying is that which lives itself out within the private breast (VRE: 267).

James's defining of "religion" in *The Varieties*, not as organized or institutional, but rather as that personal and sensory experience that might be called "spirituality," obviously bears upon current interest in spirituality. While he does not distinguish between the religious and the spiritual *per se*, as is now the case, he clearly focuses upon the inner world of religious experience. Following Neville (1978), it is important today to distinguish between the two since, though as labels they do overlap, some instances of spiritual discipline are clearly distinct from traditional religious practice. Religion for James involves: wholeness both in the sense of encompassing the body, mind, and feelings and as a total comprehension of reality, an emphasis on experience, sudden transformations, and the importance of such experience to a vital and enduring sense of self. With respect to wholeness, it should be noted that James himself is quite critical of the subject/object dualisms. While having practical meaning, such distinctions do not have ontological significance. He looks upon consciousness as an entity composed of not radically different stuff from the context it encounters. Spirituality involves a consciousness of self in relation to a larger environment and thus is, in its most fundamental sense, holistic.

Rediscovery of the "Feeling Self"

For James, the perception of bodily sensations generates feelings, which is for him a central concept in his analysis of religion. Feeling is not only the heart of emotion but the heart of his psychology. Feelings are central to his understanding of the self. Above all, as Izard observes (1990: 632), in James's view, "the self is felt, and what is felt motivates cognition and action."

In an age when themes such as the *"Saturated Self,"* the *"Depleted Self,"* and the *"Protean Self"* are widely discussed, perhaps we should consider yet another—James's "feeling self." To say that the self "feels" is to anchor it in the perception of bodily processes and to offer something of a counterpoint to the currently popular "constructionist" approach to the self in the social sciences. This is not to deny the importance of social influence and processes, but to affirm that, in its most essential state, the self is embodied by and thereby subject to feelings arising out of the body. The matter is of course complex, since feelings are themselves shaped by social construction—what Bourdieu (1977) describes as the "socially informed body." Yet it would seem that perceptions of bodily sensations are far too rich, too diverse, too dynamic and fleeting to limit their activating power simply to the labels an individual acquires through socialization. Indeed, for James, feelings are foundational not just for religion but even for consciousness, which in his earlier book on psychology he describes as "subjective life" and likens to a stream because it "feels unbroken" (James 1890: 238).

What contemporary charismatics, many evangelicals, New Agers and the dance trance of Rave culture have in common is, among other things, a high level of expressive feelings. Ecstatic worship, whether inside or outside the religious establishment, is what many people appear to be trying to find. James's notion of the "feeling self" is helpful in grasping this element of contemporary religious and spiritual quest—first, because as he saw it the self is dynamic, fluid and open to emotional expression, and second, because religion is an active and powerful agent in producing a change in feelings. The "feeling self" is a self that is transformed through its own emotional expression and, for James, there is no more likely way for this to happen than by means of religious experience.

Today, the "feeling self" begs to be reclaimed as religiously authentic. So much attention has been given to a subjective narcissistic mode of self-expressiveness in contemporary American culture that we have become suspicious of feelings, even religious feelings, as if they were ill-founded or little more than a self-preoccupation. But James teaches us quite differently: that feelings constitute the self and are central to religious life. If the express train he speaks of is to be grasped fully in its movement—that is, if religion is to be pictured as alive and dynamic—then the energy has to arise out of a religious emotion that is, above all else, felt.

One final observation: Religion, particularly in James's view, is far too pluriform to allow for simple explanations. His thought resists easy generalizations, perhaps even "central propositions," as Dittes (1973) points out. James does not use cause-and-effect language and leaves it to the reader to think with him in his explorations. He steers us away from the more visible institutional and philosophical constructions and takes us into the deeper, more mysterious realms of what lies behind them. Body, emotions and religious experience, while never rigidly formulated, serve as the essential linkages in what for him is the central reality—the force that propels the religious response. In a time of renewed debate over the categories for analyzing religion, we would do well to consider once again James's insights.

REFERENCES

Bordieu, P. (1977). *Outline of a Theory of Practice*. Cambridge: Cambridge University Press.

Buck, R. (1990). William James, the nature of knowledge, and current issues in emotion, cognition, and communication. *Personality and Social Psychology Bulletin*, 16: 612-624.

Butler, J. (1993). *Bodies That Matter*. New York: Routledge.

Delattre, R. (1990). Supply-side spirituality: A case study in the cultural interpretation of religious ethics in America. In R. Sherrill (Ed.) *Religion and the Life of the Nation*. Urbana, IL: University of Illinois Press (pp. 84-108).

Dittes, J. (1973). Beyond William James. In C.Y. Glock & P.E. Hammond (Eds.) *Beyond the Classics? Essays in the Scientific Study of Religion*. New York: Harper and Row (pp. 291-354).

Duclos, S., et al. (1989). Categorical vs. dimensional effects of facial expressions and postures on emotional experience. *Journal of Personality and Social Psychology*, 57: 100-108.

Frankenberg, R. (1986). Sickness as cultural performance: Drama, trajectory, and pilgrimage root metaphors and the making of social disease. *International Journal of Health Services*, 16: 603-626.

Goodman, F. (1986). Body posture and the religious altered state of consciousness. *Journal of Humanistic Psychology*, 26: 81-118.

Izard, C. (1990). The substrates and functions of emotional feelings: William James and current emotion theory. *Personality and Social Psychology Bulletin*, 16: 626-636.

James, W. (1920). What is an emotion? In *Collected Essays and Reviews*. London: Longmans, Green (pp. 244-275).

————— (1950). The *Principles of Psychology*, 2 vols. New York: Dover.

————— (1985). *The Varieties of Religious Experience*. New York: Collier Books/Macmillan.

Kellerman, J., Lewis, J. & J. Laird (1989). Looking and loving: The effects of mutual gaze on feelings of romantic love. *Journal of Research on Personality*, 23: 145-161.

Laird, J. & C. Bresler (1990). William James and the mechanisms of emotional experience.

Personality and Social Psychology Bulletin, 16: 636-651.

Marshall, J. (1994). Here come the Zippies! *Wired* (May): 79-134.

McGuire, M. (1988). *Ritual Healing in Surburban America*. New Brunswick, NJ: Rutgers University Press.

————— (1990). Religion and the body: Rematerializing the human body in the social sciences of religion. *Journal for the Scientific Study of Religion*, 29: 283-296.

Mellor, P. & C. Shilling (1994). Reflexive modernity and the religious body. *Religion*, 24: 23-42.

Neville, R. (1978). *Soldier, Sage, Saint*. New York: Fordham University Press.

Preston, D. (1988). *The Social Organization of Zen Practice*. Cambridge: Cambridge University Press.

Riskind, J. H. (1983). Nonverbal expressions and the accessibility of life experience memories: A congruency hypothesis. *Social Cognition*, 2: 62-86.

Riskind, J. H. & C. C. Gotay (1982). Physical posture: Could it have regulatory or feedback effects on motivation and emotion? *Motivation and Emotion*, 6: 273-298.

Roof, W. C. (1993). *A Generation of Seekers*. San Francisco, CA: Harper San Francisco.

Scarry, E. (1985). *The Body in Pain*. New York: Oxford University Press.

Schepper-Hughes, N. & M. Lock (1987). The mindful body: A prolegomenon to future work in medical anthropology. *Medical Anthropology Quarterly*, 1: 6-41.

Snodgrass, S. E., Higgins, J. G. & L. Todisco (1986). The effects of waking behavior on mood. Paper presented at the annual meeting of the American Psychological Association, Washington, D.C.

Spickard, J. (1993). For a sociology of experience. In W. Swatos (Ed.), *A Future for Religion: New Paradigms for Social Analysis*. Newbury Park, CA: Sage Publications (pp. 109-128).

Stearns, P. (1989). Social history update: Sociology of emotion. *Journal of Social History*, 22: 592-600.

Sudnow, D. (1978). *Ways of the Hand*. Cambridge, MA: Harvard University Press.

Taves, A. (1993). Knowing through the body: Dissociative experience in the African-and British-American Methodist traditions. *Journal for Religion*, 73: 200-223.

THE SOULFUL SELF OF WILLIAM JAMES

RALPH W. HOOD JR.

Interest in mysticism has always been a central focus of the psychology of religion. Not surprisingly, the earliest investigatiors in psychology not only had an interest in religion, but wrote heavily on mysticism. Perhaps James (1985, p. 329; hereafter VRE), put the issue most succinctly when he stated, "In mystic states we both become one with the Absolute and we become aware of our oneness. This is the everlasting and triumphant mystical tradition, hardly altered by differences of clime or creed."

It comes as no surprise then that resurgence of interest in the psychology of religion provides a climate hospitable to the study of mysticism. Clearly my own efforts in the psychology of religion center primarily around mysticism. Yet if there has been a change from the earliest concerns with mysticism in the psychology of religion and present concerns, it is clearly focused upon issues of measurement. Recently Gorsuch (1984) has persuasively argued that the dominant paradigm in the contemporary psychology of religion is a measurement paradigm—one that operationalizes concepts of concern to the investigator and assesses them in a variety of methodological contexts, whether correlational, quasi-experimental, or even occasionally, true experimental designs. In this light, my own efforts to study mysticism illustrate Gorsuch's claim well. They also emphasize the distinction between contemporary research and the earliest work on mysticism. Since my own efforts in this area are reviewed in several readily available sources (Hood 1985; Hutch 1982; Spilka et al. 1985; Preston 1984), I shall use this opportunity to attempt to assess the value of my research in light of my concern with the psychology of religion in general. And while it may seem curious, given my own identification with the measurement paradigm, I want to express in this brief paper a concern with the too narrow focus upon measurement in the psychology of religion, divorced from theistic considerations. I do this despite my strong agreement that measurement is essential in the psychology of religion. I merely want to insist that it be meaningful as well.

PROMISCUOUS EMPIRICISM

It has been more than two decades since James Dittes, retiring as editor of the *Journal for the Scientific Study of Religion*, noted that much of the empirical psychology of religion was rooted in a "promiscuous empiricism" (1971, p. 393). By this he meant, among other things, that much of the empirical psychology of religion, while methodologically sound, reached essentially shallow conclusions. In the specific article in which Dittes (1971) made these comments, he was responding to an empirically adequate study (after all, Dittes as editor had accepted the study for publication) in which the perpetual claim that religion was related to "deprivation" was once again empirically tested. Dittes noted appropriately that the status of this claim was at least as old as the Old Testament itself and, given the proper choice of indices, could hardly fail to be "proven." Hence, despite the rigors of empirical investigation, the outcome is at best trivial and at worst uninformative.

I have kept Dittes's article filed in the back of my mind all these years and wonder about my own empirical research on mysticism in light of his charge of "promiscuous empiricism." Indeed, otherwise favorable comments on my own research have suggested a similar charge (Hutch 1982; Preston 1984). Put simply, has the empirical study of mysticism and religious experience truly been illuminating? If I were to answer that question in terms of my own research, the answer is less favorable. For example, much of my research can be summarized in terms of three major areas. First, intrinsic, devout persons are most likely to report religiously interpreted mystical experiences, and such experiences are not necessarily reported only by church committed persons, especially when the experiences are not religiously interpreted. Second, indicators of psychopathology, if unbiased, do not relate to mysticism. Third, various conditions trigger mystical experiences depending upon the beliefs of the persons involved. Perhaps this is a too brief summary of my work, but not all that unfair (e.g., Hood 1985). And yet, while I would argue that my research has been empirically sound, I am not as sure I can argue that it has been equally illuminating. Is this not, then, "promiscuous empiricism?" After all, if we do not know significantly more about mysticism after empirical research within the measurement paradigm, is measurement per se sufficient to provide truly meaningful research? The answer is clearly no.

If there is a hidden agenda in my empirical research efforts, it is in the careful measurement of reported mystical experiences derived from an explicit philosophical perspective. In all my studies of mysticism, I treat my measurement of mysticism as operational *indicators* and not as operational *definitions*. The distinction, simply put, is that operational indicators are always to be judged by their reasonableness in indicating some measurable aspects of a phenomenon, itself never directly assessed. This is to be distinguished from simple claims to operational definitions whereby the measurement is itself synonymous with the phenomenon. My own commitment to a conceptualization of mysticism, advocated most clearly by Stace (1961), is well documented. As such, two claims are implicit in my empirical research. First, interpretations of experience can be separated from experience itself, even though, paradoxically, no experience is uninterpreted. Second, mysticism is the fundamental experiential basis upon which religions ultimately rest. Succinctly summarized, I want to argue that mystical experience is a human universal variously confronted within and without religious traditions. As such, one can seek to empirically identify the report of mystical experience and its incorporation and structuring within various interpretative schemes. Indeed, I think contemporary concern with attribution theory is on the right track insofar as attributions are interpretative schemes rooted in certain experiences. Specifically with respect to mysticism, given my claim to its universality as a human characteristic, religions are inevitable as they form at least one major interpretative frame for understanding this experience. As Spilka et al. (1985b) have recently noted, one reason religious attributions are made is that religions exist! I merely wish to add that the religions exist because of the necessity to adequately express people's inaleinable mystical natures. If this is accepted, then I think the case can be made for an escape from "promiscuous empiricism" in a manner I tried to resist for a long time, but I think no longer wise. That is to say, the empirical study of religion must proceed under the guidance of a "methodological theism" (Hood 1985).

In a seldom-noted work, Bowker (1973) traces the various scientific claims to the origin of the sense of god and notes wryly that no investigator has really taken seriously that the origin of the sense of god might be God! This I think to be a perceptive point in many senses. I shall conclude these introductory remarks, however, by focusing only upon one of these senses and using as my example Buber's telling criticism of Jung's psychology of religion. I do so to illustrate how it is that empiricism can be more than promiscuous.

As is well known, Jung repeatedly argued that he was an empiricist. In his sense, this meant referring only to phenomena as they appeared to human consciousness (what perhaps loosely can be called a "phenomenological orientation"). As such, Jung rested securely in a curious interpretation of Kant—namely, that one could study appearances only (Kant's phenomena). For Jung this meant that all attributions to God have their origin purely in human mental processes. Yet as Buber rightly notes, such a claim is curious in that it equates for psychological purposes God with self as if self in the psychological sense was also God. As Buber notes correctly, this is gnosticism. Now I have no argument with Jung's gnostic commitments except insofar as he purports to thereby escape theological issues by claims to mere empiricism. As Buber also notes correctly, to equate the phenomena of religious and mystical experience as having origins only within human consciousness, as if such were mere phenomena in the Kantian sense, is erroneous. In Buber's (1952; 80) terse and telling criticism:

> It is thus unequivocally declared here that what the believer ascribes to God has its origin in his own soul. How this assertion is to be reconciled with Jung's assurance that he means by all this "approximately the same thing Kant meant when he called the thing in itself a 'purely negative, borderline concept'" is to me incomprehensible. Kant has explained that the things in themselves are not to be recognized through any categories because they are not phenomena, but are only to be conceived of as an unknown something. However, that that phenomenon, for example, which I call the tree before my window originates not in my meeting with an unknown something but in my own inner self Kant simply did not mean.

Buber's critique of Jung is relevant to my concerns here, as Buber links religious experience to the reality of God and finds a psychology that ignores this reality incomplete (see also Day 1990). In *The Varieties of Religious Experience*, William James defines religious experience as "the feelings, acts, and experiences of individual [persons] in their solitude, so far as they apprehend themselves to stand in relation to whatever they may consider the divine" (VRE: 34). In the following discussion, I want to explore James's own case for methodological theism, focusing first on his theory of the self as presented in *The Principles of Psychology* (1981; hereafter PP); and then on his discussion of mysticism in *The Varieties*. I will argue that the "soul," excluded from *The Principles* for scientific reasons but included in *The Varieties* for religious reasons, is central to his own case for methodological theism.[1]

THE SOULLESS SELF OF *THE PRINCIPLES*

More than one scholar has noted that at least in Western thought the concept of self has been historically intertwined with the concept of God. In *The Principles*, "God talk" is always on the fringe of the discussion forever threatening to break into the text by its various metaphysical forays. The denial of the soul as unnecessary to the empirical facts of psychology is not to deny its existence on other grounds (PP: 182). Readers of *The Principles* are continually assured that they are free to accept the reality of the soul should they wish. James excludes religious discussion of the soul from *The Principles* only after arguing its "superfluity for scientific purposes" (PP: 332). The empirical data on consciousness of self discussed in *The Principles* is not further illuminated by metaphysical discussions of the soul. However, throughout *The Principles* James articulates conditions under which empirical facts might once again demand a return of the soul as a useful scientific concept. As we shall see, the empirical facts of *The Varieties* demand just such a return . In this sense, reading *The Varieties* in light of *The Principles* reveals the anticipated

---

1. While anecdotal evidence suggest *The Varieties* as the most referenced work in American psychology of religion, no real data exists. Vande Kemp (1976) found *The Varieties* the most frequently assigned book in a survey of 49 respondents teaching college courses related to the psychology of religion. However, only less than half of these (17) assigned the text. Wulff (1991: 498-501) under the subheading "The enduring influence of *The Varieties*" provides the best case for James's influence in American culture. James has always been problematic for mainstream American psychology. Coon (1992) has documented James's problematic status for early American psychology.

return of the soul, not only in James's own work, but in contemporary scientific and philosophical thought as well (Barrett, 1986; Fenn & Capps, 1995; Ward, 1993; See also Bird 1991; Bjork 1953).

James's discussion of consciousness of self in *The Principles* requires no consideration of the soul. His distinction among various selves, the material, the social, and the spiritual are all soulless. The concept of soul adds nothing to the empirical facts of self experiencing. The stream of consciousness can appropriate various me's as it does other objects. The awareness of self, of a me found in reflection, does not necessarily entail an additional awareness of a pure self or I. It is neither a logical requirement in a Kantian sense nor must it appear in reflexive consciousness as empirical awareness. James states:

> Instead then, of the stream of thought being one of *consciousness*, "thinking its own existence along with whatever else it thinks,"... it might be better called a stream of *Sciousness* pure and simple thinking objects of some of which it makes what it calls a 'Me'; and unaware of its 'pure' self in an abstract, hypothetic, or conceptual way (PP: 290-291, emphasis in original).

The postulation of a *'sciousness'* as a thinker is rightly noted by James as a metaphysical issue and not empirically required for the facts of experience discussed in *The Principles*. The pure self or I is merely a thought that at each moment is different from the last, but continuous with the last insofar as it appropriates the last, including that which it identifies as 'me' (PP: 379). The I provides continuity and the sense of personal identity heretofore problematic for both associationists and transcendentalists. James's solution is purely psychological. It is the foundation for what otherwise is misperceived as an unoriginal discussion of self.[2] The variety of empirical selves discussed are soulless. Soullessness is the very nature of self and consciousness discussed in *The Principles*:

> It is the Thought to whom the various 'constituents' are known. That Thought is a vehicle of choice as well as of cognition; and among choices it makes are these, appropriation, or repudiations, of its 'own.' But the Thought never is an object in its own hands, it never appropriates or disowns itself (PP: 323).

James noted at the beginning of his discussion of these matters that his resolution would fail to please most (PP: 334). Yet his soulless self is less conceptually clouded than either Hume's or Kant's version of the empirically absent self. The dilemma of personal identity, of continuity of self, at least in terms of its empirical facts, is denied by James to require special metaphysical considerations.

> *The sense of our own personal identity, then, is exactly like any one of our other perceptions of sameness among phenomena. It is a conclusion grounded either on the resemblance in a fundamental respect, or on the continuity before the mind, of the phenomena compared* (PP: 318, emphasis in original).

James's purely psychological solution to the problem of self identity could be reopened as a metaphysical issue only if it were denied that we have direct knowledge of the

---

2. There is a Jamesian influence yet to be critically traced in American sociological social psychology as opposed to psychological social psychology. This is especially the case in some forms of symbolic interactionism (See Schellenberg 1990).

thought as such (PP: 374). The empirical facts, assuming direct knowledge of the thought as such, are elegantly handled by the stream of consciousness metaphor. Still, the dualism of *The Principles* was explicitly provisional. Additional facts might suggest other options. Waxing metaphysical, James bemoaned the isolated soulless self that was the consequence of his positivistic psychology, rigorously followed (PP: 328). His own preference finds the ultimately more satisfying hypothesis to be some sort of *animi mundi* (PP: 328). That the self might exist as a soulful self united with a larger soulful self gains its metaphysical legitimacy in the face of empirical facts not confronted in *The Principles*.[3] The psychologist for whom James's soulless self in isolated irreducible pluralism is the final word must read through the two volumes of *The Principles* to *The Varieties*.

THE SOULFUL SELF OF *THE VARIETIES*

One can fancy an image of James off to Edinburgh to deliver the Gifford lectures with *The Principles* neatly tucked under his arm. This image helps counter the often cited claim that just as there is little religion in *The Principles* there is little of the psychology of *The Principles* in *The Varieties*. This curious claim fails to confront the fact that *The Principles* are as full of religious concerns (addressed psychologically) as *The Varieties* are full of psychological concerns (confronted religiously). Treating *The Principles* and *The Varieties* as one continuous work as I am recommending here allows us to argue the case for the anticipated soulful self that emerges when James confronts the varieties of religious experience.

James's Criteria of Mysticism

It is dangerous to go directly to James's lectures on mysticism (XVI & XVII) for the full facts to be dealt with. Dangerous since in James's own words, "Over and over again in these lectures I have raised points and left them open and unfinished until we should have come to the subject of Mysticism" (VRE: 301). It should not pass unnoticed that much of what is implied concerning mysticism earlier in the lectures that compose *The Varieties* also is on the fringes of discussions in *The Principles*. Much that was left open as a metaphysical option not demanded by the empirical data of a strictly positivistic psychology is now contained in the lectures of *The Varieties* as the essential empirical facts that a psychology of religious experience must confront (Smith 1985: xv).

The criteria James proposes to justify an experience as mystical are often quoted, despite their curious inadequacy. Two criteria are declared to be sufficient to qualify an experience as mystical; two additional criteria James claims are "less sharply marked, but are usually found" (VRE: 302).

The sufficient criteria are those that in the *Principles* characterize most of human experience—noeticism and ineffability (VRE: 302). The noetic criteria, listed second, is curious since in *The Principles* we are continually reminded how consciousness continually confronts objects that are known. Ineffability is cited first, and rightly so, since this negative criterion removes James from concerns with religious overbeliefs and theological debates for which he has little patience. His psychology avoids both the reductionistic claims of the medical materialists and the theological restrictions of the religious dogmatists. Thus, James insists mystical knowledge is participatory and cannot be acquired from descrip-

---

3. While James's positivism clashes with both associationism and transcendentalism this purely philosophical debate parallels similar theological debates found, for instance, in Vedantic and Buddhist thought (see Hood 1994b: 284-286).

tions of the experience, whether given by first of third person authorities. Thus, the authoritative nature of mystical experience is much like that of any experience. Mysticism is removed from the privileged domain of theology and immune from the reductionistic critiques of the physiologists. Mysticism is a shared participation unencumbered by language. As noted above in *The Principles*, language can mislead as much as enlighten. While some experiences are clearly capable of articulation, others are not. Constructionist claims to the linguistic structuring of experience are undermined by the claim that at least some experience is ineffable. "Even namelessness is compatible with existence" (p. 243). Thus, mysticism can reveal, "insights into depths of truth unplumbed by the discursive intellect" (VRE: 302).

That mysticism is identified by two other less typical criteria, passivity and transiency, is not particularly helpful in that these states also characterize most of human experience. In the chapter on Attention (XI) in *The Principles* we are reminded that an object directs our awareness to it as much as we direct our awareness to objects, thus, the passivity of much of human experience is well founded as a general psychological principle. As for transiency, it is almost a synonym for the stream of consciousness and characterizes the growth and development of mystical experiences no more so than experience in general. The criteria used to identify mystical states less marks them off from than injects them into the center of the stream of human experience. Mysticism is a variety of religious experience, even its "root and centre" (VRE: 301), but it remains a fit topic for general psychology. As with all religious experiences, mystical experiences form part of a study of human nature as the subtitle of *The Varieties* asserts.

James's discussion of relevant mystical states is meant to illustrate his method of serial study (VRE: 11-29; Wulff 1991: 481-483). Like other religious experiences, mystical states are to be understood serially, "studied in their germ and in their over-ripe decay, and compared with other exaggerated and degenerate kindred" (VRE: 303). James's mystical series runs from the recognition of a deeper meaning to an otherwise well known phrase to compete states of mystical union, variously described and expressed. It is worth noting that James often cites drug induced states as instances of mystical experiences, thus continuing in *The Varieties* what has already been well established in *The Principles*. To cite but one example, alcohol is perhaps one of James's best exemplars of the fallacy of the limits of medical materialism. Despite the physiological reality of intoxication, its existential and ontological importance is unscathed. In *The Principles* we read: "One of the charms of drunkenness unquestionably lies in the deepening of the sense of reality and truth which is gained therein" (p. 914). In *The Varieties* we read that the truth so found may be mystical:

> The sway of alcohol over mankind is unquestionably due to its power to stimulate the mystical faculties of human nature, usually crushed to earth by the cold facts and dry criticism of the sober hour. Sobriety diminishes, discriminates, and says no; drunkenness expands, unites, and says yes. It is in fact the great exciter of the *Yes* function in man. It brings its votary from the chill periphery of things to the radiant core. It makes him for the moment one with truth (VRE: 307, emphasis in original).

James's fascination with the anesthetics of his day, and his admiration for Benjamin Blood, who wrote several papers on the "revelations" that anesthetics produced in patients (See Hood 1992), is but part of his insistence that the consequences, not the origins, of mystical states are to be the basis of the existential judgment of their value. Perhaps even of their ontological reality as well. Here, far at the end of the mystical series, is a clue to James's real criterion of mysticism. Mysticism makes us one with truth. It is neither simply passive nor transient; neither is it merely a knowledge that is ineffable.

These despite their initial listing are not the defining criteria of mysticism. An experience of unity is the common core of mysticism. James boldly asserts: "In mystic states we both become one with the Absolute and we become aware of our oneness" (VRE: 332).

Why James would suddenly in the middle of his lecture of mysticism bring in the Absolute is problematic since he was far from a proponent of the Absolute in his time! Smith (1985: xv reminds us that in a letter to one of the great apostles of the Absolute, Royce, James wrote:

> When I compose my Gifford lecture mentally, 'tis with the design of overthrowing your system, and ruining your peace. I lead a parasitic life upon you, for my high-est flight of ambitious ideality is to become your conqueror, and go down in history as such.

The use of the Absolute to describe the one essential defining characteristic of mysti-cism is preceded by what many would cite as a prime example of introvertive mysticism. Symonds refers to an experience in which "At last nothing remained but a pure, absolute abstract self" (VRE: 306). Symonds's example of the realization of an absolute self is described by James as having "the genuine mystic ring" (VRE: 310). In a second, drug induced experience reported by Symonds, the experience is now of the sudden recogni-tion of the presence of God (VRE: 312). Both Absolute and God are terms referring to the "reality of the unseen" (VRE: 51-70). Mysticism is one variety of experience in which union with this reality occurs. That the unseen is variously referred to as God and the Absolute by James in his examples of mysticism is not accidental. Just prior to his refer-ence to union with the Absolute quoted above, James states:

> In Paul's language, I live, yet not I, but Christ liveth in me. Only when I become as nothing can God enter in and no difference between his life and mine remain out-standing (VRE: 332).

Both Absolute and God reference overbeliefs whose relevance for mystical experience is in their ability to facilitate such experiences should they be objects of belief and as metaphysical alternatives supporting the ontological claims of mystical illumination. Which is to be preferred, whether God or Absolute, is not yet an issue. Furthermore, that drug induced experiences are most cited by the exemplars illustrating Christian mysti-cism is part of James's insistence on the discontinuity of mystical states with normal con-sciousness (VRE: 308). For many it is drug states that reveal discontinuities in conscious-ness. The linking of drug elicited states with the language of God in an instance of Christian mysticism also illustrates the extent of James's complete refutation of physio-logical reductionism. That one finds union with God is the issue; not the proximate physi-ological elicitor, should one be identified. Likewise, in appealing to the major philosopher of the Absolute, Hegel, James sees his tortured metaphysics as indicative of a struggle to express in the language of the Absolute what was, "surely set to Hegel's intellect by mysti-cal feeling" (VRE: 308). For James, the language of both God and the Absolute suggest the evidential force of experience of which the overbeliefs are primarily expressive outcomes. He knows full well that both God and Absolute are code words suggesting the major lin-guistic traditions within which the Western tradition has confronted mysticism. At this stage of his discussion of mysticism, which term, which linguistic tradition is evoked, is of little concern precisely because they have no direct empirical consequences. God and the Absolute for now are mere code terms for the reality of the unseen with which the mystic experiences union. Their value is precisely to affirm the ontological reality of such a union and hence the possibility that mystical states are objective. Perry (1935 II: 331, emphasis in original) quotes James as stating in his note for *The Varieties*: "Remember, that the whole point lies in really *believing* that through a certain point or part in you you coalesce and are identical with the Eternal."

Because mystical experience is apparently so discontinuous with ordinary consciousness, James has two chalenges. First, to account for this discontinuity in light of the psychology of *The Principles*. Second, to seek conditions under which this discontinuity is less dramatic.

The discontinuity of mystical consciousness is not a problem given a Jamesian view of consciousness. The stream of consciousness whether in smooth flow or spurts selectively appropriates the past. James emphasizes that mystical states are remembered states. They are never merely interruptive, they always are remembered, valued and transforming (VRE: 303). Their passivity is precisely in their union with something greater; something not totally under personal control. The self that is overcome, is done so by a higher self with which it is continuous. Thus, the mystic both loses self (lower self; diminished self) and finds self (higher self; expanded self) which nevertheless is one self. The possibility of a higher self to which lower selves are related as parts to a whole is the empirical possibility noted in *The Principles* that, if entertained, would require additional metaphysical considerations. The centrality of mysticism to religious experiences is precisely in this type of empirical data. It thus requires additional metaphysical discussion. The passing thought is identified in *The Principles* as the thinker (p. 324). The judging thought is empirically identified as both I and me (p. 350). That there may be more to the thinker is admitted in *The Principles* as a mere metaphysical option (p. 324). In *The Varieties* it now becomes a much more lively metaphysical option given the experience of this "more" as basic empirical data of religious consciousness. Second, whether this more is merely a subjective fact within the limits of psychology as a natural science or is an objective fact in which encounter with another self truly occurs is an option James will seriously consider. There is an evidential basis to religious experience beyond its authoritativeness for the person who has the experience. To seriously consider this option obviously expands the limited horizon of psychology as a natural science. James asserts that "Consciousness of illumination is for us the essential mark of 'mystical' states" (VRE: 324). This consciousness is the remembered content of mystical experience insisted upon previously (VRE: 303) and expressed in the Western tradition under the two dominant traditions linked to God or the Absolute. The self is therefore understood to be a soulful self. *The Principles* affirmed the extra scientific meaningfulness of identifying this self (p. 291); *The Varieites* affirm this self empirically. The great faith traditions articulate this self metaphysically.

The disruptive basis of mystical states is partly due to James's use selection of primarily sporadic mystical states to illustrate mystical experience. He thus finds it imperative to cite instances of "methodologically cultivated" mystical states from the major faith traditions including, Buddhism, Christianity, Hinduism, and Islam (VRE: 317-335). His dismissal of the theologies of these faiths, their "overbeliefs," is because he finds no parallel for them in experience. The extensive tradition of Catholic classification of mystical states is dismissed with the quip that it seems to represent "nothing objectively distinct" (VRE: 324). What James wants is simply to document the universality of mystical experience and, as we shall see, the relevance of a metaphysics of the soulful self. As a fact of experience, James affirms that all mystics, whatever their tradition, experience a truth that is absolutely authoritative for them (VRE: 335). Non-mystics gain no authority from the reports of mystics' experiences, and must confront mystic truth claims critically, from the outside. Yet central to all such experiences is an awareness, sporadic or cultivated, of one's self as continuous with a "more." Mystical experiences are but one example of the continuity of self with the unseen. In mystical states unity with this unseen, whether God or Absolute, is experienced. It is not inappropriate to call such experiences an awakening of the soulful self. Its cultivation is a matter of empirical fact, but one that must be experienced. Mystical scriptures are more like musical compositions than critical texts (VRE: 333). The empirical correlates of this experience are likely to be optimism, anti-intellectualism, twice-borness, and asceticism (VRE: 331). Furthermore, such experiences truly engage the person and if they have the appropriate personality characteristics they can benefit from such experiences. However, the dark side of mysticism awaits those for whom their personality characteristics cannot withstand such experiences (VRE: 325). The possibilities of an empirical psychology of religious experience in general and mysticism in particular as sketched by James are on the whole yet to be explored (Hood 1992, 1994b). One issue remaining for consideration in this chapter is to confront the truth claims for a psychology that would recognize the experience of a soulful self.

The Evidential Force of Mystical Experience

James notes that the articulation of religious experiences in general or of mystical experiences in particular, whether in philosophical, psychological or theological terms, cannot establish their truth. Despite the unanimity of the appearance of the soulful self in mystical experiences, these experiences remain private and variously expressed. They have no specific intellectual content of their own (VRE: 337). Yet the fact of the matter is such that transcendental ideals safeguard the reality of individual mystical experience in a more generalized vocabulary (VRE: 358). As with all of James's thought, the issue is the experience that particular language engenders or facilitates, not the language itself. Theological efforts do not impress James precisely because they attempt to establish and defend by abstract reason what is in fact a matter of experience. Thus, James notes:

> In all sad sincerity I think we must conclude that the attempt to demonstrate by purely intellectual processes the truth of the deliverance of direct religious experience is absolutely hopeless (VRE: 359).

As a related point, the language of the Absolute, in its various forms, always entails a language of the soul. Whether a world soul of which the self is a part as in the *animi mundi* noted in *The Principles* (p. 328), or a personal God admitted as James's personal preference in *The Varieties* (VRE: 410-414) makes no difference at the level of legitimating the objectivity of a soulful self as opposed to its mere subjective nature. Thus, in *The Varieties*, the language of soul and the reality of the unseen order loom large as appropriate language for the facts of religious experience. It matters whether the soulful self is merely a subjective expansion in which the subconscious is confronted, or an objective expansion in which God or the Absolute is encountered, though all these hypotheses may fit the limited data of mystical experience. Metaphysically, however, both God and the Absolute offer a richer option. Mysticism must ultimately demand some form of intellectualization (VRE: 362) and accordingly can form matrimonial alliances with so many systems of thought (VRE: 337). Yet the paradox of mystical experience is that description, once removed from experience, will do nothng to foster the experience itself. Thus, as with much of Wittgenstein's philosophy, James's psychology is directed less at resolving certain questions than at making the questions disappear.

James's model of religious experience is simply enough to be elegant. It leaves open the question of the evidential force of religious experience (See Davis 1989). It does not preclude that such experiences are of the soulful self in God and indeed, suggests empirical consequences that should follow if this be true. Indeed, James's preference for God over the Absolute is largely empirical in terms of specific consequences that follow for the individual (VRE: 412-414). In a letter to James Leuba, James noted, "No reader ... could possibly guess that the only spirit I contend for is 'God'" (in Perry 1935, II: 348-349). The Absolute is too impersonal to care and leaves abstract and only apparent the reality of evil in the world. The concreteness of a personal God has consequences for motivation and action in this world. Thus, overbeliefs matter as existential forces in this world and as the generators of ontological facts.[4]

Religious experience expressed in its most lawful form is continuous with James's stream of consciousness metaphor. Ultimately what is most common and generic is succinctly stated: "...*the fact that the conscious person is continuous with a wider self through which saving experiences come*" (VRE: 405, emphasis in original). Despite his rejection of the doctrines of the Absolute as an overbelief, and his rejection of Hegel's dialectic, James notes that much of empirical fact is reflected by these overbeliefs: "The universe *is* a place where things are followed by other things that correct and fulfill them" (VRE: 355, emphasis in original). Consciousness is directed to an uneasiness which in more developed minds assumes a moral character (VRE: 400). There is a solution that in time comes about from a proper relation and connection to "the higher powers." (VRE: 400). There is personal salvation—the soulful self at rest. As James concludes, "It seems to me that all the phenomena are accurately describable in these very terms" (VRE: 400).

The social scientist is presented with a model that can trace the effects of this more in individual lives of those who experience it. They can explore historical and social variations of it in the cultural expression of this "more" and even provide empirical clarifications. James foresaw a science of religion contextualized in the comparative study of religious experiences (VRE: 342). As a working hypothesis James would even allow the "more" to be expressed simply as a "B" different from a normal consciousness, "A" (VRE: 381). If his legacy is in the methodological pluralism that characterizes contemporary studies in the psychology and religion field (Hood 1994aa), is there not a place for methodological theism? If so, what the social scientist cannot do is to lose the full force of the experience of this "more" by retreating to abstractions far removed from the data of experience. The language of unconsciousness, God, and the Absolute remain as viable options to be explored and tested by the full facts of experience. Yet when all is said and done, the truth of any overbelief is in its fruits: in the realization, I would say, of the soulful self.

REFERENCES

Barrett, W. (1983). *Death of the Soul*. New York: Anchor.
Bird, G. (1991). Humanistic understanding and physiological explanation in *The Principles*. British Journal of Psychology, 82: 195-203.
Bjork, D.W. (1983). *The Compromised Scientist: William James in the Development of American Psychology*. New York: Columbia University Press.
Bowker, J. (1973). *The Sense of God*. Oxford: Clarendon Press.
Buber, M. (1952). *Eclipse of God: Studies in the Relation Between Religion and Philosophy*. New York: Harper.
Coon, D.J. (1992). Testing the limits of sense and science: American experimental psychologists combat spiritualism, 1880-1920. *American Psychologist*, 47: 143-158.

---

4. A contemporary critical reversal of James's preference for God over the Absolute is Earle (1980).

Day, B. (1990). The compatibility of Jamesian and Jungian thought. *Journal of Psychology and Christianity*, 9: 20-26.

Davis, F.C. (1989). *The Evidential Force of Religious Experience*. Oxford: Clarendon.

Dittes, J.E. (1971). Conceptual deprivation and statistical rigor. *Journal for the Scientific Study of Religion*, 10: 392-395.

Earle, W. (1981). *Mystical Reason*. Chicago, IL: Regnery Gateway.

Fenn, R.K. & D. Capps (1995). *On Losing the Soul: Essays in the Social Psychology of Religion*. Albany, NY: State University of New York Press.

Gorsuch, R.L. (1984). Measurement: The boon and bane of investigating religion. *American Psychologist*, 39: 228-236.

Hood, R. W., Jr. (1985). Mysticism. In P.E. Hammond (Ed.) *The Sacred in a Secular Age*. Berkeley and Los Angeles, CA: University of California Press (pp. 285-297).

————— (1992). A Jamesian look at self and self loss in mysticism. *The Journal of the Psychology of Religion*, 1: 1-24.

————— (1994a). Psychology and religion. In V.S. Ramachandran (Ed.) *Encyclopedia of Human Behavior*, Vol. 3. Hillsdale, NJ: Academic Press (pp. 619-629).

————— Self and self loss in mystical experience. In T.M. Brinthaupt & R.P. Lipka (Eds.) *Changing the Self*. Albany, NY: State University of New York Press.

Hutch, R. A. (1982). Are psychological studies of religion on the right track? *Religion*, 12: 277-299.

James, W. (1981). *The Principles of Psychology*, 2 vols. In F. Burkhardt, Bowers, F. & I.K. Skrupskelis (Eds.) *The Works of William James*. Cambridge, MA: Harvard University Press.

————— (1985). *The Varieties of Religious Experience*. In F. Burkhardt, Bowers, F. & I. K. Skrupskelis (Eds.) *The Works of William James*. Cambridge, MA: Harvard University Press.

Perry, R.B. (1935). *The Thought and Character of William James*, 2 vols. Boston, MA: Little, Brown.

Preston, J. J. (1954). Empiricism and the phenomenology of religious experience. *Mentalities*, 2: 10-20.

Schellenberg, J.A. (1990). William James and symbolic interactionism. *Personality and Social Psychology Bulletin*, 16: 769-773.

Smith, J. E. (1985). Introduction to *The Varieties of Religious Experience*. Cambridge, MA: Harvard University Press (pp. xi-li).

Spilka, B., Hood, R.W. Jr. & R. L. Gorsuch (1985). *The Psychology of Religion: An Empirical Approach*. Englewood Cliffs, NJ: Prentice-Hall.

Spilka, B., Shaver, P. & L. A. Kirkpatrick (1985). A general attribution theory for the psychology of religion. *Journal for the Scientific Study of Religion*, 24: 1-20.

Stace, W. T. (1961). *Mysticism and Philosophy*. Philadelphia, PA: Lippincott; London: Macmillan.

Vande Kemp, H. (1976). Teaching psychology/religion in the seventies: Monopoly or cooperation? *Teaching of Psychology*, 3: 15-18.

Ward, K. (1993). *Defending the Soul*. Chatham, NY: One World Publishers.

Wulff, D. (1991). *Psychology of Religion*. New York: John Wiley.

THE DARK SIDE OF MYSTICISM: DEPRESSION AND "THE DARK NIGHT"

MARY JO MEADOW

Most people writing about mysticism emphasize mystical exaltation, ecstasy and union with God, divinity, value. Such experiences—the crown of mystical endeavor—are surely important aspects of mysticism. However, mystics also acknowledge periods of dryness, darkness, and religious despair—the keenly felt absence of God. These features seldom receive scholarly consideration in spite of their importance in virtually all mystics' experience.

Psychologists have studied mystical states simply as altered states of consciousness, and also in relation to drug experience and psychotic episodes. Some writers consider both drugs and mysticism self-chosen ways of diving into the depths of the same inner sea in which the schizophrenic person struggles and drowns (Campbell 1972). The Group for the Advancement of Psychiatry, in their 1976 report "Mysticism: Spiritual Quest or Psychic Disorder?," concluded that distinguishing between mysticism and certain psychiatric disorders is virtually impossible (Goleman and Davidson 1979). Most psychological studies, spanning more than three-fourths of a century, emphasize mystical exaltation.

Psychologist William James (1961; hereafter VRE) considered insanity the opposite side of the coin of mysticism. In both, there is the same sense of importance in small events, the same words having new and exciting meanings that other people do not discern, the same feeling of being controlled by external powers, the same sense of mission, the same exalted emotion. James also pointed out differences: in insanity, the emotion is pessimistic compared to mystical optimism; there are desolations instead of consolations; the meanings are dreadful instead of wonderful; and the powers are enemies rather than friends.

Recognized mystics also report desolation as well as consolation, dryness as well as the dew of mystical grace, yearning as well as fulfillment, entombment in the awful continuing ordinariness of frustrated longing as well as upliftedness to a personal heaven. These aspects of mysticism might more aptly be compared to such psychological states as depression, despair, meaninglessness, or futility than to psychotic episodes. Here, there are not hidden meanings in things, but an apparent absence of meaning. There is no exalted emotion, but a deadly and despairing yearning for some emotional anointing, for watering of one's dryness. External powers seem to have withdrawn their presence or ceased to exist. Events do not have added importance, but seem to have lost all importance. Life itself lacks purpose or coherence, and is devoid of any sense of mission or direction.

This article explores relationships between mystical periods of aridity and suffering—"the dark night of the soul"—and clinical depression. Material from the lives and writings of two contemporary figures who were not formally associated with any religious tradition illustrates the discussion. Simone Weil and Dag Hammarskjöld are readily acknowledged to be mystics by most scholars in the field. The paper also discusses the possible necessity of mysticism in some lives.

THE MYSTICAL DARK NIGHT

Although mystics give differing descriptions of their voyage, they apparently agree

---

Originally published in *Pastoral Psychology*, 33 (1984): 105-125.

upon some commonalities. Five steps outline the general mystical voyage: (1) awakening, (2) purification, (3) illumination, (4) the dark night of the soul, and (5) the unitive state of spiritual marriage. This paper is concerned with the second and fourth steps. (General references for this material are Arintero 1949-51; Garrigou-LaGrange 1947-48; and Underhill 1955).

The Early Mystical Life

The mystic's initial task is a conscious decision to purify life of aspects contrary to mystical endeavor. This consists of active striving against deliberate sin, cultivation of an awareness of God, practice of some meditative technique to focus consciousness on God, and various other ritual, ascetic, and spiritual disciplines according to the particular path being followed. The time of active striving involves some anguish over the costs of the voyage, but gives a sense of mastery over one's situation.

In the second stage, all sense of competence disappears. The individual feels overwhelmed by personal failure and inadequacy. Prayer becomes difficult, and consciousness focuses on subtle faults of which one was previously unaware. The individual feels overwhelmed by her or his own evilness, and may believe that God has withdrawn support. Writers of mystical theology warn against mistaking this relatively benign trial for the more rigorously purging dark night of the soul, which is characteristic of a more advanced state. Perseverance in this initial trial leads to the first stages of mystical prayer. One enjoys scattered episodes of peace in being wordlessly in the presence of God. Virtue also becomes easier as the many outbreaks of anger, gluttony, greed, and other faults diminish.

The Later Mystical Life

The dark night of the soul reflects advanced spirituality. Here, the mystical path is complicated by the apparent loss of the very basis for spiritual endeavor itself; religious meaning disappears. The mystic feels completely abandoned by God, incapable of faith or hope, and heavily burdened by the demands of religious love and perseverance. Completely alone, bereft of any consolation, one faces the task of continuing on the path. Religious literature reflects the terrible anguish of this period: "How much longer will you forget me, Yahweh? Forever? How much longer will you hide your face from me? How much longer must I endure grief in my soul, and sorrow in my heart by day and by night?" (Ps. 13:1-2, NJB) Similarly: "God, you are my God, I am seeking you, my soul is thirsting for you, my flesh is longing for you, a land parched, weary and waterless"(Ps. 63:1).

The Indian poet Tagore describes the same experience: "The rain has held back for days and days, my God, in my arid heart. The horizon is fiercely naked—into the thinnest cover of a soft cloud, not the vaguest hint of a distant cool shower ... Call back, my lord, call back, this pervading silent heat, still and keen and cruel, burning the heart with dire despair" (Tagore 1971: 53-54). Also from Tagore: "Ah, love, why dost thou let me wait outside at the door all alone?... It is only for thee that I hope. If thou showest not thy face, if thou leavest me wholly aside, I know not how I am to pass these long, rainy hours. I keep gazing on the far away gloom of the sky, and my heart wanders wailing with the restless wind" (37).

Mystics consider perseverance in this often very prolonged period of distress necessary for the final crown of mystical attainment, the ecstasy that has been compared to drug experience and psychosis. Mystical literature often seems to suggest that sheer perseverance—should one attain the dark night—will necessarily lead to mystical union. This paper raises two questions concerning this contention. Does one who experiences an agony of longing for God necessarily eventually pass to mystical ecstasy? Is one who experiences this intense longing for God necessarily far advanced in the spiritual life?

Within a normal range, people differ in basic optimism—with feelings of confidence, happiness, and positive expectations of life and the future—and pessimism—with self-doubt, frequent "blue" feelings, forebodings of unhappiness, and dissatisfaction with life and the future. This paper is not concerned with temporary depression, reactions to particular events in life, but with individuals who appear to have a depressive life cycle.

Mental health professionals agree on the common symptoms of clinical depression. The typically depressed person is deeply sad and lonely. Life seems empty and lacks meaning; the future is bleak. Often, there is great fatigue and a general slowdown in thinking, speaking, and acting. Anxiety, shame, and guilt are also common. The depressed person likely has negative attitudes toward self, others, and the world. All tasks feel like a burden for which one is inadequate. Life holds no joy or delight.

As depression deepens, there may be severe problems with concentration and problem solving. Sleeping and eating disorders are common. Sometimes strong hypochondriacal concerns appear. An extremely negative attitude toward oneself—even to the point of seeing oneself as vile and despicable—is common. The depressed person may feel guilty of unpardonable sins. In extreme cases, delusions and/or suicide may occur.

GENETIC/BIOCHEMICAL UNDERSTANDING OF DEPRESSION

Psychologists disagree about the bases for depressive life-styles. Genetically based, biochemical factors seem clearly to be at work in some cases. Ancient documents attribute to Hippocrates and Galen classifications of people that include a biologically based melancholic group (Gray 1978: 173). Numerous other biologically based explanations of depression have since arisen. We also know that treatment with appropriate medications often reduces the wide mood swings of some individuals (Kolb 1977: 464-469) and that electroconvulsive therapy lifts some depressions. Four other explanations of depression consider depressive life-styles as learned behavior which can—theoretically, at least—be modified without somatic treatment.

1. Claiming Depression

Temporary depressions often seem triggered by some kind of loss: loss of love or emotional support, personal or economic failures, or the loss of security produced by new responsibilities (Cameron 1963: 415). Silvano Arieti (1978: 221-222) has described a depressive life-style focusing on poignant sensitivity to loss. In this "claiming depression," the depressed person lays claim to a "lost paradise," and any unfulfilled desire leads to depression. These people want to be dependent on some dominant other responsible for meeting their needs and keeping them from feeling deprived. They generally hold unexpressed hostility toward others failing to satisfy them and feel they do not get what they should have. Treatment consists of getting the person beyond using dependency and hostile expectations to get what she or he wants.

2. Self-Blaming Depression

Arieti (1978: 223-225) also describes a "self-blaming" depression. This commonly accepted interpretation sees depression as anger turned inward against oneself. Freud postulated a "death instinct" which could either be turned inward against oneself or else manifest as aggression against others. Depression thus results from having turned aggressive impulses toward others inward against oneself (Gray 1978: 177). This produces strong feelings of guilt and unworthiness, and desire to punish oneself.

In self-blaming depression, concerns about sin, duty, punishment, and guilt dominate. One reacts to disappointments with self-accusation. Arieti maintains that such depressed people try to retrieve losses by expiating instead of insisting upon their right to certain goods. The person chooses guilt and suffering because they leave one feeling the power of self-redemption by suffering, instead of being dependent upon another. Treatment consists of getting the person to recognize how feelings of loss and anxiety are translated into self-blame; one then learns to face and deal with anxiety.

O. H. Mowrer (1961) believes self-blame in depression is usually related to the person's real guilt. Depressed people often blame themselves for small or insignificant peccadillos to avoid facing deeper underlying guilt. Mowrer's treatment begins with an opportunity for the person to confess what the real guilt is. Next comes admitting to important people in one's life the real truths about oneself, repairing—to the extent of one's ability—any damage done to others, and amending one's conduct in the future.

3. Helplessness and Depression

Arieti's models of depression consider emotion the basis of depression. Two other recent understandings emphasize the cognitive components of depression. Seligman's (1975) work views depression as learned helplessness. People who acquire a generalized expectancy that they are not able to control their outcome in life are especially prone to depression (Depue and Monroe 1978). Seligman (1975: 106) noted many symptom similarities between depressed persons and animals in whom learned helplessness had been experimentally induced: passivity, lack of aggression, negative cognitive sets, and disturbances of social, sexual, and eating behavior. Being unable to control one's outcomes prolongs feelings of powerlessness, hopelessness, and pessimism about the future. This model says treatment should consist of corrective learning experiences in which the depressed person exercises power with positive outcomes.

4. Attributions and Depression

Aaron Beck (1967) says that depression is best understood as resulting from cognitive distortions: the person incorrectly attributes certain characteristics to some of her or his experiences. These emphasize unfavorable aspects of oneself, others, the world, and the future. Trivial problems are magnified, difficulties seem unsolvable, and change is impossible. The depressed person has acquired a habit of automatically having negative cognitions which seem logical and irrefutable. Treatment consists of teaching the person to substitute other more optimistic cognitions in place of those leading to depression.

These four models are not meant by their proposers to be mutually exclusive; indeed, all can be seen as complementary and alternative frameworks for understanding. In actual work with clients, therapists often find different models particularly appropriate for different clients. All these models help focus on some aspects of depressive life-styles for which we can examine the lives of mystics.

OUR ILLUSTRATIVE FIGURES

We now look briefly at the writings and lives of our mystics for themes related to various interpretations of depression.

Dag Hammarskjöld

Dag Hammarskjöld (1905-1961) had strong tendencies toward a mystical vision of life. Early in life, the study of philosophy and theology greatly interested him (Soderberg 1962: 36). He dedicated himself to serving causes greater than himself as a self-surrender without anxiety about outcomes (Miller 1961: 21-22). Hammarskjöld died in an airplane crash while on United Nations business. Shortly before the flight, he spoke with a friend about the demands of mystical love (Soderberg 1962: 97).

In a program for Edward R. Murrow's "This I Believe," Hammarskjöld stated his personal faith: "The full explanation of how man should live ... I found in the writings of those great medieval mystics for whom 'self-surrender' had been the way to self-realization, and who in 'singleness of mind' and 'inwardness' had found strength to say yes also to every fate life had in store for them ... Love ... meant simply an overflowing of the strength with which they felt themselves filled when living in true self-oblivion ... whatever it brought them personally of toil, suffering—or happiness" (1962: 24). For the dedication of the meditation room of the United Nations, he stated, "When we come to our deepest feelings and urgings we have to be alone, we have to feel the sky and the earth, and hear the voice that speaks within us" (Miller 1961: 20). In a pamphlet explaining this room, he said, "It is for those who come here to fill the void with what they find in their center of stillness" (Hammarskjöld 1962: 161).

Hammarskjöld was deeply sensitive to loss and loneliness throughout his life; these themes dominate in his journal *Markings* (1964). He stated, "What makes loneliness an anguish is not that I have no one to share my burden, but this: I have only my own burden to bear" (p. 85). Further: "Alone beside the moorland spring, once again you are aware of your loneliness—as it is and always has been. As it always had been—even when, at times, the friendship of others veiled its nakedness (p. 116). Loneliness led him to suicidal ruminations: "to be sure, you have to fence with an unbuttoned foil: but, in the loneliness of yesterday, did you not toy with the idea of poisoning the tip" (p. 8). Later, he wrote, "So *that* is the way in which you are tempted to overcome your loneliness—by making the ultimate escape from life" (p. 86). His journal noted accounts of several suicides he had observed (pp. 27-28).

Hammarskjöld was also highly sensitive to his own failings. He once complained of himself: "so, once again, you chose for yourself—and opened the door to chaos. The chaos you become whenever God's hand does not rest upon your head" (Hammarskjöld 1964: 104). He wrote elsewhere, "When all becomes silent around you, and you recoil in terror—[you] see that your work has become a flight from suffering and responsibility, your unselfishness a thinly disguised masochism ... Gaze steadfastly at the vision until you have plumbed its depths" (p. 16).

Themes of helplessness also appear: "Slow and gray—He searches every face. But the people aimlessly streaming along the gray ditches of the streets are all like himself—atoms in whom the radioactivity is extinct, and force has tied its endless chain around nothing—In the dim light he searches every face, but sees only endless variations on his own meanness" (Hammarskjold 1964: 24). Later he wrote, "How am I to find the strength to live as a free man, detached from all that was unjust in my past and all that is pretty in my present, and so, daily, to forgive myself?" (p. 150).

Negative expectations of himself, others, and the future were common attributions made by Hammarskjöld: "Isn't the void which surrounds you when the noise ceases your just reward for a day devoted to preventing others from neglecting you?" (1964: 12). Similarly: "Your contempt for your fellow human beings does not prevent you, with a well-guarded self-respect, from trying to win their respect" (p. 41). He noted: "What I ask for is absurd: that life shall have a meaning. What I strive for is impossible: that my life shall acquire a meaning. I dare not believe. I do not see how I shall ever be able to believe: that I am not alone" (p. 86).

Simone Weil

Simone Weil (1909-1943) appears to have been born with an unusually deep sensitivity. Her awareness of other people's deprivations led her to practice austerities even as a child. She considered herself stupid and ugly, although she was clearly a brilliant intellectual. At 14, contemplating her own acute sense of absolute unworthiness, she was suicidal. Later in life, although her family was well able to support her, she insisted on taking jobs of exhausting physical labor to be with the common person. She was intensely concerned with the social and political problems of her times.

Reading a poem about the unworthiness of a guest at a feast precipitated Weil's first mystical experience. She had read nothing of the mystical literature before this time and later was grateful for her ignorance. She had refused to kneel until literally forced to her knees by a power from without stronger than her resistance. Throughout her life, she considered herself a reluctant and unworthy intimate of God. Weil daily recited the Lord's Prayer in Greek with a concentration that regularly transported her to mystical ecstasy. Her writings emphasize a theme of "waiting for God."

Another central theme in Weil's works is eating and not eating (Weil 1973: 35). Her spirituality stressed that one must be content to be externally hungry and welcome it, refusing to eat what is forbidden to make up for felt lack. Her concerns for social injustice and maintaining pure desire for God expressed themselves behaviorally in bouts of fasting and semistarvation. Weil died in England in a sanitarium for treatment of tuberculosis. The cause of death is given as starvation from refusing to eat because of mental imbalance. Some people with her during the last days report that she apparently tried to eat, but was unable to do so.

Weil was intensely alone throughout her life. She wrote: "It is not by chance that you have never been loved ... To want to escape from being lonely is cowardice. Friendship ought not to cure the sorrows of loneliness but to double its joys. Friendship is not to be sought for, dreamed about, longed for, but exercised (it is virtue)" (Weil 1970: 43; Weil's punctuation). She wrote Father Perrin, a priest with whom she corresponded and counseled: "I think that, except you, all those human beings for whom I have made it easy to hurt me through my friendship have amused themselves by doing so ... They did not behave like this from malice, but as a result of ... this animal nature within them" (Weil 1973: 92).

Weil strongly longed for passivity: "The most beautiful life possible has always seemed to me to be one where everything is determined, either by the pressure of circumstances or by impulses ... where there is never any room for choice" (Weil 1973: 100). She claimed that "men can never escape from obedience to God ... The only choice given to me ... is to desire obedience or not to desire it" (p. 133). Forced compliance would appeal to her: "We experience the compulsion of God's pressure, on condition that we deserve to do so ... We have to abandon ourselves to that pressure" (pp. 44-45).

Weil's intense feelings of guilt and unworthiness lasted her lifetime. She wrote: "I am an instrument already rotten. I am too worn out ... I have never read the story of the barren fig tree without trembling. I think that it is a portrait of me" (Weil 1973: 100). Weil expected little good from herself, others, life, or the future. Another quotation indicates her understanding of Providence: "A blind mechanism, heedless of degrees of spiritual perfection, continually tosses men about and throws some of them at the very foot of the Cross ... It is in his Providence that God has willed that necessity should be like a blind mechanism" (pp. 24-25).

SPIRITUALITY AND TEMPERAMENT

At the turn of the century, psychologist William James (VRE) related basic emotional temperament to religiousness. He concluded that people with a proclivity to melancholy—whom he called "sick soul" types—are constituted to be far more religiously sensitive than those of more sanguine nature. Sick souls have a low threshold for mental distress, are deeply sensitive to internal discord, suffer from negative feelings about themselves, and brood about possible future ills. James said that the most complete religions are essentially religions of deliverance in which the pessimistic elements are well developed; only sick souls can most fully appreciate the deliverance that they offer. The superficiality of the more "healthy-minded" insulates them from emotional contact with experience that predisposes one to religious or spiritual needs: lack, evil, suffering, anguish, and sorrow.

One can easily agree with James that some sensitivity to discord and anguish may be a precondition for deeply developed religiousness. Existential anxiety, "cosmic empathy," and awareness of life's darker aspects are probably prerequisite to mysticism. Individuals lacking such sensitivity, though, can certainly be depressed. Their depression would probably be related to minor losses and frustrations, crushed personal ambitions, petty matters of everyday life, and other such individual agendas. Such mundane depression might indicate an awareness of and capacity for suffering that could eventually become desire for God but, in itself, bears no relationship to the fully developed anguish of mystics. Maslow considered such suffering a sign of spiritual disorder if it did not transcend itself. He wrote, "It is better to consider neurosis as related rather to spiritual disorders, to loss of meaning, to doubts about the goal of life, to grief and anger over a lost love, to seeing life in a different way, to loss of courage or hope, to despair over the future, to dislike for oneself, to recognition that one's life is being wasted, or that there is no possibility of joy or love, etc. These are all falling away from full humanness" (Maslow 1971: 31).

Hammarskjöld and Weil surely fit James's "sick soul" type in some ways, whether their "depression" was neurotic or not. Weil said of herself: "If I am sad, it comes primarily from the permanent sadness that destiny has imprinted forever upon my emotions, where the greatest and purest joys can only be superimposed and that at the price of a great effort of attention" (1973: 76). From Hammarskjöld we have: "At least he knew this much about himself—I know what man is—his vulgarity, lust, pride, envy,—and longing. Longing—among other things, for the Cross" (1964: 55). Maslow summed up this idea in saying, "I have a vague impression that the transcenders are less 'happy' than the healthy ones. They can be more ecstatic, more rapturous, and experience greater heights of 'happiness' (a too weak word) than the happy and healthy ones. But I sometimes get the impression that they are as prone and maybe more prone to a kind of cosmic-sadness ... over the stupidity of people, their self-defeat, their blindness, their cruelty to each other, their shortsightedness" (1971: 284).

While mystics show evidence of depression, Maslow has captured the flavor of an additional note that is struck. The anguish experienced, the loss felt, the guilt suffered, the meanings extinguished, the impotence endured—To be considered mystical suffering, all must have as their referent something of the cosmic order, of yearning for divinity or God. Guilt must be more than a fear of punishment; it must include awareness of being in opposition to cosmic order. The yearning must be for the Ultimate—not for petty satisfactions. The mystics have experienced Augustine's "you have made us for yourself, and our heart is restless until it rests in you" (Augustine 1960: 43).

MYSTICISM AND DEPRESSION

We have seen in the lives of Hammarskjöld and Weil evidence that psychiatry could easily consider symptoms of depression. Are mystics chronically depressed individuals who manage occasionally to break through to mystical joy as scattered islands in their gloom? Can we develop any criteria to sort out the wheat from the chaff? These issues raise more questions than answers.

1. Mysticism and Loss

Mystics' intense awareness of ultimate human aloneness and emptiness shows their sensitivity to loss. They interpret their longings as an absence of God rather than other goods, however. From Hammarskjöld we have: "Did'st Thou give me this inescapable loneliness so that it would be easier for me to give Thee all?" (1964: 166). Weil claimed, "The longing to love the beauty of the world in a human being is essentially the longing for the Incarnation ... The Incarnation alone can satisfy it" (1973: 171).

If an expressed yearning for the Ultimate is a necessary prerequisite for mysticism, it is not a sufficient one. Various longings can easily be translated into longing for God. Some scholars (see Clark 1958: 278-84) see mysticism as a sublimation of needs for sex, love, security, or escape. Boisen pointed out that "the idea of God stands for something which is operative in the lives of all men, even though they may not call themselves religious. It is the symbol of that which is supreme in the interpersonal relationships and ... that fellowship without which he cannot live" (1970: 203).

Thus, God may simply be the name under which other longings are subsumed. Dag Hammarskjöld understood this: "Your cravings as a human animal do not become prayer just because it is God whom you ask to attend to them" (1964: 11). Psychologist Gordon Allport described transformation of lesser desires: "Prayer is continuous with hope, as hope is continuous with fear. Religious activity thus grows imperceptibly out of desire. The mind finds itself gradually ... seeking to add to its natural powers a reasonable complement" (1973: 56). As a counterpoint to Boisen and a continuation of Allport's theme, Weil says, "If love finds no object, the lover must love his love itself, perceived as something external. Then one has found God" (1970: 260). For this to be factually true in a given life, one's behavior should evidence that God is the true focus of desire. Weil claims that "all sins are attempts to fill voids" (p. 160) and insists that "anyone who, at the moment when he is thinking of God, has not renounced everything, without any exception, is giving the name of God to one of his idols" (p. 217).

2. Mysticism and Guilt

Mystics throughout history have been highly sensitive to their own failings. A mystic's ethical sensitivity—as opposed to neurotic self-blaming—should be reflected in genuine efforts to govern one's life ethically. This should result in transcending the preoccupation with one's own guilt and utter lack that paralyzes appropriate conduct. Weil noted that "the great obstacle to the loss of personality is the feeling of guilt. One must lose it" (1970: 208). Her own success at this task is not pronounced, although somewhat implicit in such statements as "when we have the feeling that on some occasion we have disobeyed God, it simply means that for a time we have ceased to desire obedience" (Weil 1973: 133). If awareness of personal fault is "genuine" rather than neurotic, it should lead beyond mere confession to further events. Mowrer (1961) discussed continuing honesty about oneself with salient others, reparative expiation, and amendment of conduct. Weil certainly accomplished these further steps.

Failure to transcend preoccupation with personal ego-centered guilt is written of by James, who complains of those who go about professing their smallness and sinfulness with the greatest of pride. He pointed out in one saint "her voluble egotism; her sense, not of radical bad being, as the really contrite have it, but of her 'faults' and 'imperfections' in the plural; her stereotyped humility and return upon herself" (James, [1902]1961: 276). This feeling of radical badness, rather than scattered particular flaws, is strongly apparent in our examples. Hammarskjöld noted: "Guilt—it is not the repeated mistakes, the long succession of petty betrayals ... but the huge elementary mistake, the betrayal of that within me which is greater than I—in a complacent adjustment to alien demands" (1964: 47). Weil wrote of herself, "Even if I believed in the possibility of God's consenting to repair the mutilations of my nature, I could not bring myself to ask it of him" (1973: 100).

Traditionally, the mystics' awareness of personal guilt also extends to a general awareness of human foibles and a feeling for the common misery of humankind in attempting reasonable self-management. Hammarskjöld wrote, "We can reach the point where it becomes possible for us to recognize and understand Original Sin, that dark counter-center in our nature ... that something within us which rejoices when disaster befalls the very cause we are trying to serve, or misfortune overtakes even those whom we love" (1964: 149).

In spite of their subjective feelings of failure, inadequacy, and sinfulness, the ethical imperative demands that mystics continue to meet obligations to others and their life-work. There may be brief periods of incapacitation because of intense suffering, but the life pattern as a whole should show consistent application of self to one's perceived duty. In more classically psychological terms, mystics should have transcended ego-centeredness, for task-centeredness. Such task-orientation is seen in Hammarskjöld's "Be grateful as your deeds become less and less associated with your name, as your feet ever more lightly tread the earth" (1964: 146). Also: "*Dedicated*—for my destiny is to be used and used up according to Thy will" (p. 123).

Weil wrote: "If still persevering in our love, we fall to the point where the soul cannot keep back the cry, 'My God, why hast thou forsaken me?' If we remain at this point without ceasing to love, we end by touching something that is not affliction, not joy, something that is the central essence ... the very love of God" (1973: 89). This criterion of perseverance in one's tasks cannot seem as sufficient, however, for agreeing that one is a mystic. Hammarskjöld warns us: "Work as an anesthetic against loneliness, books as a substitute for people—! You say you are waiting, that door stands open. For what? ... a fate beyond companionship?" (1964: 82). Work and business *can* be running away rather than dedicated service.

3. Mysticism and Passivity

The line between helpless passivity regarding one's life and general religious acceptance of all that befalls one is thin. We have already established that though our figures showed tendencies toward passivity and feelings of impotence, they also conducted their lives according to their understanding of duty. They were prestigious accomplishers in their endeavors.

Most mystics manifest a pronounced submission to life that extends even to welcoming and embracing pain, rather than fighting against it as something alien. Although James emphasized that deliverance features of religiousness attract the "sick soul," clearly, any religiousness which remains primarily a search for personal deliverance is not a developed religiousness. In mystics, the emphasis shifts from "may I be delivered" to "thy will be done," and even to delight in enduring all of one's lot as reflecting God's will. The poet Tagore captured this attitude: If thou speakest not I will fill my heart with thy silence and endure it ... head bent low with patience" (1971: 37-38).

Willed and chosen passivity in relation to God is strong in both Weil and Hammarskjöld. The latter wrote: "It is not we who seek the Way, but the Way which seeks us. That is why you are faithful to it, even while you stand waiting, so long as you are prepared, and act the moment you are confronted by its demands" (1964: 120). Also: "You are not the oil, you are not the air—merely the lens in the beam. You can only receive, give, and possess the light as a lens does" (p. 155). Maslow described the general attitude of acceptance common in mystical awareness: "Because he becomes more unmotivated, that is to say, closer to non-striving, non-needing, non-wishing, he asks less for himself ... The unmotivated human being becomes more god-like" (1964: 67).

Weil wrote: "Our misery gives us the infinitely precious privilege of sharing in this distance placed between the Son and his Father ... Even the distress of the abandoned Christ is a good. There cannot be a greater good for us on earth than to share it. God can never be perfectly present to us here below ... but he can be almost in extreme application. This is the only possibility of perfection for us on earth" (1973: 127). Weil had reservations about acceptance. She said, "I believe in the value of suffering, so long as one makes every (legitimate) effort to escape it" (1970: 3; Weil's parentheses). She renounced the luxury of yielding responsibility for her life in a letter to Father Perrin: "There are times when I am tempted to put myself entirely in your hands and ask you to decide for me. But, when all is said and done, I cannot do this. I have not the right" (Weil 1973: 56). She commented further: "What Christ meant when he advised his friends to bear their cross each day was not, as people seem to think nowadays, simply that one should be resigned about one's little daily troubles—which, by an almost sacrilegious abuse of language, people sometimes refer to as crosses ... To bear one's cross is to bear the knowledge that one is entirely subject to ... blind necessity in every part of one's being, except for one point in the soul which is so secret that it is inaccessible to consciousness" (Weil 1968: 185). Weil concludes: "Having absolutely relinquished every kind of existence, I accept existence, of no matter what kind, solely through conformity to God's will" (1970: 360).

Our figures expressed highly negative views of self, others, the world, and expectations for the future. Yet, in addition to those less sanguine interpretations, they tend to see all that happens in terms of ultimate divine purposes or goals, no matter how painful or distressing an event might appear. Mystics commonly impose higher order meanings upon the apparent chaos of life.

Hammarskjöld urged himself to keep alive his religious interpretations: "Never let success hide its emptiness from you, achievement its nothingness, toil its desolation. And so keep alive the incentive to push on further, that pain in the soul which drives us beyond ourselves" (1964: 55). He speculated: "Perhaps a great love is never returned. Had it been given warmth and shelter by its counterpart in the other, perhaps it would have been hindered from ever growing to maturity. It 'gives' us nothing. But in its world of loneliness, it leads us up to summits with wide vistas—of insight" (p. 42).

Weil frequently interpreted pain in terms of her vision:

This infinite distance between God and God, this supreme tearing apart, this agony beyond all others, this marvel of love, is the crucifixion. (1973: 123-24).

He whose soul remains ever turned toward God though the nail pierces it finds himself nailed to the very center of the universe ... It is at the intersection of creation and its Creator. This point of intersection is the point of intersection of the arms of the Cross (135-36).

It is the purpose of affliction to provide the occasion for judging that God's creation is good. (1968: 193).

It is in affliction itself that the splendor of God's mercy shines, from its very depths, in the heart of its inconsolable bitterness. (1973: 89).

Such insistence on religious meaning could simply be a defense such as denial or isolation—ways of deceiving oneself in a partially unconscious fashion. Gordon Allport (1973) noted that mature religiousness necessarily requires heuristic faith—that it acknowledges doubt. Hammarskjöld queried: "Is the bleakness of this world of mine a reflection of my poverty or my honesty, a symptom of weakness or of strength, an indication that I have strayed from my path, or that I am to follow it?—Will despair provide the answer?" (1964: 86).

Awareness of the "risk" of religious faith—even of the uncertainties associated with the mystical vision itself—was pondered by Weil. She commented: "The whole problem of mysticism and kindred questions is that of the degree of value of sensations of presence" (Weil 1970, 198). She reasoned: "If God should be an illusion from the point of view of existence, He is the sole reality from the point of view of the good... I am in accord with the truth if I wrench my desire away from everything which is not a good, so as to direct it solely towards the good, without knowing whether the good exists or not" (p.157). Elsewhere, she expressed strong doubts about the survival of the soul (p. 152).

The genuineness of investment in religious frameworks of meaning can be measured indirectly by conduct. However firm or uncertain one's belief may appear, behavior reflects the values one is trying to make operative in life. Allport ([1950] 1973: 145) noted that "sometimes we designate unrest that has not found its polarization of 'divine discontent'." Yet, he was very clear in insisting that vividness of longing, or use of religious interpretation, does not constitute the religious intention. Desire may be the original impetus, but an intention requires productive striving.

William James, reflecting on the intricate connection between belief and behavior, said: "There are, then, cases where a fact cannot come at all unless a preliminary faith exists in its coming ... *where faith in a fact can help create the fact* ... In truths dependent on our personal action, then, faith based on desire is ... possibly an indispensable thing" (1956: 25). To believe or manifest commitment to a belief, "we need only in cold blood ACT as if the thing in question were real, and keep acting as if it were real and it will infallibly end by growing into such a connection with our life that it will become real" (ibid.).

Hammarskjöld wrote of making goals operative: "O how much self-discipline, nobility of soul, lofty sentiments, we can treat ourselves to when we are well-off and everything we touch prospers—Cheap: Scarcely better than believing success is the reward of virtue" (1964: 56). He said further: "to reach perfection, we must all pass, one by one, through the death of self-effacement" (p. 25). Characteristically for Weil, action-oriented faith involves waiting for God: "The only choice before man is whether he will or will not ... stay motionless, without searching, waiting in immobility and without even trying to know what he waits ... it is absolutely certain that God will come all the way to him" (Weil 1968: 159). However differently mystics might state it, they believe one must not merely mouth religious interpretations of life but also act in accord with them.

NECESSITY, RISKS, AND DEMANDS OF MYSTICISM

For some people, mysticism may be the most viable alternative to shipwreck. These individuals have intense spiritual needs, much as other individuals may have different strong needs.

Characteristics Likely Contributing to Mystical Need

Cosmic Sadness

A temperamental sadness appears to be an underlying note in mystics. They show great sensitivity to loss, transience, change, vulnerability, insecurity, and other "unsolvable" problems of life. A sufficiently keen sensitivity may, on its own, make mysticism necessary; the individual may find genuine comfort in nothing other than the ultimate satisfier: the divine. Weil echoed this position: "The man who has known pure joy, if only for a moment ... is the only man for whom affliction ... is no punishment; it is God himself holding his hand and pressing it rather hard. For, if he remains constant, what he will discover buried deep under the sound of his own lamentations is the pearl of the silence of God" (1968: 198). Awareness of such need is also strong in Hammarskjöld.

High-Motivational Intensity

Highly passionate individuals, who strongly feel motivational pushes, also likely need mysticism. Although some very passionate individuals find other outlets to absorb their energies, for some only the Ultimate may be sufficiently large. For high-intensity people, the option may be between utter depravity and sanctity. Highly charismatic or forceful people may distort aspirations for sanctity unless they maintain continuing awareness of that greater than self.

Hammarskjöld felt intensely his own strong inclinations: "Upon your continual cowardice, your repeated lies, sentence will be passed on the day when some exhibition of your weakness ... deprives you of any further opportunities to make a choice—and justly. Do you at least feel grateful that your trial is permitted to continue, that you have not yet been taken at your word?" (1964: 72). Weil wrote: "One might conclude that there are some souls with a natural deficiency which irremediably unfits them for the service of God. And I am one of them. Is there any remedy? ... The only way is, if a seed has fallen into a hollow place in a stone, to water it and keep on doing so whenever the water evaporates ... Detachment is even more rigorously necessary than for the souls which are good ground. For, if thorn and weed absorb a few drops of the water which has to be renewed continually, the wheat will inevitably shrivel ... Literally, it is total purity or death" (1970: 348).

Strong Abilities

Weil and Hammarskjöld had strong intellectual capabilities and high levels of talent. Some mystics have lacked these features, but ability probably adds to need for mysticism. As with motivational intensity, many high-ability people find other outlets. Ability heightens the temptation to an excessively narcissistic self-involvement though, and some people may avoid that pitfall only with the felt awareness of "smallness" that mysticism gives. The highly intelligent psychologist of religion Gordon Allport explained his own religious involvement: "Humility and some mysticism, I felt, were indispensable for me; otherwise I would be victimized by my own arrogance" (Boring and Lindzey 1967: 7). This exceptional man supports the contention being made here.

Awareness of being talented may also produce feelings of indebtedness. Maslow hypothesized that self-actualized individuals might further need to transcend self in some way. This need may be related to a heightened awareness of one's good fortune in having been blessed beyond the average of all persons. Hammarskjöld wrote: "Atonement, for the guilt you carry because of your good fortune: without pity for yourself or others, to give all you are, and thus justify, at least morally, what you possess, knowing that you only have a right to demand anything of others so long as you follow this course" (1964: 50).

Certainly not all individuals of heightened emotional sensitivity, strong motivational intensity, and high talent and/or capacity actually need mysticism. Such characteristics however, might interact multiplicatively with each other to raise one's level of need. Individuals high in only one of these characteristics may not be especially prone to such need; cosmic sadness is likely the most compelling single need. The interaction of moderate levels of two of these characteristics may produce considerable need. An individual with at least moderate to high levels of all these conditions should have considerable need.

William James, commenting on unappealing manifestations of religiousness, blamed them on relative deficiencies in other human attributes. He wrote: "It is hard to imagine an essential faculty too strong, if only other faculties equally strong be there to cooperate with it in action... Spiritual excitement takes pathological forms whenever other interests are too few and the intellect too narrow" (VRE: 271). Conversely, individuals of strong intellect, high talent, deep emotionality, and intense volition may be most able to "contain" mystical experience. They may further need it to prevent excessive grandiosity and self-preoccupation.

Clearly, Weil and Hammarskjöld showed characteristics suggesting they needed mysticism. They were poignantly aware of their need for spiritual involvement. In some ways, it was their "salvation." The same may well be true of other individuals of similar qualities.

The Demands and Risks of Mysticism

No mystics claim that the path is easy. That the results are not assured, fewer are willing to admit. An ancient Bengali saying states: "The sides of the mountain are strewn with the bones of those who fail to reach the top." Mystics note the risks of despair, failure to persevere, resentment, and being ground to pieces by suffering. Hammarskjöld admitted tendencies to resent being an "outsider" who could not enjoy life as simply as most people: "In spite of everything, your bitterness because others are enjoying what you are denied is always ready to flare up" (1964: 47). "I feel that it is necessary and ordained that I should be alone, a stranger and an exile in relation to every human circle without exception" (Weil 1973: 54).

Both Hammarskjöld and Weil were aware of having at some point said "yes" to their calling. Weil wrote: "Over the infinity of space and time, the infinitely more infinite love of God comes to possess us ... If we consent, God puts a little seed in us and he goes away again ... no more to do ... except to wait. We only have not to regret the consent we gave him" (1973: 133). Hammarskjöld reported: "I don't know Who—or what—put the question, I don't know when it was put. I don't even remember answering. But at some moment I did answer Yes to someone—or something—and from that hour ... I have known what it means 'not to look back'" (1964: 205). He was aware of the cost of such a decision: "He who has surrendered himself to it knows that the Way ends on the Cross—even when it is leading him through the ... triumphal entry in Jerusalem" (p. 91).

CONCLUSIONS

Trying to evaluate these individuals in the different darknesses they inhabited produces awesome problems. Darkness has so many meanings. It stands simply for being bereft or alone, for loss, loneliness, and longing for satisfaction and closeness. Darkness also stands for being in sin, in error of conduct. How does one evaluate another's self-accusation in this regard, the attribution to oneself of guilt and unworthiness? Darkness also stands for ignorance and/or error, for misinterpreting or misunderstanding what is going on around oneself. Darkness stands for being in danger, for being helpless and impotent. These four connotations of darkness are mirrored in the theories of depression discussed above. Yet, the darkness inherent in human existence goes beyond simple theories of emotional disturbance to something far more radical and profound.

Darkness stands for other uncomfortable things. It stands for being confused, unable to see clearly, not knowing—a common experience for all mystics. Darkness eventually stands for death—death either as the ultimate of being cut-off, aloneness, loneliness, vulnerability, and extinction—or death as the termination of self-preoccupation, petty concerns, and seeking the tinsel rather than the gold of existence—as being born into the goodness of darkness.

Darkness thus also has positive connotations. It stands for a welcome solitude, a retreating within oneself to recharge and revitalize oneself. It stands for peace and rest—hard earned retirement from striving and effort. In the lives of mystics over the centuries, darkness stands for the visitation of God. For mystics, darkness means all of the above—both the positive and the negative. Darkness contained terrible aloneness, devastating self-knowledge, and the awareness of evil and personal impotence. Darkness also held the light of truth, intimacy with God, and perfect peace in the midst of terrible suffering; darkness revealed Goodness, Truth, and Beauty.

How can one judge that which comes in the darkness? Is it heavenly or diabolical? Is it merely a chemical imbalance in the brain? Is it truth or delusion? What can one know for sure? In the lives of the great mystics are both profound certainty and agonizing uncertainty. The common trial of the dark night is the terrible suffering in loss of the religious framework of meaning itself, in the inability to believe in the reality of their own experiences, the inability to hope and love. Well might one fear the darkness—the darkness in which devil and angel, insanity and God, both come. Well might one tremble at human limitation, fallibility, and vulnerability. Well might one pray: "Deliver us from evil."

One never reaches higher than one aims. Aspiration to the vision of God requires the attendant risks. One who prays, "Give us this day our daily bread"—give us the sustaining vision of God—must be prepared to drink the chalice drunk by other God-lovers. In "fear and trembling" they went forth, in courageous acceptance of risk they went, in openness to grace they went. They went forth; the silent attentiveness they trusted was nearness to God—into the darkness—and waited.

REFERENCES

Allport, G. W. (1973). *The Individual and His Religion: A Psychological Interpretation.* New York: Macmillan.

Arieti, S. (1978). *On Schizophrenia, Phobias, Depression, Psychotherapy, and the Farther Shores of Psychiatry.* New York: Brunner-Mazel.

Arintero, J. G. (1949-51). *The Mystical Evolution*, 2 vols. J. Aumann (Trans.). St. Louis, MO: Herder.

Augustine, St. (1960). *Confessions.* John K. Ryan (Trans.). New York: Image Books.

Beck, A. T. (1967). *Depression: Causes and Treatment.* Philadelphia, PA: University of Pennsylvania Press.

Boisen, A. T. (1970). *Crises in Personality Development.* In W. Sadler (Ed.) *Personality and Religion.* New York: Harper (pp. 191-205).

Boring, E. G. & G. Lindzey (Eds.) (1967). *A History of Psychology in Autobiography*, Vol. 5. New York: Appleton-Century-Crofts (pp. 1-25).

Cameron, N. (1963). *Personality Development and Psychopathology.* Boston, MA: Houghton Mifflin.

Campbell, J. (1972). *Myths to Live By*. New York: Viking.

Clark, W.H. (1958). *The Psychology of Religion: An Introduction to Religious Experience and Behavior*. New York: Macmillan.

Depue, R.A. & S.M. Monroe (1978). Learned helplessness in the perspective of the depressive disorders: conceptual and definitional issues. *Journal of Abnormal Psychology*, 87: 2-20.

Garrigou-LaGrange, R. (1947-48). *The Three Ages of the Interior Life*, 2 vols. M.T. Doyle (Trans.) St. Louis, MO: Herder.

Goleman, D. & R.J. Davidson (Eds.) (1979). *Consciousness: Brain, States of Awareness, and Mysticism*. New York: Harper and Row.

Gray, M. (1978). *Neuroses: A Comprehensive and Critical View*. New York: Van Nostrand Reinhold.

Hammarskjöld, D. (1962). *Servant of Peace*. W. Foote (Ed.) New York: Harper.

————— (1964). *Markings*. L. Sjoberg and W.H. Auden (Trans.) New York: Knopf.

James, W. (1956). *The Will to Believe and Other Essays in Popular Philosophy*. New York: Dover.

————— (1961). *The Varieties of Religious Experience: A Study in Human Nature*. New York: Collier.

Jones, A. (Ed.) (1966). *The New Jerusalem Bible*. Garden City, NY: Doubleday.

Kolb, L. C. (1977). *Modern Clinical Psychiatry*. Philadelphia, PA: Saunders.

Maslow, A. H. (1964). *Religions, Values, and Peak Experiences*. Columbus, OH: Ohio State University Press.

————— (1971). *The Farther Reaches of Human Nature*. New York: Viking.

Miller, R. I. (1961). *Dag Hammarskjöld and Crisis Diplomacy*. Washington, D.C.: Oceania Publications.

Mowrer, O. H. (1961). *The Crisis in Psychiatry and Religion*. Princeton, NJ: Van Nostrand.

Petrement, S. (1976). *Simone Weil: A Life*. R. Rosenthal (Trans.) New York: Random House.

Rees, R. (1966). *Simone Weil: A Sketch for a Portrait*. Carbondale, IL: Southern Illinois University Press.

Seligman, M. (1975). *Helplessness: On Depression, Development, and Death*. San Francisco, CA: W. H. Freeman.

Soderberg, S. (1962). *Hammarskjöld: A Pictorial Biography*. New York: Viking.

Tagore, R. (1971). *Gitanjali*. New York: Macmillan.

Underhill, E. (1955). *Mysticism: A Study in the Nature and Development of Man's Spiritual Consciousness*. New York: Meridian.

Weil, S. (1968). *On Science, Necessity, and the Love of God*. R. Rees (Ed. and Trans.) New York: Oxford University Press.

————— (1970). *First and Last Notebooks*. R. Rees (Ed.) New York: Oxford University Press.

————— (1973). *Waiting for God*. E. Crauford (Trans.) New York: Harper and Row.

WILLIAM JAMES'S TERMINAL DREAM

ERIK H. ERIKSON

To return to the second of our great initial witnesses we will quote what is probably the most incisive report of an identity confusion in dreams—incisive no doubt just because the dreamer could reassert his positive identity, that of a researcher, and remember and record the dream the next day (James 1910). The date of *his* dream is important, too, for it was probably the last dream recorded and certainly the last publicly reported in James's life; he died half a year later at the age of sixty-eight. No wonder, then, that in this dream identity confusion is part of an inner storm denoting a loss of hold on the world— the kind of storm which Shakespeare in King Lear, according to dramatic laws of representation, projects on nature and yet clearly marks as an inner storm. James had this dream in a period when he was seeking to break out from the bonds of "natural" psychology and to understand certain mystical states in which man transcends his own boundaries. He complains, however, that this dream was the "exact opposite of mystical illumination" and thus permits us to claim it as a product of the conflict between man's lasting hopes for a higher Integrity and his terminal despair.

In fact, James illustrates much of what we have been saying here in descriptive terms so close to our generalizations that it seems necessary to say that this dream came to my attention only recently. No doubt, however—and this is why I had reason to refer to him in the introduction to the Harvard doctors' book on emotional problems among students (Erikson 1961)—James knew from personal experience what we have described as "borderline" psychotic states in these pages. However, apparently, he never came as close to a truly psychotic experience as in this dream—a fact which I ascribe to the depth of "ultimate concerns" at this stage of his life. He introduces his dream account as follows:

> I despair of giving the reader any just idea of the bewildering confusion of mind into which I was thrown by this, the most intensely peculiar experience of my whole life. I wrote a full memorandum of it a couple of days after it happened and appended some reflections. Even though it should cast no light on the conditions of mysticism, it seems as if this record might be worthy of publication, simply as a contribution to the descriptive literature of pathological mental states. I let it follow, therefore, as originally written, with only a few words altered to make the account more clear.

Since I would not wish to interrupt this account with astonished comments, I will ask the reader to take note of the clarity with which the characteristics of an acute identity confusion appear in this dream: the discontinuity of time and space; the twilight between waking and sleeping; the loss of ego boundaries and, with it, the experience of being dreamed by the dream rather than actively "having" it; and many other criteria which will occur to the reader:

> San Francisco, Feb. 14th 1906.—The night before last, in my bed at Stanford

---

Reprinted from *Identity: Youth and Crisis* (New York: W.W. Norton, 1968: 204-207). This material is preceded by a discussion of Sigmund Freud's dream of Irma as illustrative of Freud's identity problems in the stage of middle adulthood (generativity vs. stagnation). James's dream is illustrative of James's identity problems in the period of old age (integrity vs. despair).

University, I woke at about 7:30 a.m., from a quiet dream of some sort, and whilst "gathering my waking wits," seemed suddenly to get mixed up with reminiscences of a dream of an entirely different sort, which seemed to telescope, as it were, into the first one, a dream very elaborate, of lions, and tragic. I concluded this to have been a previous dream of the same sleep; but the apparent mingling of two dreams was something very queer, which I had never before experienced.

On the following night (Feb. 12-13) I awoke suddenly from my first sleep, which appeared to have been very heavy, in the middle of a dream, in thinking of which I became suddenly confused by the contents of two other dreams that shuffled themselves abruptly in between the parts of the first dream, and of which I couldn't grasp the origin. Whence come *these dreams*? I asked. They were close to *me*, and fresh, as if I had just dreamed them; and yet they were far away *from the first dream*. The contents of the three had absolutely no connection. One had a cockney atmosphere, it had happened to someone in London. The other two were American. One involved the trying on of a coat (was this the dream I seemed to wake from?), the other was a sort of nightmare and had to do with soldiers. Each had a wholly distinct emotional atmosphere that made its individuality discontinuous with that of the others. And yet, in a moment, as these three dreams alternately telescoped into and out of each other, and I seemed to myself to have been their common dreamer, they seemed quite as distinctly *not* to have been dreamed in succession, in that one sleep. *When*, then? Not on a previous night, either. *When*, then, and *which* was the one out of which I had just awakened? I *could no longer tell:* one was as close to me as the others, and yet they entirely repelled each other, and I seemed thus to belong to three different dream-systems at once, no one of which would connect itself either with the others or with my waking life. I began to feel curiously confused and *scared*, and tried to wake myself up wider, but I seemed already wide-awake. Presently cold shivers of dread ran over me: *am I getting into other people's dreams?* Is this a "telepathic" experience? Or an invasion of double (or treble) personality? Or is it a thrombus in a cortical artery? and the beginning of a general mental "confusion" and disorientation which is going on to develop who knows how far?

Decidedly I was losing hold of my "self," and making acquaintance with a quality of mental distress that I had never known before, its nearest analogue being the sinking, giddying anxiety that one may have when, in the woods, one discovers that one is really "lost." Most human troubles look towards a terminus. Most fears point in a direction and concentrate towards a climax. Most assaults of the evil one may be met by bracing oneself against something, one's principles, one's courage, one's will, one's pride. But in this experience all was diffusion from a centre, and foothold swept away, the brace itself disintegrating all the faster as one needed its support more direly. Meanwhile vivid perception (or remembrance) of the various dreams kept coming over me in alternation. Whose? *whose?* WHOSE? Unless I can *attach* them, I am swept out to sea with no horizon and no bond, getting *lost*. The idea aroused the "creeps" again, and with it the fear of again falling asleep and renewing the process. It had begun the previous night, but then the confusion had only gone one step, and had seemed simply curious. *This* was the second step— where might I be after a third step had been taken?

And now to that aspect of the account which, I feel, reinstates (as did Freud's dream) the dreamer's *activity* in the terms of his professional identity. Having come close to being a "patient" and feeling close to life's "terminus," he now assumes the psychologist's prerogative of "objective" empathy and systematic compassion, and this, at first, in words with which we would have been more than glad to conclude our own description of identity confusion:

> At the same time I found myself filled with a new pity towards persons passing into dementia with *Verwirrtheit,* or into invasions of secondary personality. *We* regard them as simply *curious;* but what *they* want in the awful drift of their being out of its customary self, is any principle of steadiness to hold on to. We ought to assure them and reassure them that we will stand by them, and recognize the true self in them, to the end. We ought to let them know that we are with *them* and not (as too often we must seem to them) a part of the world that but confirms and publishes their deliquescence.
>
> Evidently I was in full possession of my reflective wits; and whenever I thus objectively thought of the situation in which I was, my anxieties ceased. But there was a tendency to relapse into the dreams and reminiscences, and to relapse vividly; and then the confusion recommenced, along with the emotion of dread lest it should develop farther.
>
> Then I looked at my watch. Half-past twelve! Midnight, therefore. And this gave me another reflective idea. Habitually, on going to bed, I fall into a very deep slumber from which I never naturally awaken until after two. I never awaken, therefore, from a midnight dream, as I did tonight, so of midnight dreams my ordinary consciousness retains no recollection. My sleep seemed terribly heavy as I woke tonight. Dream states carry dream memories—why may not the two succedaneous dreams (whichever two of the three *were* succedaneous) be memories of *twelve o'clock dreams of previous nights,* swept in, along with the just-fading dream, into the just-waking system of memory? Why, in short, may I not be tapping in a way precluded by my ordinary habit of life, *the midnight stratum* of my past?
>
> This idea gave great relief—I felt now as if I were in full possession of my *anima rationalis* ... it seems, therefore, merely as if the threshold between the rational and the morbid state had, in my case, been temporarily lowered, and as if similar confusions might be very near the line of possibility in all of us.

And even as one often feels (and especially in the case of the Irma dream) that Freud's dreams were dreamed to reveal the nature of dreams, so James ends by reporting that this dream, which was "the exact opposite of mystical illumination," was permeated with "the sense that reality was being uncovered"—a sense which he found in itself to be "mystical in the highest degree." And, in his eagerness for and closeness to transcendence, he ended by feeling that his dream had been dreamed "in reality"—by another "I," by a mysterious stranger.

REFERENCES

Erikson, E. (1961). Introduction to *Emotional Problems of the Student.* G. B. Blaine & C. C. McArthur (Eds.). New York: Appleton (pp. xiii-xxv).

James, W. (1910). A suggestion about mysticism. *Journal of Philosophy, Psychology and Scientific Methods,* 7: 85-92.

V. THE STRUGGLE FOR A LIVING RELIGION

THE BEDROCK OF EXPERIENCE:
AN ASSESSMENT OF JAMES'S PROPOSALS FOR A
CRITICAL SCIENCE OF RELIGION

JOHN CAPPS

INTRODUCTION

Though he has already shown that religious experiences possess a unique intensity, in the closing lectures of *The Varieties* James returns to the question of their objective truth. First, he concludes that even though mystical states "tell us of the supremacy of the ideal, of vastness, of union, of safety and of rest," they nevertheless "wield no authority" (1990; 386; hereafter VRE) on the question of whether these qualities actually exist. Subsequently, applying a pragmatic standard borrowed from Peirce, James finds philosophical reasoning on the issue to be sterile and ultimately unconvincing:

> Conceptual processes can class facts, define them, interpret them; but they do not produce them, nor can they reproduce their individuality... I think we must conclude that the attempt to demonstrate by purely intellectual processes the truth of the deliverances of direct religious experience is absolutely hopeless (VRE: 408).

Finally, in his concluding lecture James problematizes the application of impersonal scientific methods to the personal subject matter of religious experiences: since these experiences entail—by definition—an individualistic relationship to a "more" they necessarily depend upon a dimension of reality that falls outside the particular expertise and subject-matter of science. Nonetheless, this wider reality still makes an assignable difference in individual lives, leading James to conclude that

> [W]e have in *the fact that the conscious person is continuous with a wider self through which saving experiences come*, a positive content of religious experiences which, it seems to me, *is literally and objectively true as far as it goes* (VRE: 460).

Thus, given the inability of mysticism, philosophy and science to determine the truth of religious subject-matter, we find that James has shifted his emphasis from the objective truth of religious experiences to the particular awareness of a difference made in one's life.

This is a questionable move, for the reason that it is not clear what James can mean by now characterizing the content of religious experiences as "objectively true as far as it goes"—at the outset, this would seem to be not very far at all. In other words, James appears to avoid the difficulties associated with objective truth by resorting to the opposite extreme, by casting truth in subjective terms, dependent solely on one's introspective understanding of a handful of privileged experiences. James may yet be justified in pursuing this line of reasoning; unfortunately, by failing to develop this idea further he makes it difficult to distinguish his standpoint from less appealing alternatives. Thus, if truth is *merely* a subjective concept, the status of James's own claims are placed in doubt: either he must rely—inconsistently—on an additional, smuggled-in criterion of truth, or it is difficult to see how he avoids a commitment to relativism or voluntarism. James's position is not helped, furthermore, by his distrust of both philosophy and science. By questioning their ability to provide an adequate rational foundation for religious experiences, James is left to rely only on the *consequences* of these episodes. As a result, his many case-studies amount to little more than an inductive argument for the subjective value of a certain kind of emotion.

In what follows, I will re-examine James's position with respect to both philosophy and science. After discussing arguments that he lapses into either an unpragmatic dogmatism or an indefensible relativism, I will investigate the presence of a critical dimension implicit in *The Varieties*. It will be my contention that James is here offering—as he does elsewhere—a naturalistic reconception of the roles played by philosophy and science, thereby allowing him to opt out of the traditional debate between a "tough minded" dogmatism and a "tender-minded" relativism. By bringing these roles to the forefront, I hope to shed light, ultimately, on James's understanding of the overlapping roles played by the philosophy, science, and psychology of religion.

REALISM AND RELATIVISM: ALTERNATE READINGS OF *THE VARIETIES*

In this section I will address the question of whether James has in fact committed himself to a form of either realism or relativism. I use these terms advisedly, however, to indicate a wide range of philosophical perspectives. Thus while no single philosopher may fit these categories precisely, I mean them more to suggest a constellation of ideas that underlie (or that, after critical scrutiny, are indistinguishable from) commonplace philosophical doctrines. In this way I have in mind something like the distinction James draws between "tough-minded" and "tender-minded" attitudes in his *Pragmatism* (1978: 13): the former characterized by empiricism, sensationalism and materialism, the latter by rationalism, intellectualism, and idealism. For James's purposes, and for my purposes here, it is not necessary that these classifications fit actual thinkers; what is important is that these categories roughly indicate the extremes of a continuum along which philosophical thinking normally takes place: from a reliance on material facts on the one hand to an emphasis on ideas and mental operations on the other. That James can be placed at either end of this continuum is due, I will contend, to the fact that the debate is framed in such a two-dimensional, dualistic manner; thus, I will argue in the final section that James is not so much trying to occupy an untenable position *between* the two sides of this issue as he is trying to formulate a critical perspective *outside* it. However, before reaching this positive conclusion, it will be necessary to examine those interpretations of James that would commit him to either realism or relativism.

The same intuition gives rise to both readings: while toleration is certainly desirable and necessary, it seems as though we nevertheless need an objective standard capable of distinguishing authentic and beneficial (or at least neutral) religious experiences from those that clearly are not. This is not a question of giving one religion precedence over another, but rather a matter of distinguishing religious experiences that lead to positive expressions of faith from those, for instance, which might lead one to join a cult or deny Darwinism.

Within the context of James's *The Varieties*, to be sure, his emphasis on the inherently personal aspect of religious experiences could lead to the conclusion that while a particular cult, say, might give just cause for alarm, it would be presumptuous nevertheless to pass judgment on the religious experiences of a particular individual. The latter, it could be argued, are that person's business alone; as a result, no matter how personally harmful or pathetic these experiences might be, an outside observer is prevented from passing judgment so long as these experiences fail to affect the welfare of others. Admittedly, there is a kernel of truth to this argument: it captures the importance we place on an individual's right to privacy and self-determination. All the same, however, this argument fails to hold generally: it is not so easy to separate purely private experiences from those that have public consequences. Because the private sphere often spills over into the public (and vice versa), it would be disingenuous to arbitrarily isolate it from ethical and epistemological investigations. The status of most experiences is unclear; even leaving open the possibility of those that are *completely* private, we must be prepared to subject ambiguous cases (which, I suspect, would constitute the vast majority today) to questions of rightness and veracity.

Thus, even granting the fact that individual religious experiences are not directly analogous to the larger religious movements through which they often find their expression, the intuition persists that these individual experiences must still be the objects of continuous critical inquiry. This, however, appears to be in conflict with James's attitude toward the case-studies contained in *The Varieties*: despite his frequent apologies for their often extreme and eccentric quality, he generally casts their "truths" in a positive light (even though these episodes might now appear to be exemplars of anti-social, delusional, and even self-destructive behavior). It is this seemingly unwarranted optimism that then raises the question of James's philosophical commitments. As mentioned earlier, two sorts of responses seem possible: either 1) James can avoid making explicit value judgments since his choice of case-studies *already* reflects an implicit standard, or 2) he is simply obligated to give *any* religious experience the benefit of the doubt. That is, either James has operated dogmatically in excluding those religious experiences that fail to meet his unstated criterion, or he has forsaken the possibility of giving his work a normative grounding, instead adopting a relativistic point of view.

Turning our attention to the first possibility, we might ask the question: on what basis would such dogmatism be justified? In other words, when James writes that "immediate luminousness, in short, philosophical reasonableness, and moral helpfulness are the only available criteria" (VRE: 25); for making spiritual judgments, we ought to ask: luminous, reasonable, and helpful according to whom? I believe one answer to this question lies in the intellectual debt owed by James to Charles Sanders Peirce, evident in his later paraphrase of Peirce's theory of meaning:

> To develop a thought's meaning we need therefore only determine what conduct it is fitted to produce; for conduct is for us its sole significance; and the tangible fact at the root of all our thought-distinctions is that there is no one of them so fine as to consist in anything but a possible difference in practice (VRE: 399).

According to this pragmatic criterion, the philosophical reasonableness of a particular belief is a function of the consequences it holds in practice. It is easy to extend the argument, furthermore, to conclude that a belief that fails to make a difference is not only meaningless—and hence philosophically unreasonable—but also unilluminating and unhelpful. Of course, this pragmatic standard is still too vague: a given belief may have a variety of consequences—intended and unintended, positive and negative, public and private—such that it becomes necessary to distinguish the practical consequences (that is, the meanings) that are intrinsic to a belief from those that are not. In other words, it becomes a question of determining the *truth* of a belief.

In "How to Make Our Ideas Clear," (1992) the article already referred to by James, Peirce offers the following answer to this question:

Different minds may set out with the most antagonistic views, but the progress of investigation carries them by a force outside of themselves to one and the same conclusion ... The opinion which is fated to be ultimately agreed to by all who investigate, is what we mean by the truth, and the object represented in this opinion is the real. That is the way I would explain reality (pp. 138-9).

Thus, a belief's true meaning, according to Peirce, is that which makes the most difference in bringing the believer to the opinion "which is fated to be ultimately agreed to by all who investigate." Peirce, however, is definite on the question of what constitutes proper investigation: as becomes clear in his article "The Fixation of Belief" nothing less than a rigid scientific method is acceptable. In contrast with methods relying on tenacity, authority or *a priori* rules, science presupposes that the objects of its study behave in a law-like manner, independently of how we may want to think of them. Consequently, scientific method is a method of discovery; the meaning of our beliefs is not in our control and we are led to the truth by a "force" outside of ourselves.

In other words, Peirce is in some sense both a pragmatist and a realist: though his theory of meaning depends on the practical difference a belief makes, his theory of truth depends on there being "Reals" whose "characters are entirely independent of our opinions about them" (p. 120). By defining the subject matter of science in terms of practical verifiability, Peirce both accounts for and guarantees its continued success. However, it seems unlikely that James would be willing to follow Peirce along this realist path. Even though he devotes the third lecture of *The Varieties* to defending the "reality of the unseen", he avoids assigning independent attributes to this additional "something there" (p. 59). Furthermore, in his lecture on "The Value of Saintliness" he discusses the "empirical evolution" of religious ideas:

Nothing is more striking than the secular alteration that goes on in the moral and religious tone of men, as their insight into nature and their social arrangements progressively develop. After an interval of a few generations the mental climate proves unfavorable to notions of the deity which at an earlier date were perfectly satisfactory: the older gods have fallen below the common secular level, and can no longer be believed in (VRE: 300-1).

For James, the "mental climate" is as important as the physical; in comparison, Peirce's scientism appears unnecessarily narrow. As a result, James's attitude toward the unseen "more" is much more humanistic and historically oriented than Peirce's; there is less a sense that the genuine traits of reality are simply waiting to be discovered by means of an impartial scientific method. Instead, what characteristics do come to be identified with the "more" results from an evolving recognition of human capacities. These traits are, to some extent at least, placed there *by us*.

If Peirce's realism commits him to a theory of truth that is a combination of correspondence and consensus *in extremis*, James's ontology is, in comparison, much less well defined. There is not the sense, as there is sometimes with Peirce, that James views nature in terms of a single, ultimate reality. Taken as a whole, the case-studies of *The Varieties* share little more than a family resemblance; more suggestive than descriptive, they each point toward a "something more" without it ever being clear that it is in each case the same. James's attitude is fallibilistic, even skeptical: ever-conscious of the shortcomings of science, he emphasizes the ongoing role we play in constituting what is, for us, real.

Thus, despite his adherence to a pragmatic theory of meaning, James does not seem committed to the same realist ontology as Peirce. As a result, while Peirce can measure beliefs against settled opinions verified by scientific methods, James lacks such an independent standard especially when it comes to the private contents of religious experiences. However, if he is innocent of relying on this form of positivistic dogma—admittedly, a common one—the question still remains whether he is guilty of resorting to the opposite extreme: namely, relativism. As noted earlier, James's skepticism regarding the applicability of philosophy and science, coupled with the generally positive tone of his case-studies, leads to the suspicion that *The Varieties* lacks a normative, regulative foundation. Of the two criticisms of James offered here, this is the more familiar and the most serious.

Though their rejection of *a priori* ethical and epistemological standards is by now a commonplace of post-modernism, pragmatists have often been accused of failing to offer an adequate substitute for these foundational principles. As John Patrick Diggins writes:

> [James] could never bring himself to believe that the things that mattered most could emanate from any source other than our subjective selves ... There is no moral order in which objective truth resides, and facts in themselves can make no demands upon our passional nature, which has more to do with the impulses of desire than with the imperatives of duty (1994: 136).

Accordingly, the pragmatist position seems rather bleak: in place of a "moral order" and "objective truth", we seem now to be left at the mercy of passion and desire. This move clearly holds disastrous consequences for both ethics and epistemology; with respect to the study of religious experiences, furthermore, it seems to leave us in the position alluded to at the beginning of this section. Originating in our subjective selves, responding only to inclination and whim, these experiences can no longer be held accountable to standards of either veracity or propriety.

Nor does it seem as if James does much to assuage such fears. Already we have seen his generally skeptical attitude toward both philosophy and science. Far from grounding religious experiences in logical relationships, "intellectualist" philosophers have been unable to reach agreement among themselves, their systematic distinctions and deductions failing to capture the sense of vitality that is central to the phenomenon. Likewise, philosophers of a more Hegelian bent, positing an absolute Spirit in communion with finite human consciousness, do little by such transcendental maneuvers to make religious experiences any more comprehensible, much less verifiable. If anything, science is of even less help; as James makes clear throughout, the scientific tendency to focus on origins and causes, to offer explanations in terms of impersonal physical laws and relationships, not only fails to account for the ineffable quality of religious experiences, it fails even to take them seriously.

By turning away from philosophical deduction and scientific explanation, James of course wishes to emphasize the consequences of religious experiences. But his is a questionable ploy: not only does it seem possible to balance his positive case-studies with more pathological examples (as he does himself, to some extent, in his lecture on "The Value of Saintliness"), but even his own illustrations seem prone to a wide range of interpretations. As he notes, saintly attributes are different only in degree from their opposite vices; "whenever other interests are too few and the intellect too narrow" (VRE: 310), devotion becomes fanaticism, asceticism leads to mortification, purity becomes seclusion, and so on. With this in mind, the examples James gives of saintly behavior are open to multiple readings: do John Woolman's concerns regarding dye reflect a pure soul, or a foolish consistency (270-1)? In literally turning the other cheek, is Richard Weaver acting charitably or merely naively (p. 259)? And does George Müller's faith in petitionary prayer (pp. 419-422) allow him to devalue selfishly the charitable contributions made by others on his behalf?

"Relativism" clearly carries a pejorative connotation: it is hardly a term one would use to describe oneself. Rather, employed in an accusatory tone, it functions largely as a challenge, demanding of its target some regulative ideal or mechanism supporting a particular philosophical perspective. In James's case, however, it is not clear what can play this role. We have already seen that he avoids following Peirce in the direction of a realism based on scientific method. On the other hand, however, his mistrust of philosophical reasoning raises the possibility alluded to by Diggins: the moral order of nature is reduced to passion and desire, objective truth giving way to the supremacy of will. Thus, even conceding that "relativism" may be unnecessarily tendentious a term, it is small consolation to cast James as a voluntarist instead.

"PURE EXPERIENCE" AND JAMES'S NATURALIZATION OF PHILOSOPHY AND SCIENCE

As we have already seen, James does not find Peirce's realism attractive; furthermore, he is equally disenchanted with rationalism, Hegelian idealism, and scientific positivism. However, rather than resort to a voluntarist posture, in this section I will discuss the question of whether his strategy in *The Varieties* contains a coherent regulative component. I will argue that it does, but to do so will involve re-examing—and possibly reconstructing—James's attitude toward the proper function of both philosophy and science.

My point of entry is a passage referred to earlier which, without being a rigorous argument, provides clues to James's overall perspective. As we saw, James assumes an evolutionary standpoint in his discussion of changing human conceptions of god; thus "the original factor in fixing the figure of the gods must always have been psychological" (VRE: 301)—religious images are chosen on the basis of how well they fit the exigencies of a constantly changing social structure and developing self awareness. As a result, "the gods we stand by are the gods we need and can use, the gods whose demands on us are reinforcements of our demands on ourselves and on one another" (p. 303). However, there is nothing limiting this point of view to theology: James's outlook applies as well to any of the ideas, structures, and expectations that gain currency within communities. With respect to the question under discussion, philosophy and science underwent a similar transformation in the 17th century as nature began to be seen less in terms of a hierarchic "great chain of being" and more in mechanistic terms, as composed of atomistic parts obeying physical laws. Like images of god, our conceptions of these disciplines have had to adapt to prevalent social and psychological forces.

If we take this evolutionary perspective as a general feature of James's thinking, it is well to keep in mind three points. Most obviously, first of all, evolution implies a frank awareness of the fallibility of our current ideas, standards, and practices. No matter how well these may presently help us cope, there is no escaping the conclusion that changing circumstances may render them ill-suited, obsolete, even hazardous. Second, there is no point of view from which to equate evolution with a linear, teleological progress. Evolution is simply adaptation to changes within the present environment and, at the time, there can be no guarantee that a particular adaptation will be successful. We must wait and see, and even then be less than completely optimistic: successfully responding to one challenge may mean occupying such a narrow niche that further demands cannot be adequately met. Finally, though evolution is the result of particular deviations from the norm, it is not an individual, but a large-scale phenomenon. In other words, evolution is to be distinguished from simple mutation in that it can be correlated to crises experienced on the level of groups, communities, and species. This is not to say that evolutions are actually caused by the problems that they then seek to overcome; rather, that in hindsight they act as the transition leading from one general way of dealing with the world to another. In retrospect these transitions may even seem revolutionary.

Keeping these characteristics in mind, it is possible to shed light on the changing role James sees for philosophy and science. Like the ideas present in religious experiences, the expectations surrounding these disciplines must also be self-consciously fallible, cast in terms that avoid the language of teleological progress, and meet needs at a general (not merely particular) level. However, even though absolute certainty on philosophical and scientific issues is no longer a tenable aim—not only is there nothing in their results to warrant this judgment, but the nonlinear development of new investigative methods precludes even knowing for certain if we are on the right track—skepticism is not the inevitable result. Rather, the recognition of philosophical and scientific limits becomes an opportunity for a critical self-awareness:

> [T]o admit one's liability to correction is one thing, and to embark upon a sea of wanton doubt is another. ... If we claim only reasonable probability, it will be as much as men who love the truth can ever at any given moment hope to have within their grasp. Pretty surely it will be more than we could have had, if we were unconscious of our liability to err (VRE: 304).

One final point, corresponding to the third characteristic of an evolutionary outlook. In the above passage and elsewhere, I believe that James's use of "we" should be taken literally, not as idle editorializing. That is, despite his emphasis on the individual character of experience in general and religious experiences in particular, there is also a sense that how these experiences come to be understood and brought to resolution depends on social and not merely psychological factors. When, consequently, James proposes to "test saintliness by common sense" (p. 303) this should be taken both as an affirmation of our individual rationality (in contrast with sophisticated theorization) and, more importantly, as a recognition of the intellectual standards that members of the same community often hold implicitly in common.

Emphasizing the evolutionary dimension of James's thought helps bring to light the expectations he might reasonably be supposed to hold for both philosophy and science. We are not yet at the point, however, of understanding what shape exactly these two disciplines ought to take. To address this latter question, then, I wish to return to the final pages of his lecture "Philosophy". There, having concluded that a purely intellectual philosophy fails to capture the unique character of religious experiences, he instead proposes that philosophy be made into a "science of religions", one that might "eventually command as general a public adhesion as is commanded by a physical science" (VRE: 409). There are problems, however, with this formulation: James appears to gloss over the differences between two distinct roles that he assigns to philosophy. Thus, on the one hand, James sees philosophy performing a largely critical function, removing the "local and accidental" from religious definitions and eliminating conflicts with established principles: "by confronting the spontaneous religious constructions with the results of natural science, philosophy can also eliminate doctrines that are now known to be scientifically absurd or incongruous" (p. 408). This amounts primarily to keeping religion separate from science, to keeping religious beliefs—in miracles or creationism, for instance—from taking precedence over physics and biology, and is simply the flip-side of James's desire to prevent science from performing an equally solipsistic reduction. On the other hand, however, James evidently envisions philosophy playing a more constructive role:

Sifting out in this way unworthy formulations, she can leave a residuum of conceptions that at least are possible. With these she can deal as *hypotheses*, testing them in all the manners, whether negative or positive, by which hypotheses are ever tested. ... She can perhaps become the champion of one which she picks out as being the most closely verified or verifiable (pp. 408-9).

It is in this matter of testing and verification that James sees a science of religions coming closest to a physical science, such as optics (his own example). However, it is not at all clear how such testing can take place: the hallmark of a physical science, after all, is that its laws are—to a large extent, at least—*empirically* verifiable. But in the case of religious principles this avenue has already been closed off by James's desire to keep the positive contents of religion and science distinct. What is more, there is no reason to suppose that religious "hypotheses" can be judged according to traditional scientific standards of simplicity and consistency; on the contrary, religious formulations often owe their ineffable quality to the fact that they are bewildering and paradoxical.

As a result, we seem to be left in much the same position as before: even treating science and philosophy as fallible, culturally sensitive disciplines, it is still not clear how their methods can be brought to bear on the contents of religious experiences in a critical, regulative manner. However, this may simply be begging the question: is it reasonable in the first place to expect scientific methods to play such a role? My suspicion is that it is not, more by virtue of the nature of scientific methodology than by anything having to do with religious experiences per se. As many historians and philosophers of science have suggested (Latour 1987, Feyeraband 1993), science may well be best understood in terms of practice, that is, in terms of the social and technological forces that contribute both to the formulation and solution of a problem situation. There is not the sense (as there is, for instance, with Peirce) that nature is a book for which we simply need an unerring method in order to decipher its secrets. Rather, "nature" is the end product of a process involving elements as diverse as the search for funding, the construction of new instruments and the interpretation of resulting data, and, in many cases, flashes of counter-intuitive insight. Similarly, there is no single "scientific method" applicable to a wide range of phenomena, this illusion being due instead to the reconstructive rhetoric of scientific articles.

I think James would be sympathetic with this demystification of science—it is consistent with his debunking of "medical materialism," for instance—but, for important reasons, I think he would also recognize that the reputation of science is not completely undeserved. For, despite the often crass factors that enter into its practice, science still offers a reliable means of dealing with the world: more dependable, certainly, than wishful thinking or random guesswork. This reliability—though admittedly imperfect—can be easily explained, furthermore, on pragmatic grounds: we naturally fasten onto those aspects of our experience that would seem to ensure our continued safety, comfort and success. It is not necessary to suppose that these regularities reflect the intrinsic order of nature or fit *a priori* rational categories; their test lies simply in the direction in which they guide our thoughts and actions. Thus, in *Pragmatism*, James writes:

Our experience meanwhile is all shot through with regularities. One bit of it can warn us to get ready for another bit, can 'intend' or be 'significant' of that remoter object. The object's advent is the signficance's verification. ... By 'realities' or 'objects' here, we mean either things of common sense, sensibly present, or else common-sense relations, such as dates, places, distances, kinds, activities, (1978: 99).

By reducing the reliability of science to the regularity of experience, it might appear that James is once again recasting inquiry in subjective terms. To some extent this is the case: our experiences are necessarily fashioned by idiosyncratic psychological factors as well as by contingent social and historical circumstances. But I do not think this is cause for alarm: while there may well be disagreement over whether a particular scientific hypothesis is successful, not only is reliability a patently general criterion (it is inconceivable that one would knowingly choose an unreliable hypothesis), but the means of its testing seem perfectly clear (the more reliable hypothesis is that one which most often leads to promised results). Reliability, in other words, is as near a universal criterion as we might hope to have.

There are two lessons to be drawn from this digression. First, it would be a mistake to expect religious "hypotheses" to be verified in the same way as scientific laws. Again, this is due to the fact that it is imprecise to speak of a uniquely scientific method, as if all hypotheses were verifiable in the same manner. Second, it is worth emphasizing James's reliance on "experience" as the source of the regularities that do underlie reliable inferences. What distinguishes this attitude from mere empiricism, however, is that James does not maintain the dualism between a subjective knower and an objective fact of the matter:

> *Experience, I believe, has no such inner duplicity; and the separation of it into consciousness and content comes, not by way of subtraction, but by way of addition.* ... [A] given undivided portion of experience, taken in one context of associates, play[s] the part of a knower, of a state of mind, of 'consciousness'; while in a different context the same undivided bit of experience plays the part of a thing known, of an objective 'content', (James 1987: 1144-1145, emphasis in original).

In rejecting the dualistic categories of subject and object in favor of "pure experience"—a move consonant with his notion of a "stream of consciousness"—James avoids the question of whether consciousness accurately captures its own content. Rather, experience is "the instant field of the present":

> [I]t is plain, unqualified actuality or existence, a simple *that*. In this *naif* immediacy it is of course *valid*; it is *there*, we act upon it; and the doubling of it in retrospection into a state of mind and a reality intended thereby, is just one of the acts (1987: 1151).

As such, pure experience is not within our conscious control, being instead the result of a contingent personal history crossing paths with a given physical chain of events. At this level, there is no question of whether an experience is accurate or not; it simply is what it is. Only when we seek to divide the experience into subjective and objective elements is it possible for error and bias to creep in. Pure experience thus functions for James as a sort of bedrock principle, a limit beyond which further investigation is both unthinkable and unnecessary.

To make this all somewhat more concrete, it is helpful to return to James's use of experience in The Varieties. Once again, in the section where he introduces a "standard of theological probability", he goes on to write:

> [T]his very standard has been begotten out of the drift of common life. It is the voice of human experience within us, judging and condemning all gods that stand athwart the pathway along which it feels itself to be advancing (VRE: 302).

In light of the foregoing, James's reference to experience is not as suspect as it might first appear. In effect, this allusion reflects his commitment to subverting the traditional dualism between rationalism and empiricism: by concentrating on this more basic level, James is attempting to opt out of the debate between those who place their standards in the operations of human reason, and those who find them only in nature. Even so, it is not clear how experience—in James's sense—can play the regulative role that he envisions. In other words, we come back to the same question: is this emphasis on experience simply a capitulation to either realism or relativism?

I admit there is this risk; still, James's conception of experience is such that a reduction to either one of these philosophical stances is not inevitable. By positing a layer of pure experience logically prior to the conceptualization of subject and object, James gives precedence to our natural, unmediated awareness of our surroundings and to our unsophisticated reactions toward it. This prioritization of the natural, even instinctive, is consistent with James's evolutionary point of view, noted earlier: from this perspective, not only does the distinction between mind and matter break down, but our experience—in all its "naif immediacy"—gains *prima facie* validity for having so far proved reliable. With respect to philosophy, this means paying greater attention to how we do *in fact* think and act prior to addressing the question of how we *ought* to. Naturalizing epistemology and ethics in this way, furthermore, means that philosophy's relation to other disciplines must be rethought. No longer can philosophy presume only to pass judgment on the methods and arguments of other specialties; in investigating concrete circumstances of thinking and acting, philosophy must pay attention, for instance, to both sociology and psychology. And even though it retains a critical function, the relationship between philosophy and these other disciplines need not beg the question; as standards and practices mutually inform and determine each other, the process may best be visualized by a helix, not a circle.

In this roundabout way, proceeding from James's notion of philosophy as a "science of religions", to an analysis of the function of scientific method, and lastly to a discussion of the primacy of experience, we can finally begin to shed light on the regulative role that philosophy might play with respect to religious experiences. Earlier, we saw that James assigns two separate functions to philosophy: first, that of limiting the conflict between science and religion, and second, that of testing religious "hypotheses" by whatever standards are current. This second function we found problematic insofar as it implies the application of scientific methods to religious subject-matter. Not only would this blur the distinction between two realms of experience that James otherwise wishes to keep separate, but it also depends on scientific method meeting expectations that seem excessively optimistic. If philosophy cannot perform this latter function, however, our attention must be drawn all the more to the former. The question, then, is this: can philosophy, in articulating the boundary between science and religion, adequately perform a regulative role with respect to religious experiences?

That it can is due to the manner in which these boundaries are set. For James, as we saw, experience places a limiting condition on philosophy; in addition, however, it too obeys a principle of evolution. As far as religious experiences go, then, there is no reason to expect particular instances to remain paradigmatic beyond their own historical context. This is why many of James's own examples appear anachronistic; but this does not mean that present-day substitutes could not be found. On the other hand, the reason why these examples seem outmoded is not due so much to the fact that they can be given a scientific explanation, as to the fact that the boundary between science and religion is constantly in flux. As a result, the sorts of experiences that one may reasonably be expected to have, and that properly qualify as religious experiences, also undergo change. For someone to have the same experiences as John Woolman or George Muller would today seem rather absurd simply because the field of our experiences is that much broader.

To put it slightly differently, as the sciences show themselves capable of addressing some questions but not others, not only do the possibilities for experience change, but so do the possibilities for the sense of a "more" and a "wider self" that lie just beyond our conscious selves. It is here, finally, that the interdependence of the philosophy, science, psychology, and sociology of religion is most evident. That is, in attempting to set the boundaries between the sciences and religion, philosophy must not only take to heart the lesson of James's naturalism—concentrating on how it is that we do think and act prior to conceiving how it is that we *ought* to—but in doing so it must also assume an attitude of critical attentiveness toward developments in the psychology and sociology of religion.

Because there is no wholly independent point of view from which to judge the development—or evolution—of these sciences, their insights must always remain fallible, open to change. As a result, there is no perspective from which to judge absolutely the veracity or propriety of a particular religious experience. But this is not to say that a judgment cannot be made despite its inevitable contextualization. Rather, such judgments can and must take place on the basis of current experience, that is, on the basis of our reactions to the continuing innovations, discoveries, and insights of each of the sciences. Emphasizing experience in this way allows for a dynamic reconceptualization of the relationship between our philosophical standards and our scientific practices. Because there is no independent standard against which to measure philosophy and science, their efficacy and reliability must be measured by their ability to keep pace with each other.

To summarize, this essay has been devoted to examining James's understanding of the role played by philosophy and science with respect to religious experiences. Beginning with the concluding lectures of *The Varieties*, it has examined the possibility that James's philosophical perspective commits him to latent forms of either realism or relativism. That he can be declared innocent of these charges is due to the fact that he naturalizes both philosophy and science, grounding them in a pure experience that is prior both to the formulation of subjective and objective spheres as well as to the dilemmas and controversies that ensue. As a result, however, any regulative role to be performed by these disciplines must fail to meet a traditional standard of absolute certainty. Rather, consonant with James's evolutionary outlook, a standard of "theological probability" can make no pretense either to being infallible or to representing constant teleological progress. But this is not tantamount to skepticism or relativism; instead, recognizing the historical situatedness of these standards leads to a critical awareness of their connection with contemporary human experience, and to the constant interplay between standards and practices. To conclude, then, I wish to note what I hope is by now evident: in addition to its position within the psychology of religion, James's text also possesses a philosophical richness due to its crucial re-appraisal of both philosophy and science: a richness that is made all the more ironic, though by no means lessened, by its ostensibly religious subject-matter.

REFERENCES

Diggins, J. P. (1994). *The Promise of Pragmatism.* Chicago, IL: the University of Chicago Press.

Feyeraband, P. (1993). *Against Method*, 3rd. ed. London: Verso Press.

James, W. (1978). *Pragmatism and the Meaning of Truth.* Cambridge, MA: Harvard University Press.

————— (1987). Does "consciousness" exist? *Writings 1902-1910.* New York: The Library of America (pp. 1141-1158).

————— (1990). *The Varieties of Religious Experience.* New York: The Library of America.

Latour, B. (1987), *Science in Action.* Cambridge, MA: Harvard University Press.

Pierce, C. (1992). In N. Houser & C. Kloesel (Eds.) *The Essential Pierce,* Vol. 1. Bloomington, IN: Indiana University Press.

PRAYER, MELANCHOLY
AND THE VIVIFIED FACE OF THE WORLD

DONALD CAPPS

In 1904, James Bissett Pratt (1973) sent William James a questionnnaire on the subject of religious belief. One of the questions concerned prayer and it consisted of two parts. The first part asked, "Do you pray, and if so, why? That is, is it purely from habit, and social custom, or do you really believe that God hears your prayers?" James's answer to this part of the question was brief, "I can't possibly pray—I feel foolish and artificial." The second part asked, "Is prayer with you one-sided or two-sided—i.e. do you sometimes feel that in prayer you receive something—such as strength or the divine spirit—from God? Is it a real communion?" Having answered the first part of the question in the negative, James did not write a response to the second part. This is the only question in the questionnaire that James left unanswered.

Pratt also posed questions about the meaning of God for the respondent and how the respondent experiences God. To the question, "Is He a person?" James responded, "He must be cognizant and responsive in some way." To the question, "How do you apprehend his relation to mankind and to you personally? If your position on any of these matters is uncertain, please state the fact." James responded, "Uncertain."

James's negative but forthright answer to Pratt's question "Do you pray, and if so, why?" and his simple one word response—"Uncertain"—to Pratt's question about how God is apprehended prepare us for his discussion of prayer in *The Varieties*. They suggest, at the very least, that prayer is a matter of considerable struggle for James, that anything he may have to say about prayer will be hedged with caution and reserve. These answers to Pratt's questions are particularly interesting in light of the fact that Pratt's manner of posing the question is quite compatible with James's own discussion of prayer in *The Varieties*. His questions could well have been derived primarily, even exclusively, from James's discussion of prayer, and since Pratt's questionnaire was distributed just two years after *The Varieties* was published, we can well imagine that James's discussion of prayer was his primary source for his own questions on prayer.

James's discussion of prayer occurs in the nineteenth (of twenty) lectures in *The Varieties* (1982: 463-477; hereafter VRE). It follows his lecture on philosophy and precedes the lecture on general conclusions. This lecture bears the title "Other Characteristics," implying that it will be concerned with some aspects of personal religion that were not important enough to have a full lecture devoted exclusively to them, and because this lecture comes so close to the end of the lecture series, it gives the impression of being an effort to tie up a few loose ends. It might even serve a defensive purpose. If potential critics wanted to fault James for failing to deal with one or another feature of personal religion that they considered important, he could rightfully claim that he at least made an effort to include it and that he may well have wanted to treat it at greater length had the lecture series been even more ambitous than it already was. In any case, a lecture on "Other Characteristics" does not raise high expectations and, if one were informed of the title in advance, this might well be the lecture in the series that one would be most tempted to miss. The previous lecture on philosophy ends with the brief sentence, "In my next lecture I will try to complete my rough description of religious experience; and in the lecture after that, which is the last one, I will try my own hand at formulating conceptually the truth to which it is a witness" (VRE: 457). Of the two, the final lecture sounds considerably more important than the penultimate one, with its quite modest goal of trying "to complete my rough description of religious experience." That the "Other Characteristics" lecture has received little comment in scholarly interpretations of *The Varieties* indicates that it has, for the most part, been quickly skipped over by readers, even serious readers, of *The Varieties*.

Yet, for all its apparent insignificance in the lecture series as a whole, lecture nineteen is actually one of the most important, largely because the central topic is that of prayer.

PRAYER AS THE VERY SOUL AND ESSENCE OF RELIGION

James begins the lecture by noting that his long excursion through mysticism and philosophy now brings him back to where he had arrived at the conclusion of the lectures on saintliness, i.e. to "the uses of religion, its uses to the individual who has it, and the uses of the individual himself to the world" (p. 458). At the conclusion of the final lecture on saintliness, he had noted that by abandoning "theological criteria" in favor of criteria derived from "practical common sense and the empirical method," he had been able to make a strong case for the uses of religion, its uses to the individual who has it, and the uses of such an individual to the world (cf. Hutch article in this volume for discussion of this issue). He had especially taken note of the uses of such individuals to the "world's welfare," and had observed that the great saints are immediate successes in this regard while the lesser saints are "at least heralds and harbingers and...leavens also of a better mundane order" (p. 377). On this basis, he had issued this invitation:

> Let us be saints, then, if we can, whether or not we succeed visibly and temporarily. But in our father's house are many mansions, and each of us must discover for himself the kind of religion and the amount of saintship which best comports with what he believes to be his powers and feels to be his truest mission and vocation (VRE: 377).

The issue, finally, is not whether we are well or ill-adapted to this world (only the healthy-minded believe that to be the case), but whether, in our exercise of the powers we possess, we have made our contribution toward "a better mundane order." He recognizes that there is at least a paradox, and perhaps even an outright contradiction, in his concluding thus, for how is it that religion, which "believes in two worlds and an invisible order," is here being "established by the adoption of its fruits to this world's order alone?" (p. 377). It is to address this problem that he makes his excursion first into mysticism and then into philosophy.

But, now, in lecture nineteen, he is back to the issue of the uses of religion. If, however, the lectures on saintliness focused especially on the uses of the religious person to the world, this lecture will be much more concerned with the uses of religion to the person who has it. It will address the question of what my religion does *for me*, and will therefore take on the question of whether personal or "egotistic" religion is an inferior form of religion (p. 500). This penultimate lecture is therefore far more important than it might initially appear, for it addresses the question of whether religion that has its uses to the individual is less genuine or less true than religion (the religion of saintliness) that enables the individual to be of use to the world.

The first several paragraphs in the lecture focus on the role that the aesthetic life plays in determining the individual's choice of religion. Here James discusses at some length the aesthetic appeal of religion to John Henry Newman (who Zaleski in her article in this volume says was a puzzlement to James "perhaps because he senses that Newman is a kindred spirit facing him from the other side of the looking-glass"; Newman, she says, is "Ecclesiastical Man," a designation that one would never use for James himself). This discussion of the aesthetic appeal of religion centers on the inadequacy of an "individual religion" for persons of Newman's type, for their "inner need is rather of something institutional and complex, majestic in the hierarchic interrelatedness of its parts, with authority descending from stage to stage, and at every stage objects for adjectives of mystery and splendor, derived in the last resort from the Godhead who is the fountain and culmination of the system" (p. 460).

James next identifies the three "other characteristics" that he intends to discuss in the lecture—sacrifice, confession and prayer—features of religion that in "most books on religion ... are represented as its most essential elements" (p. 462). He gives only brief attention to sacrifice, only a single paragraph, noting that sacrifices to God are omnipresent in primeval worship, but that ritual sacrifice has been eliminated from the major world religions, though in Christianity, the idea of sacrifice "is preserved in transfigured form in the mystery of Christ's atonement" (p. 462). What these religions do is to "substitute offerings of the heart, renunciations of the inner self, for all those vain oblations" (p. 462).

His comments on confession are equally brief, also only one paragraph, and are concerned to make the point that confession, while not nearly as widespread as sacrifice has been, "corresponds to a more inward and moral stage of sentiment. It is part of the general system of purgation and cleansing which one feels one's self in need of, in order to be in right relations to one's deity" (p. 462).

These brief paragraphs on sacrifice and confession set the stage for his much more lengthy consideration of prayer as they focus on the renunications and cleansings of "the inner self." As we will see, James will be concerned with prayer as "inward communion or conversation." He begins his discussion of prayer with the observation that there has been much talk about prayer lately, especially against prayers for better weather and for the recovery of sick people. He agrees that prayer for better weather is of no avail, for "every one now knows that droughts and storms follow from physical antecedents, and that moral appeals cannot avert them" (p. 464). Prayer for the sick is a different matter, for "if any medical fact can be considered to stand firm, it is that in certain environments prayer may contribute to recovery, and should be encouraged as a therapeutic measure. Being a normal factor of moral health in the person, its omission would be deleterious" (p. 463).

Thus, James makes clear to the audience that he is not an opponent of prayer, but that he believes prayer serves mainly the personal needs of individuals as it cannot directly influence the natural world. This does not mean, however, that prayer has no connection with the natural world, for, as he will go on to argue, it directly influences our ability to respond to the world around us. His point for the moment, though, is that we should not join the scientific despisers of prayer, for it is a *medical* fact that prayer may contribute to the recovery of the individual and, furthermore, "petitional prayer is only one department of prayer," and when prayer is taken "in the wider sense as meaning every kind of inward communion or conversation with the power recognized as divine," prayer, in that sense, is quite beyond scientific criticism (p. 464).

James next makes his vivid and unequivocal statement that "prayer in this wide sense is the very soul and essence of religion" (p. 464). As the liberal French theologian, Auguste Sabatier, has written:

Religion is an intercourse, a conscious and voluntary relation, entered into by a soul in distress with the mysterious power upon which it feels itself to depend, and upon which its fate is contingent. This intercourse with God is realized by prayer. Prayer is religion in act; that is, prayer is real religion. It is prayer that distinguishes the religious phenomenon from such similar or neighboring phenomenon as purely moral or aesthetic sentiment. Religion is nothing if it be not the vital act by which the entire mind seeks to save itself by clinging to the principle from which it draws its life. This act is prayer, by which term I understand no vain exercise of words, no mere repetition of certain sacred formulae, but the very movement itself of the soul, putting itself in a personal relation of contact with the mysterious power of which it feels the presence,—it may be even before it has a name by which to call it. Wherever this interior prayer is lacking, there is no religion; wherever, on the other hand, this prayer rises and stirs the soul, even in the absence of forms or of doctrines, we have living religion (VRE: 464).

James follows this quote from Sabatier with the assertion that "the entire series of our lectures proves the truth of M. Sabatier's contention. The religious phenomenon, studied as an inner fact, and apart from ecclesiastical or theological complications, has shown itself to consist everywhere, and at all its stages, in the consciousness which individuals have of an intercourse between themselves and higher powers with which they feel themselves to be related" (p. 465). If this intercourse is not "a give and take relation," if nothing is "really transacted while it lasts," and if "the world is no whit different for its having taken place," then prayer, "taken in this wide meaning of a sense that *something is transacting*, is of course a feeling of what is illusory" (p. 465). Then, all that would remain would be, at most, "some inferential belief that the whole order of existence must have a divine cause" (p. 465). This, however, would reduce the believer to a spectator at a play, "whereas in experiential religion and the prayerful life, we seem ourselves to be actors, and not in a play, but in a very serious reality" (p. 466). Thus prayer, if it be real, is an experience—as long as it lasts—of inward communion or conversation with "the power recognized as divine," and the genuineness of religion "is thus indissolubly bound up with the question whether the prayerful consciousness be or be not deceitful," for the "conviction that something is genuinely transacted in this consciousness is the very core of living religion" (p. 466).

As to *what* is transacted, there have been great differences of opinion throughout the course of human history. James is quick to acknowledge that "the unseen powers" have been supposed to do things "which no enlightened man can nowadays believe in" (p. 466). He even entertains the possibility that "the sphere of influence in prayer is subjective exclusively, and that what is immediately changed is only the mind of the praying person" (p. 466). While his willingness to entertain this possibility may seem inconsistent with his assertion that, in prayer, "something is transacting," there is a difference between saying that "intercourse" takes place between the praying person and the higher power with which the person is related, and assigning "influence." It is quite plausible that the "influence" that occurs in prayer would be exclusively that of a change in the mind of the praying person, and that this change would not be attributable to any direct "influence" exerted by the power to whom the prayer is addressed. In fact, it is only in petitionary prayer that the praying person seeks to exert influence on the higher power, and James has already noted that petitional prayer is only one department of prayer. What ultimately matters, therefore, is not whether there is evidence of divine influence but that, through prayer, "things which cannot be realized in any other manner come about: energy which but for prayer would be bound is by prayer set free and operates in some part, be it objective or subjective, of the world of facts" (p. 466).

In support of his view that, even if we are unable to determine whether some influence other than subjective is involved, this does not in itself invalidate prayer, James quotes from a letter written by the late Frederic W.H. Myers to a friend, which reads in part:

If we then ask to *whom* to pray, the answer (strangely enough) must be that *that* does not much matter. The prayer is not indeed a purely subjective thing;—it means a real increase in intensity of absorption of spiritual power or grace;—but we do not know enough of what takes place in the spiritual world to know how the prayer operates;—*who* is cognizant of it, or through what channel the grace is given (VRE: 467).

Thus Myers contends that just because we do not know how the divine "influence" works does not mean that prayer is "a purely subjective thing." But James is more cautious, proposing that the "question of the truth or falsehood of the belief that power is absorbed" he deferred until the next lecture. In the meantime, he will focus for the remainder of the present lecture on "concrete examples" of the prayerful consciousness.

He begins with George Müller of Bristol, England, a man who could well have been discussed in his lectures on saintliness, for Müller was indefatigable in his efforts to equip Christian missionaries for work overseas, in making Christian literature available to the masses at home and abroad, and in building and overseeing several orphanages and schools. James, however, is interested here in Müller's "prayerful life," and in this regard his judgment of Müller is quite negative, for Müller's prayers "were of the crassest petitional order" (p. 467). According to his biographer, Müller refused to borrow money but paid for everything in cash. This means that he might not know from one day to the next whether he would be able to feed the children in his orphanage. Yet, by his own attestation, the money always arrived in the nick of time, and no one went hungry. Once, when he received the sum he needed to carry on his work, he wrote in his diary:

> It is impossible to describe my joy in God when I received this donation. I was neither excited nor surprised; for I *look out* for answers to my prayers. *I believe that God hears me.* Yet my heart was so full of joy that I could only *sit* before God, and admire him, like David in 2 Samuel vii. At last I cast myself flat down upon my face and burst forth in thanksgiving to God and in surrendering my heart afresh to him for his blessed service (VRE: 470).

As the money he received was a large sum earmarked for his building fund for a certain house, his reference to David is specifically to verse 18, "Then King David went in and sat before the Lord, and said, 'Who am I, O Lord God, and what is my house, that thou hast brought me thus far?"

James considers Muller's to be an extreme case of the prayerful consciousness, especially "in the extraordinary narrowness of the man's intellectual horizon. His God was, as he often said, his business partner. He seems to have been for Müller little more than a sort of supernatural clergyman interested in the congregation of tradesmen and others in Bristol who were his saints ...." (p. 470). God, as perceived by Müller, was "unpossessed of any of those vaster and wilder and more ideal attributes with which the human imagination elsewhere has invested him." Müller's "intensely private and practical conception of his relations with the Deity continued the traditions of the most primitive human thought" (pp. 470-471). In a footnote to this observation that Müller's conception of his relations with the Deity was most primitive, James provides an example of "an even more primitive style of religious thought," the case of an English sailor who, as a prisoner on a French ship, set upon the crew of seven Frenchmen, killed two and made the others his prisoners, and brought home the ship. His account of this feat is replete with references to his prayers to God to help him, with each request resulting in his discovery of a weapon near at hand with which to assault an adversary.

While obviously intrigued by these two examples of prayer, James is also offended by them, not because the two men engage in petitionary prayer (as he has already expressed his support for petitionary prayer in the case of the sick), but because their prayers are so crassly instrumental. These men's prayers, he asserts, claim that the "unseen powers" do things "which no enlightened man can nowadays believe in" (p. 466). His next case, that of the German pietist C. Hilty, fares considerably better. Hilty's book on happiness had been previously cited by James in the chapter on the religion of healthy-mindedness, so James's insertion of his case here should alert us to the fact that Hilty uses prayer in support of an essentially healthy-minded religious attitude. According to James, Hilty is a good illustration of the prayerful life followed by innumerable Christians for whom "persistence in leaning on the Almighty for support and guidance" brings with it "proofs, palpable but much more subtle, of his presence and active influence" (p. 472). His account is too lengthy to quote in full, but its basic point is that if one allows God to take over the control of one's life, things tend to work out surprisingly well. One finds oneself "settling one's affairs neither too early nor too late" and "persons are sent to us at the right time, to offer or ask for what is needed, and what we should never have had the courage or resolution to undertake of our own accord" (p. 473).

James suggests that Hilty's account shades "into others where the belief is, not that particular events are tempered more towardly to us by a superintending providence, as a reward for our reliance, but that by cultivating the continuous sense of our connection with the power that made things as they are, we are tempered more towardly for their reception" (p. 474). The change, in other words, is essentially subjective:

The outward face of nature need not alter, but the expressions of meaning in it alter. It was dead and is alive again. It is like the difference between looking on a person without love, or upon the same person with love. In the latter case intercourse springs into new vitality. So when one's affections keep in touch with the divinity of the world's authorship, fear and egotism fall away; and in the equanimity that follows, one finds in the hours, as they succeed each other, a series of purely benignant opportunities. It is as if all doors were opened, and all paths freshly smoothed. We meet a new world when we meet the old world in the spirit which this kind of prayer infuses (VRE: 474).

Here, James introduces what had been a key issue in his earlier lectures on the healthy-minded and the sick-soul temperaments, namely, the individual's sense of the natural world or "the mundane order of things," especially as to whether this world is benignantly or hostilely disposed toward oneself. In a footnote, James quotes at some length a passage from the writings of the Greek stoic, Epictetus, who discerns the providence of God in all the seemingly mundane processes of nature:

"Good Heaven!" says Epictetus, "any one thing in the creation is sufficient to demonstrate a Providence, to a humble and grateful mind. The mere possibility of producing milk from grass, cheese from milk, and wool from skins; who formed and planned it? Ought we not, whether we plough or eat, to sing this hymn to God? Great is God, who has supplied us with these instruments to till the ground; great is God, who has given us hands and instruments of digestion; who has given us to grow insensibly and to breathe in sleep. These things we ought forever to celebrate ...." (VRE: 474).

Epictetus accuses those who do not sing this hymn to God of being blind and insensible, and therefore nominates himself, "a lame old man," to lead the singing, for "what else can I do ... but sing hymns to God? Were I a nightingale, I would act the part of the nightingale; were I a swan, the part of a swan. But since I am a reasonable creature, it is my duty to praise God ... and I call on you to join the same song" (p. 474).

James associates this spirit of "cultivating the continuous sense of our connection with the power that made things as they are" with the healthy-minded temperament, for it is also the spirit of "mind-curers, of the transcendentalists, and of the so-called 'liberal' Christians'" (p. 474). This spirit is expressed in James Martineau's sermon entitled "Help Thou Mine Unbelief," in which Martineau asserts:

> Depend upon it, it is not the want of greater miracles, but of the soul to perceive such as are allowed us still, that makes us push all the sanctities into the far spaces we cannot reach. The devout feel that wherever God's hand is, *there* is miracle; and it is simply an indevoutness which imagines that only where miracle is, can there be the real hand of God ... It is no outward change, no shifting in time or place; but only the loving meditation of the pure in heart, that can reawaken the Eternal from the sleep within our souls: that can render him a reality again, and reassert for him once more his ancient name of "the living God" (VRE: 475).

James himself concludes, "When we see all things in God, and refer all things to him, we read in common matters superior expressions of meaning. The deadness with which custom invests the familiar vanishes, and existence as a whole appears transfigured" (pp. 475-476).

PRAYER AND THE MELANCHOLY SPIRIT

Mind-curers, transcendentalists and liberal Christians are all "healthy-minded" types. Perhaps, then, we are not surprised that they would find themselves disposed, as Martineau puts it, to "discern beneath the sun, as he rises any morning, the supporting finger of the Almighty" (p. 475). But what about the sick-soul, the melancholiac for whom the world that surrounds us is either indifferent or hostile? That Martineau's sermon is entitled "Help Thou Mine Unbelief" suggests that it may be addressed precisely to those who do not experience this world as reflective of the "supporting finger of the Almighty," for he goes on to describe the one who now discerns the Almighty behind the rising sun as *recovering* "the sweet and reverent surprise with which Adam gazed on the first dawn in Paradise" (p. 475). He is speaking, in part at least, to those who have lost the perception of the world as disclosing the reality of God. It is not that the world has changed, for "The universe, open to the eye today, looks as it did a thousand years ago" (p. 475). It is the perceiver who has changed, and it is the perceiver who can change again. As James puts it, "The deadness with which custom invests the familiar vanishes, and existence as a whole *appears* transfigured" (p. 476). What we are witnessing in this case is "the state of a mind thus awakened from torpor" (p. 476).

Thus, the sick or melancholic soul can also have experience of the world as transfigured. The difference between the healthy-minded and the sick-soul may be in the fact that for the one the sense of the world being upheld by the supporting arms of God is more habitual whereas for the other this perception is more occasional. In support of this distinction between the habitual and the occasional, James cites the following example from the autobiographical recollections of the Catholic philosopher, Fr. A. Gratry. The experience occurred, according to James, in Fr. Gratry's "youthful melancholy period":

> One day I had a moment of consolation, because I met with something which seemed to me ideally perfect. It was a poor drummer beating the tattoo in the

streets of Paris. I walked behind him in returning to the school on the evening of a holiday. His drum gave out the tattoo in such a way that, at that moment at least, however peevish I were, I could find no pretext for fault-finding. It was impossible to conceive more nerve or spirit, better time or measure, more clearness or richness, than were in this drumming. Ideal desire could go no farther in that direction. I was enchanted and consoled; the perfection of this wretched act did me good. Good is at least possible, I said, since the ideal can thus sometimes get embodied (VRE: 476).

Later, in his lecture on "Conclusions," James comments on the emotion that "overcomes temperamental melancholy and imparts endurance to the Subject, or a zest, or a meaning, or an enchantment and glory to the common objects of life," and adds a footnote in which a correspondent credits Fr. Gratry with having aroused a profound happiness in him through their conversation that very morning (pp. 505-506).

If, for Gratry, his melancholic mood was lifted by the symbols and sounds of the drummer beating the tattoo in the streets of Paris, the main character in a novel by Sénancour had a similar experience, also on the streets of Paris, when he came across a flower—a yellow jonquil—blooming on a March day:

It was the strongest expression of desire: it was the first perfume of the year. I felt all the happiness destined for man. This unutterable harmony of souls, the phantom of the ideal world, arose in me complete. I never felt anything so great or so instantaneous. I know not what shape, what analogy, what secret of relation it was that made me see in this flower a limitless beauty .... I shall never inclose in a conception this power, this immensity that nothing will express; this form that nothing will contain; this ideal of a better world which one feels, but which, it seems, nature has not made actual (VRE: 477).

These illustrations indicate that it is the sick-soul for whom such epiphanies are especially poignant and meaningful, for through them, the world suddenly appears transfigured. The "ideal" world that seemed so impossible of realization, so transcendentally removed, is suddenly present, so close that it can be seen and felt.

James goes on to remind his listeners that he had already drawn attention to this experience of "the vivified face of the world" in his lectures on conversion, and cites a passage in the conversion lecture that contrasted the experience of the convert with that of the melancholiac:

A third peculiarity of the assurance state [in conversion] is the objective change which the world often appears to undergo. "An appearance of newness beautifies every object," the precise opposite of that other sort of newness, that dreadful unreality and strangeness in the appearance of the world, which is experienced by melancholy patients, and of which you may recall my relating some examples (VRE: 248).

In both instances, in the lecture on conversion and now in his discussion on prayer, he footnotes the passage in the earlier "Sick-Soul" lecture in which he had alluded to "transformations in the whole expression of reality." Anticipating his lecture on conversion, he contrasts there the experience of the convert and the melancholiac:

When we come to study the phenomenon of conversion or religious regeneration, we shall see that a not infrequent consequence of the change operated in the subject is a transfiguration of the face of nature in his eyes. A new heaven seems to shine upon a new earth. In melancholiacs there is usually a similar change, only it is in the reverse direction. The world now looks remote, strange, sinister, uncanny. Its color is gone, its breath is cold, there is no speculation in the eyes it glares with (VRE: 151).

Thus, the world can be experienced in both forms—now with vivified face and shining, now remote, strange and eyes glaring—which causes one to wonder: "If the natural world is so double-faced and unhomelike, what world, what thing is real? An urgent wondering and questioning is set up, a poring theoretic activity, and in the desperate effort to get into right relations with the matter, the sufferer is often led to what becomes for him a satisfying religious solution" (p. 152).

In the lecture on prayer, however, the effort is much less theoretic, much less a matter of conscious thought or active will, and far more a matter of yielding to the sights and sounds around us. The energy, so to speak, comes from without, not from within:

As a rule, religious persons generally assume that whatever natural facts connect themselves in any way with their destiny are significant of the divine purpose with them. Through prayer the purpose, often far from obvious, comes home to them, and if it be "trial," strength to endure the trial is given. Thus at all stages of the prayerful life we find the persuasion that in the process of communion energy from on high flows in to meet demand, and becomes operative within the phenomenal world. So long as this operativeness is admitted to be real, it makes no essential difference whether its immediate effects be subjective or objective. The fundamental religious point is that in prayer, spiritual energy, which otherwise would slumber, does become active, and spiritual work of some kind is effected really (VRE: 477).

Whatever the ultimate source of the energy may be, it is experienced in prayer as originating outside of the individual and as occurring in direct relation to the prayerful one's receptivity and yielding.

In light of James's suggestion that, in prayer, the divine purposes "come home" to us, his answer to the final question in Pratt's questionnaire is especially illuminating: "What do you mean by a 'religious experience'"? James responds, "Any moment of life that brings the reality of spiritual things more 'home' to one" (Pratt 1973: 125). The purpose of prayer, then, is not to effect an actual change in the natural world. Our prayers have no effect on droughts and storms. But prayer, as "the vital act by which the entire world seeks to save itself by clinging to the principle from which it draws its life" (p. 464), or as "the very movement itself of the soul putting itself in a personal relation of contact with the mysterious power of which it feels the presence," even perhaps before it has a name by which it call it (p. 464), such prayer opens itself to the world that surrounds it (the seen world) and so to the unseen world to which the seen world is vivid testimony. In prayer, understood in its widest sense as "inward communion," the spiritual world "comes home" to us, a lovely image, especially coming from a man who spent so much of his life away from home. For the one for whom the perception of the unseen world behind the seen world is not an habitual experience—which is to say, for the melancholiac—it will be those experiences in which the natural world beckons oneself out of oneself—the drummer's tattoo, the yellow jonquil on a March day—that will bring the unseen world home again. Thus, through the "vivified face of nature" the unseen world shows its own benignant face as well.

SCIENCE AND THE MELANCHOLIC MOOD

In his final lecture, "Conclusions," James identifies the three beliefs that are integral to the religious life understood in its broadest sense. These are:

1. That the invisible world is part of a more spiritual universe from which it draws its chief significance.
2. That union or harmonious relation with that higher universe is our true end.
3. That prayer or inner communion with the spirit thereof—be that spirit "God" or "law"—is a process wherein work is really done, and spiritual energy flows in and produces effects, psychological or material, within the phenomenal world (p. 485).

Thus, it is through prayer that one opens oneself to the unseen world and allows spiritual energy to make a difference in the visible or phenomenal world. In commenting on the central role that this accords prayer in the religious life, James asserts that the scientific attitude of the day is the greatest threat to religion because it takes the view that prayer is merely a survival from more primitive times when our ancestors believed that they could "coerce the spiritual powers" to "get them on our side," especially in "our dealings with the natural world" (p. 495). While James shares the scientific community's critique of such efforts to coerce the spiritual powers, he distances himself from its insistence that we replace animistic views of the natural world as found in religion with science's "mathematical and mechanical modes of conception" (pp. 496-497). If science claims that such views of the natural world are mere "survivals" of a more primitive way of thinking, James cautions that the natural world possesses such "picturesquely striking" features that our ancestors would surely have viewed these "as the more promising avenue to the knowledge of Nature's life" than the thin, pallid, uninteresting ideas "that guide science's approach to nature" (e.g., considerations of weight, movement, velocity, direction, position, etc.):

> Well, it is still in these richer animistic and dramatic aspects that religion delights to dwell. It is the terror and beauty of phenomena, the "promise" of the dawn and of the rainbow, the "voice" of the thunder, the "gentleness" of the summer rain, the "sublimity" of the stars, and not the physical laws which these things follow, by which the religious mind still continues to be most impressed (VRE: 497-498).

In effect, science and the melancholic mood share in common the sense that the natural world is dead and lifeless, and it is the religious temperament, with its perception of the "vivified face of nature," that experiences the world as dramatically, yes, animistically alive. The very fact that science shares the melancholic perception of the world as indifferent does not in itself invalidate science, but it surely calls into question science's superior attitude toward religion. Thus, prayer, which is of critical importance to the religious perception of the natural world as transfigured, is not only the core of religion but also a basis for its claims against the scientific view that religion is a mere survival of more primitive ways of thinking. The individual's perception of the phenomenal world is very much a subjective matter. For some, the world is warm and inviting, for others it is cold and sinister. But there is an objective factor as well, in that the world "out there" is not an undifferentiated mass, but has features that stand out from the rest, and are, so to speak, more "animated" than its other features. For those who are religious, these are the very features of the world that have the feel of divine presence. The reality of God is perceptible behind the promise of the dawn, the voice of the thunder, the gentleness of the summer rain, the sublimity of the stars.

AUTOMATISMS AND THE EXPERIENCE OF OBJECTIVITY

If we take James's answer to Pratt's questions on prayer at face value, then we must conclude that he does not identify himself among those who pray: "I can't possibly pray —I feel foolish and artificial." We do, however, know that he struggled throughout his life with melancholy (see my article in this volume), and that he would therefore identify himself with those for whom the world is not habitually perceived as spiritually alive, but rather with those who, like Fr. Gratry, on occasion experience the world in this way. If he does not pray, does this mean that he cannot attest personally to the role that religion plays in the transfiguring of the world? If to pray makes him feel foolish and artificial—perhaps because it seems much like talking to himself—does this mean that he has no personal experience of religion enabling him to see the world transfigured, its face vivified?

For the answer to this question, we need to return to the "Other Characteristics" lecture and consider the section that follows the discussion of prayer and concludes the lecture. Here he introduces the "last aspect of the religious life which remains for me to touch upon," the fact that the "manifestations" of religion "frequently connect themselves with the subconscious part of our existence" (pp. 477-478). He then proceeds to discuss the role that "automatisms" have played in the lives of religious individuals. In *The Principles of Psychology* (1950, I: 394-396), he had considered at some length the phenomenon of automatic writing, and had cited the case of a Rhode Island journalist, author and man of affairs who had a large collection of manuscripts automatically produced while his conscious mind was directed toward other matters. For James, the best explanation for this phenomenon is the duality of mind, perhaps attributable to the fact that the brain consists of two hemispheres. In considering automatisms in *The Varieties*, he cites the "whole array of Christian saints and heresiarchs" who experienced automatisms of one kind or another: visions, voices, rapt conditions, guiding impressions, "openings," dreams and trances. Whatever form these may take, such automatisms corroborate belief:

> Incursions from beyond the transmarginal region have a peculiar power to increase conviction. The inchoate sense of presence is infinitely stronger than conception, but strong as it may be, it is seldom equal to the evidence of hallucination. Saints who actually see or hear their Saviour reach the acme of assurance. Motor automatisms, though rarer, are, if possible, even more convincing than sensations. The subjects here actually feel themselves played upon by powers beyond their will. The evidence is dynamic; the God or spirit moves the very organs of their body (VRE: 478).

Reminiscent of his earlier discussion of automatic writing in *The Principles*, James adds a footnote to this comment in *The Varieties* about the spirit moving the very organs of the body by citing another example of automatic writing, where the arm actually seemed to be activated independently, as if by another agency besides the arm. While many religious leaders make no claim to be writing or speaking under the "inspiration" of God or some other spiritual agency, many others do. An especially noteworthy example is Philo of Alexandria, who describes his inspiration as follows:

> Sometimes, when I have come to my work empty, I have suddenly become full; ideas being in an invisible manner showered upon me, and implanted in me from on high; so that through the influence of divine inspiration, I have become greatly excited, and have known neither the place in which I was, nor those who were present, nor myself, nor what I was saying, nor what I was writing; for then I have been conscious of a richness of interpretation, an enjoyment of light, a most penetrat-

ing insight, a most manifest energy in all that was to be done; having such effect on my mind as the clearest ocular demonstration would have on the eyes (VRE: 481).

In "Conclusions," James suggests that much of what occurs in the subconscious is insignificant: Imperfect memories, silly jingles, inhibitive timidities, etc., comprise a large part of it. Yet, his earlier discussions of conversion, mystical experience and prayer have revealed "how striking a part invasions from this region play in the religious life," and the fact of these "invasions" prompts him to propose, "as an hypothesis, that whatever it may be on *its farther side*, the 'more' with which in religious experience we feel ourselves connected is on its *hither* side the subconscious continuation of our conscious life" (p. 512). On the one hand, this hypothesis preserves contact with science as it begins with a recognized psychological fact. On the other hand, it vindicates the theologian's contention that the religious person is moved by an external power,

> for it is one of the peculiarities of invasions from the subconscious region to take on objective appearances, and to suggest to the Subject an external control. In the religious life the control is felt as "higher"; but since on our hypothesis it is primarily the higher faculties of our own hidden mind which are controlling, the sense of union with the power beyond us is a sense of something, not merely apparently, but literally true (VRE: 512-513).

Thus, for James, the automatisms of which he writes in the chapter on "Other Considerations" are objective to the one who experiences them, and it is their felt objectivity that the religious individual is most conscious of, and most concerned to affirm.

James himself had considerable experience of automatisms throughout his life. In his account of the "French sufferer" experience in his lecture on "The Sick Soul," the scripture-texts that entered his mind and kept him from going really insane were undoubtedly automatisms. The terminal dream that Erikson discusses (in this volume) is another example. What seems to distinguish James from the religious individuals considered in the automatisms section of the lecture on "Other Characteristics," however, is that he finds himself unable to ascribe the "objectivity" to his own experiences that they ascribe to theirs. It is not that he rejects the idea that these "invasions" come from some outside agency which one may call "spiritual" or even "divine," but neither is he prepared to affirm that his own experiences of this nature involve "more" than the effects of his own subconscious mind (its "hither" side only).

PUTTING A FACE ON THE WORLD

Yet, at the very least, James is a most appreciative observer of the religious. Religious experience is, for him, but once removed, as he has gotten ever so close to persons who have had such experiences without having any himself, at least of which he is aware. To Pratt's question, "If you have had no such experience [of God's presence], do you accept the testimony of others who claim to have felt God's presence directly?," he responded, "Yes! The whole line of testimony on this point is so strong that I am unable to pooh-pooh it away. No doubt there is a germ in me of something similar that makes response." In *The Principles*, in commenting on the religious life in his chapter on "Will," he notes that "just as our courage is so often a reflex of another's courage, so our faith is apt to be, as Max Müller somewhere says, a faith in some one else's faith" (1950, II: 579). Thus, in *The Varieties*, he has provided a portrait gallery of religious persons (Davis, in her article in this volume, counts over 200 such portraits), and has placed himself, inconspicuously and surreptitiously, among them (as "French Sufferer" and "intimate Friend"; see my article in this volume). We would surely not look for him at the center of the exhibit, but neither has he chosen to exclude himself from it. His own self-inclusion in the portrait gallery that he creates in *The Varieties* implies both similarity and difference between himself and his subjects: "That shape am I, potentially." As Richard Brilliant writes of the portrait artist, Francis Bacon:

> Francis Bacon's portraits of popes, friends, patrons, of himself, all seem to look alike, as if he were seeking to express himself through their contorted images. To the degree to which they can be distinguished from one another, each portrait retains its own integrity; to the degree that they resemble one another, they implicate the artist in each image as if he mirrored his own anxious appearance in their faces (Brilliant 1991: 156).

The metaphor of the portrait is perhaps, then, a particularly apt way of describing what James has accomplished in *The Varieties*, not only because he nearly became an artist specializing in portraiture, but also because portraiture illustrates his point about the world "out there" not being an undifferentiated mass, but as having features that stand out from the rest, as being more animated than the other features. For the portrait artist, it is the face especially, that portrays the "life" of the subject. Brilliant believes that the attention the face draws to itself goes back to our earliest experience of being infants in our mother's arms:

> The dynamic nature of portraits and the "occasionality" that anchors their imagery in life seem ultimately to depend on the primary experience of the infant in arms. That child, gazing up at its mother, imprints her vitally important image so firmly on its mind that soon enough she can be recognized almost instantaneously and without conscious thought; spontaneous face recognition remains an important instrument of survival, separating friend from foe, that persists into adult life. A little later a name, "Mama" or some other, will be attached to the now familiar face and body, soon followed by a more conscious acknowledgment of her role vis-à-vis the infant as "mother" or "provider," and finally by an understanding of her character, being loving and warmly protective towards the infant (in an ideal world, of course!). Eventually the infant will acquire a sense of its own independent existence, of itself as a sentient being, responding to others, and possessing, as well, its own given name. Here are the essential constituents of a persons's identity: a recognized or recognizable appearance; a given name that refers to no one else; a social, interactive function that can be defined; in context, a pertinent characterization; and a consciousness of the distinction between one's own person and another's, and of the possible relationship between them. Only physical appearance is naturally visible, and even that is unstable. The rest is conceptual and must be expressed symbolically. All these elements, however, may be represented by portrait artists who must meet the complex demands of portraiture as a particular challenge of their artistic ingenuity and empathetic insight (Brilliant 1991: 9).

If the impetus for portraiture begins with the infant's perception of the face of the mother, and with the desire to put a name to this familiar face, portraiture is inherently relational: "Making portraits is a response to the natural human tendency to think about oneself, of oneself in relation to others, and of others in apparent relation to themselves and to others. To put a face on the world catches the essence of ordinary behavior in the social context; to do the same in a work of art catches the essence of the human relationship and

262

consolidates it in the portrait through the creation of a visible identity sign by which someone can be known, possibly for ever" (Brilliant 1991: 14).

In noting that religion preserves an animated view of the world against the pressures of science to limit the world to its mathematical and mechanical conceptions only, James spoke of the "vivified face of nature." Religion is dedicated, as it were, to putting a face on the world. In "The Reality of the Unseen" lecture, he laments the fact that "'Science' in many minds is genuinely taking the place of a religion," and notes that "laws of nature" are replacing the "feeling of objective presence" in the world, a presence that was only half-metaphoric, "just as even now we may speak of the smile of the morning, the kiss of the breeze, or the bite of the cold, without really meaning that these phenomena of nature actually wear a human face" (pp. 57-58). In a footnote to this passage, he quotes B. de St. Pierre's observation that "Nature is always so interesting, under whatever aspect she shows herself, that when it rains, I seem to see a beautiful woman weeping. She appears the more beautiful, the more afflicted she is" (p. 58). For religion, there is a certain "objective" truth in this view of nature as a beautiful woman weeping, a view that is not so much imposed upon nature but excited by it: "*Nature* is always so interesting, under whatever aspect *she* shows herself."

In his discussion in *The Principles* of the role that sense perceptions play in effecting belief, James contends that

no object which neither possesses [sensible] vividness in its own right nor is able to borrow it from anything else has a chance of making headway against vivid rivals, or of rousing in us that reaction in which belief consists. On the vivid objects we *pin*, as the saying is, our faith in all the rest; and our belief returns instinctively even to those of them from which reflection has led it away (James 1950, II: 301-302).

To illustrate his point, he cites the role played by portraits or photographs of a dead or distant friend in enabling us to "realize" the person's existence. Indeed, "To many persons among us, photographs of lost ones seem to be fetishes" as the "mere materiality of the reminder is almost as important as its resemblance" to the loved one (p. 304). What such portraits and photographs do is to heighten our awareness of the reality of the one who is no longer physically present. The portrait and photograph also, of course, testify to the objective reality of the one being portrayed. As Brilliant points out, "The very fact of the portrait's allusion to an individual human being, actually existing outside the work, defines the function of the art work in the world and constitutes the cause of its coming into being" (1991: 8). Furthermore, "Portraiture challenges the transiency or irrelevancy of human existence and the portrait artist must respond to the demands formulated by the individual's wish to endure" (Brilliant 1991: 14); or, we should add, by the wish that the loved one who is the subject of the portrait may endure.

If portraits and photographs have such a powerful influence on our capacity to believe, so do words, but only if they are sensibly vivid. As James goes on to note: "Some persons, the present writer among the number, can hardly lecture without a black-board: the abstract conceptions must be symbolized by letters, squares or circles, and the relations between them by lines. All this symbolism, linguistic, graphic, and dramatic, has other uses too, for it abridges thought and fixes terms. But one of its uses is surely to rouse the believing reaction and give to the ideas a more living reality" (1950, II: 305).[1]

---

1. James confesses that he is not a very good "visualizer" himself. In his chapter on "Imagination" in *The Principles*, in commenting on persons who can give lifelike descriptions of what they have seen, he says in a footnote, "I am myself a good draughtsman, and have a very lively interest in pic-

What James has given us in *The Varieties*, then, are word portraits that provide a vivid sense of their subjects' lives among us, precisely so that we, in reading about their faith, may, in a reflexive way, have a faith of our own. *The Varieties* succeeds in this sense to the extent that its word portraits are vivid, thereby compelling our attention. Where there is such sensible vividness, there will be living religion, for where sensibly vivid objects claim our attention, the reality of spiritual things is brought home to us. Religion dares to put a face on the visible world, and thereby, like portraiture, engenders belief in a reality "actually existing outside the work." Three beliefs, according to James, summarize in the broadest way the characteristics of the religious life, and the first of these is "That the visible world is part of a more spiritual universe from which it draws its chief significance" (p. 485).

For those whose souls are of "sky-blue tint," their "affinities are rather with flowers and birds and all enchanting innocencies than with dark human passions" (p. 81). For James, the "face" of the visible world was considerably more threatening, which is why he could speak of his mother as seeming to him to be "a perfect paradox in her unconsciousness of danger" (p. 161). But nature herself is a "perfect paradox," in that when she reveals herself as "a beautiful woman weeping," she evokes in us the faith that there is an unseen world where every human tear is wiped away (Revelation 21: 4). In turn, she enables us to believe that we have a self, and one that is worthy of our care. As James writes in *The Principles of Psychology* (1950, I: 319): "To have a self that I can *care for*, nature must first present me with some *object* interesting enough to make me instinctively wish to appropriate it for its *own* sake ...."

REFERENCES

Brilliant, R. (1991). *Portraiture*. Cambridge, MA: Harvard University Press.
James, W. (1950). *The Principles of Psychology*, 2 vols. New York: Dover.
———— (1982). *The Varieties of Religious Experience*. New York: Penguin Books.

---

tures, statues, architecture and decoration, and a keen sensibility to artistic effects. But I am an extremely poor visualizer, and find myself often unable to reproduce in my mind's eye pictures which I have most carefully examined" (1950, II: 53). Later, in another footnote, he writes, "I am myself a very poor visualizer, and find that I can seldom call to mind even a single letter of the alphabet in purely retinal terms. I must trace the letter by running my mental eye over its contour in order that the image of it shall have any distinctness at all. On questioning a large number of other people, mostly students, I find that perhaps half of them say they have no such difficulty in seeing letters mentally. Many affirm that they can see an entire word at once, especially a short one like 'dog,' with no such feeling of creating the letters successively by tracing them with the eye" (p. 61). James's confessions may indicate that he lacks the very ability that is necessary to "see" the phenomenal world, but it may just as well mean that his ability to see the phenomenal world is not in question, that what he cannot do is "see" the world out there *in here*, i.e., in his mind. Which means that he needs the visible world to stimulate thought, and that, conversely, he cannot think if, in a melancholic mood, the world out there offers no stimulation to thought. This would be consistent with his view that the natural world is necessary to make the spiritual or unseen world come alive and make its own reality felt.

IS LIFE WORTH LIVING?*

WILLIAM JAMES

When Mr. Mallock's book with this title appeared some fifteen years ago, the jocose answer that "it depends on the *liver*" had great currency in the newspapers. The answer which I propose to give to-night cannot be jocose. In the words of one of Shakespeare's prologues,—

> "I come no more to make you laugh; things now,
> That bear a weighty and a serious brow,
> Sad, high, and working, full of state and woe,"—

must be my theme. In the deepest heart of all of us there is a corner in which the ultimate mystery of things works sadly; and I know not what such an association as yours intends, nor what you ask of those whom you invite to address you, unless it be to lead you from the surface-glamour of existence, and for an hour at least to make you heedless to the buzzing and jigging and vibration of small interests and excitements that form the tissue of our ordinary consciousness. Without further explanation or apology, then, I ask you to join me in turning an attention, commonly too unwilling, to the profounder bass-note of life. Let us search the lonely depths for an hour together, and see what answers in the last folds and recesses of things our question may find.

I.

With many men the question of life's worth is answered by a temperamental optimism which makes them incapable of believing that anything seriously evil can exist. Our dear old Walt Whitman's works are the standing text-book of this kind of optimism. The mere joy of living is so immense in Walt Whitman's veins that it abolishes the possibility of any other kind of feeling:—

> "To breathe the air, how delicious!
> To speak, to walk, to seize something by the hand!...
> To be this incredible God I am!...
> O amazement of things, even the least particle!
> O spirituality of things!
> I too carol the Sun, usher'd or at noon, or as now, setting;
> I too throb to the brain and beauty of the earth and of all the growths of the
>   earth...
> I sing to the last the equalities, modern or old,
> I sing the endless finales of things,
> I say Nature continues—glory continues.
> I praise with electric voice,
> For I do not see one imperfection in the universe,
> And I do not see one cause or result lamentable at last."

---

*An address to the Harvard Young Men's Christian Association. Published in the *International Journal of Ethics,* October, 1895, and subsequently in *The Will to Believe and Other Essays in Popular Philosophy* (Longmans, Green and Company, 1897).

So Rousseau, writing of the nine years he spent at Annecy, with nothing but his happiness to tell:—

"How tell what was neither said nor done nor even thought, but tasted only and felt, with no object of my felicity but the emotion of felicity itself! I rose with the sun, and I was happy; I went to walk, and I was happy; I saw 'Maman,' and I was happy; I left her, and I was happy. I rambled through the woods and over the vine-slopes, I wandered in the valleys, I read, I lounged, I worked in the garden, I gathered the fruits, I helped at the indoor work, and happiness followed me everywhere. It was in no one assignable thing; it was all within myself; it could not leave me for a single instant."

If moods like this could be made permanent, and constitutions like these universal, there would never be any occasion for such discourses as the present one. No philosopher would seek to prove articulately that life is worth living, for the fact that it absolutely is so would vouch for itself, and the problem disappear in the vanishing of the question rather than in the coming of anything like a reply. But we are not magicians to make the optimistic temperament universal; and alongside of the deliverances of temperamental optimism concerning life, those of temperamental pessimism always exist, and oppose to them a standing refutation. In what is called 'circular insanity,' phases of melancholy succeed phases of mania, with no outward cause that we can discover; and often enough to one and the same well person life will present incarnate radiance to-day and incarnate dreariness to-morrow, according to the fluctuations of what the older medical books used to call "the concoction of the humors." In the words of the newspaper joke, "it depends on the liver." Rousseau's ill-balanced constitution undergoes a change, and behold him in his latter evil days a prey to melancholy and black delusions of suspicion and fear. Some men seem launched upon the world even from their birth with souls as incapable of happiness as Walt Whitman's was of gloom, and they have left us their messages in even more lasting verse than his,—the exquisite Leopardi; for example; or our own contemporary, James Thomson, in that pathetic book, *The City of Dreadful Night*, which I think is less well-known than it should be for its literary beauty, simply because men are afraid to quote its words,—they are so gloomy, and at the same time so sincere. In one place the poet describes a congregation gathered to listen to a preacher in a great unillumined cathedral at night. The sermon is too long to quote, but it ends thus:—

"'O Brothers of sad lives! they are so brief;
A few short years must bring us all relief:
Can we not bear these years of laboring breath?
But if you would not this poor life fulfil,
Lo, you are free to end it when you will,
Without the fear of waking after death.'—

"The organ-like vibrations of his voice
thrilled through the vaulted aisles and died away;
The yearning of the tones which bade rejoice
Was sad and tender as a requiem lay:
Our shadowy congregation rested still,
As brooding on that 'End it when you will.'

"Our shadowy congregation rested still,
As musing on that message we had heard,
And brooding on that 'End it when you will,'
Perchance awaiting yet some other word;
When keen as lightning through a muffled sky
Sprang forth a shrill and lamentable cry:—

"'The man speaks sooth, alas! the man speaks sooth;
We have no personal life beyond the grave;
There is no God; Fate knows nor wrath nor ruth:
Can I find here the comfort which I crave?

" 'In all eternity I had one chance,
One few years' term of gracious human life,—
The splendors of the intellect's advance,
The sweetness of the home with babes and wife;

" 'The social pleasures with their genial wit;
The fascination of the worlds of art;
The glories of the worlds of Nature lit
By large imagination's glowing heart;

" 'The rapture of mere being, full of health;
The careless childhood and the ardent youth;
The strenuous manhood winning various wealth,
The reverend age serene with life's long truth:

" 'All the sublime prerogatives of Man;
The storied memories of the times of old,
The patient tracking of the world's great plan
Through sequences and changes myriadfold.

" 'This chance was never offered me before;
For me the infinite past is blank and dumb;
This chance recurreth never, nevermore;
Blank, blank for me the infinite To-come.

" 'And this sole chance was frustrate from my birth,
A mockery, a delusion; and my breath
Of noble human life upon this earth
So racks me that I sigh for senseless death.

" 'My wine of life is poison mixed with gall,
My noonday passes in a nightmare dream,
I worse than lose the years which are my all:
What can console me for the loss supreme?

" 'Speak not of comfort where no comfort is,
Speak not at all: can words make foul things fair?
Our life's a cheat, our death a black abyss:
Hush, and be mute, envisaging despair.

"This vehement voice came from the northern aisle,
Rapid and shrill to its abrupt harsh close;
And none gave answer for a certain while,
For words must shrink from these most wordless woes;
At last the pulpit speaker simply said,
With humid eyes and thoughtful, drooping head,—

" 'My Brother, my poor Brothers, it is thus:
This life holds nothing good for us,
But it ends soon and nevermore can be;
And we knew nothing of it ere our birth,
And shall know nothing when consigned to earth:
I ponder these thoughts, and they comfort me.'"

"It ends soon, and never more can be," "Lo, you are free to end it when you will,"— these verses flow truthfully from the melancholy Thomson's pen, and are in truth a consolation for all to whom, as to him, the world is far more like a steady den of fear than a continual fountain of delight. That life is *not* worth living the whole army of suicides declare,—an army whose roll-call, like the famous evening gun of the British army, follows the sun round the world and never terminates. We, too, as we sit here in our comfort, must 'ponder these things' also, for we are of one substance with these suicides, and their life is the life we share. The plainest intellectual integrity,—nay, more, the simplest manliness and honor, forbid us to forget their case.

"If suddenly," says Mr. Ruskin, "in the midst of the enjoyments of the palate and lightnesses of heart of a London dinner-party, the walls of the chamber were parted, and through their gap the nearest human beings who were famishing and in misery were borne into the midst of the company feasting and fancy free; if, pale from death, horrible in destitution, broken by despair, body by body they were laid upon the soft carpet, one beside the chair of every guest,—would only the crumbs of the dainties be cast to them; would only a passing glance, a passing thought, be vouchsafed to them? Yet the actual facts, the real relation of each Dives and Lazarus, are not altered by the intervention of the house-wall between the table and the sickbed,—by the few feet of ground (how few!) which are, indeed, all that separate the merriment from the misery."

II

To come immediately to the heart of my theme, then, what I propose is to imagine ourselves reasoning with a fellow-mortal who is on such terms with life that the only comfort left him is to brood on the assurance, "You may end it when you will." What reasons can we plead that may render such a brother (or sister) willing to take up the burden again? Ordinary Christians, reasoning with would-be suicides, have little to offer them beyond the usual negative, "Thou shalt not." God alone is master of life and death, they say, and it is a blasphemous act to anticipate his absolving hand. But can *we* find nothing richer or more positive than this, no reflections to urge whereby the suicide may actually see, and in all sad seriousness feel, that in spite of adverse appearances even for him life is still worth living? There are suicides and suicides (in the United States about three thousand of them every year), and I must frankly confess that with perhaps the majority of these my suggestions are impotent to deal. Where suicide is the result of insanity or sudden frenzied impulse, reflection is impotent to arrest its headway; and cases like these belong to the ultimate mystery of evil, concerning which I can only offer considerations tending toward religious patience at the end of this hour. My task, let me say now, is practically narrow, and my words are to deal only with that metaphysical *tedium vitae* which is peculiar to reflecting men. Most of you are devoted, for good or ill, to the reflective life. Many of you are students of philosophy, and have already felt in your own persons the skepticism and unreality that too much grubbing in the abstract roots of things will breed. This is, indeed, one of the regular fruits of the over-studious career. Too much questioning and too little active responsibility lead, almost as often as too much sensualism does, to the edge of the slope, at the bottom of which lie pessimism and the nightmare or suicidal view of life. But to the diseases which reflection breeds, still further reflection can oppose effective remedies; and it is of the melancholy and Weltschmerz bred of reflection that I now proceed to speak.

Let me say, immediately, that my final appeal is to nothing more recondite than religious faith. So far as my argument is to be destructive, it will consist in nothing more than the sweeping away of certain views that often keep the springs of religious faith compressed; and so far as it is to be constructive, it will consist in holding up to the light of day certain considerations calculated to let loose these springs in a normal, natural way. Pessimism is essentially a religious disease. In the form of it to which you are most liable, it consists in nothing but a religious demand to which there comes no normal religious reply.

Now, there are two stages of recovery from this disease, two different levels upon which one may emerge from the midnight view to the daylight view of things, and I must treat of them in turn. The second stage is the more complete and joyous, and it corresponds to the freer exercise of religious trust and fancy. There are, as is well known, persons who are naturally very free in this regard, others who are not at all so. There are persons, for instance, whom we find indulging to their heart's content in prospects of immortality; and there are others who experience the greatest difficulty in making such a notion seem real to themselves at all. These latter persons are tied to their senses, restricted to their natural experience; and many of them, moreover, feel a sort of intellectual loyalty to what they call 'hard facts,' which is positively shocked by the easy excursions into the unseen that other people make at the bare call of sentiment. Minds of either class may, however, be intensely religious. They may equally desire atonement and reconciliation, and crave acquiescence and communion with the total soul of things. But the craving, when the mind is pent in to the hard facts, especially as science now reveals them, can breed pessimism, quite as easily as it breeds optimism when it inspires religious trust and fancy to wing their way to another and a better world.

That is why I call pessimism an essentially religious disease. The nightmare view of life has plenty of organic sources; but its great reflective source has at all times been the contradiction between the phenomena of nature and the craving of the heart to believe that behind nature there is a spirit whose expression nature is. What philosophers call 'natural theology' has been one way of appeasing this craving; that poetry of nature in which our English literature is so rich has been another way. Now, suppose a mind of the latter of our two classes, whose imagination is pent in consequently, and who takes its facts 'hard;' suppose it, moreover, to feel strongly the craving for communion, and yet to realize how desperately difficult it is to construe the scientific order of nature either theologically or poetically,—and what result *can* there be but inner discord and contradiction? Now, this inner discord (merely as discord) can be relieved in either of two ways: The longing to read the facts religiously may cease, and leave the bare facts by themselves; or, supplementary facts may be discovered or believed-in, which permit the religious reading to go on. These two ways of relief are the two stages of recovery, the two levels of escape from pessimism, to which I made allusion a moment ago, and which the sequel will, I trust, make more clear.

III

Starting then with nature, we naturally tend, if we have the religious craving, to say with Marcus Aurelius, "O Universe! what thou wishest I wish." Our sacred books and traditions tell us of one God who made heaven and earth, and, looking on them, saw that they were good. Yet, on more intimate acquaintance, the visible surfaces of heaven and earth refuse to be brought by us into any intelligible unity at all. Every phenomenon that we would praise there exists cheek by jowl with some contrary phenomenon that cancels all its religious effect upon the mind. Beauty and hideousness, love and cruelty, life and death keep house together in indissoluble partnership; and there gradually steals over us, instead of the old warm notion of a man-loving Deity, that of an awful power that neither hates nor loves, but rolls all things together meaninglessly to a common doom. This is an uncanny, a sinister, a nightmare view of life, and its peculiar *unheimlichkeit*, or poisonousness, lies expressly in our holding two things together which cannot possibly agree,—in our clinging, on the one hand, to the demand that there shall be a living spirit of the whole; and, on the other, to the belief that the course of nature must be such a spirit's adequate manifestation and expression. It is in the contradiction between the supposed being of a spirit that encompasses and owns us, and with which we ought to have some communion, and the character of such a spirit as revealed by the visible world's course, that this particular death-in-life paradox and this melancholy-breeding puzzle reside. Carlyle expresses the result in that chapter of his immortal 'Sartor Resartus' entitled 'The Everlasting No.' "I lived," writes poor Teufelsdröckh, "in a continual, indefinite, pining fear; tremulous, pusillanimous, apprehensive of I knew not what: it seemed as if all things in the heavens above and the earth beneath would hurt me; as if the heavens and the earth were but boundless jaws of a devouring monster, wherein I, palpitating, lay waiting to be devoured."

This is the first stage of speculative melancholy. No brute can have this sort of melancholy; no man who is irreligious can become its prey. It is the sick shudder of the frustrated religious demand, and not the mere necessary outcome of animal experience. Teufelsdröckh himself could have made shift to face the general chaos and bedevilment of this world's experiences very well, were he not the victim of an originally unlimited trust and affection towards them. If he might meet them piecemeal, with no suspicion of any whole expressing itself in them, shunning the bitter parts and husbanding the sweet ones, as the occasion served, and as the day was foul or fair, he could have zigzagged toward an easy end, and felt no obligation to make the air vocal with his lamentations. The mood of levity, of 'I don't care,' is for this world's ills a sovereign and practical anaesthetic. But, no! something deep down in Teufelsdröckh and in the rest of us tells us that there is a Spirit in things to which we owe allegiance, and for whose sake we must keep up the serious mood. And so the inner fever and discord also are kept up; for nature taken on her visible surface reveals no such Spirit, and beyond the facts of nature we are at the present stage of our inquiry not supposing ourselves to look.

Now, I do not hesitate frankly and sincerely to confess to you that this real and genuine discord seems to me to carry with it the inevitable bankruptcy of natural religion naively and simply taken. There were times when Leibnitzes with their heads buried in monstrous wigs could compose Theodicies, and when stall-fed officials of an established church could prove by the valves in the heart and the round ligament of the hip-joint the existence of a "Moral and Intelligent Contriver of the World." But those times are past; and we of the nineteenth century, with our evolutionary theories and our mechanical philosophies, already know nature too impartially and too well to worship unreservedly any God of whose character she can be an adequate expression. Truly, all we know of good and duty proceeds from nature; but none the less so all we know of evil. Visible nature is all plasticity and indifference,—a moral multiverse, as one might call it, and not a moral universe. To such a harlot we owe no allegiance; with her as a whole we can establish no moral communion; and we are free in our dealings with her several parts to obey or destroy, and to follow no law but that of prudence in coming to terms with such of her particular features as will help us to our private ends. If there be a divine Spirit of the universe, nature, such as we know her, cannot possibly be its *ultimate word* to man. Either there is no Spirit revealed in nature, or else it is inadequately revealed there; and (as all the higher religions have assumed) what we call visible nature, or this world, must be but a veil and surface-show whose full meaning resides in a supplementary unseen or *other* world.

I cannot help, therefore, accounting it on the whole a gain (though it may seem for certain poetic constitutions a very sad loss) that the naturalistic superstition, the worship of the god of nature, simply taken as such, should have begun to loosen its hold upon the educated mind. In fact, if I am to express my personal opinion unreservedly, I should say (in spite of its sounding blasphemous at first to certain ears) that the initial step towards getting into healthy ultimate relations with the universe is the act of rebellion against the idea that such a God exists. Such rebellion essentially is that which in the chapter I have quoted from Carlyle goes on to describe:—

" 'Wherefore, like a coward, dost thou forever pip and whimper, and go cowering and trembling? Despicable biped!... Hast thou not a heart; canst thou not suffer whatsoever it be; and, as a Child of Freedom, though outcast, trample Tophet itself under thy feet, while it consumes thee? Let it come, then; I will meet it and defy it!' And as I so thought, there rushed like a stream of fire over my whole soul; and I shook base Fear away from me forever ...

"Thus had the Everlasting No pealed authoritatively through all the recesses of my being, of my Me; and then was it that my whole Me stood up, in native God-created majesty, and recorded its Protest. Such a Protest, the most important transaction in life, may that same Indignation and Defiance, in a psychological point of view, be fitly called. The Everlasting No had said: 'Behold, thou art fatherless, outcast, and the Universe is mine;' to which my whole Me now made answer: 'I am not thine, but Free, and forever hate thee!' From that hour," Teufelsdröckh-Carlyle adds, "I began to be a man."

And our poor friend, James Thomason, similarly writes:—

"Who is most wretched in this dolorous place?
I think myself; yet I would rather be
My miserable self than He, than He
Who formed such creatures to his own disgrace.

The vilest thing must be less vile than Thou
From whom it had its being, God and Lord!
Creator of all woe and sin! abhorred,
Malignant and implacable! I vow

That not for all Thy power furled and unfurled,
For all the temples to Thy glory built,
Would I assume the ignominious guilt
Of having made such men in such a world."

We are familiar enough in this community with the spectacle of persons exulting in their emancipation from belief in the God of their ancestral Calvinism,—him who made the garden and the serpent, and pre-appointed the eternal fires of hell. Some of them have found humaner gods to worship, others are simply converts from all theology; but, both alike, they assure us that to have got rid of the sophistication of thinking they could feel any reverence or duty toward that impossible idol gave a tremendous happiness to their souls. Now, to make an idol of the spirit of nature, and worship it, also leads to sophistication; and in souls that are religious and would also be scientific the sophistication breeds a philosophical melancholy, from which the first natural step of escape is the denial of the idol; and with the downfall of the idol, whatever lack of positive joyousness may remain, there comes also the downfall of the whimpering and cowering mood. With evil simply taken as such, men can make short work, for their relations with it then are only practical. It looms up no longer so spectrally, it loses all its haunting and perplexing significance, as soon as the mind attacks the instances of it singly, and ceases to worry about their derivation from the 'one and only Power.'

Here, then, on this stage of mere emancipation from monistic superstition, the would-be suicide may already get encouraging answers to his question about the worth of life. There are in most men instinctive springs of vitality that respond healthily when the burden of metaphysical and infinite responsibility rolls off. The certainty that you now may step out of life whenever you please, and that to do so is not blasphemous or monstrous, is itself an immense relief. The thought of suicide is now no longer a guilty challenge and obsession.

"This little life is all we must endure;
The grave's most holy peace is ever sure,"—

says Thomson; adding, "I ponder these thoughts, and they comfort me." Meanwhile we can always stand it for twenty-four hours longer, if only to see what to-morrow's newspaper will contain, or what the next postman will bring.

But far deeper forces than this mere vital curiosity are arousable, even in the pessimistically-tending mind; for where the loving and admiring impulses are dead, the hating and fighting impulses will still respond to fit appeals. This evil which we feel so deeply is something that we can also help to overthrow; for its sources, now that no 'Substance' or 'Spirit' is behind them, are finite, and we can deal with each of them in turn. It is, indeed, a remarkable fact that sufferings and hardships do not, as a rule, abate the love of life; they seem, on the contrary, usually to give it a keener zest. The sovereign source of melancholy is repletion. Need and struggle are what excite and inspire us; our hour of triumph is what brings the void. Not the Jews of the captivity, but those of the days of Solomon's glory are those from whom the pessimistic utterances in our Bible come. Germany, when she lay trampled beneath the hoofs of Bonaparte's troopers, produced perhaps the most optimistic and idealistic literature that the world has seen; and not till the French 'milliards' were distributed after 1871 did pessimism overrun the country in the shape in which we see it there to-day. The history of our own race is one long commentary on the cheerfulness that comes with fighting ills. Or take the Waldenses, of whom I lately have been reading, as examples of what strong men will endure. In 1485 a papal bull of Innocent VIII. enjoined their extermination. It absolved those who should take up the crusade against them from all ecclesiastical pains and penalties, released them from any oath, legitimized their title to all property which they might have illegally acquired, and promised remission of sins to all who should kill the heretics.

"There is no town in Piedmont," says a Vaudois writer, "where some of our brethren have not been put to death. Jordan Terbano was burnt alive at Susa; Hippolite Rossiero at Turin; Michael Goneto, an octogenarian, at Sarcena; Vilermin Ambrosio hanged on the Col di Meano; Hugo Chiambs, of Fenestrelle, had his entrails torn from his living body at Turin; Peter Geymarali of Bobbio in like manner had his entrails taken out in Lucerna, and a fierce cat thrust in their place to torture him further; Maria Romano was buried alive at Rocca Patia; Magdalena Fauno underwent the same fate at San Giovanni; Susanna Michelini was bound hand and foot, and left to perish of cold and hunger on the snow at Sarcena: Bartolomeo Fache, gashed with sabres, had the wounds filled up with quicklime, and perished thus in agony at Fenile; Daniel Michelini had his tongue torn out at Bobbo for having praised God; James Baridari perished covered with sulphurous matches which had been forced into his flesh under the nails, between the fingers, in the nostrils, in the lips, and all over the body, and then lighted; Daniel Rovelli had his mouth filled with gunpowder, which, being lighted, blew his head to pieces; ... Sara Rostignol was slit open from the legs to the bosom, and left so to perish on the road between Eyral and Lucerna; Anna Charbonnier was impaled, and carried thus on a pike from San Giovanni to La Toree."[1]

Und dergleichen mehr! In 1630 the plague swept away one-half of the Vaudois population, including fifteen of their seventeen pastors. The places of these were supplied from Geneva and Dauphiny, and the whole Vaudois people learned French in order to follow their services. More than once their number fell, by unremitting persecution, from the normal standard of twenty-five thousand to about four thousand. In 1686 the Duke of Savoy ordered the three thousand that remained to give up their faith or leave the country. Refusing, they fought the French and Piedmontese armies till only eighty of their fighting men remained alive or uncaptured, when they gave up, and were sent in a body to Switzerland. But in 1689, encouraged by William Of Orange and led by one of their pastor-captains, between eight hundred and nine hundred of them returned to conquer their old homes again. They fought their way to Bobi, reduced to four hundred men in the first half year, and met every force sent against them; until at last the Duke of Savoy, giving up his alliance with that abomination of desolation, Louis XIV, restored them to comparative freedom,—since which time they have increased and multiplied in their barren Alpine valleys to this day.

What are our woes and sufferance compared with these? Does not the recital of such a fight so obstinately waged against such odds fill us with resolution against our petty powers of darkness,—machine politicians, spoilsmen, and the rest? Life is worth living, no matter what it bring, if only such combats may be carried to successful terminations and one's heel set on the tyrant's throat. To the suicide, then, in his supposed world of multifarious and immoral nature, you can appeal—and appeal in the name of the very evils that make his heart sick there—to wait and see *his* part of the battle out. And the

---

1. Quoted by George E. Waring in his book on Tyrol. Compare A. Berard: Les Vaudois, Lyon, Storck, 1892.

consent to live on, which you ask of him under these circumstances, is not the sophistical 'resignation' which devotees of cowering religions preach: it is not resignation in the sense of licking a despotic Deity's hand. It is, on the contrary, a resignation based on man-liness and pride. So long as your would-be suicide leaves an evil of his own unremedied, so long he has strictly no concern with evil in the abstract and at large. The submission which you demand of yourself to the general fact of evil in the world, your apparent acquiescence in it, is here nothing but the conviction that evil at large is *none of your busi-ness* until your business with your private particular evils is liquidated and settled up. A challenge of this sort, with proper designation of detail, is one that need only be made to be accepted by men whose normal instincts are not decayed; and your reflective would-be suicide may easily be moved by it to face life with a certain interest again. The senti-ment of honor is a very penetrating thing. When you and I, for instance, realize how many innocent beasts have had to suffer in cattle-cars and slaughter-pens and lay down their lives that we might grow up, all fattened and clad, to sit together here in comfort and carry on this discourse, it does, indeed, put our relation to the universe in a more solemn light. "Does not," as a young Amherst philosopher (Xenos Clark, now dead) once wrote, "the acceptance of a happy life upon such terms involve a point of honor?" Are we not bound to take some suffering upon ourselves, to do some self-denying service with our lives, in return for all those lives upon which ours are built? To hear this question is to answer it in but one possible way, if one have a normally constituted heart.

Thus, then, we see that mere instinctive curiosity, pugnacity, and honor may make life on a purely naturalistic basis seem worth living from day to day to men who have cast away all metaphysics in order to get rid of hypochondria, but who are resolved to owe nothing as yet to religion and its more positive gifts. A poor half-way stage, some of you may be inclined to say; but at least you must grant it to be an honest stage; and no man should dare to speak meanly of these instincts which are our nature's best equipment, and to which religion herself must in the last resort address her own peculiar appeals.

IV

And now, in turning to what religion may have to say to the question, I come to what is the soul of my discourse. Religion has meant many things in human history; but when from now onward I use the word I mean to use it in the supernaturalist sense, as declar-ing that the so-called order of nature, which constitutes this world's experience, is only one portion of the total universe, and that there stretches beyond this visible world an unseen world of which we now know nothing positive, but in its relation to which the true significance of our present mundane life consists. A man's religious faith (whatever more special items of doctrine it may involve) means for me essentially his faith in the existence of an unseen order of some kind in which the riddles of the natural order may be found explained. In the more developed religions the natural world has always been regarded as the mere scaffolding or vestibule of a truer, more eternal world, and affirmed to be a sphere of education, trial, or redemption. In these religions, one must in some fashion die to the natural life before one can enter into life eternal. The notion that this physical world of wind and water, where the sun rises and the moon sets, is absolutely and ultimately the divinely aimed-at and established thing, is one which we find only in very early religions, such as that of the most primitive Jews. It is this natural religion (primitive still, in spite of the fact that poets and men of science whose good-will exceeds their perspicacity keep publishing it in new editions tuned to our contemporary ears) that, as I said a while ago, has suffered definitive bankruptcy in the opinion of a circle of persons, among whom I must count myself, and who are growing more numerous every day. For such persons the physical order of nature, taken simply as science knows it, cannot be held to reveal any one harmonious spiritual intent. It is mere *weather*, as Chauncey Wright called it, doing and undoing without end.

Now, I wish to make you feel, if I can in the short remainder of this hour, that we have a right to believe the physical order to be only a partial order; that we have a right to supplement it by an unseen spiritual order which we assume on trust, if only thereby life may seem to us better worth living again. But as such a trust will seem to some of you sadly mystical and execrably unscientific, I must first say a word or two to weaken the veto which you may consider that science opposes to our act.

There is included in human nature an ingrained naturalism and materialism of mind which can only admit facts that are actually tangible. Of this sort of mind the entity called 'science' is the idol. Fondness for the word 'scientist' is one of the notes by which you may know its votaries; and its short way of killing any opinion that it disbelieves in is to call it 'unscientific.' It must be granted that there is no slight excuse for this. Science has made such glorious leaps in the last three hundred years, and extended our knowledge of nature so enormously both in general and in detail; men of science, moreover, have as a class displayed such admirable virtues,—that it is no wonder if the worshippers of science lose their head. In this very University, accordingly, I have heard more than one teacher say that all the fundamental conceptions of truth have already been found by science, and that the future has only the details of the picture to fill in. But the slightest reflection on the real conditions will suffice to show how barbaric such notions are. They show such a lack of scientific imagination, that it is hard to see how one who is actively advancing any part of science can make a mistake so crude. Think how many absolutely new scientific conceptions have arisen in our own generation, how many new problems have been formulated that were never thought of before, and then cast an eye upon the brevity of science's career. It began with Galileo, not three hundred years ago. Four thinkers since Galileo, each informing his successor of what discoveries his own lifetime had seen achieved, might have passed the torch of science into our hands as we sit here in this room. Indeed, for the matter of that, an audience much smaller than the present one, an audience of some five or six score people, if each person in it could speak for his own generation, would carry us away to the black unknown of the human species, to days without a document or monument to tell their tale. Is it credible that such a mushroom knowledge, such a growth overnight as this, *can* represent more than the minutest glimpse of what the universe will really prove to be when adequately understood? No! our science is a drop, our ignorance a sea. Whatever else be certain, this at least is certain,—that the world of our present natural knowledge *is* enveloped in a larger world of *some* sort of whose residual properties we at present can frame no positive idea.

Agnostic positivism, of course, admits this principle theoretically in the most cordial terms, but insists that we must not turn it to any practical use. We have no right, this doctrine tells us, to dream dreams, or suppose anything about the unseen part of the universe, merely because to do so may be for what we are pleased to call our highest interests. We must always wait for sensible evidence for our beliefs; and where such evidence is inaccessible we must frame no hypotheses whatever. Of course this is a safe enough position in *abstracto*. If a thinker had no stake in the unknown, no vital needs, to live or languish according to what the unseen world contained, a philosophic neutrality and refusal to believe either one way or the other would be his wisest cue. But, unfortunately, neutrality is not only inwardly difficult, it is also outwardly unrealizable, where our relations to an alternative are practical and vital. This is because, as the psychologists tell us, belief and doubt are living attitudes, and involve conduct on our part. Our only way, for example, of doubting, or refusing to believe, that a certain thing *is*, is continuing to act as if it were *not*. If, for instance, I refuse to believe that the room is getting cold, I leave the windows open and light no fire just as if it still were warm. If I doubt that you are worthy of my confidence, I keep you uninformed of all my secrets just as if you were unworthy of the same. If I doubt the need of insuring my house, I leave it uninsured as much as if I believed there were no need. And so if I must not believe that the world is divine, I can only express that refusal by declining ever to act distinctively as if it were so, which can only mean acting on certain critical occasions as if it were *not* so, or in an irreligious way. There are, you see, inevitable occasions in life when inaction is a kind of action, and must count as action, and when not to be for is to be practically against; and in all such cases strict and consistent neutrality is an unattainable thing.

And, after all, is not this duty of neutrality where only our inner interests would lead us to believe, the most ridiculous of commands? Is it not sheer dogmatic folly to say that our inner interests can have no real connection with the forces that the hidden world may contain? In other cases divinations based on inner interests have proved prophetic enough. Take science itself! Without an imperious inner demand on our part for ideal logical and mathematical harmonies, we should never have attained to proving that such harmonies lie hidden between all the chinks and interstices of the crude natural world. Hardly a law has been established in science, hardly a fact ascertained, which was not first sought after, often with sweat and blood, to gratify an inner need. Whence such needs come from we do not know: we find them in us, and biological psychology so far only classes them with Darwin's 'accidental variations.' But the inner need of believing that this world of nature is a sign of something more spiritual and eternal than itself is just as strong and authoritative in those who feel it, as the inner need of uniform laws of causation ever can be in a professionally scientific head. The toil of many generations has proved the latter need prophetic. Why *may* not the former one be prophetic, too? And if needs of ours outrun the visible universe, why *may* not that be a sign that an invisible universe is there? What, in short, has authority to debar us from trusting our religious demands? Science as such assuredly has no authority, for she can only say what is, not what is not; and the agnostic "thou shalt not believe without coercive sensible evidence" is simply an expression (free to any one to make) of private personal appetite for evidence of a certain peculiar kind.

Now, when I speak of trusting our religious demands, just what do I mean by 'trusting'? Is the word to carry with it license to define in detail an invisible world, and to anathematize and excommunicate those whose trust is different? Certainly not! Our faculties of belief were not primarily given us to make orthodoxies and heresies withal; they were given us to live by. And to trust our religious demands means first of all to live in the light of them, and to act as if the invisible world which they suggest were real. It is a fact of human nature, that men can live and die by the help of a sort of faith that goes without a single dogma or definition. The bare assurance that this natural order is not ultimate but a mere sign or vision, the external staging of a many-storied universe, in which spiritual forces have the last word and are eternal,—this bare assurance is to such men enough to make life seem worth living in spite of every contrary presumption suggested by its circumstances on the natural plane. Destroy this inner assurance, however, vague as it is, and all the light and radiance of existence is extinguished for these persons at a stroke. Often enough the wild-eyed look at life—the suicidal mood—will then set in.

And now the application comes directly home to you and me. Probably to almost every one of us here the most adverse life would seem well worth living, if we only could be *certain* that our bravery and patience with it were terminating and eventuating and bearing fruit somewhere in an unseen spiritual world. But granting we are not certain, does it then follow that a bare trust in such a world is a fool's paradise and lubberland, or rather that it is a living attitude in which we are free to indulge? Well, we are free to trust at our own risks anything that is not impossible, and that can bring analogies to bear in its behalf. That the world of physics is probably not absolute, all the converging multitude of arguments that make in favor of idealism tend to prove; and that our whole physical life may lie soaking in a spiritual atmosphere, a dimension of being that we at present have no organ for apprehending, is vividly suggested to us by the analogy of the life of our domestic animals. Our dogs, for example, are in our human life but not of it. They witness hourly the outward body of events whose inner meaning cannot, by any possible operation, be revealed to their intelligence,—events in which they themselves often play the cardinal part. My terrier bites a teasing boy, for example, and the father demands damages. The dog may be present at every step of the negotiations, and see the money paid, without an inkling of what it all means, without a suspicion that it has anything to do with *him*; and he never *can* know in his natural dog's life. Or take another case which used greatly to impress me in my medical-student days. Consider a poor dog whom they are vivisecting in a laboratory. He lies strapped on a board and shrieking at his executioners, and to his own dark consciousness is literally in a sort of hell. He cannot see a single redeeming ray in the whole business; and yet all these diabolical-seeming events are often controlled by human intentions with which, if his poor benighted mind could only be made to catch a glimpse of them, all that is heroic in him would religiously acquiesce. Healing truth, relief to future sufferings of beast and man, are to be bought by them. It may be genuinely a process of redemption. Lying on his back on the board there he may be performing a function incalculably higher than any that prosperous canine life admits of; and yet, of the whole performance, this function is the one portion that must remain absolutely beyond his ken.

Now turn from this to the life of man. In the dog's life we see the world invisible to him because we live in both worlds. In human life, although we only see our world, and his within it, yet encompassing both these worlds a still wider world may be there, as unseen by us as our world is by him; and to believe in that world *may* be the most essential function that our lives in this world have to perform. But "*may* be! *may* be!" One now hears the positivist contemptuously exclaim; "what use can a scientific life have for maybes?" Well, I reply, the 'scientific' life itself has much to do with maybes, and human life at large has everything to do with them. So far as man stands for anything, and is productive or originative at all, his entire vital function may be said to have to deal with maybes. Not a victory is gained, not a deed of faithfulness or courage is done, except upon a maybe; not a service, not a sally of generosity, not a scientific exploration or experiment or textbook, that may not be a mistake. It is only by risking ours persons from one hour to another that we live at all. And often enough our faith beforehand in an uncertified result *is the only thing that makes the result come true.* Suppose, for instance, that you are climbing a mountain, and have worked yourself into a position from which the only escape is by a terrible leap. Have faith that you can successfully make it, and your feet are nerved to its accomplishment. But mistrust yourself, and think of all the sweet things you have heard the scientists say of *maybes*, and you will hesitate so long that, at last, all unstrung and trembling, and launching yourself in a moment of despair, you roll in the abyss. In such a case (and it belongs to an enormous class), the part of wisdom as well as of courage is to *believe what is in the line of your needs*, for only by such belief is the need fulfilled. Refuse to believe, and you shall indeed be right, for you shall irretrievably perish. But believe, and again you shall be right, for you shall save yourself. You make one or the other of two possible universes true by your trust or mistrust,—both universes having been only *maybes*, in this particular, before you contributed your act.

Now, it appears to me that the question whether life is worth living is subject to conditions logically much like these. It does, indeed, depend on you the liver. If you surrender to the nightmare view and crown the evil edifice by your own suicide, you have indeed made a picture totally black. Pessimism, completed by your act, is true beyond a doubt, so far as your world goes. Your mistrust of life has removed whatever worth your own enduring existence might have given to it; and now, throughout the whole sphere of possible influence of that existence, the mistrust has proved itself to have had divining power. But suppose, on the other hand, that instead of giving way to the nightmare view you cling to it that this world is not the *ultimatum*. Suppose you find yourself a very well-spring, as Wordsworth says, of—

"Zeal, and the virtue to exist by faith
As soldiers live by courage; as, by strength
Of heart, the sailor fights with roaring seas."

Suppose, however thickly evils crowd upon you, that your unconquerable subjectivity proves to be their match, and that you find a more wonderful joy than any passive pleasure can bring in trusting ever in the larger whole. Have you not now made life worth living on these terms? What sort of a thing would life really be, with your qualities ready for a tussle with it, if it only brought fair weather and gave these higher faculties of yours no scope? Please remember that optimism and pessimism are definitions of the world, and that our own reactions on the world, small as they are in bulk, are integral parts of the whole thing, and necessarily help to determine the definition. They may even be the decisive elements in determining the definition. A large mass can have its unstable equilibrium overturned by the addition of a feather's weight; a long phrase may have its sense reversed by the addition of the three letters *n-o-t*. This life is worth living, we can say, *since it is what we make it, from the moral point of view;* and we are determined to make it from that point of view, so far as we have anything to do with it, a success.

Now, in this description of faiths that verify themselves I have assumed that our faith in an invisible order is what inspires those efforts and that patience which make this visible order good for moral men. Our faith in the seen world's goodness (goodness now meaning fitness for successful moral and religious life) has verified itself by leaning on our faith in the unseen world. But will our faith in the unseen world similarly verify itself? Who knows?

Once more it is a case of *maybe*; and once more *maybes* are the essence of the situation. I confess that I do not see why the very existence of an invisible world may not in part depend on the personal response which any one of us may make to the religious appeal. God himself, in short, may draw vital strength and increase of very being from our fidelity. For my own part, I do not know what the sweat and blood and tragedy of this life mean, if they mean anything short of this. If this life be not a real fight, in which something is eternally gained for the universe by success, it is no better than a game of private theatricals from which one may withdraw at will. But it *feels* like a real fight,—as if there were something really wild in the universe which we, with all our idealities and faithfulness, are needed to redeem; and first of all to redeem our own hearts from atheisms and fears. For such a half-wild, half-saved universe our nature is adapted. The deepest thing in our nature is this *Binnenleben* (as a German doctor lately has called it), this dumb region of the heart in which we dwell alone with our willingness and unwillingness, our faiths and fears. As through the cracks and crannies of caverns those waters exude from the earth's bosom which then form the fountain-heads of springs, so in these crepuscular depths of personality the sources of all our outer deeds and decisions take their rise. Here is our deepest organ of communication with the nature of things; and compared with these concrete movements of our soul all abstract statements and scientific arguments—the veto, for example, which the strict positivist pronounces upon our faith—sound to us like mere chatterings of the teeth. For here possibilities, not finished facts, are the realities with which we have actively to deal; and to quote my friend William Salter, of the Philadelphia Ethical Society, "as the essence of courage is to stake one's life on a possibility, so the essence of faith is to believe that the possibility exists."

These, then, are my last words to you: Be not afraid of life. Believe that life is worth living, and your belief will help create the fact. The 'scientific proof' that you are right may not be clear before the day of judgment (or some stage of being which that expression may serve to symbolize) is reached. But the faithful fighters of this hour, or the beings that then and there will represent them, may then turn to the faint-hearted, who here decline to go on, with words like those with which Henry IV. greeted the tardy Crillon after a great victory had been gained: "Hang yourself, brave Crillon! we fought at Arques, and you were not there."

AN ANNOTATED BIBLIOGRAPHY ON WILLIAM JAMES'S

THE VARIETIES OF RELIGIOUS EXPERIENCE,

WITH A LIST OF ENGLISH-LANGUAGE EDITIONS, AUDIO RECORDINGS, AND TRANSLATIONS

DAVID M. WULFF

A. English-language editions

1902 Longmans, Green: New York, London, and Bombay (xii + 534 pages). The first edition is dated June, 1902. The second, slightly revised edition, dated August, 1902, incorporated seven minor plate changes; a few additional minor changes were made in subsequent printings. The final, thirty-eighth printing by Longmans, Green was published in 1935. Unless otherwise indicated, the editions listed below are reprintings of the text of the Longmans, Green edition as it stood at the time of James's death in 1910.

1936 Modern Library (Random House): New York (xviii + 526 pages). ("1994 Modern Library edition": xxi + 582 pages)

1958 Mentor (New American Library/Dutton Signet): New York (444 pages). Foreword by Jacques Barzun.

196-? Dolphin (Doubleday): Garden City, N.Y. (478 pages).

1960 The Fontana Library (Collins): London and Glasgow (508 pages). With an introduction by Arthur Darby Nock.

1961 Collier (Macmillan): New York (416 pages). With an introduction by Reinhold Niebuhr.

1963 University Books: New Hyde Park, N.Y. (xlii + 626 pages). With an introduction by Joseph Ratner and ten appendices of related writings by James. The text of *The Varieties* is a photo-reproduction of the Longmans, Green edition and follows the original pagination.

1978 Image Books: New York (516 pages)

1982 Penguin: New York (xlii + 534 pages). Edited and with an introduction by Martin E. Marty. A photo-reproduction of the Longmans, Green edition.

1985 Harvard University Press: Cambridge (li + 669 pages). The definitive edition of *The Varieties* and a volume in *The Works of William James,* with an introduction by John E. Smith and 216 pages of supplementary material consisting of the following: (1) notes on the text of *The Varieties,* which encompasses pages 11-414 of this edition; (2) appendixes of notes, drafts, and letters pertaining to *The Varieties;* (3) a note on the editiorial method used in preparing *The Works;* (4) a history of the preparation of James's Gifford Lectures, an account of their printing, a description of the manuscript printer's copy for Lecture XIX and part of Lecture XX, a discussion of the oral delivery of these two lectures, and remarks on the problems of editing this edition of *The Varieties;* (5) a record of the emendations made in this edition to the copy-text (the first 1902 printing); (6) a list of the variant readings that differ from the edited text in the authoritative documents recorded for the book; (7) a record of all alterations James made during the writing and revising of the manuscript; and (8) a note on word-division.

1987 Literary Classics of the United States: New York. In William James, *Writings, 1902-1910* (pages 3-477), with a chronology and notes on the text by Bruce Kuklick. *A* reprinting of the original, June, 1902, edition that incorporates all of the changes indicated in James's annotated copy but not the numerous additional corrections of the Harvard University Press edition.

1990 Vintage Books/Library of America: New York. With an introduction by Jaroslav Pelikan (xviii + 517 pages).

1991 Triumph Books: New York (406 pages). With an introduction by Eugene Kennedy.

1992 Classics of Psychiatry & Behavioral Sciences Library (Gryphon Editions): Birmingham, Alabama (xii + 534 pages). A leather-bound and gold-stamped photo-reproduction of the revised, August, 1902, edition "privately printed for the members of the Classics of Psychiatry & Behavioral Sciences Library."

1992 Notable American Authors Series. Reprint Services Corporation: Irvine, California. (Reprint of 1902 edition.)

B. Audio recordings

1975 Halvorson Dixit: [U.S.]. 14 cassettes.

1990 Audio Scholars: Mendocino, California. 2 cassettes (abridged recording); read by Eric Bauersfeld.

1992 Audio Book Contractors: Washington, D.C. 12 cassettes.

C. Translations

Although the following list of translations was made as inclusive as possible, it should not be taken as exhaustive, especially of non-European translations. Reprintings of translations are noted only if they contain substantial changes. It should be noted that translations of *The Varieties* were commonly abridged.

Czech
Druhy náboženské zkušenosti. Translated by Josef Hrusa. Prague: Melantrich A.S., 1930.

Danish
Religiøse Erfaringer; en Undersøgelse af den menneskelige Natur. An abridged edition translated by Edv. Lehmann and Christine Mønster, with a foreword by Harald Høffding. Copenhagen: V. Pio, 1906. Second, revised, and enlarged edition, 1911.
Religiøse Erfaringer. A revised translation by Thomas Hee Andersen with Høffding's foreword and a new introduction by Villiam Grønbaek. Copenhagen: Jespersen & Pio, 1963.

Dutch
Varianten van religieuze beleving; Een onderzoek naar de menselijke aard. Translated by J. Dutric, with an introduction by G. J. Overduin. Zeist: De Haan; Arnhem: van Loghum Slaterus; Antwerpen: Standaard Boekhandel, 1963.

French
L'experience religieuse; essai de psychologie descriptive. Translated by Frank Abauzit, with a preface by Emile Boutroux. Paris: Felix Alcan, 1906. Second, revised and corrected edition, 1908. Third, revised and corrected edition, 1931.

German
Die religiöse Erfahrung in ihrer Mannigfaltigkeit: Materialien und Studien zu einer Psychologie und Pathologie des religiösen Lebens. Translated and introduced by Georg Wobbermin.

Leipzig: J. C. Hinrichs, 1907. Second, improved edition, with revised introduction, 1914.

Die Vielfalt religiöser Erfahrung; Eine Studie über die menschliche Natur. Translated, edited, and provided with an afterword by Eilert Herms. Olten: Walter-Verlag, 1979. Bookclub edition: Zurich: Buchclub Ex Libris, 1982.

Hebrew
ha-Havayah ha-datit le-sugeha: mehkar be-teva'ha-adam. Translated by Yaakov Koplivits, with an introduction by P. Tiberger and edited by Y. Even-Shemuel. Jerusalem: Mosad Bialik, 709 [1948 or 1949].

Italian
Le varie forme dela coscienza religiosa; studio sulla natura umano. Translated by G. C. Ferrari and M. Calderoni, with a preface by Roberto Ardigo. Torino: Fratelli Bocca, 1904. Second edition: Milan: Fratelli Bocca, 1945.

Norwegian
Religiøs røynsle i sine ymse former; ein etterrøknad ym mannanaturi. Translated by Ola Raknes. Oslo: Norske samleget, 1920.

Persian
Dīn va ravān. Translated by Mahdi Quimi. Qum: Dar al-Fikr, 1359 [1980 or 1981].

Polish
Dóswiadczenia religijne. Translated and introduced by Jan Hempel; translation checked by Rafaf Radziwillowicz. Warsaw: Gebethnera i Wolffa, 1918. Second edition, with a new introduction by Andrzej Nowicki: Warsaw: Ksiazka i Wiedza, 1958.

Russian
Mnogoobrazie religioznago opyta. Translated by V. G. Malakhievoi-Mirovich and M. V. Shik, and edited by S. V. Lur'e. Moscow: Izd. zhurnala "Russkaia mysl'," 1910.

Spanish
Fases del sentimiento religioso; estudio sobre la naturaleza humano (3 vols.). Translated by Miguel Domenga Mir. Barcelona: Carbonell y Esteva, 1907-1908.

Swedish
Den religiösa erfarenheten i dess skilda former. Translated by Ivar Norberg. Stockholm: P. A. Norstedt & Söners, 1906. Reprinted in 1956, with a new introduction by Erland Ehnmark (Stockholm: Svenska Bokförlaget Norstedts), and in 1974, with a revised translation by Karl Hylander and introductions by Hans Akerberg and Erland Ehnmark (Lund: Studentlitteratur, 1974).

D. Reviews
Berle, A.A.
1903 The Psychology of Christian Experience. *BibliothecaSacra* 60:1-27.
James's reckless reliance on self-descriptions of religious experience, some written years after the event, is one of the worst cases of the credulity of science the reviewer has ever known. Moreover, all efforts at classification in the area of spiritual experience are grotesque and unreal, for as Jesus demonstrates, communion with God is

above such process. Finally, James's insistence that conversion, if it genuinely represents transformation, ought to be reflected in some perceptible radiance, recalls those who thumbed their noses at Christ on Calvary. And even while graciously conceding that the vast majority of Christian converts do show changed lives, James maintains that the same results may be secured through the agency of demons or Alexander Dowie's Zionism. If James can be so manifestly wrong in the region of ordinary religious discipline we have the soundest reason for distrusting all the rest.

Bishop, W. S.
1902 Religion within the bounds of strict psychology. *The Sewanee Review* 10:493-497.
As a pyschological work accenting the subjective side of religion, *The Varieties* is both suggestive and illuminating—in large measure because of the author's powers of acute analysis and brilliant exposition. As a work that does not pretend, on the other hand, to contribute to theological knowledge, it offers little to religious faith. Yet in allowing his sources to speak of their experience in their own words, James provides a valuable mass of testimony to the power of religious belief on the human heart.

Boutroux, Émile
1908 William James et l'expérience religieuse. *Revue de Metaphysique et de Morale* 16: 1-27.
Of the manifestations of the contemporary mystical spirit that seeks the inspiration of living reality without the constraints of tradition, the finest is the doctrine of religious experience put forth by the learned psychologist and profound thinker William James. For James, religious experience is just as useful and authentic as scientific experience. It is even more immediate, concrete, extensive, and deep. Furthermore, it is presupposed by scientific experience. Thanks to the psychological theory of the subconscious, religious experience is also a point of support in science itself. It develops in the same way as science and is in harmony with it.

Coe, Goerge Albert
1903 [Review of *The Varieties*]. *Philosophical Review* 12:62-67.
In this exceedingly varied and richly detailed work, which is filled with suggestive opinions and penetrating insights, one great idea stands out: religion resides among our vital functions. That the work attains this trustworthy conclusion—the treatment of which constitutes a distinctive and permanent contribution to the psychology of religion—testifies to the fact that James comes to view religion from a much broader perspective than he establishes at the outset of this work. Morbid growths nevertheless remain prominent, and there is a corresponding failure properly to recognize religion as a universal human phenomenon. A large task remains for the projected volume on the philosophy of religion.

Delacroix, Henri
1903 Les variétés de l'experience religieuse par William James. *Revue de Metaphysique et de Morale* 11:642-669.
This beautiful work, which serves with others to reintegrate the study of religion into the study of human nature, cannot easily be summarized; the richness of its documentaiton, the character of its bold and positive method, the acuteness of observation, the breadth of views laid out—all elude analysis. Although James describes the infinite nuances of his subject matter with remarkable virtuosity and sympathy, it must be added that the religious experience he studies, derived as it is from biography, autobiography, and questionnaires, is at bottom a very limited and

modern one. Nowhere is the historical question addressed. Furthermore, his somewhat obscure thesis that religion has its origin in the individual affective life underestimates the role in the shaping of religious tradition of intelligence as it confronts the external world.

Flournoy, Theodore
1902 [Review of *The Varieties*]. *Revue Philosophique* 54:516-527. Reprinted in *The Philosophy of William James*, 217-244, by T. Flournoy and translated by E. B. Holt and W. James, Jr. New York: Henry Holt, 1917.

In this masterly work written by a keen psychologist and an extraordinarily original philosopher, the realm of religious experience receives at last the consideration it deserves. As one reads this empirical and pragmatic work, every page of which testifies to the rare temper of the author's mind, one does not know whether to praise James more for the breadth and richness of his knowledge or for the admirable openness that allows him to understand and appreciate the diverse manifestations of the religious life.

Gardner, P.
1902 [Review of *The Varieties*]. *Hibbert Journal* 1:182-187.

If imperfect or perverted reasoning have many times led the author astray, *The Varieties* must nevertheless be praised for its wonderfully sympathetic appreciation of all possible forms of religious experience. It is the most valuable contribution yet to the psychology of religion.

Gorsuch, Richard, and Bernard Spilka
1987 Retrospective review: *The Varieties* in historical and contemporary contexts. *Contemporary Psychology* 32:773-778.

The importance of *The Varieties* lies in its being a social document that represents the values and feelings of a broad spectrum of Americans. James actually contributed very few new ideas to the psychology of religion, but instead referenced other scientists for his most basic distinctions. He selected his cases from other researchers simply to show the principles he believed had already been established by contemporary nomothetic science. His use of his contemporaries' data lacks the tables and statistical analyses that were already typical of the psychology of religion in his day. Although many of James's terms and conclusions have been widely influential in psychology, it is his concern with integrating his philosophy with the psychology of religion that has made his work most successful. It has also been influential in demonstrating the possibility of approaching religion objectively from both psychological and philosophical perspectives.

Hay, David
1985 Re-review: William James's *The varieties of religious experience*. *The Modern Churchman* NS27(2):45-49.

More than eighty years after it was written, *The Varieties* remains the most widely respected account of religious experience in the English language. In spite of certain shortcomings, notably the conflation of an extraordinarily wide range of religious testimony in the notion of the saving experience and the neglect of the social dimension of religion, *The Varieties* is still a riveting book to read. Many of James's claims for religious experience have today a greater plausibility than at almost any other time in this century.

Hibben, John
1903 {Review of *The Varieties*]. *Psychological Review* 10:180-186.

In largely restricting this inductive study of *The Varieties* of religious experience to the extreme cases, James overlooks the commonplace experiences that together form a stream of influence conserving and promoting all forms of social good. Moreover, it is only in the light of these ordinary experiences that the abnormal can be adequately evaluated. Problematical, too, is James's hypothesis of the subliminal region, for this unkown sphere may as likely be a source of delusion as of the divine. While these and many other conceptions will provoke differences of opinion, the work wil undoubtedly prove a valuable and permanent contribution to our understanding of religious experience and human nature.

Leuba, James Henry
1904 Professor William James's interpretation of religious experience. *International Journal of Ethics* 14:322-339.

In many respects a marvelous book, *The Varieties* is not a systematic treatise on the religious life but a further step in the author's preparation of a system of Pluralistic Idealism. James surveys only those religious phenomena—conversion and mystical experiences—that promise support for the notion that the universe is in fact a multiverse of spiritual beings. With remarkable skill, he fills the book with imaginary shadows of spirit-agents, transforming even simple, natural things into mysterious happenings. James is certainly right in claiming that the subjective aspects of mystical experiences are absolutely authoritative and hence cannot be denied; but all inferences about the origins of these experiences are surely amenable to the criticisms of rational consciousness. Whereas *The Varieties* is filled with testimony that may seem to the uncritical reader to support the notion of spiritual intervention, the work provides no empirical evidence whatsoever for this hypothesis. Most if not all of the striking phenomena that have supported popular faith in spiritism have today been made intelligible by psychology, bringing them into conformity with the rest of our empirical knowledge.

Margreth, Jakob
1909 Amerikanische Religionspsychologie, in ihrer Grundlage geprüft. *Der Katholik; Zeitschrift für katholische Wissenschaft und kirchliches Leben* 40:223-229.

In scarcely any other work known to the reviewer are fundamental questions taken so lightly as by James. This pragmatic and fundamentally anti-intellectual work is so flawed, in fact, that it would be a waste of time to review its contents. It may be noted, however, that like many others working in this field, James possesses only a fragmentary knowledge of the Catholic mystics. The great systematizers of asceticism and mysticism are sparsely represented; moreover, James neglects the rich ecclesiastical material that would have taught him much about the concept of holiness, which he badly understands, and the difference between true and false mystics. In any case, the essence of religion is not accessible to empirical and experimental means.

Muirhead, J. H.
1903 Professor William James's philosophy of religion. *International Journal of Ethics* 13:236-246.

In terms of sympathy, erudition, psychological address, and analytical insight, no other living writer was better qualified than James for the task he undertook. The chapters on saintliness in particular are a model of all that a psychological discussion engaged with the highest object should be—full, sympathetic, sane, convincing, abounding in practical suggestiveness. Hardly less striking, however, are this work's defects as a contribution to philosophy. While James seems in some of his declarations to affirm the idealist position, his misrepresentation of it raises doubts that he understands the idealist contention regarding the implications of experience. And his effort to rest religious faith on the results of psychical research fails, for the relatively undifferentiated Subliminal cannot be substituted for the Sublime.

Oesterreich, K.
1908 [Review of the German translation of *The Varieties*]. *Kantstudien* 13:474-478.
In its working through of a comprehensive and widely drawn collection of self-reported testimonies on religious states and especially in its delineation of specific religious types, *The Varieties* has become a standard work in the psychology of religion. Whereas this very good translation of James's work will allow it to receive in Germany the attention it deserves, the absence of any indication of the condensations and omissions makes problematical the use of the translation in the place of the original.

Ostwald, Wilhelm
1903 [Review of *The Varieties*]. *Annalen der Naturphilosophie* 2:142-143.
Drawing on exceptionally rich and variegated observation material taken from the most diverse sources, James provides us with an unusually fascinating and valuable essay on the collective psyche. It is "interesting" in the best sense of the word.

Rashdall, H.
1903 [Review of *The Varieties*]. *Mind* 12:245-250.
As a piece of literature and psychological research, *The Varieties* is of the highest interest and of unquestionable vivacity and open-mindedness. But as a work of philosophy it is flimsy and superficial. James fails to consider how his conclusions regarding religion, notably his emphasis on feeling, are the result of his almost exclusive emphasis on abnormal experiences. He deliberately abandons the search for truth and hands religion and morality over to the sway of willful caprice. Many other minds require a relgious outlook that is grounded, rather, in reflective thought.

Runze, Georg
1904 [Review of *The Varieties*]. *Zeitschrift für Psychologie und Physiologie der Sinnesorgane* 37:129-143.
Certain expectations of *The Varieties*'s readers will be richly fulfilled: the clear style, the fresh and lively presentation, the richness of material, the wisely rendered judgments, and above all, the conjoining of the otherwise divergent themes of the affective-mystical and the practical-ethical as a postulate in a new philosophy of religion. On the other hand, those more exact thinkers who approach problems in the psychology of religion by means of rigorous research will be disappointed. The tangible results are slight and neither new nor unassailable. One finds little of the material one might expect from the book's promising title; rather, it is largely limited to a collection of materials for a pathology of religious aesthetics and affective mysticism.

Sewall, Frank
1903 Professor James on religious experience. *The New-Church Review* 10:243-264.

In maintaining that the religious character exists in either one of two extreme forms—acute fever or dull habit—James overlooks the genuine and perfectly normal form of religion that Swedenborg defines as the presence of God with man. A real religious experience bears no relation to the eccentricities of mind and conduct with which James entertains his readers. Given the impression that James looks upon religion as intrinsically pathological, we do not wonder that he left Swedenborg out of the ranks of religious geniuses. Certain of James's conclusions, however, accord with Swedenborg's views.

Starbuck, Edwin D.
1904 The varieties of religious experience. *The Biblical World* NS 24:100-111.
This masterful work, which exemplifies the author's rare ability to combine literary excellence and scientific accuracy, gives to the scientific study of religion a secure and dignified footing. In terms of analysis and inference, this empirical work leaves nothing to be desired. With respect to the selection of data, however, questions must be raised. The extreme examples that James preferred are impossible to interpret apart from systematic knowledge of the processes of ordinary experience, which may play a much larger role in determining the course of religious history. Moreover, in relying on the specialists in religion, James comes to position religion chiefly among the pheonomena of feeling. While he has performed a vast service in overthrowing the unwarranted claims of intellectualism in religious process, the feelings may themseves be by-products. Further analysis of James's cases would show the underlying life-movements to be the vital part of the experience. Such a reconception of the role of the feelings would leave intact and perhaps making more comprehensible the most original, profound, and far-reaching of James's conclusions—that the subconscious self is the fountainhead of religion.

Stevens, George B.
1903 [review of *The Varieties*]. *American Journal of Theology* 7:114-117.
James's quaint and witty characterizations of abnormal and bizarre manifestations of religious sentiment make *The Varieties* the most unconventional and raciest treatment of the philosophy of religion to date. His extremely brief conclusion that there is something there "other and larger than our conscious selves" constitutes the rather slim volume of dogma that the empiricist so far has to offer.

Troeltsch, Ernst
1904 [review of *The Varieties*]. *Deutsche Literaturzeitung* 25:3021-3027.
A well-known master of psychology, James possesses a genuine understanding of the intimate manifestations of religion. His *The Varieties* is a book of highest interest; it is original and clever, rich in facts and the sense of reality, and important in its treatment of the material. Were there room for critical remarks in this review, they would note, from the psychological perspective, the undervaluation of thought, will, and the ethical in religion as well as the neglect of the psychology of institutional religion. From the perspective of the theory of knowledge, attention would be given to the fundamental problems of rationalism and irrationalism and of general concepts and particular facts.

E. Articles, books, and book chapters
Adams, James Luther
1980 Letter from Friedrich von Hügel to William James. *Downside Review* 98(332):214-236.

In a letter discovered in Houghton Library by Adams, von Hugel acknowledges his indebtedness to James in the writing of his own *The Mystical Element in Religion* (1908), but he also notes his dissatisfaction with James's separation of religious experience from its institutional-historical contexts and from the analytic and speculative activity of the mind; with his favorable estimation of spiritualistic phenomena and experiences; and with his use of pragmatism for apprehending religious facts and experience. Adams places this letter in its context, explores James's emphasis on the private and personal, and otherwise notes the strengths and limitations of *The Varieties*.

Åkerberg, Hans
1972 The significance of William James's psychology of religion today. *Studia Theologica* 26:141-158.
  The continuing importance of James's *The Varieties* lies in its delimitation of the subject, religion; its description of the sick soul; its study of sudden conversion; and its treatment of mystical experience. A renewed study of *The Varieties* may open new research perspectives.
1980a William James och "The Varieties." Några princip-och metodlinjer. In *William James då och nu*, edited by Olof Pettersson and Hans Åkerberg, 11-21. Lund: Doxa.
  With its emphasis on the individual and on religious development, *The Varieties* not only succeeded in refuting the medical materialism of James's day but also established two corresponding fundamental trends in the psychology of religion.
1980b Dynamisk undervisning. En psykologisk analys av William James's religionspedagogiska metodik. In *William James då och nu*, edited by Olof Pettersson and Hans Åkerberg, 187-204.
  James's dynamic model of religious pedagogy provides a timeless method for all educational work and has the potential for stimulating scientific research on the personal qualities that make for successful teaching.

Alexander, Gary T.
1979 Psychological foundations of William James's theory of religious experience. *Journal of Religion* 59:421-434.
  Contrary to what Dittes asserts, James did draw upon some of his earlier psychological analyses in the writing of *The Varieties*. In particular, he makes explicit use of his general model of the stream and field of consciousness. James's investigation of religious experience provides a bridge from the descriptive, functional psychology of the *Principles* to his explorations into the nature of the universe and the individual's relation to it.
1980 William James, the sick soul, and the negative dimensions of consciousness: A partial critique of transpersonal psychology. *Journal of the American Academy of Religion* 48: 191-205.
  Although contemporary transpersonal psychologists place James's view of consciousness at the center of their tradition, James would likely characterize their optimistic notion of consciousness as a once-born or healthy-minded view. However attractive such a philosophy may be, James considers it inadequate, for it denies the essential reality of evil. Moreover, the transpersonal emphasis on the immediacy of experience and the efficacy of technique fails to take into account the substantive role that traditional religious beliefs have played in the development of the very spiritual psychologies that fascinate them. Most serious, from James's perspective, is the failure of the transpersonal view to address critically its implicit metaphysic,

leading to a confusion of the study of consciousness with the experience of consciousness, a critical issue for the relation between psychology and the religious consciousness. James himself never confused the essentially descriptive task of psychology with the normative analysis of philosophy. Transpersonal psychology runs the risk of functioning as a religious perspective in itself and thus forfeiting its claim to being a science.

Allen, Gay Wilson
1965 James's *The varieties of religious experience* as introduction to American Transcendentalism. *Emerson Society Quarterly* No. 39:81-85.
James's *The Varieties* proves to be the best book for conveying the spirit of the American Transcendentalist movement. Although not himself a Transcendentalist, James not only provides an entree into Transcendental religious experience but also sums up, through his own over-beliefs, the Transcendentalist conception of the religious life.

Bixler, Julius S.
1926 *Religion in the Philosophy of William James*. Boston: Marshall Jones Co.
The fundamental tension in James's work is not between modern science and traditional religion but between two competing views of salvation, one accenting human autonomy and the other emphasizing the dependence of human well-being on deity. James's conception of deity developed in three stages, the second of which is expressed in *The Varieties*. Here, the mood of peace and security takes equal place with the active, strenuous mood that is accented in "The Will to Believe."

Boisen, Anton T.
1953 The present status of William James's psychology of religion. *Journal of Pastoral Care* 7:155-157.
The observed decline in the psychology of religion, 50 years after the publication of *The Varieties*, is only a recession. New interests in the problems of personality, particularly the psychopathological, promise to lead us back to the central insights of James, who is only now beginning to come into his own.

Bozzo, Edward George
1977 James and the valence of human action. *Journal of Religion of Health* 16:26-43.
The aim of this essay is to clarify James's use of the metaphor "the center of energy," which is employed and amplified chiefly in *The Varieties*. Used in diverse imagistic contexts, the metaphor suggests both a system of ideas or interests, which focus and channel the energy, and affective or emotional processes, which are the energy's source. In the case of conversion, for example, James says that religious ideas that were previously peripheral come to take a central place in consciousness, forming a new center of energy. Given the limitations of scientific psychology's general laws, James felt compelled to employ metaphor, imagination's instrument of insight, to cast light on religious phenomena.

Browning, Don
1975 William James's philosophy of the person: The concept of the strenuous life. *Zygon* 10:162-174.
According to James's implicit philosophy of the person, human beings are in their

highest form when they adopt the "strenuous mood," an ascetic attitude of active care and concern for the future. This vision of the good person is extended in *The Varieties*, where the strenuous mood is represented by the sick soul's decision to confront the necessity of transforming oneself and one's world in radical ways. The fullest exemplification of the strenuous mood is found in the lives of saints. In living the strenuous life, the saints increase our capacity to envision and some day to live in an ideal world of justice and love.

1979 William James's philosophy of mysticism. *Journal of Religion* 59:56-70.
The revived interest in mystical experiences raises a variety of questions regarding the relation of mysticism and the ethical life. As James helps us to see, that relation depends on the form of mysticism. Monistic or unitive mysticism, like philosophical monism, generally undermines the moral point of view, for by utterly collapsing all distance between God and the individual and thus eliminating individual selfhood, these positions render impossible the freedom and agency necessary for moral action. James advocated instead a pluralistic mysticism, which, depending on the overbeliefs associated with it, may support a moral point of view. Wayne Proudfoot's notion of the numinous-type mystical experience, according to which God is given a particularly social definition, comes close to representing James's views.

1980 Mysticism, Saintliness, and the Strenuous Life. In *Pluralism and personality; William James and some contemporary cultures of psychology*. Chapter 11, pp. 237-270. Lewisburg, PA: Bucknell University Press.
In *The Varieties* and his other religious writings, James synthesizes a mystical view of life with an ethical one. Life in the modern world requires of us, says James, the "strenuous life" or "strenuous mood." The mystical experience may contribute to this life a broader sense of sympathetic relatedness to the whole of the world at the same time that it brings feelings of relaxation and security. It thereby charges the ethical act with a heightened sense of spontaneity and joy while mitigating the strain of the ethical mode of existence. In spite of the selectivity of James's phenomenology of religious experience, *The Varieties* is a book still relevant to the choices facing our present age.

Bruns, Gerald L.
1984 Loose talk about religion from William James. *Critical Inquiry* 11:299-316.
Instead of speaking in the straightforward and unequivocal language of the scientist, James addresses his listeners with a studied indefiniteness, encouraging them to adopt a hermeneutical attitude that accords with their own points of view. As a pragmatist who views naming as a complicated and forever unfinished business, James employs the language of psychology in a rhetorical fashion, never quite making it his own and leaving it open to reinterpretation, second thoughts, and new sources of understanding. In accord with modern-day hermeneutics, James affirms that the "previous truths" that help to compose reality for us are social constructions and thus historical and contingent. In making sense of the religious feeling in the documents in *The Varieties*, most of which are phrased in the traditional language of theological discourse, James seeks to recognize and preserve the helpful relation to the world that is for him the heart of human truth. Thus rather than substituting psychology for theology, James constructs a model of religious experience that incorporates both psychological and religious perspectives.

Busch, Karl August
1911 *William James as Religionsphilosoph*. Göttingen: Vandenhoeck & Ruprecht.

James's analytical and descriiptive psychology of religion, which is perhaps more widely discussed in Germany than in America, is a great step forward that merits our unreserved appreciation. Clarification of the field's methodology still remains, however, on the distant horizon.

Chamberlain, Gary L.
1971 The drive for meaning in William James's analysis of religious experience. *Journal of Value Inquiry* 5:194-206.
Herbert Fingerette's analysis of the process of integration and the discovery of meaning, in his *The Self in Transformation*, may serve as a loose framework for discussing James's own effort to analyze the processes by which individuals find meaning in life. These include the healthy-minded and sick-souled therapies of integration, with conversion representing the process of meaning-discovery and integration and mysticism signaling their attainment.

Clark, John H.
1986 William James's model of mysticism. In *Current issues in the psychology of religion; Proceedings of the third symposium on the psychology of religion in Europe,* edited by J. A. van Belzen and J. M. van der Lans, 102-111. Amsterdam: Rodopi.
Given James's arranging of his examples of mysticism in order of increasing religious significance, one would expect that his four "marks" or criteria of mystical experiences would occur more frequently toward the latter end of his series than toward the beginning. An examination of his 43 examples shows, however, that there is a sharp drop following the 26th example. After attempting to locate James's examples on his own map of mental states, the author concludes that James's dimension of religious significance is interrupted by a limiting state, at which point the mystics are more concerned with other aspects of their experience.

Clark, Walter Houston
1965 William James: Contributions to the psychology of religious conversion. *Pastoral Psychology* 16(Sept.): 29-36.
James's contribution to the psychology of religious conversion consisted less of substantive findings than of particular attitudes and insights, including his emphasis on individual experience and its consequences, the use of extreme cases, and his respect for the role of the subliminal region.

Coolidge, Mary L.
1950 Some vicissitudes of the once-born and of the twice-born. *Philosophy and Phenomenological Research* 11: 75-87.
Appealing today to the two types of individuals distinguished in *The Varieties*, the once-born or healthy-minded and the twice-born or sick souled, are two philosophical movements. On the one hand is American empirical naturalism, which is thoroughly once-born, extraverted, and optimistic. On the other hand is the sick-souled European atheistic existentialism represented by Sartre. James would have responded with interest and sympathy to both of these contrasting modes of thought.

Crooks, Ezra B.
1913 Professor James and the psychology of religion. *The Monist* 23: 122-130.
The Varieties, which established the psychology of religion as a clearly defined and widespread movement, employs a method more fruitful than the questionnaires of

Hall's students at Clark. Yet the cases James used are so exceptional that they provide no basis for general conclusions about religion. Moreover, James offers little formal psychological analysis of these cases, and what he does say tells us more about his own inner life than about his subjects. The great value of *The Varieties* lies, rather, in James's reflections on the religious life, which are based on his profound and sympathetic understanding of religion as a whole. If the psychology of religion is to penetrate into the meaning of religion it must include this method of interpretation by intimate personal reference.

Crozier, John Beattie
1902 The problem of religious conversion. Professor James's Gifford lectures. *Fortnightly Review* 78: 1004-1018.

James's conclusion that religious conversion signals direct and immediate contact with God or other spiritual agencies is contradicted (1) by the predictable diversity of content, which varies in accord with the teachings of the individuals' religious traditions; (2) by the absence of new insights into the laws of this world; and, most decisively, (3) by the methods that induce such states in uncultured and refined minds alike. Religious conversion and related phenomena are due, rather, to the disruption of the organized centers of the brain, so that one part is isolated, and detached from another. The outcome, although a balm for perplexed and broken spirits, would be a disaster for civilization if universalized.

Day, Bryon
1990a The compatibility of Jamesian and Jungian thought. *Journal of Psychology and Christianity* 9(3):20-26.

James and Jung show several similarities in their respective approaches to religious experience and ethics. Following the hermeneutical principle that the method of interpretation should be appropriate to its object, both combine an introverted and tender-minded approach with an empirical one. Both view the subconscious portion of the psyche as the medium of access to religious experience. Both take the emotional and the intuitive to be fundamental to such experience. And both believed that individual ethics, in contrast to conventional morality, develops out of personal religious experience and should be elevated in terms of personal authenticity and genuineness of community. There is much to be gained, both theoretically and practically, from placing Jung's personality theory within James's philosophical framework.

1990b Convergent themes across Jamesian and Jungian thought. *Journal of Counseling and Development* 68:438-442.

The convergence of the perspectives of James and Jung on religious experience and ethics, delineated in the previous article, extends even further, for they are likewise similar in their views on the nature of the human psyche and on epistemology. If Jung was not systematically influenced by James, he at least demonstrates a philosophical temperament broadly consistent with James's.

Deconchy, Jean-Pierre
1969 La définition de la religion chez William James; Dans quelle mesure peut-on l'opérationaliser? *Archives de Sociologie des Religions* 27:51-70.

According to James's definition of religion in *The Varieties,* the essence of religion lies neither in its social or institutional aspects, nor in intellectual, philosophical, or theological operations, nor in psychopathological behavior. It lies, rather, in experience.

Phenomenologicaally, religious experience consists of three levels of disclosure: a realistic one, of an invisible world and the divine; a subjective one, of feelings of optimism; and a genetic one, of sudden conversion. The fruits of religious experience are threefold: saintliness, interior illumination, and logical satisfaction. For those who wish to operationalize religion, James's approach presents difficulties, both because of the ambiguities of phenomenology and because reference to groups is crucial for systematic observation. James evidenced no concern for these methodological issues.

Disbrey, Claire

1989 George Fox and some theorites of innovation in religion. *Religious Studies* 25:61-74.

According to James, new religious traditions have their origins in the private experience of religious innovators, whose efforts to conceptualize and communicate their ineffable perceptions of spiritual reality result in new theological formulations. Whereas George Fox, the founder of the Society of Friends, is offered by James as an outstanding example of this process, a careful examination of Fox's journals and other contemporary sources leaves James's theory in tatters. Fox's experiences were not significantly different from his contemporaries, and he did not reject the religious concepts of his day. What he left his followers was not primarily a new set of doctrines but a method of reaching truth, the Quaker practice of corporate worship. Empiricist-biased theories of religious innovation, such as James presents, have been repeatedly discredited by an accumulation of theoretical criticisms of empiricism. The sort of experiences the empiricists describe cannot be the source of concepts and beliefs; likewise, they cannot serve as evidence for a supernatural realm or as a means of criticizing and renewing religious institutions.

Dittes, James E.

1973 Beyond William James. In *Beyond the classics? Essays in the scientific study of religion*, edited by Charles Y. Glock and Phillip E. Hammond, 291-354. New York: Harper & Row.

What James offers in *The Varieties* is not a set of central propositions but a distinctive philosophical outlook or spirit. His famous types, his analysis of mysticism, his discussion of saintliness, his championing of religion as *sui generis*—all of these, although offered at first as firm propositions, were later qualified or renounced. More important than these particulars are the principles of pluralism and pragmatism that they represent. Rather than going beyond William James, contemporary psychology of religion has ignored and bypassed him. His spirit does not inspire it. From James's perspective, we see that today's unreflective adulation of and obedience to empiricism, objectivity, and generalizability has jmade them into golden calves. A careful reading of James compels us to reexamine our received faith in such virtues.

Edie, James M.

1968 William James and the phenomenology of religious experience. In *American Philosophy and the Future*, edited by Michael Novak, 247-269. New York: Charles Scribner's Sons. Reprinted in James M. Edie, *William James and phenomenology*, 49-64. Bloomington: Indiana University Press, 1987.

Rather than studying the historical and philological origins of religious meanings and symbols, in the manner of the disciples of Husserl, James explored the foundations of such meanings in naive, unreflective experience. In so doing, he was the first to attempt a true phenomenology of religious experience. The way he opened but left incompletely explored has been unaccountably neglected by his successors.

Ferm, Dean William

1973a Taking God seriously (with the help of William James). *Christian Century* 90:596-600.

Can we still affirm the basic theological premise, the existence of a transcendent personal God? This premise is denied by those who argue that we can know nothing beyond what language can tell us, just as it is covertly dismissed by pop-mystics inspired by Carlos Castaneda. In contrast, *The Varieties*—always fresh and illuminating like his other writings—offers inspiration for a few basic principles for a contemporary theism: that there is a reality beyond man, a transcendent "Other" who cares about us and seeks to make us whole; that God's reality is best known through personal experiences of illumination; and that it is far better to settle for vagueness in expression than to deny the reality of what language seeks to encompass. (See Sawyer 1973 for response)

1973b Reality of the "divine." *Christian Century* 90:1182.

Although it is true that James had no finished theology, he may yet be considered a theist, defined as one who believes in a personal and transcendent being or "other." Furthermore, his postulate of the existence of God can be justified not merely on affective grounds but also on the basis of immediate experience, the practical consequences for human life, the subjective character of human needs, and the implications of the teleological dimension of human thought. Contemporary theology would do well to start with James's insistence on the legitimacy of taking religious experience as evidence for the reality of the "divine." (A rejoinder to Sawyer 1973.)

Forsyth, James

1982 Psychology, theology, and William James. *Soundings* 65:402-416.

James's analysis of religious experience as an experience of self-transcendence (the "wider self") provides a basis for dialogue between psychology and theology. Understood psychologically as wholeness and theologically as salvation, self-transcendence is a subject matter that psychology and theology have in common.

Fuller, Andrew R.

1994 William James. In *Psychology and religion: Eight points of View* (3rd ed.), Chapter 1, 1-33. Lanham, Md.: Rowman & Littlefield.

A summary of James's essay "The Will to Believe" and a systematic overview of *The Varieties* underscores his concern with religious questions of everyday existence, with a personal God of the heart. Accenting the rights, and intelligence, of feeling and the priority of firsthand, personal religious experience, James opens himself to criticism, especially for discounting ordinary religiousness and for positing a culture-free mystical experience. Nevertheless, in allowing for the ambiguities and mysteriousness of existence, James gives the psychologists of religion room to breathe. With a voice truly his own, James is remarkably contemporary.

Geels, Anton

1980 William James och drogforskningen. Några linjer i forskningsdebatten. In *William James då och nu*, edited by Olof Pettersson and Hans Akerberg, 129-151.

James's reflections on the role of drugs in the induction of religious experience today provide a starting point and an inspiration for systematic research on altered states of consciousness.

Gilmore, Ronald M.

1973 William James and religious language: Daughters of earth, sons of heaven? *Église et Theologie* 4:359-390.

The twenty lectures composing *The Varieties* owed much to the influences—intellectual, social, and religious—of James's father, but they reflect even more the author's own tortured search for personal and intellectual moorings. Out of the searing experiences of the 1860s emerged a new understanding: that feeling, not discursive intelligence, is the way to the real, and that feeling carries with it its own warrant. Whereas intelligence can provide words and plausibility, it can neither engender nor secure religious experience. While seeking to pass on this crucial understanding to his auditors at Edinburgh, James at the same time lashed out at the ghosts from his own past.

Hyers, Conrad

1983 Once-born, twice-born Zen: William James and the Rinzai and Soto schools of Japanese Buddhism. In *Traditions in Contact and Change*, edited by Peter Slater and Donald Wiebe, 187-199. Waterloo: Wilfred Laurier University Press.

James's typology of once-born and twice-born forms of religious experience, although developed in a Western, largely Christian context, may serve to elucidate the contrasts between Rinzai and Soto Zen Buddhism. The better-known Rinzai school, which seeks to precipitate an ecstatic experience of enlightenment through unrelenting concentration on one's *koan* and daily *sanzen* session with the master, was founded by the suffering, sick-souled Hakuin, who struggled through the "Great Doubt" and "Great Death" before suddenly experiencing the "Great Joy." The contrasting Soto school, which stresses nothing beyond the act of "just-sitting" in meditation and allowing one's buddha-mind to manifest itself, was founded by the once-born dogen, who was troubled by external, philosophical problems rather than internal conflict and melancholy. Whereas the radical differences in the religious experience of these founders seems to have been consequential in the areas of Zen training and pedagogical techniques, the effects seem minimal in the areas of religious perspective and teaching.

Jantzen, Grace M.

1989 Mysticism and experience. *Religious Studies* 25:295-315.

James's narrow definition of mystical experience, with its emphasis on such phenomena as seizures, ecstasies, visions, and levitations, does not accord with the views and experience of Bernard of Clairvaux and Julian of Norwich, who together serve as paradigms of Christian mysticism. Thus James's position is misguided and inadequate, and so also is much of the subsequent literature on mysticism, given James's enormous influence.

Johnson, Roger A.

1987 Idealism, empiricism, and "other religious": Troeltsch's reading of William James. *Harvard Theological Review* 80:449-476.

Troeltsch, a philosophical idealist who was nonetheless fascinated with empiricism, showed his long-standing interest in the empirical psychology of religion as early as 1894. But it was *The Varieties* that particularly attracted him. The assumptions he held in common with James allowed him to appropriate into his idealist philosophy the whole of James's psychology of religion.

Jones, James W.

1989 Personality and epistemology: Cognitive social learning theory as a philosophy of science. *Zygon* 24:23-38.

Lacking categories with which to analyze the material he gathered in *The Varieties*, James is unable to move beyond phenomenological description. A way forward is offered by cognitive social learning theory, which suggests that we comprehend James's temperamental types in terms of cognitive schemata and encoding strategies.

Kent, Stephen A.

1987a Psychological and mystical interpretations of early Quakerism: William James and Rufus Jones. *Religion* 17:251-274.

In spite of its reductionistic tendency, *The Varieties* was quickly seized upon by Quaker scholars, especially the historian Rufus Jones, as an important resource for interpreting George Fox, their founder, as well as their tradition as a whole. Missing from James and the Quaker interpreters, however, is a consideration of the historical and cultural forces that helped to shape the Quaker tradition. Modern historical scholarship and a social-psychological perspective suggest a variety of reinterpretations, including especially the framework of relative deprivation. (See Naulty, 1989, for a discussion.).

1987b Psychology and Quaker mysticism: The legacy of William James and Rufus Jones. *Quaker History* 76:1-17.

James's remarks on the mental instability, personal power, and religious insights of George Fox, in the context of his high praise for the Quaker tradition, have been cited to substantiate the claims of two competing interpretations of Quakerism: the mystical, which locates the tradition's origins in direct intuitions of God, and the psychological, which accents the psychodynamics of the tradition's early leaders. However, both James and the proponents of these two alternative interpretations have failed to situate the Quaker tradition in its socio-cultural context. Located within the millenarian context of mid-17th century beliefs, the facts utilized by mystical and psychological interpreters gain new salience. Continuing refinements in social history and historical sociology make doubtful the independent adequacy of either interpretive approach.

1989 Mysticism, Quakerism, and relative deprivation: A sociological reply to R. A. Naulty. *Religion* 19:157-178.

While Kent cannot refute the claim that Quaker mysticism was real (i.e., was a genuine experience of God) it is more plausible to explain it as a purely social product, a human expression of the mystics' socio-cultural location and experience. That James was a moderate reductionist is demonstrated by various evidence, including his equation of mystical experience with the subconscious self. Various early Quaker statements of frustrated reformist aspirations suggest that relative deprivation theory is indeed applicable to this tradition, just as it is to early Christianity. The counter-example of St. Bernard of Clairvaux fails on two counts, for the Quakers adamantly dissociated themselves from the Catholics, and Bernard rigorously recruited for the Second Crusade when the Turks reasserted their hegemony. Similarly, Sufism—which had its great appeal among the disprivileged segments of Islam—arose out of disappointment in and resistance to the government.

Levinson, Henry Samuel

1981 *The religious investigations of William James.* Chapel Hill: University of North Carolina Press.

The Varieties is the critical segment in a series of religious investigations that spanned nearly 35 years of James's life. Failing to find a cure for his religious disease in either personal tenacity or philosophy, James turned instead to the newly emerging science of religion. His Gifford Lectures, reviewed and commented on here in detail, constituted his own "crumblike contribution" to this new science, which, like James himself, had been influenced by Darwin's evolutionary perspective. His work on these lectures advanced his own religious investigations in various ways, but many issues, including the problem of religious truth, were left unresolved. These he addressed during the eight, highly productive years that still lay ahead.

Long, Charles H.
1976 The oppressive elements in religion and the religions of the oppressed. *Harvard Theological Review* 69:397-412.
Like Troeltsch, James was unable to come to terms with what Otto later characterized as the *mysterium tremendum*—the awesome, overwhelming, and dreadful element present in every religious experience. An historical-sociological approach, such as we find in W. E. B. DuBois, is necessary to grasp this element and its vicissitudes, especially in the religions of the oppressed, including the religion of American Blacks. The common structural elements of religious experience bear the weight of their histories and situations.

Malone, Michael T.
1983 Traditionalist-renewalist tensions: William James and a modest conciliatory proposal. *Anglican Theological Review* 65:167-176.
James's distinction of the healthy-minded and the divided soul may serve to help traditionalist and renewalist Episcopalians to understand each other. The traditionalists, who affirm the church's historical ethos as the healthiest setting for individual spiritual growth, correspond to the healthy-minded type. The renewalists, who are caught up in a new evangelical fervor of commitment and devotion, are the divided souls. Both groups should consider whether their emotional constitutions and personal histories do not leave them with blind spots.

May, Robert M.
1991 William James on "The varieties of religious experience." In *Cosmic consciousness revisited; The modern origins and development of a western spiritual psychology*, Chapter 2, 71-94. Rockport, MA: Element.
Following a brief introduction to James's life and his psychology of consciousness, May provides a summary-overview of *The Varieties* in the framework of R. M. Bucke's notion of cosmic consciousness.

Moore, Jared S.
1913 The religious significance of the philosophy of William James. The *Sewanee Review* 21:41-58.
James's studies in religion, which culminate in *The Varieties*, form a transition from his psychological period (1880-1900) to his philosophical one (1900-1910). The semipantheistic and decidedly mystical "Gifford philosophy" of *The Varieties*, which conceives of the world as a continuum out of which individuals are only temporarily differentiated, is seriously inconsistent with the pluralistic and non-mystical "Hibbert philosophy" found in earlier and later writings. James was a forceful writer but not a profound one.

Moore, John M.

1938 *Theories of religious experience, with special reference to James, Otto, and Bergson.* New York: Round Table Press.

William James inaugurated the modern discussion of religious experience and explicitly formulated the widespread assumption that it is the creative source or originative aspect of religion. Yet such a view is weak both historically and psychologically. Religious rites, doctrines, and institutions antedate and condition all the personal experiences of which we have any record. Religious experience is certainly important, but it cannot exist by itself, and it is not the source of religion.

Muelder, Walter G.

1942 William James and the problems of religious empiricism. *The Personalist* 23:159-171.

Because James conceived of religion as originating in the experience of individuals, his empirical observations from the outset were pluralistic and nonsystematic, an approach that has raised a number of issues and problems. Many of these arise from his ambiguous treatment of feeling, which he posited to be the most important ingredient in religious experience. His various uses of the term introduce divergent and not easily reconcilable elements into his religious thinking. Although his views on mysticism have likewise roused much analytical criticism, they have nevertheless been enormously influential. In opening the door to religious faith, he also opened it to much credulous irrationalism.

Naulty, R. A.

1989 Stephen A. Kent and the mysticism of the early Quakers. *Religion* 19:151-156.

Kent's (1987b claims that Quaker mysticism is only reputed and that James reduced mysticism to psychology are found to be insupportable. The mysticism of George Fox and his immediate followers was unmistakably real; furthermore, its similarity in form to mysticism occurring in other cultural contexts belies Kent's assertion that the content of these experiences was bounded by the cultural dimensions of mid-17th-century England. The relative deprivation interpretation in particular is challenged by the case of St. Bernard of Clairvaux, whose like-kind of mysticism occurred in a context of personal and cultural success, as well as by the instances of Pascal and the Sufis. (See Kent, 1989, for his reply.)

Nilsson, Lars

1980 Expansiv tro. Den religiösa mognadsprocessen i William James's religionspsykologi. In *William James då och nu*, edited by Olof Pettersson and Hans Akerberg, 81-127. Lund: Doxa.

James's reflections on the growth and differentiation of the religious life contribute fundamentally to the enduring significance of *The Varieties*. These reflections are here discussed in relation to the psychological sources of the religious sentiment, James's typology of the healthy-minded and the sick soul, the process of conversion, and the notion of saintliness.

Paulsell, William O.

1989 William James and Bernard of Clairvaux on mystical experience. *Studies in Formative Spirituality* 10:171-180.

A comparison of James's *The Varieties* with the descriptions of religious experience by the twelfth-century mystic Bernard of Clairvaux demonstrates that the two were of one mind regarding the basic characteristics of mystical experience. Both saw it as indescribable, productive of knowledge, transient, and passive.

Pearson, Fred

1974 How the energy crisis can keep us in moral fighting trim. *Christian Century* 91:256-259.

The current fuel shortage may be viewed as offering us James's moral equivalent of war, a social device that will keep us in moral fighting trim. The succession of renunciations that James found in the lives of saints—first amusements and conventional society and then business and family duties—if taken to heart today would surely improve our manliness, as we laid aside the stock market, meetings at the Holiday Inn, garage sales, and television. We had better make the most of this moral opportunity, however, for the new fuels promised us will allow us once again to be profligate to our heart's content. We may be confident that Americans will heroically embrace the strenuous life for the sake of the years of waste that lie ahead.

Perry, Ralph Barton

1935 *The Thought and Character of William James, Vol. 2, chs. 69-70 (pp. 323-351).* Boston: Atlantic-Little, Brown.

At the same time that the Gifford Lectures sprang from James's filial piety and from his own experience of crisis, they also expressed the psychological interests, especially in exceptional mental states, that had governed James in the nineties. Prepared during a difficult period of invalidism and despair, the lectures were an unequivocal success, restoring James's confidence in himself. In them, he stationed himself at the center of the believer's consciousness and tried to convey its warmth and appeal as they were originally felt. While underscoring the uniqueness of religious experience he also defended its claims.

Pettersson, Olof and Hans Akerberg, eds.

1980 *William James då och nu; Några religionspsykologiska studier.* Lund: Doxa.

See abstracts for chapters by Akerberg, Geels, and Nilsson.

Proudfoot, Wayne

1989 From theology to a science of religions: Jonathan Edwards and William James on religious affections. *Harvard Theological Review* 82:149-168.

The consequential shift in Western theology and philosophy of religion from traditional theological terms to phenomenological ones is illustrated by Jonathan Edwards and William James. A comparison of Edward's *Treatise Concerning Religious Affections* (1746) and James's *The Varieties* suggests that Edwards is the more astute psychologist, for he provides a thicker and more nuanced account of the religious affections. Yet Edwards had the advantage of working exclusively within his own tradition whereas James sought to represent a range of beliefs and practices that were not his own. The contemporary scholar of religion must retain James's distinction between the subject's views and those of the observer while also incorporating the thick description and nuanced analysis of Edwards.

Rambo, Lewis R.

1982 Evolution, community, and the strenuous life: The context of William James's "Varieties of religious experience." *Encounter* 43:239-253.

Properly to understand *The Varieties*, and in particular its moral dimensions, one must place this work in the context of the explicitly ethical essays, articles, and speeches that James wrote between 1880 and 1910. An examination of a number of these writings demonstrates that the strenuous life, which long preoccupied James, lies at the core of his normative vision. In *The Varieties*, James reserves his highest praise for the saint, who not only embodies the strenuous life but also serves as an example for others to emulate. Although recognizing the aberrant quality of some religious lives, James asserts that the most complete form of the strenuous life can be achieved only through religion.

Ramsey, Bennett

1993 *Submitting to freedom; The religious vision of William James.* New York: Oxford University Press.

The Varieties is best understood as a kind of third volume to James's *Principles of Psychology,* a continuing exploration of the marginal streams of consciousness and of their impact on the definition and depiction of the self of ordinary consciousness. The religious stories of *The Varieties* broke through the images and the story of the self in the *Principles,* revealing to James another self of a vastly other world, filled with connections. The religious self was in a commerce, a self-with-a-god. When James ended his Gifford Lectures, he did so with a new psychological world before him, a world that was more genuinely constructive yet one that still needed to be filled out. The filling out of that new world constituted the remaining work of James's career.

Ruf, Frederick J.

1991 *The creation of chaos; William James and the stylistic making of a disorderly world.* Albany: State University of New York Press.

The festival of variety that marks all of James's work serves to create a world that is chaotic, a term that here designates a religious orientation that functions to disorient readers in relation to themselves, their surroundings, and their destination. In *The Varieties,* James depicts a religious view that recognizes, tolerates, and even creates the chaotic—in its recognition of evil and the insecurity it brings; in the disorder and confusion of the sick soul; in the flooding of the field of consciousness in conversion; and in the subtle disapproval of the saint's flight from variety and confusion. Furthermore, the voice of *The Varieties* does not merely report these views but insistently believes in them, engaging the reader to a degree that may eclipse concern with the analysis of religious experience. Joining in are other living voices, some more extreme and affecting than James's own. This continuing interruption of voices threatens to tear *The Varieties* apart, creating a disruptive chaos that many readers likely find disturbing. Yet is through this disorientation that James encourages us to "front" life and thereby find a new, more adequate orientation.

Sawyer, Edward H.

1973 Ferm's appeal to William James: Use or misuse? *Christian Century* 90:923-924.

James's cautious and minimal statements are misused by Ferm in his argument for theism. One may legitimately "use" James to try to establish that God-talk includes a referent "other and larger than our conscious selves." But one "misuses" him when one appeals to his writings for help in establishing theism. Traditional assertions of theism fall into James's category of "over-beliefs," which go beyond what experience requires. James limited himself to what may be called beliefs, a minimal and fundamental core of assertions about the "unseen region." When we test the theistic hypothesis against the criteria that James sets forth in his essay "*The Will to Believe,*" we find that this hypothesis may be neither live nor forced, and that, pragmatically speaking, it promises only to make the theist feel more comfortable. (See Ferm's 1973b rejoinder.)

Schmidt, Wilhelm E.

1908 *Die verschiedenen Typen religiöser Erfahrung und die Psychologie.* Gutersloh: Bertelsmann.

James's comparison of religious expressions to pathological phenomena is profoundly misleading, for religion stands wholly independent of other factors. The testimony of a persons's own inner being unequivocally certifies religion as fundamentally a phenomenon of health, not illness. Moreover, we can know nothing of the subconscious incubation and maturing of motives by which James explains the phenomenon of conversion. True religious conversion, to the contrary, entails a fully conscious break with the person's former ways, achieved through self-determination and passionate inner struggle. James is likewise mistaken in separating personal and institutional religion, for each presupposes and conditions the other.

Smith, John E.

1983 William James's account of mysticism: A critical appraisal. In *Mysticism and religious traditions,* edited by Steven T. Katz, 247-279. Oxford: Oxford University Press.

James's treatment of mysticism, including his distinguishing of mysticism's features and types as well as his estimate of the validity of its claims, suffers from a superabundance of rich fare that has not been thoroughly digested. *The Varieties*'s descriptive bias, which led James to concentrate on the force of mystical experience in the life of individuals and to subordinate the conceptual order to personal feeling, accounts for his neglect of "rationalistic mysticism" as represented by Bonadventure, Nicholas of Cusa, and Spinoza. Furthermore, James paid insufficient attention to the relation between the mystical goal and the path by which it is reached. In many forms of mysticism a large part of the meaning of the final vision derives from trying to understand what was negated, transcended, or absorbed along the way. And in overlooking the important distinction between organization and community, James greatly underestimated the importance of the social dimension in religion.

Strandberg, Victor

1981 *Religious psychology in American literature: A study in the relevance of William James.* Madrid: Jose Porrua Turanzas; Potomac, Md.: Studia Humanitatis.

When the religious psychologies of James, Freud, and Jung are compared, James's proves to be the most open and empirical as well as the most capable of embracing the whole range of religious experiences. To demonstrate the continuing relevance of *The Varieties,* James's healthy-minded/sick soul typology as well as his insights regarding conversion, mysticism, and saintliness are applied to thirty major American writers. The resulting illumination of these literary personalities, whose writings are presumed to be confessional and self-affirming, leaves James more securely in possession of his towering place in American literary history.

Strout, Cushing

1971 The pluralistic identity of William James; A psychohistorical reading of *The varieties of religious experience. American Quarterly* 23:135-152.

Such variety as can be found in James's *The Varieties* derives chiefly from the many-sidedness of its author's lively personality. James's various fragmented identities— the patient, the healer, the scientist, the believer, the reformer, and the metaphysician—were all vitally and symbolically connected to the vigorous but troubled personality of his father, with whom James over-identified and from whose example he struggled to emancipate himself. Psychobiography thus becomes the best way to account for the eccentricities of the highly popular *The Varieties*, including its odd vocabulary, the urgency of its themes, and the distribution of its sympathies. It helps us, too, to see the strategic place of *The Varieties* in the developing identity of one of America's most original philosophers.

Strug, Cordell
1974 Seraph, snake, and saint: the subconscious mind in James's *Varieties. Journal of the American Academy of Religion* 42:505-515.
    Illustrating the submerged assumptions, hazy distinctions, and awe-inspiring overstatements that make *The Varieties* so troublesome a text is James's conception of the subconscious mind. The subconscious is put to good use early in *The Varieties*, in James's analysis of conversion; but when he suggests that the gods may exist on the "farther side" of the subconscious, his fuzzy conception turns into a rotten apple that spoils his conclusion.

Taylor, Eugene I.
1978 Psychology of religion and Asian studies: The William James legacy. *Journal of Transpersonal Psychology* 10:67-79.
    At least three main streams of influence shaped James's thoughts on religious experience as they appear in *The Varieties*: (1) Academic scholarship in the history of comparative religions; (2) The rise of the metaphysical or mind-cure movement in popular American culture; and (3) Interest in the psychology of religion within the broader discipline of academic psychology. James's legacy for us is a widely inclusive eclecticism that will require creative dialogue both within and between the disciplines, especially psychology, religion, and Asian Studies, and the training of translators capable of bridging the specialized languages.

Tracy, David
1988 The question of criteria for inter-religious dialogue: A tribute to Langdon Gilkey. In *The whirlwind in culture; Frontiers in theology,* edited by Donald W. Musser and Joseph L. Price, 246-261. Bloomington, IN: Meyerstone Books.
    With his great interest in religion's variety, and the multiplicity and subtlety of his responses to it, James qualifies as the classic early modern student of religious pluralism. Since his day, historians and anthropologists of religion have exponentially increased our awareness of the variety of religion, and theologians in every tradition are increasingly pressed to make the issue of religious pluralism central in their thinking. Even with this explosion of work, we may fruitfully return to James, and especially to his classic *The Varieties*, for criteria that, once reformulated, may prove fruitful for serious inter-religious dialogue. His category of "immediate luminousness" can be usefully shifted to the wider hermeneutical category of "suggestive possibility," the criteria for coherence will today be more flexible but no less rational, and the criteria of ethical—and by implication, social and political—consequences for action will likewise require refinement in the face of challenges that James could not have anticipated.

Tumulty, Peter
1990 Judging God by "human" standards: Reflections on William James's *Varieties of religious experience. Faith and Philosophy* 7:316-328.

James's proposal in *The Varieties* that we judge religion according to human standards would be objected to by religious fundamentalists on two counts: (1) a truly religious person must be prepared to sacrifice everything, including reason itself, on the altar of faith; and (2) James removes human standards from criticism by religion, thus closing off one of the major historical sources for reason's own development. But according to the principle of autonomy, reason must judge the limits to its own operations, and as in the case of friendship, the very elevating of our standards of evaluation and of ourselves may become the standard by which we judge.

Uren, A. Rudolph

1928 James's "The Varieties of Religious Experience." In *Recent religious psychology; A study in the psychology of religion,* Chapter 5, 61-84. Edinburg: T. & T. Clark.

The Varieties is a piece of seductive writing that, for sheer witchery, is incomparable in the psychology of religion literature. When we are able to break the spell, however, certain grave defects become apparent. The most fundamental of these defects is James's basing of his whole argument on extreme cases; he never seems to differentiate the typical from the aberrational, and exceptional cases are taken to be characteristic of the religious life as a whole. Other defects follow: a religious life is denied to that vast multitude of persons who represent the prophetic rather than the mystical type of religious experience; the melancholic temperament receives more than its share of attention whereas the active temperament is given no place at all; the religious experience of the intellectual type is unrepresented; the examples of the conversion experience are nearly all of ancient date; and whereas James seeks in the facts of religious experience an empirical warrant for the transcendental hypothesis, his notion of the subconscious stands as a sufficient explanation in itself. Nevertheless, as a work of genius, *The Varieties* is replete with penetrating insights and analyses. James's distinctive contribution to the psychology of religion is his powerful forthsetting of the value of religion for human life.

Vincent, Gilbert, ed.

1985 Lettres de Bergson à F. Abauzit. *Revue d'histoire et de philosophie religieuses* 65:381-394.

Bergson, who frequently corresponded with James and expressed great admiration for his *The Varieties*, initially agreed to write a preface for the French translation. Less than two months later he withdrew from the project. These letters to Frank Abauzit, the translator, reveal to us that Bergson finally refused to write the invited essay because of his unhappiness with the quality of Abauzit's translation. Like James, Bergson believed that the stylistic particularities of a text are intimately related to the formulation of its thought.

Walle, A. H.

1992 William James's legacy to Alcoholics Anonymous: An analysis and a critique. *Journal of Addictive Diseases* 11:91-99.

Inspired by *The Varieties*, the founders of Alcoholics Anonymous have bequeathed to the organization a recovery program that is directed to a certain type of person (the sick-souled individual) and that fosters a specific type of religious experience (self-surrender). This model may be too narrowly conceived to be effective with all of the varieties of alcoholism.

Wulff, David M.

1991 William James and his legacy. In *Psychology of religion; Classic and contemporary views,*

Chapter 10, 467-518. New York: John Wiley & Sons.

James's *The Varieties*, which reflects the author's philosophic standpoint as well as his own inner experience, possesses a threefold agenda. First, it is a descriptive work that seeks by means of personal documents and the method of serial study to help others to understand the remarkable inner experiences of religious experts. James's typology of the healthy-minded and the sick soul is the chief fruit of this phenomenological analysis. Second, *The Varieties* is a work of existential judgment, an investigation into the origins of religious experience. Of the metaphors that James uses toward this end, the subconscious self stands out. Third, *The Varieties* is a work of spiritual judgment, an exercise in assessing religion's fruits for life. At its best, James concludes, religion yields a level of human excellence otherwise unobtainable. Although *The Varieties* has been the subject of much criticism—most frequently, for its emphasis on exceptional experience—and has not been systematically influential, it has retained to this day its status as the field's one great classic.

Zaleski, Carol

1993-1994 Speaking of William James to the cultured among his despisers. *Journal of the Psychology of Religion* 2-3:127-170.

This essay is an experiment in making *The Varieties* more usable, by reading James in such a way as to answer the chief objections that have been raised against this classic work. Where it does not appear to be possible to defend James, it is considered whether his thought is in principle corrigible, and hence of more than historical interest for interpreters of religion. Seven charges are considered: (1) James's account of religious experience is marred by excessive individualism, privatism, and elitism; (2) He gives undue emphasis to feeling; (3) He overlooks ordinary and wholesome forms of piety; (4) He wrongly posits the existence of raw, uninterpreted experience; (5) He equates truth simplistically with emotional expediency; (6) He is trying to construct an empirical argument for the existence of God; and (7) He presents a reduced and unworthy image of God. That James's understanding of religious experience may bear correction today is no sign that his understanding is obsolete. He may, in fact, be considered the forerunner of all that is liberating in post-modernism, without any of its nihilistic bravado or despair.

Note: Additional, minor reviews and related works, including doctoral dissertations, are listed in Ignas K. Skrupskelis, *William James: A Reference Guide* (Boston: G. K. Hall & Co., 1977).

ABOUT THE CONTRIBUTORS

Joseph F. Byrnes is Professor of History at Oklahoma State University in Stillwater, Oklahoma. He received his master's degree from the University of Notre Dame and his doctorate from The University of Chicago. He is the author of several books, including *The Virgin of Chartres: An Intellectual and Psychological History of the Work of Henry Adams* and *The Psychology of Religion.* His special interest is nineteenth-and twentieth-century interpretations of medieval religion and art. He is currently engaged in the study of French religious history from the Revolution to the present.

Donald Capps is Professor of Pastoral Theology at Princeton Theological Seminary in Princeton, New Jersey. He received his doctorate from The University of Chicago and holds an honorary doctorate in theology from the University of Uppsala in Sweden. He is the author of several books, including *The Depleted Self: Sin in a Narcissistic Age* and *The Child's Song: The Religious Abuse of Children.* He has been editor of the Journal for the Scientific Study of Religion and President of the Society for the Scientific Study of Religion.

John Capps is a doctoral candidate in Philosophy at Northwestern University in Evanston, Illinois. He received his B.A. degree from St. Johns College in Annapolis, Maryland, His interests include theory of knowledge, philosophy of science and American pragmatism.

Richard Chiles is Professor of Psychology at Jackson State University in Jackson, Mississippi. He received his master's degree from the University of North Dakota and his Ph.D. from Northwestern University in Evanston, Illinois. He has pursued further theological studies at St. Thomas University in Rome. He is a member of the Chicago Center for the Study of Groups and Organizations and a regular consultant for group relations conferences cosponsored by the Center, The University of Chicago and Northwestern University.

Patricia H. Davis is Assistant Professor at Perkins School of Theology at Southern Methodist University in Dallas, Texas. She has an M.A. in religious studies from Indiana University and the Ph.D. from Princeton Theological Seminary where she specialized in pastoral theology, psychology of religion and women's studies. She wrote her doctoral dissertation on Cotton Mather's role in the Salem witchcraft trials.

John Dewey taught philosophy at The University of Chicago and Columbia University in New York. He received his doctorate in philosophy from John Hopkins University in Baltimore, Maryland. He is best known for his application of a philosophy of experience and process to educational theory and practice. He died in 1952 at the age of 93. His works include *How We Think, Democracy and Education, School and Society,* and *Experience and Nature.* His major work on religion is *A Common Faith,* written in 1933, which includes discussion of religion and the religious, faith and its object, and the human abode of the religious function.

James E. Dittes is Professor of Pastoral Theology at Yale Divinity School and Professor of Psychology at Yale University in New Haven, Connecticut. He received his B.D. degree from Yale Divinity School and his doctorate in psychology from Yale University. His recent books include *The Male Predicament* and *When Work Goes Sour.* He has been editor of the *Journal for the Scientific Study of Religion,* and Executive Secretary and President of the Society for the Scientific Study of Religion. He has studied in Rome as a Fulbright

Scholar, and has held a Guggenheim Fellowship and a Senior Faculty Fellowship from the National Endowment for the Humanities.

Erik H. Erikson was Professor of Human Development at Harvard University in Cambridge, Massachusetts, from 1960 to his retirement in 1970. He died on May 12, 1994, at the age of 91. He is the author of numerous books, including *Childhood and Society, Young Man Luther, Identity: Youth and Crisis,* and *Gandhi's Truth.* He was associated with the Psychoanalytic Institute in Vienna prior to his emigration to the United States in 1933 and was a protege of Anna Freud. He is best known for his theory of the human life cycle and for his encouragement of interdisciplinary studies in psychology and history.

Ralph W. Hood Jr. is Professor of Psychology at the University of Tennessee in Chattanooga. He is the coauthor of *The Psychology of Religion: An Empirical Approach* and the editor of *The Handbook of Religious Experience.* He has been President of Division 36 (Psychology of Religion) of the American Psychological Association and a recipient of its William James Award. He is an editor of *The International Journal for the Psychology of Religion* and also current editor of *The Journal for the Scientific Study of Religion.*

Richard A. Hutch is Reader in Religion and the Human Sciences in the Department of Studies of Religion and the Deputy Dean of the Faculty of Arts at the University of Queensland in Brisbane, Australia. He received his doctorate from The University of Chicago and his B.D. degree from Yale University. In addition to over sixty articles on psychology of religion, death and dying, and biography studies (including women religious leaders), he is the author of *Religious Leadership: Personality, History and Sacred Authority* and *Emerson's Optics: Biographical Process and the Dawn of Religious Leadership.*

Janet L. Jacobs is Associate Professor of Women Studies and sociology at the University of Colorado in Boulder, where she also completed her doctorate in sociology. She is author of *Divine Disenchantment: Deconverting from New Religious Movements* and *Victimized Daughters: Incest and the Development of the Female Self.* Her primary areas of research include religion and women, and religion and family violence. She is a member of the executive council of the Society for the Scientific Study of Religion.

Roger A. Johnson is Elisabeth Luce Moore Professor in the Religion Department at Wellesley College in Wellesley, Massachusetts. He received his doctorate from Harvard University and is author of several books, including *Critical Issues in Modern Religion, Views From the Pews: Christian Beliefs and Social Attitudes,* and the editor of *Psychohistory and Religion: The Case of Young Man Luther.* He has been a visiting professor at the Chinese University of Hong Kong.

Mary Jo Meadow is Professor of Psychology and Director of Religious Studies at Mankato State University, Mankato, Minnesota. She received her Ph.D. from the University of Minnesota in clinical and personality psychology. She is co-author with Richard D. Kahoe of *Psychology of Religion: Religion in Individual Lives,* and author of *Gentling the Heart: Buddhist Loving-Kindness Practice for Christians* and *Through a Glass Darkly: A Spiritual Psychology of Faith.* She has served as president of Divisions 32 (Humanistic Psychology) and 36 (Psychology of Religion) of the American Psychological Association.

Troels Nørager is Professor of Psychology of Religion and Pastoral Theology at Aarhus University in Aarhus, Denmark, where he also received his doctorate. He is author of *Theories of Socialization and the Problem of Anthropological Normativity* and *System* and *Life World: Habermas' Construction of Modernity.* He has studied with Jurgen Habermas in

Frankfurt, Germany, and has held an American Council of Learned Societies Fellowship for study in the United States. He is currently working on a comparative study of Jonathan Edwards, William James, and C. G. Jung dealing with the language of religious experience.

Mark Ralls is a Ph.D. candidate at Princeton Theological Seminary, pursuing an interdisciplinary program of studies in practical and systematic theology. He received his M.Div. degree from Duke University. His special area of interest is theological anthropology.

Wade Clark Roof is the J.F. Rowny Professor of Religion and Society at the University of California at Santa Barbara. He is the author, most recently, of *A Generation of Seekers: The Spiritual Journeys of the Baby Boom Generation.* He has been Executive Secretary of the Society for the Scientific Study of Religion and is currently President of the Society. He has conducted major sociological surveys of contemporary religion in America. His interests are in the sociology and psychology of religion.

Sarah McFarland Taylor is a Rowny Fellow and doctoral student in the Religion in America program at the University of California at Santa Barbara. She received her master's degree from Dartmouth College in Religious Studies and her bachelor's degree from Brown University. Her research interests are in popular religion and American culture and issues of gender and religion.

David M. Wulff is Professor of Psychology at Wheaton College, Norton, Massachusetts. He received his Ph.D. in personality psychology at the University of Michigan in 1969 and was awarded an honorary Doctor of Theology in 1993 from the University of Lund, Sweden. He is the author of *Psychology of Religion: Classic and Contemporary Views*, which has not only been translated into Swedish but also been awarded the Quinquennial Prize by the International Commission for Scientific Psychology of Religion.

Carol Zaleski is Associate Professor in the Department of Religion and Biblical Literature at Smith College in Northampton, Massachusetts. She teaches philosophy of religion, psychology of religion, and world religions. She received her doctorate from Harvard University. She is the author of *Otherworld Journeys: Accounts of Near-Death Experience in Medieval and Modern Times* and is currently working on a book entitled *On Seeing Angels: Towards a Theory of Religious Experience.*